MW00784309

From Maps to Metaphors

During the summers of 1792-4 George Vancouver and the crew of the British naval ships *Discovery* and *Chatham* mapped the northwest coast of North America from Baja California to Alaska. Vancouver's voyage was the last, and longest, of the great Pacific voyages of the late eighteenth century. Taking the art and technique of distant voyaging to a new level, Vancouver eliminated the possibility of a northwest passage, and his remarkably precise surveys completed the outline of the Pacific.

But to map an area is to appropriate it, and Vancouver's charts of the northwest coast were part of a process of economic exploitation and cultural disruption. Although he and the other great navigators of his age exercised no control over the ideas and enterprises spawned by their voyages, their names have come to symbolize the consequences of European expansion – good or bad.

From Maps to Metaphors grew out of the Vancouver Conference on Exploration and Discovery, held to observe the bicentennial of Vancouver's arrival on the Pacific northwest coast. Its aim is to bring to light much of the new research on the discovery of the Pacific, as well as to illuminate the European and Native experience. The chapters are written from a variety of perspectives, and provide new insights on many aspects of Vancouver's voyage – from the technology Vancouver employed to the complex political and power relationships among European explorers and the Native leadership.

ROBIN FISHER is a professor and chair of the Department of History at the University of Northern British Columbia. HUGH JOHNSTON is a professor in the Department of History at Simon Fraser University. Both are widely published historians.

From Maps to Metaphors

.

THE PACIFIC WORLD
OF GEORGE VANCOUVER

.

Edited by Robin Fisher
and Hugh Johnston

UBC PRESS / VANCOUVER

ISBN 0-7748-0470-X

Canadian Cataloguing in Publication Data

Main entry under title:

From maps to metaphors

  Selected papers from the Vancouver Conference on Exploration and Discovery,
April 22-26, 1992.

  Includes bibliographical references and index.
  ISBN 0-7748-0470-X

  1. Vancouver, George, 1757-1798 – Journeys – British Columbia – Pacific Coast.
2. Vancouver, George, 1757-1798 – Journeys – United States – Pacific Coast.
3. Northwest Coast of North America – Discovery and exploration – British. 4. Pacific
Area – Discovery and exploration – British. I. Fisher, Robin, 1946- II. Johnston,
Hugh J.M., 1939- III. Vancouver Conference on Exploration and Discovery (1992:
Simon Fraser University)

FC3821.F76 1993   910'.9164'3   C93-091889-4
F1088.F76 1993

UBC Press gratefully acknowledges the ongoing support to its publishing program from
the Canada Council, the Province of British Columbia Cultural Services Branch, and the
Department of Communications of the Government of Canada.

Book design: George Vaitkunas
Typefaces: Minon and Gill Sans
Printed and bound in Canada by D.W. Friesen & Sons Ltd.

UBC Press
University of British Columbia
6344 Memorial Road
Vancouver, BC V6T 1Z2
(604) 822-3259
(604) 822-6083

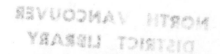

Contents

Illustrations and Maps

Illustrations

Maps

Acknowledgments

The conference that generated this book received the generous encouragement and financial support of many corporations and individuals. The editors would particularly like to thank Jack V. Christensen, Douglas L. Cole, and H. Leslie Smith for their guidance and help over a long time. They also thank all of the participants at the Vancouver Conference on Exploration and Discovery, without whom this book would not be possible.

From Maps to Metaphors

How the Squamish Remember George Vancouver

*The following is an account of the Squamish's first
encounter with GeorgeVancouver, as told by
Squamish historian Louis Miranda (1892-1990),
and presented at the Vancouver Conference
on Exploration and Discovery by Chief Philip Joe*

Vancouver's journal records that my ancestors who greeted him 'conducted themselves with the greatest decorum and civility.' He certainly liked the fish given and did not mind parting with a few iron tools in exchange. Vancouver took a look around the inlet and then headed into Howe Sound where an incident occurred that you may not be so familiar with, but which has been preserved in Squamish oral tradition.

As my elders tell the story, early one morning in the month called *Tim-kwis-KWAS* 'hot time,' an old man living near the mouth of the Squamish River had gone down to wash. As he raised his head, he saw an 'island' where no island had been before. The old man was alarmed and ran back to his house to wake his relatives. 'There is an island in the sound – a floating island,' he told them. The old man knew it was an island for it had skeletons of trees thrusting skyward. But it was like no island he had ever seen. Word was sent up the Squamish River for the people to come and see the mysterious floating island.

It was decided that the men would go out in their canoes to see the island. As they grew near, they saw that it wasn't a floating island at all, but a very large canoe, a strange canoe. Soon, men appeared and walked around the canoe. But what strange men they were! Every part of their body was covered except for their faces, which were white. My people scrutinized them. Finally, some of the elders came up with an explanation – these people are from the land of the dead. And they are wrapped in their burial blankets!

One of the dead people stepped forward. He had smoke coming

from his mouth and it appeared that he was eating fire. The man motioned for my ancestors to go on board. They were hesitant, of course, but after much discussion, one brave young man decided that he would go, and others followed. Instantly, the dead man in the canoe extended his hand. 'Oh, he wants to play the "pulling fingers" game,' the Squamish men told one another. One man stepped forward, spit in his palm, rubbed his hands together, and thrust out his crooked finger. The fire-eating dead man shook his head no, no. 'A stronger opponent is wanted,' the Squamish decided. Another man stepped forward, spit on his hand and got ready to play the game. Again the white man shook his head, no. More Squamish men stepped forward, spit, and extended their finger, until only one man remained – a strong man from up the Squamish River. My people could see that the strangers were talking amongst themselves and we can only assume that they must have decided that this unusual behaviour was the Indian way of greeting. So the white man stepped forward to link fingers with the strong man of Squamish. The Squamish man pulled. He pulled hard. Oh, the smoke-blowing dead man hollered in pain as his finger was disconnected! Some of the Squamish had been sceptical of the strangers. Then they knew. 'Dead people don't feel pain, and this one is certainly having some!'

Fear of the strangers vanished. The Squamish looked around the strange, large canoe and when it came time to leave they climbed down into their own canoes. The white people lowered into the canoes some presents, including a barrel and a few boxes.

Back at the village the people huddled around as the men opened the treasure. When they pried the top from the barrel they were pleased to see that it contained good thick hair and face oil, much better than the deer tallow and salmon oil they had in storage. All hands dipped into the barrel and smeared it onto their faces and hair. But soon the oil began to thicken. Their hair got stiff! Their faces got thick! And they could hardly move their jaw! They ran for the water and washed it off. The gift of molasses was then emptied onto the ground.

My people had hoped that the second gift might be less trouble. Inside the box were shiny round pieces that attracted the attention of the women – who saw their value as ornaments – and the children – who thought they made fine toys. For the box of silver coins had no other value to the Squamish in 1792.

The story passed down by my ancestors tells how Vancouver provided gifts of pilot biscuits, whisky, and white flour —unfamiliar foods that they used with results that were initially comical, although history has recorded a less jovial aftermath.

Viewing the explorers' ships as 'floating islands' and the men, themselves, as 'dead people' was not a perspective unique to the Squamish. Our relatives – the Nanaimo Indians – were also visited one night by floating islands. In addition to the fire-eating habit of the strangers, they saw that their feet were wooden and made a great deal of noise when they walked! The Nanaimo people's barrel of molasses was used to mend their canoes, but it was soon found that molasses was as poor a canoe pitch as it was a hair oil.

Apparently Vancouver then sailed north, for his travels up the coast can be traced by the elders' stories of mysterious floating islands that appeared offshore, and then, just as quickly as they arrived, sailed beyond the next point.

Many of you have investigated the naming of the landscape by Vancouver and his Spanish counterparts. But perhaps you are not aware that the Squamish commemorated the historic 1792 meeting in Howe Sound by thereafter referring to the site by the Squamish name *Whul-whul-LÁY-ton*, meaning 'Whiteman place.'

Indian stories and place names, like explorers' journals, are reminders of history that provide a glimpse into another era. As I hope my people's story has demonstrated, our mutual histories since 1792 have been inexorably entwined, although recalled from different perspectives.

This country, which so inspired the explorers and challenged the map makers, was the homeland of the Squamish and our neighbours the Musqueam and the Seleelwat. These beaches gave us shellfish, crabs, and eel grass. The forests and flatlands provided deer, large herds of elk, bear, and mountain goats. Food plants were harvested, and the trees supplied the wood for our houses, canoes, weapons, and ceremonial objects. The bark of red cedars was stripped to make our clothes. The inlet waters provided us with a wide variety of fish and sea mammals, and salmon returned regularly to the streams. And just as Captain Vancouver was said to have shared his molasses, biscuits, and flour, so our people shared our natural resources with those who followed in the wake of the floating islands.

Introduction

Robin Fisher and Hugh Johnston

The Squamish were the first group of Canadian Native people to meet Captain George Vancouver after his expedition left Birch Bay in June 1792. Peter Puget, Vancouver's lieutenant, recorded the event in his daily log on 13 June, and Vancouver mentions it in his published journals.[1] The Squamish have their own recollection of this moment, and when Chief Philip Joe related it during the first day of Simon Fraser University's Vancouver Conference, he reminded us that history is a matter of perspective. Our understanding of the past depends on what we know, and what we make of what we know. George Vancouver came to the Pacific to gather scientific information, but he was not simply a collector of data. His account of his voyage, and even his meticulous maps and charts of the northwest coast of North America, reflected his personality and his culture. He saw and observed according to the limits of his vision. And then, almost immediately, Vancouver's information was used, and misused, by others to develop their own conceptions of the Pacific world. In this process of vision and revision, Vancouver's maps have been made into metaphors.

Although Vancouver and the other great navigators of his age exercised no control over the ideas and enterprises spawned by their voyages, their names have always been employed to symbolize the consequences of European expansion – good or bad. Today the impact of European explorers on the Pacific and its peoples is a matter of conflicting interpretation, with the more negative views gaining currency. In the public arena this development has created a striking ambivalence: on the 200th anniversary of Vancouver's voyage, the mayor and council of the city of Vancouver supported commemorative events which determinedly avoided recognizing Vancouver himself. The city no longer wished to be reminded of the navigator for whom it was named. Unfortunately, the man has been associated with acts and attitudes that he himself would have criticized. His name, and his work, have come to represent much more than his own record of accomplishments and failures.

Vancouver's voyage was the last, and longest, of the great Pacific voyages of the second half of the eighteenth century. Adding the years that he served with Cook to his own voyage of nearly four-and-a-half years, Vancouver probably spent more time in the Pacific than any other European sailor of his day. By mapping the northwest coast of North America, he eliminated the possibility of a northwest passage and completed the outline of the Pacific. His charts offered empirical knowledge in place of speculation about the shape of the world's last uncharted mid-latitude coastline. His account, entitled *A Voyage of Discovery to the North Pacific Ocean and Round the World; in which the Coast of North-West America has been Carefully Examined and Accurately Surveyed ...*, conscientiously provided details 'in a way calculated to *instruct*, even though it should fail to *entertain*.'[2] He furnished the hard evidence of his own observations, and his cartography was definitive. The true significance of his voyage, like the voyages of others, remains open to question; but, for any attempt to reconstruct an image of the Pacific region and its peoples in the eighteenth century, the log books, journals, and specimens brought back to Europe by Vancouver and his contemporaries are invaluable sources of information.

Vancouver came to the Pacific in command of a British naval expedition that reached New Zealand in November 1791 and the northwest coast of North America on 17 April 1792. His instructions were twofold: to make a detailed survey of the northwest coast to prove or disprove the existence of a northwest passage connecting the Atlantic and Pacific oceans; and to negotiate with Spanish representatives on restoring property and trading rights that the British claimed at Nootka Sound and in the region. Thus his mission involved both hydrography, at which he was stunningly successful, and diplomacy, at which he achieved little.

In passing through southern waters, he surveyed an extensive reach of the southern coast of Australia and parts of the south island of New Zealand. By the time he arrived off the northwest coast of North America he had spent three weeks at Dusky Bay, New Zealand, a month in Tahiti, and two weeks in the Hawai'ian Islands. He devoted the next three summers to investigating the northwest coast through all of its 'twistings and windings.'[3] At the end of each summer, he sailed to the Spanish port of Monterey, California, to receive dispatches and supplies sent out from Britain; but he and his crew passed the winters of 1792-3 and 1793-4 in the Hawai'ian Islands. Thus, they were in constant contact with the people of the Pacific, especially in Hawai'i and on the northwest coast of North America. And in developing relationships with these people – economic, political, and cultural – they were carrying on work Cook had begun not many years earlier.

During the entire voyage, Vancouver lost only five men out of a total complement of 145. This achievement, along with his remarkably precise surveys, ought to have earned him more recognition than it did. True, his successes were the product of experience accumulated by many captains within the British navy over a long time, but Vancouver took the art and technique of distant voyaging to a new level. He had learned from a master, Cook, with whom he had first served as a midshipman at the age of fourteen. He had sailed on Cook's second and third great Pacific voyages and had first visited the northwest coast in 1778, when Cook spent a month refitting at Nootka Sound before sailing north into Alaskan waters. During the ten years between returning from Cook's last Pacific expedition and leading his own, Vancouver had risen through the ranks of the British navy and served on a number of ships, particularly in the Caribbean Sea. He was thirty-three in December 1790 when appointed to command the *Discovery* – three and a half months before it departed from Falmouth, along with the smaller tender *Chatham*, on its great Pacific voyage – and he was well prepared for the task ahead.

Charting the northwest coast began with a running survey north from a point near Cape Cabrillo on the California coast to the Olympic Peninsula. Then Vancouver entered the Strait of Juan de Fuca and anchored at Discovery Bay. The anchorage was well named, for there he discovered the enormity of the task ahead. He and his boat crews, examining the adjacent coast, took five days just to survey Port Townsend and Hood Canal. As he continued to chart the tangled waterways around

Puget Sound, he realized that, if the rest of the coast were like this, mapping it would not be a simple matter of conducting running surveys from the *Discovery* and *Chatham*. Rather it was likely to involve long hours, days, weeks, and, in the end, months, of back-breaking work in small boats, rowing up and down the inlets and around the islands in a painstaking effort to put the convoluted coastline on paper. Having surveyed Puget Sound, Vancouver and his expedition headed north to discover that the task would not get any easier.

Each summer, as Vancouver and his crews carefully charted the coast from Baja California, in the south to Cook Inlet in the north, the routine was the same. *Discovery* and *Chatham* would anchor in a sheltered cove where the crews could gather supplies and take astronomical observations to help to fix the exact location. Meanwhile the boat crews would fan out from this focal point to survey the coastline. When they returned, often after more than two weeks at the oars, another stretch of the northwest coast would be added to the chart. Then the vessels would move to another anchorage to repeat the process.

During the first season in 1792 the expedition established the insularity of Vancouver Island and worked as far north as Burke Channel. In the second season, in the spring of 1793, picking up where they left off, the boat crews slowly unravelled the tangled skein of inlets and islands that make up the coast between Vancouver Island and the Alaska panhandle. The expedition ended the second year's work at Cape Decision in Sumner Strait. Returning for a third and final survey season in 1794, Vancouver reversed the pattern of the previous years and worked from north to south. His boat crews carried out a detailed survey of Cook Inlet – where they encountered Russian fur traders – and Prince William Sound, before the expedition moved down the Alaskan coast. Vancouver's chart of the northwest coast was completed at Port Conclusion at the southern tip of Baranof Island in late August 1794.

While on the coast, Vancouver and his men were in frequent contact with Native people, although never with any one group for long. In these encounters, Vancouver himself was not particularly perceptive. Even at Nootka Sound, where he spent more time than at any other place on the coast, he was unimpressed with the people and their culture. His limitations as an ethnographer were, however, compensated for by others, particularly the botanist Archibald Menzies. Initially Vancouver tended to associate other coastal groups with the people of Nootka Sound, but as the expedition moved further north, even Vancouver gradually came to appreciate the great variety of cultures in the region. He was not completely indifferent. Vancouver certainly understood that his survey work depended on the cooperation, or at least the tacit compliance, of the local inhabitants. So he was very concerned that misunderstanding should not lead to violence and, except for one or two encounters in the north between his men and the Tlingit, he was successful in avoiding it.

Nor should we jump to the conclusion that Vancouver's attitude was the same toward all Pacific people. His relatively unenthusiastic accounts of the cultures of the northwest coast contrast with his lively and engaged reporting on the Hawai'ians. After the first and second seasons on the northwest coast, the expedition sailed south to spend part of the winter in Hawai'i. With more time on his hands, Vancouver took a greater interest in Hawai'ian matters. He tried unsuccessfully to negotiate a truce between the warring factions on the Islands and, in the process, established an association with the powerful leader Kamehameha. Interested in obtaining outside support in his struggle to gain control of the entire island chain, Kamehameha agreed to Vancouver's suggestion that Hawai'i be 'ceded' to Britain. Whatever one makes of this so-called cession, clearly Vancouver was much more interested in, and involved with, the Hawai'ian people than those of the northwest coast.

On the face of it, Vancouver had more diplomatic success with the Hawai'ians than with the Spanish. The second reason that he was sent to the Pacific was to settle the details of a disagreement between Spain and Britain over who was to have the right to exploit the resources of the Pacific. The Spanish arrest of some British trading vessels at Nootka Sound in 1789 had led to an international incident that brought the two nations to the brink of war. They found a face-saving device by signing the Nootka Sound Convention which affirmed the right of both parties to navigate, trade, or settle on the northwest coast. It also provided for the formal restoration of the land and buildings said to belong to British subjects and taken over by Spain in 1789. Vancouver was to arrange the exact details of this restitution with Spanish representatives at Nootka Sound itself.

On a personal level, Vancouver's dealings with Juan Francisco de la Bodega y Quadra, the senior Spanish officer at Nootka in 1792, were very cordial. Personal conviviality did not, however, resolve the restitution issue. Quadra was only prepared to hand over a tiny piece of land at Friendly Cove. Vancouver decided that he could not accept this 'small pittance' without approval from Britain.[4] After an inconclusive exchange of letters between the two, the matter was submitted back to London and Madrid. Part of Vancouver's problem was that he was never given clear instructions by his government and he was unwilling to act on his own. Quadra was replaced as the Spanish commander at Nootka and those who followed him were less amiable personalities. For these reasons, Vancouver left the northwest coast in 1794 with the issue unresolved.

Both Vancouver and his published account, A Voyage of Discovery, failed to receive the attention they deserved in the years following his return to Britain. Vancouver himself was broken in health by the end of his voyage, and, in the short time left to him, he laboured away in obscurity in the quiet village of Petersham on the book that would chronicle his life's work. On the wider public stage his reputation was sullied by powerful critics. A demeaning row with his former midshipman, now Lord Camelford, achieved notoriety in London and detracted attention from the achievements of the voyage. More substantially, Vancouver suffered from the disapprobation of Joseph Banks, the powerful and influential president of the Royal Society.

Vancouver's A Voyage of Discovery was not published until two or three months after his death in May 1798.[5] When it appeared, it received mixed reviews. The Naval Chronicle commented sonorously that Vancouver's Voyage would 'always rank high among those works which are considered as naval classics by professional men.' Robert Barrie, one of Vancouver's midshipmen, wrote caustically that 'it is one of the most tedious books I have ever read.'[6] Most reactions lay somewhere between these extremes and the Voyage did attract a wide readership. Within three years it had been published in four different languages and a new English edition appeared in 1801. But Vancouver's account of his voyage never achieved the notoriety of, say, James Cook's Voyages. In many ways a comparison is unfair. Vancouver was a more prosaic explorer than Cook. He was not the first European to 'discover' any major piece of land. His work was less flashy because he was left to complete what others had begun; this he did by persistence and sheer hard work. In Canada, where his name designates a large island and the country's third

largest city, he has not been not well remembered. Vancouver's charts of
the northwest coast were so accurate that they were still being used by
sailors more than a century after he died, but few gave much thought to
the man who had drawn them.

George Vancouver began to reappear in the historical memory in the
1930s. In Britain, George Godwin published a biography in 1930 and the
British Columbia historian, F.W. Howay, wrote a brief account published
in 1932.[7] Articles on aspects of his voyage began to turn up in historical
journals, particularly on the west coast of North America and in Hawai'i.
In 1960 a respectable biography by Bern Anderson entitled *Surveyor of
the Sea* appeared.[8] But an extensive scholarly evaluation of Vancouver
and his achievements had to wait until 1984 and the publication of W.
Kaye Lamb's Hakluyt Society edition of Vancouver's account of his voyage under the title, *A Voyage of Discovery to the North Pacific Ocean and
Round the World, 1791-1795*.

Lamb's edition of Vancouver has provided the basis for recent scholarship. Bound in four volumes, it begins with a long introduction which
stands as by far the best account of Vancouver, his voyage, and its context. The original manuscript of Vancouver's journal having been lost,
the text is taken from the second edition published in 1801 with minor
corrections by John Vancouver, who had worked closely with his brother
George on the first edition. It also includes copious annotations, generous appendices of related documents, and many illustrations from the
voyage. Its publication was a major contribution to the literature on the
European exploration of the Pacific in general and the early history of
the northwest coast in particular. Like Vancouver, Lamb set out detailed
directions for others to sail by.

By the early 1990s when the History Department at Simon Fraser
University was considering holding an international conference on the
bicentennial of Vancouver's arrival on the northwest coast, views of
Vancouver and other European explorers had shifted again. The Native
people of North America had forcefully reminded us that they had little
reason to celebrate the coming of Europeans to their land. They had
been making this point for generations, but significant numbers of non-
Natives were only now beginning to take notice. It was no longer possible to 'celebrate' the arrival of European explorers like George Vancouver
with enthusiasm. Compared with the controversy surrounding prepara-

tions for the Christopher Columbus quincentennial, a Vancouver bicentennial seemed like a minor side show, yet the two were linked in public consciousness. Caught up in big generalizations about the uniformly disastrous impact of early European contact, few wished to recognize the differences between the east coast in 1492 and the west coast in 1792.

To map an area is to appropriate it. To fix the convolutions of the northwest coast on a grid of lines of latitude and longitude is to begin to bring it under control. Vancouver's charts of the northwest coast were a part of a process of economic exploitation and, eventually, cultural disruption. But appropriation did not begin or end with Vancouver and, even among the well-intentioned, it continues today. Throughout much of 1992 Ronald Wright's book, *Stolen Continents: The 'New World' Through Indian Eyes Since 1492*, was on the best-seller list in Canada. This book, like others published in the quincentennial year, chronicles a history of Native people in North America that is seen as a straight and unrelieved downhill run from 1492 to the present day.[9] The periods and places of cooperation and accommodation between Natives and newcomers are forgotten in the scramble to present a politically palatable version of the past. The notion that one can see through the eyes of people from different cultures living 500 years ago and then presume to speak on their behalf involves a conceit greater than anything either Columbus or Vancouver possessed. Even sympathetic Europeans still have difficulty in understanding the need to listen to, rather than speak for, Native people.

There is no denying the oppression and suffering of the Native people of the Pacific region, and around the globe, from the time of their first encounter with Europeans; but as non-Natives strive to write the so-called 'history of the other side' they sometimes forget their own.[10] The achievements of European explorers are downplayed. Certainly for Vancouver the wheel had come full circle by 1992 as, once again, he was disparaged or ignored, just as he had been in the years after he returned from his voyage. The bicentennial of his coming to the northwest coast did not receive the same recognition as the Cook bicentennial had received fourteen years earlier. One reason was an increased consciousness among civic politicians and the public of Native issues and Native perspectives. A Vancouver event no longer seemed appropriate. But laundering history for public consumption does not lead to a better understanding of the past. History must constantly be reinterpreted, but ought not be denied.

The chapters in this book are concerned with European and Native experience. In the first, Ben Finney argues that European explorers did make genuine discoveries about the Pacific. They learned things that were not known by Europeans or even understood by the people of the Pacific. During three voyages to the Pacific, Cook discovered Polynesia – recognizing that dispersed within a huge triangle of ocean formed by the points of New Zealand (Aotearoa), Easter island (Rapa Nui), and Hawai'i were people sharing a similar language and culture. In the same sense Vancouver could be said to have discovered the northwest coast of North America, for it was he who established that it was a continuous line, unbroken by any passage to the Atlantic. His chart of the northwest coast was produced in response to questions raised in Europe that could not have been answered by any one indigenous group.

Of course, the European questions were often based on misconceptions. In mapping the northwest coast of America, armchair theoreticians constructively interacted with those who did the practical and arduous surveying itself. Glyndwr Williams shows the process at work after Cook's visit to the coast in 1778. Cook had discounted any possibility of a navigable passage through the continent, but when it became apparent that there were huge gaps on his chart of the coast, geographers returned again to the mysterious and sketchy accounts of the early voyages of de Fuca and de Fonte, with their promise of a great western sea or a system of passages through a great archipelago occupying much of what we now know to be continental land mass. Vancouver's careful surveys proved the theoreticians wrong, but they at least had framed the question and given purpose to his mission.

What the Europeans found depended on what they were looking for. Although Vancouver has been criticized for missing the mouths of the Columbia and Fraser rivers, we learn from Andrew David how important it is to examine Vancouver's Admiralty instructions before judging his results. He was to look for a navigable passage between 30° and 60° north without attempting a minute examination of the entire coast or continuing his survey of any river or inlet once he had determined that it could not be navigated by an ocean-going vessel. Vancouver, David says, was brilliantly successful given the limits of his instructions, the length of the coastline he covered, and the technology available to him. His work has to be placed within a context. He made an incremental advance in a project that had occupied Europeans for centuries – mapping distant regions of the world – and the design and capabilities of his mission were determined largely by what had gone before.

Technology illustrates the nature of Vancouver's contribution. In calculating longitudes, he employed dead reckoning, lunar observation, and chronometers. Alun C. Davies draws attention to this combination of old and new technologies. Advances did not come in giant leaps, he observes, but in small steps. Chronometers were the instruments of the future, but the best of them were not reliable enough to gain Vancouver's complete trust. Improvements to chronometers came as experience directed and encouraged development. Vancouver's extended trial of chronometers supplied by the leading makers of the day both publicized the instrument and showed where further improvement was needed.

Maritime technology also enters James Gibson's discussion of Russian activity in the North Pacific. Again we see incremental developments and a historical inheritance of fixed ideas that was not easily shaken. In seeking to account for what he describes as a slow and tentative Russian exploitation eastward from the Kamchatka peninsula, Gibson offers several related lines of explanation. The Russians were a continental people for whom the ocean was more a boundary than an invitation to go further. Their logistical problems in maintaining bases on the Pacific were immense, and they were easily diverted by opportunities and challenges on their land frontiers. Finally, Russia was comparatively backward in the sciences and deficient in skills essential to exploring and mapping maritime regions.

The arrival of the British in the North Pacific underscored the weakness of the Russian position. For, in contrast to the Russians, the British had an idea of the value of the Pacific and the means to realize that idea. Alan Frost marshals evidence of Britain's singular capacity and will to act; and he offers the British response to Spain in the confrontation over Nootka Sound as a striking demonstration of Britain's global reach. He also sees Britain's behaviour in this crisis as the expression of a well-developed policy aimed at opening up the Pacific to the independent traders of all nations. In adopting this view, he challenges those who have looked for an imperial plan in British ventures in the Pacific and found only a series of reactions to immediate crises and concerns. The British government of the time, he argues, conceived of a commercial empire based on a free trade system centred in the Pacific, and this conception informed its efforts throughout the Pacific region.

Christon Archer reminds us that European vision was refracted through Pacific reality. The Spanish, like all other European explorers on the northwest coast, had to cope with the power of the Native peoples. Thus their plans for missionary work based on experience with Native people in the south were quickly abandoned on the northern coast. The Spanish did, however, attempt to appropriate Native people to assert hegemony over the northwest coast. When it suited them, they sought alliances with Native leaders, particularly at Nootka Sound, and tried to manipulate Native evidence to bolster their claims to the area against those of Britain.

If Europeans thought that Native people were pawns in their power games, the northwest Natives also manipulated the Europeans. Yvonne Marshall shows that the European visitors were often unwitting puppets as Native leaders pulled the strings. Maquinna, the ranking leader at Nootka Sound, was involved in diplomatic manoeuvring of his own both within the Nootka Sound confederacy and in his relations with other leaders on the west coast of Vancouver Island, and he used his relationship with Vancouver and Quadra to bolster his position. Marshall also traces a clear line of continuity between the Native diplomacy at Nootka Sound in 1792 and current political organization among the Nuu-chah-nulth people.

Victoria Wyatt draws attention to the need to listen to the voices of Native people if we are to write a history that includes their contribution. The Native voice is often absent from the written record, forcing historians to tune their ears to other sources. For cultures that do not use the written word, art can speak through metaphor. In discussing northwest coast art during the time of Vancouver and after, Wyatt shows the strength and inventiveness of the artistic tradition. Within that tradition, artists explored new materials, tried new contexts for artistic expression, and, faced with these often perplexing newcomers on their shores, began to play with new metaphors. Wyatt tentatively suggests that the way in which Europeans were depicted reveals a sharp dividing line, in the minds of northwest coast artists, between their world and that of the newcomers.

Anne Salmond also urges us to see the 'exploration' of the Pacific from the viewpoint of the people who were already there. She has employed the letters and journals of the governor of the convict colony of Norfolk Island to reconstruct the experiences of two Maori, Tuki and Huru, whose lives were changed immeasurably when Vancouver's ships passed through New Zealand waters. Using European sources, she tells a memorable story of early contact between cultures that opens a door to our perception of what this meant from the Maori side. The events that she describes were minor in European history, but they profoundly affected the lives of Tuki and Huru.

Clearly, the written record is still a basic source, whether we are studying European or Native cultures. But to use this record effectively, we need to understand how it came to exist. In his history of the journal kept by the botanist and surgeon Archibald Menzies, W. Kaye Lamb illustrates the range of motives that prompted individuals to keep written records throughout long voyages. Menzies was a protegé of the influential Joseph Banks, who did not like Vancouver. The journal that Menzies maintained during his voyage with Vancouver was both adversarial and competitive. It was adversarial because it was maintained as a weapon against Vancouver in the event of an altercation (which inevitably occurred); and it was competitive because Banks and Menzies hoped to publish their journal before Vancouver got his to press. Lamb's account of the evolution of the Menzies journal shows how even the first-hand accounts of Pacific voyages were rewritten to serve interests other than providing scientific information.

Every account brought back from the Pacific was grist for the mill of the European imagination. As Europeans strove to interpret what they learned about the Pacific and its peoples, they defined things according to their own constructs. K.R. Howe looks at the long history of speculation about the origins and cultures of the Polynesians. In a sense, knowledge of the Pacific created for Europeans the problem of redefining themselves. The ultimate conclusion in defining the 'other' in order to establish the 'self' was the notion that the Polynesians had Caucasian origins.

David Mackay follows a related theme, the real and the imagined Pacific. The explorations of the likes of Cook and Vancouver were driven by myths, or metaphors, of new lands. Scientific discoveries often meant that these expectations were not fulfilled. Nevertheless, new metaphors were developed based on interpreting, and misinterpreting, the information gathered about the Pacific. As Mackay observes, Europeans have never completely abandoned their assumption that the bounty of the Pacific was limitless.

The explorer's work, it seems, is never finished. Every step in amassing hard, empirical evidence is followed by a new leap in imagination. Cook may have identified a Polynesian world and Vancouver delineated the northwest coast, thereby demolishing certain myths. But their work only led to further speculation and new questions. George Vancouver devoted nearly five years to a voyage to the Pacific, and when he returned he presented the British admiralty with a set of superb, detailed, and, for that matter, 'accurate' charts of the northwest coast of North America. In what remained of his life he wrote an account of his *Voyage of Discovery* to accompany the charts. He was determined to provide more than merely 'an abstract, of our proceedings.' Instead, he wrote a detailed, day-to-day narrative in the hope of making 'the history of our transactions on the north-west coast of America *as conclusive as possible,* against all speculative opinions.'[11] The chapters in this book illustrate, in a variety of ways, reasons why this hope could not be realized. He had represented the northwest coast on paper and drawn its contours within straight lines of latitude and longitude. But he was not the only witness to his expedition; his was not the only point of view; and he could not determine the use made of his information and experience. Consciously or not, he was involved in an interplay between maps and metaphors – an interplay that has continued to the present day.

James Cook and the European Discovery of Polynesia

Ben Finney

On Saturday, 7 October 1769, HMS *Endeavour* sailed slowly westward through uncharted waters of the South Pacific. This lone British vessel, commanded by Lieutenant James Cook of the Royal Navy, was thirteen months out of England on a scientific mission: to observe the transit of Venus across the face of the sun in order to measure the distance between earth and sun, and then to search for the fabled southern continent, the *Terra Australis* thought by many geographers of that day to lie somewhere in the southern ocean. Once Cook had completed the astronomical observations at Tahiti, he sailed south into chill waters and stormy seas. After reaching latitude 40° south, Cook turned north to seek better weather, then headed west to sweep across the ocean in search of the continent that geographers theorized must be there to balance the greater land mass of the Northern Hemisphere.

For some days prior to that October Saturday, the sight of multitudes of birds, pieces of driftwood, bits of floating seaweed, and seawater 'paler than common' had raised hopes that a land mass lay ahead. At two in the afternoon the lookout spotted land, although those on deck did not see anything until it was silhouetted against the red sunset. After an anxious night, the *Endeavour* sailed into a spacious bay ringed by green, wooded hills. 'Certainly the continent we are in search for,' wrote Joseph Banks, the expedition's natural historian.[1] But it was not a continent, nor even an island never before seen by European eyes. Over a century earlier, the Dutch navigator Abel Tasman had coasted along the opposite, western shore of this island, now known as the North Island of New Zealand.

Yet, in human terms Cook's landfall turned out to be far more important than merely chancing upon an unknown island. It might even approach the significance of finding a new continent. *Endeavour*'s landfall on New Zealand began a cultural discovery that, in three successive Pacific voyages under Cook's command, was to define Polynesia. It proved to be a new oceanic world undreamt of by European geographers, a huge triangular section of the globe the size of the better part of Europe and Asia combined that was populated by an uncommonly handsome people belonging to, as Cook phrased it, the 'same Nation.'

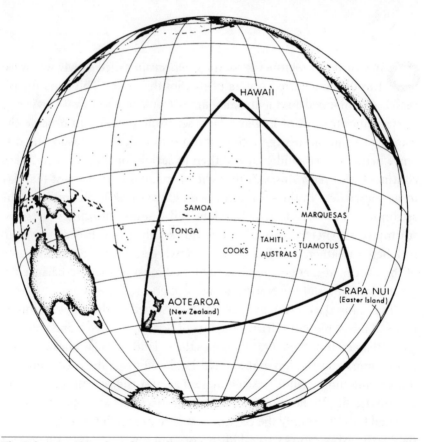

The Polynesian Triangle. A few small Polynesian settlements lie outside this triangle. The current indigenous names, Aotearoa and Rapa Nui, are used for New Zealand and Easter Island, respectively.

In fact, it might even be argued that this was Cook's greatest discovery. After all, the results of the main tasks assigned to him by the Admiralty during his three Pacific voyages – observing the transit of Venus, and searching for a southern continent and then a northwest passage – were essentially disappointing. Cook himself had been deeply chagrined to find that optical effects had made it virtually impossible to time the transit of Venus accurately. And, however geographically significant it was to report that he had not found a southern continent and a northwest passage, how much more exciting it would have been to confirm that he had. Furthermore, it is obviously false to claim that Cook discovered Hawai'i, New Zealand, or any other Pacific island. Canoe voyagers had preceded him by many centuries to each and every one of the mid-Pacific islands he chanced upon. Yet, it can be argued that during his three Pacific expeditions Cook literally discovered Polynesia, a great cultural province of humankind not only unknown to the outside world, but also not fully recognized by the Polynesians themselves.

To appreciate how Cook came to recognize this widespread maritime culture, we need to return to the *Endeavour*'s landfall on New Zealand, or Aotearoa, to use its modern Maori name. The bay into which the English expedition slowly sailed turned out to be inhabited: houses, canoes, and then people reminiscent of the Tahitians came into view. Once ashore, in what Tahitian they had learned during their stay at Tahiti, Cook and other expedition leaders tried hailing the people, who were gathered defensively across a river after one of them had been shot as he was about to loft a spear. 'But,' Cook recorded in his journal, 'they answered us by flourishing their weapons over their heads and danceing, as was supposed the war dance,' which caused the English to retire from the bank until a party of marines arrived. Then Cook, along with a Tahitian named Tupaia (Tupia to the English) who was sailing back to England aboard the *Endeavour*, returned to the river's edge. There, recorded Cook, 'Tupia spoke to them in his own language and it was an [a]greeable surprise to us to find that they perfectly understood him.'[2]

During Cook's circumnavigation of Aotearoa, Tupaia was to prove invaluable time and time again in establishing communication between the English and Maori, preventing or at least decreasing any bloodshed between the two groups, and thereby greatly aiding Cook and his crew to obtain the water and foodstuffs they needed for their survival. The

Tahitian could communicate with the Maori because their languages were so closely related, being members of the East Polynesian sub-group of the Polynesian language family. This kinship, so evident in Tupaia's performance, was further confirmed by a comparative vocabulary of basic Maori and Tahitian terms drawn up by the expedition's naturalist Joseph Banks, which clearly demonstrated the relationship. To Cook and Banks it was obvious that the 'South-sea Islanders' of Tahiti and the people of Aotearoa 'had one Origin or Source' not only because of the virtual identity of the languages, but also because they shared the same customs and 'notions of the creation of the World Mankind &c as the people of the South Sea Islands have.'[3]

Recognizing that people of 'one Origin or Source' were spread over the 2,000 miles between Tahiti and Aotearoa was just the beginning of this tale of Polynesian discovery. On his second voyage into the Pacific with *Resolution* and *Adventure*, directed primarily to probing the high latitudes of the Southern Hemisphere to confirm, or once and for all to lay to rest, the existence of a *Terra Australis*, Cook and his crew made a further cultural-linguistic discovery showing that people of this 'Nation' were distributed thousands of miles to the east as well as to the west of Tahiti.

After leaving England, Cook had first sailed along the edge of the ice in the high latitudes of the Indian Ocean. Then, after wintering over in Aotearoa and cruising through tropical Polynesian waters, in the late Austral spring he headed south once more. At latitude 71°10' huge 'ice islands' and an impenetrable wall of ice beyond them forced Cook to return north.[4] At that point, Cook could have honourably headed to Cape Town for rest, repairs, and supplies and then sailed back to England to report that no trace of an unknown continent had been found to the north of the limit of ice in either the Indian or Pacific oceans. But he wanted to explore the high latitudes of the South Atlantic to settle the question of *Terra Australis* for once and for all. Furthermore, while waiting for the next summer season to do so, Cook wanted to make still another sweep across the tropical South Pacific, for, as he wrote in his journal, it 'would have been betraying not only want of perseverance, but judgement, in supposing the South Pacific Ocean to have been so well explored that nothing remained to be done in it.'[5]

In particular, Cook wanted to locate islands reported by previous European navigators but 'imperfectly explored,' and then fix their precise locations on the map. The *Resolution* carried one of the first working chronometers, and Cook could also precisely determine their longitude by the difficult 'lunar distances' method of observation.[6] One of the first tasks was to find a small island the Dutch navigator Jacob Roggeveen had chanced upon one Easter Sunday in 1722. This was not easy. Roggeveen had been able to determine the island's latitude by measuring the angle of the noonday sun but, since neither the chronometer nor the lunar distances method had been invented, he was only able to estimate its longitude by dead reckoning. Accordingly, Cook sailed up to the island's latitude, taking care to be well to the east of its estimated longitude, then sailed due west for three days before being rewarded by the first sight of land in 103 days. Upon spying through the glass the characteristic 'Idols' mentioned by Roggeveen, Cook was sure he had found Easter Island, or Rapa Nui as its Polynesian inhabitants now call it.

Although the Dutch navigator had briefly described the islanders in his report, he had not supplied any information that would have made the English think that the people living there spoke, like the Maori of Aotearoa, a language closely related to Tahitian. The first clue to such a linguistic kinship came when a group of Rapa Nui paddled its small canoe alongside the *Resolution* and 'immediately called out for a rope, naming it by the same word as the Tahiteans.'[7] Then the curious actions of the first man to board the *Resolution* provided dramatic support to the suspicions of these amateur philologists. So impressed was the islander by the ship's great length that the first thing he did upon climbing aboard was to measure it by fathoming it with his outstretched arms from bow to stern. In so doing, wrote Cook, the man called out the 'numbers by the same names as they do at Otaheite [Tahiti].'[8] This obvious linguistic relationship, plus the similarity of the physical appearance of the people and their customs with those of the Tahitians and Maori, led Cook to proclaim that 'it is extraordinary that the same Nation should have spread themselves over all the isles in the Vast Ocean from New Zealand to this Island which is almost a fourth part of the circumference of the Globe.'[9]

Actually, the islands of Polynesia form a huge triangle that extends across the equator into the North Pacific, and Cook had really only traced the base leg formed by the southernmost Polynesian islands of Aotearoa and Rapa Nui. It would take a third expedition – this time devoted to searching for a passage around North America through which

British ships might reach Asia by a direct northerly route – for Cook to chart the northernmost extension of this seafaring nation that had preceded European navigators into the Pacific.

When, after a stop at Tahiti, Cook headed toward the northwest coast of North America, he had no reason to expect that people akin to these 'South Sea Islanders' had spread into the North Pacific. The Tahitians themselves told Cook that they knew of no islands to the north or northwest of them. On 24 December 1777, soon after crossing the equator, the English chanced upon an atoll of the Northern Line group, which they called Christmas Island because they celebrated the holiday there. This discovery, however, gave them no cause to imagine that the Polynesian nation extended that far north, for they did not see any signs of human habitation on this dry, desolate island, apparently missing the remains of structures that archaeologists now say indicate Polynesians temporarily occupied the island.

After observing a solar eclipse from Christmas Island, and stocking up on turtles from the abundant population there, Cook and his men headed toward the northwest coast. But strong northeast trade winds encountered above 7° latitude forced their ships, the *Resolution* and *Discovery,* just far enough to the west of north for them to intersect with the western end of the Hawai'ian chain. On 18 January 1778, lookouts spotted the peaks of Oahu and Kauai. Had the 'South Sea Islanders' reached these northerly isles? That question must have been uppermost in the minds of the English when they approached Kauai. However, as they coasted along Kauai's south shore, Cook wrote that there was 'some doubt whether or no[t] the land before was inhabited' – until canoes were spied coming off the shore. When the islanders reached the ships, the English were, in Cook's words, 'agreeably surprised to find them of the same Nation as the people of Otaheite and the other islands we had lately visited.'[10] As at Aotearoa and Rapa Nui, the linguistic tie was unmistakable to all those on board who knew Tahitian: Lieutenant King recorded in his journal how they caught the 'sound of Otaheite words in their speech, & on asking them for hogs, breadfruit, yams, in that Dialect, we found we were understood, & that these were in plenty on shore.'[11] The English now realized that the 'South Sea Islanders' had indeed spread across the equator into the Northern Hemisphere.

That, briefly, is the tale of how, in three epic voyages, Cook and his shipmates charted the Polynesian triangle and recognized that the people whose islands form its points – Aotearoa, Rapa Nui, and Hawai'i – shared a linguistic, cultural, and physical identity with those of Tahiti, the Marquesas, Tonga, and other islands within the triangle visited during the three expeditions.

This cultural charting of the Polynesian nation was a genuine discovery. Even though Spanish, Dutch, and English ships had been sailing through the Polynesian triangle for 250 years after Magellan's first crossing in 1519, no one aboard seems to have had the slightest inkling that they were traversing the oceanic realm of a people of common origin, who spoke closely related languages and shared a unique cultural heritage. Nor, apparently, did the Polynesians on any single or group of islands comprehend the full extent of their own maritime civilization. On first contact with the Europeans, the people of Aotearoa, Rapa Nui, and Hawai'i remembered their various homelands located at the centre of the triangle, but only in legend, for contacts between them and the more central islands, such as the Marquesas, Tahiti, and Rarotonga, had by then ceased. Likewise, although those at the centre knew about the islands around them for a considerable radius, their knowledge about the more peripheral islands was at best vague.

Why was Cook the one to make this Polynesian discovery, and not any of the navigators who sailed the Pacific before him? It would be tempting to credit Cook's superb seamanship, navigational skills, and dogged perseverance and leave it at that. But a new motivation for undertaking exploratory voyages as well as advances in seafaring provided the opportunity for Cook's qualities to shine. If Cook had not been repeatedly sent into the Pacific to explore, and if he had not had well-found ships, the latest navigational advances, and new ideas about how to defeat scurvy, he probably would not have made this great discovery. In particular, being 'employ'd as a discoverer' by the Admiralty set Cook apart from the Europeans who had sailed the Pacific before him. With few exceptions, his predecessors did not do so to explore the ocean (much less its islands and peoples), but essentially to get to the other side, and as quickly as possible, before too many on board succumbed to scurvy or just plain starvation. They belonged to the first age of discovery, when the search for routes to the riches of Asia, and the exploitation of these routes – and those to and from the unexpectedly discovered New World of the Americas – drove Europeans to cross the seas. Cook was a pioneer of what Goetzman calls the second, scientific age of discovery, during which the maritime nations of Europe, and later the United States, sent out expeditions to explore unknown seas and then report back on the lands they found, their resources, their flora and fauna, and their peoples.[12]

The groundwork for discovering Polynesia was laid at Tahiti. This island was known to Europe after Captain Samuel Wallis had chanced upon it in 1767, and it was chosen as the observation site for the transit of Venus. Cook arrived on 13 April 1769 and stayed for three months, observing the transit of Venus and taking on water and food for the rest of the voyage. Staying so long on one island was unprecedented. No previous European navigator who had sailed through Polynesian waters had stayed anywhere near that long on any island, and above all, none had tried so hard to learn the local language and customs, and make friends with the people, as did Cook and others aboard the *Endeavour*.

In part this long stay on Tahiti and the effort to establish good relations with the Tahitians and learn something about them was dictated by the nature of the mission and Cook's penchant for preparation. Cook realized that the establishment of friendly relations with the Tahitians was basic to his mission's success. He and his assistants needed to make their astronomical observations unmolested, and he required Tahitian cooperation to feed his crew and fill the ship with food and water for the remainder of the voyage. But the attention paid to the Tahitians was also integral to the new type of scientific exploration being pioneered on this voyage. The extension of Enlightenment curiosity into the Pacific meant that the people living on the oceanic islands were as much, if not more, a focus of study as were the local landforms, plants, and animals.

Joseph Banks, the expedition's young and wealthy naturalist, seems to have taken the lead in studying the Tahitians. Banks, who had some training in philology, readily picked up rudimentary Tahitian, and compiled a list of Tahitian words. Then he compared Tahitian with vocabularies of other island languages which were contained in various compilations of voyages and other texts on the *Endeavour*. This comparison revealed that languages that were spread from Tahiti westward to Indonesia, and even across the Indian Ocean to Madagascar, were related, an early recognition of what linguists now call the Austronesian language family: the most widespread language family in the world until Europeans began expanding overseas.[13]

Banks, Cook, and the other scientists and officers on that first voyage must have spent many hours talking about language relationships, as well as the physical characteristics and cultural practices of the islanders. This linguistic and anthropological inquiry was continued on the subsequent voyages, with leading roles being assumed by the 'natural philosophers' Johann Forster and his son George on the second voyage, and by the linguistically able surgeon William Anderson on the third voyage.[14] Cook obviously learned from these and other apt students on board and incorporated their findings in his journal. Cook, however, went beyond Banks, the Forsters, and the others. He developed a working knowledge of Tahitian and made linguistic-cultural observations and hypotheses on not one, but all three, voyages. Furthermore, Cook injected needed nautical sense into the conjectures about how people speaking related languages could have spread so far over the ocean.

Cook's contribution, as a mariner, to our understanding of Polynesian migration is not commonly appreciated. Largely on the basis of linguistic comparisons, Banks and Cook hypothesized that the ancestors of the 'South Sea Islanders' had migrated eastward into the Pacific from the 'East Indies,' that is, from the islands which roughly comprise modern Indonesia, island Malaysia, and the Philippines. Cook realized, however, that this hypothesis, which is still basic to thinking about Polynesian migration, raised a critical issue of seamanship: how could people sailing in canoes without keels or centreboards push thousands of miles from Southeast Asia to the eastern Pacific against the southeast trade winds? Whereas other students of Polynesian migration, including most notably Thor Heyerdahl,[15] were to conclude that the easterly trade winds would have prevented canoe voyagers from ever sailing eastward into the Pacific and that therefore Polynesia had not been settled from the Asian side of the ocean, Cook thought otherwise.

Cook was deeply influenced by what he had learned about Tahitian canoes, seamanship, and navigation from Tupaia, the learned Tahitian who had befriended the English. Tupaia told Cook that Tahiti was surrounded for a considerable distance by islands, and that the people of these islands spoke the same language (actually, related languages) as the Tahitians. Based upon the bearings and sailing times to the islands furnished by Tupaia, Cook was able to draw a map of all these islands, which, when corrected for misunderstandings about directional terms, arguably indicates that the Tahitians knew about islands in the Australs, Tuamotus, Marquesas, Cooks, and Samoa, as well as Rotuma located even farther to the west. Cook also understood Tupaia to say that the Tahitians sailed back and forth between many of these islands and Tahiti, using celestial navigation. This puzzled the English navigator. Although he accepted that the Tahitians were capable of navigating without instruments and that Tahitian canoes could sail well reaching across the wind or running before it, he did not think their craft were weatherly enough to sail directly into the wind. Since the return voyages from the Cooks, Samoa, and other islands to the west of Tahiti would, Cook thought, have to be made by tacking against the easterly trade winds, he wondered how the Tahitians were able to make these voyages.

Tupaia, we learn from Cook's journals, set the English navigator at ease by explaining to him 'that during the Months of Novr Decemb^r & January Westerly winds with rain prevail,' and that whenever the Tahitians wanted to sail to the east they waited for the seasonal westerly winds. This not only solved the puzzle of how Tupaia and other contemporary Tahitians could sail back and forth across Polynesian seas, but

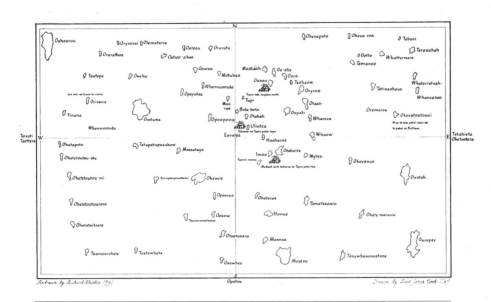

Captain James Cook's 'Chart of the Islands Surrounding Tahiti from Directions Furnished by Tupaia' (redrawn by Richard Rhodes)

also was the crucial bit of intelligence Cook needed to make sense of the evident linguistic relationship of the Tahitians and the peoples of the 'East Indies.' Since 'the inhabitants of the Islands know very well how to make proper use of the winds,' Cook proposed that their ancestors had sailed from the 'East Indies,' using westerly wind shifts to work their way, island by island, across the Pacific.[16] This prescient suggestion, contained in just a few lines in Cook's journal, has only recently been supported by archaeological excavations revealing the island-by-island progress of canoe voyagers into the mid-Pacific, and by the voyage of the reconstructed canoe *Hokule'a* from Samoa to Tahiti, demonstrating how seasonal westerly wind shifts can be used to sail eastward against the trade winds.[17]

Cook's appreciation of the deep-sea handling of the Polynesians' canoes, their skill at navigating over long stretches of open ocean with only 'the Sun serving them for a compass by day and the Moon and Stars by night,'[18] and their ability to exploit wind shifts to sail wherever they wanted contrasts greatly with the opinions of such earlier European navigators as Pedro Fernandez de Quiros and Jacob Roggeveen, who also struggled to comprehend how stone-age peoples could have reached these mid-ocean islands.

In 1595, the Spanish expedition under the command of Alvaro de Mendaña left Peru bound for the western Pacific with a party of colonists determined to settle the Solomon Islands, an archipelago Mendaña had briefly explored in 1567. While sailing across the eastern Pacific, the Spanish chanced upon an archipelago of rugged, volcanic islands northeast of Tahiti, which their commander christened Las Marquesas de Mendoza after the wife of his patron, the viceroy of Peru. In his journal, the expedition's navigator, Quiros, expressed surprise at finding people of such a seemingly low level of technology on islands so far out into the ocean. Because the Marquesans had neither ships nor the compass, Quiros adjudged them to be 'a people without skill or the possibility of sailing to distant parts,' whose ancestors, therefore, could not possibly have sailed over the sea to reach these islands.[19] Accordingly, he hypothesized that just to the south of the Marquesas must be a continent or a chain of closely spaced islands stretching from Asia across the South Pacific that had enabled the Marquesans' ancestors to move far enough east to make a short crossing to the Marquesas.[20]

When Roggeveen had visited Rapa Nui 125 years later, he was even more puzzled by how people could have reached this lovely island. Not only was the island just a speck of land lost in the immense Pacific, but the islanders had only tiny paddling canoes pieced together from whatever scraps of wood were left after some 1,500 years of human occupation and consequent deforestation. Because their canoes were so small and leaky, and because the islanders lacked the compass, he could only conclude that they had been brought there by some outside agency. After speculating that the Spanish might have brought them there from South America, or that they might be direct descendants of Adam, who 'had bred there naturally from generation to generation,' Roggeveen gave up, declaring that 'the ability of human understanding is powerless to comprehend by what means they could have been transported' to the island.[21]

Even Cook's French contemporary, Julien Crozet, who visited Aotearoa in 1772 as an officer on the ill-fated expedition of Captain Nicholas Thomas Marion du Fresne, utterly dismissed the possibility that the Maori ancestors could have sailed there on their own. Crozet, who had a list of Tahitian words gathered when Louis-Antoine de Bougainville had stopped at Tahiti a year before Cook, recognized that the languages of the Maori and the Tahitians were closely related and that both peoples must therefore share a common origin. But where Cook assumed that this tie could be explained through canoe voyaging, Crozet could only imagine that a great volcanic cataclysm had rent asunder a once populated continent: 'People so widely separated and without a knowledge of the art of navigation do not speak the same language unless they were once the same people and inhabited perhaps the same continent, of which the volcanic shocks have only spared us the mountains and their savage inhabitants.'[22]

Just as it would be a mistake to attribute to Cook personally all the linguistic and anthropological findings from each of the many islands and archipelagos visited during his three voyages of Polynesian discovery, so it would be an exaggeration to claim that he settled once and for all the question of how Polynesia had been settled. The eastward, island-by-island progression into the Pacific from the 'East Indies' that Cook wrote about at Tahiti was an inspired guess made early in the first voyage, well before the full extent of this oceanic culture was known. After reaching Hawai'i on his third voyage in early 1778, and realizing that this maritime nation extended into the Northern Hemisphere as well as across the South Pacific, Cook penned that famous question in his journal: 'How shall we account for this Nation spreading itself so far over this vast ocean?'[23] However, he did not then attempt to answer it, and because of his own fateful miscalculation the next year at Kealakekua Bay, Cook was forever denied the opportunity to do so.

Nonetheless, Andrew Sharp, who in the 1950s and 1960s argued long and hard that the Polynesian islands had been settled by innumerable involuntary drift voyages and other maritime accidents,[24] seized upon a remark made by Cook earlier during the third voyage to proclaim that Cook himself fathered the accidental settlement theory. Before turning north, the expedition had touched on the small island of Atiu in the archipelago later to be called the Cook Islands. There Ma'i, a Tahitian on board the *Resolution* whom the English called Omai, met four fellow Tahitians who told him how, while sailing from Tahiti to neighbouring Ra'iatea, they had missed their landfall and drifted many days to the southwest before fetching up on Atiu. After recounting in his journal this tale of involuntary drift voyaging, Cook tersely commented that 'this circumstance very well accounts for the manner the inhabited islands in this Sea have been first peopled; especially those which lay remote from any Continent and from each other.'[25]

Although Sharp claimed that this sentence proved that Cook dismissed the possibility that the islands had been settled through intentional voyaging, as his earlier remarks made at Tahiti suggest, John Beaglehole, Cook's editor and biographer, disagreed.[26] He proposed that if Cook had survived the third voyage to return to England where he could have reflected on the question posed, he probably would have concluded, like Anderson, the surgeon on the third voyage, that voyages of both 'design' and 'accident' accounted for the settlement of the many islands of Polynesia.[27]

Cook did not distinctively label the cultural region he had charted; he and his colleagues called the inhabitants 'South Sea Islanders' or 'Indians' and labelled the whole simply as a 'Nation.' The term *Polynesia* was in the geographical literature of the time. It had been coined in 1756 as *Polynésie*, by the French magistrate and scholar Charles de Brosses, who had combined the Greek roots for 'many' and 'islands' to label the entire insular region of the Pacific.[28] Not till a half century had passed after Cook's last voyage was the term delimited in its current sense by the

French navigator Jules-Sébastien-César Dumont-d'Urville. In a paper read before the Geographical Society of Paris, he subdivided the insular Pacific into three regions: *Polynésie*, for the islands within the triangle formed by Hawai'i, Rapa Nui, and Aotearoa; *Melanésie*, named for the dark-skinned peoples of New Guinea and islands extending eastwards toward Polynesia; and *Micronésie*, composed of the tiny islands north of Melanesia.[29]

However geographically tidy this tripartite division might have been, it has been more of an impediment than an aid to understanding the prehistory of the Pacific and its cultural diversity. Where Polynesia is remarkably homogeneous, having been populated in recent millennia by people of one origin, Micronesia is demonstrably more diverse, and Melanesia exemplifies human diversity itself. For example, despite the region's name, the skin tones of Melanesians are anything but uniformly black. The blue-black people of Bougainville and Buka islands regard their lighter-hued counterparts of mainland Papua New Guinea as 'red-skins,' and communities of brown-skinned Polynesians are sprinkled throughout the region.

Melanesia's physical diversity, also reflected strongly in its multiplicity of languages, stems from the great time the region has been occupied, with all the opportunities for micro-evolution this implies, as well as a much more complex migrational history than elsewhere in the Pacific. Polynesians can be traced to one main movement into the mid-Pacific dating back some 3500 years, and Micronesia appears to have been populated by just two similarly recent migrational thrusts. In contrast, since the first people reached Melanesia at least 40,000 years ago during the last ice age, this region has witnessed numerous migratory movements. All this rich history of migration and diversification was masked, however, by the static division of the Pacific Islands into Melanesia, Micronesia, and Polynesia. Indeed, much recent progress in understanding Melanesia's prehistory has been accomplished by ignoring Dumont-d'Urville's labels.

To be sure, Cook's discovery of the Polynesian nation contributed to this unfortunate classification scheme, but he himself was not guilty of it. He never attempted to chart the whole Pacific anthropologically; if anything, his observations from those Melanesian islands that he did visit are filled with references to the diverse peoples found there. During his second voyage, Cook explored the archipelago he named the New Hebrides (now Vanuatu) and chanced upon a long, mountainous island he called New Caledonia. Here Cook sailed clean out of homogenous Polynesia into a new island world marked by multiple tongues, physical types, and customs. In his journal, Cook remarks on how much the islanders on Vanuatu and on New Caledonia differed in language and appearance with each other as well as from the Polynesians, with one intriguing exception.[30] The English recognized that a group of people encountered on Tanna Island in Vanuatu spoke a language close to Tongan and looked as though they had some Polynesian admixture.

When, therefore, during his third voyage Cook penned in his journal the question of how to account for the great spread of the Polynesians, he did not delimit this nation solely to the islands contained within the triangle marked off by Hawai'i, Rapa Nui, and Aotearoa. He recognized that these seafaring people had spread at least as far as Tanna, and he correctly surmised that such outliers must extend farther to the 'west beyond the Hebrides.'[31] In fact, the westernmost Polynesian settlement is on the atoll of Nukuria to the northeast of New Guinea between New Britain and Bougainville. Since Nukuria is at longitude 155° west, and Rapa Nui is at longitude 109° east, this means that the Polynesians had colonized islands spread over 96 degrees of longitude, or over one-quarter of the globe.[32]

Today, to credit Cook for culturally charting Polynesia is to sail against the winds of both indigenous reawakening and anthropological fashion. Anyone who has ever been called the 'British Columbus' must now come under heavy fire. During the 1992 quincentennial of his voyage to the New World, Christopher Columbus was excoriated as the bringer of death, destruction, and colonialism to the Native Americans. Now Cook is being demonized by some islanders as the man who introduced whipping, kidnapping, and more lethal punishments to those who would not play by English rules; who carried syphilis, gonorrhoea, tuberculosis, and other epidemic illnesses into previously disease-free populations; and who by so accurately charting the islands opened this hitherto isolated Eden to the ravages of western imperialism.[33] Even in scholarly circles outside of Polynesia, Cook's reputation as an observer of island peoples is now being dismissed. How, critics such as the social anthropologist Gananach Obeyesekere ask, could a man who could not speak any of the island languages fluently, who physically punished islanders for theft, and who took lives to defend the British right to land on islands and reprovision have presumed to say anything about people he so misunderstood and abused?[34]

Anti-Cook sentiments are not altogether new in the Pacific. After all, the Hawai'ians at Kealakekua Bay killed Cook while he was attempting to take their high chief hostage to get back a stolen boat, and nineteenth-century American missionaries and their Hawai'ian converts damned Cook for his hubris in allowing himself to be worshipped as a personification of the god Lono, as well as for introducing sexually transmitted diseases.[35] Furthermore, it has long been widely accepted that Cook did not know enough Tahitian or any other Polynesian language to inquire deeply into the inner workings of the Polynesian societies he encountered – as Cook himself had confessed to none other than Boswell.[36] And, however much the opiate of discovery exhilarated those who sailed on the *Endeavour, Resolution, Adventure,* and *Discovery,* it was not without some pangs of regret for the inevitable costs to the islanders that would open their world to outside influences and temptations. As George Forster, that true child of the Enlightenment, expressed it after the second voyage: 'If the knowledge of a few individuals can only be acquired at such a price as the happiness of nations, it were better for the discoverers, and the discovered, that the South Sea had still remained unknown to Europe and its restless inhabitants.'[37]

Yet, such criticisms and regrets cannot erase the record left by a sailor from one small, but expansionary, Atlantic island nation – a record of discovery of an immense world of another seafaring people, and of marvel at how these people could have sailed their canoes so far and wide over the world's greatest ocean. In particular, we who have sailed on reconstructed Polynesian canoes, in the wake of those who first explored the Pacific, respect his effort to describe what he saw and learned and to give credit to the seafaring accomplishments of the true discoverers of all the many islands of the open Pacific.

Myth and Reality: The Theoretical Geography of Northwest America from Cook to Vancouver

Glyndwr Williams

On 20 October 1778, in the last letter he wrote to the Admiralty before his death, Captain James Cook described his failure to find a northwest passage along the Pacific coast of North America. From April to August of that year, he wrote, 'We were upon a Coast where every step was to be considered, where no information could be had from Maps, either modern or ancient ... we met with many obstacles before we got through the narrow Strait that divides Asia from America ... [but] ... on the 17th of August in the Latitude 70°45' Longitude 198° East, we were stopped by an impenetrable body of ice.'[1] The disappointment was the greater since Cook's journal makes it clear that he had no faith in those mysterious voyages of Juan de Fuca in 1592 and Bartholomew de Fonte in 1640 which had supposedly come across great straits stretching east toward the Atlantic.[2] Sailing past Cape Flattery on the night of 22 March, Cook wrote, 'It is in the very latitude we were now in where geographers have placed the pretended *Strait of Juan de Fuca*, but we saw nothing like it, nor is there the least probability that iver such thing exhisted.'[3] On 30 April, with the ships storm-tossed and well offshore in latitude 53° north, Cook wrote that he would have preferred to be closer in since this was the location of 'the pretended Strait of Admiral de Fonte,' but that 'for my own part, I give no credet to such vague and improbable stories.'[4] His only hope of a passage, he told the Admiralty, was to return again to that desolate northern strait soon to be named after Bering, though with 'little hopes of succeeding.' His pessimism was justified: for after his death at

Hawai'i in February 1779 the ships returned north, only to fall five leagues short of the distance reached the previous year. The sole consolation for the crews was that on the homeward run they obtained high prices at Canton for the sea otter skins they had traded along the American coast.

As news of the expedition slowly filtered back to England, the shocking news of Cook's death held centre stage but the geographical results of the voyage also drew interest. Two maps, both published abroad in 1781, offered very different interpretations of Cook's explorations. P.S. Pallas, the celebrated German scientist resident at St Petersburg, then the Russian capital, had seen the expedition's 1778 and 1779 dispatches when they reached St Petersburg on their way to England. From these he constructed a map which showed Bering Strait ('Cook Strasse') and Alaska in roughly correct form and, running away to the southeast, a rudimentary, but solid, coastline. A more convoluted map was issued by Jean-Nicolas Buache de Neuville, nephew of Philippe Buache, whose maps of the 1750s had laid the foundations of the theoretical geography of the northwest coast based on the de Fuca and de Fonte accounts. Although Buache de Neuville concluded that a northwest passage probably existed, Cook's experiences clearly persuaded most people otherwise. As one newspaper noted, 'the most sanguine, theoretical or practical navigators will give up, probably for ever, all hopes of finding out a passage.'[5]

Such views were confirmed when the official three-volume edition of the voyage was published in June 1784. It included the first public account of Samuel Hearne's overland journey of 1771-2 from Hudson Bay to the Arctic Ocean, a telling argument against the existence of a passage in temperate latitudes. Cook's forthright comments on the de Fuca and de Fonte narratives (rendered even more acerbic by the busy editorial pen of Douglas) could also be read by all. An annotated translation of the Mourelle journal describing Spanish explorations on the northwest coast of America in 1775 had recently been published, together with the first reliable account in English of the Russian exploring and trading voyages.[6] All in all, as John Reinhold Forster remarked, it was difficult to see where there was room for the straits and rivers of 'the narrative or rather reverie of de Fonte.'[7] Henry Roberts' map of northwest America which accompanied the official account showed an uncompromisingly solid coastline, though it also revealed how far Cook was offshore for much of his northward haul from Nootka.

If Cook's voyage seemed to have destroyed hopes of a navigable passage between the Pacific and Atlantic oceans, it drew attention to the demand in China for the furs of the northwest coast. In the official account, James King confirmed that the finest sea otter skins fetched more than 100 dollars each at Canton. The quest for beaver had drawn men westward across the North American continent from one ocean almost to within sight of the other. The maritime traders were quick to respond to the lure of the sea otters of the North Pacific, though the Russian fur traders or *promyslenniks*, who came after Bering, had already reached far along the Aleutian chain and into the Gulf of Alaska in search of the 'soft gold' of the sea otter pelts.[8] By the mid-1780s British merchants in India and China were fitting out expeditions for the northwest coast, and others from Europe and New England followed. Commerce rather than exploration was the priority, but these were not mutually exclusive objectives. As King had written in the official account, vessels trading in Cook's River might go on to 'trace the coast with great accuracy from the latitude of 56° to 50°, the space from which we were driven out of sight of land by contrary winds.'[9] Such detailed survey work was never carried out by the traders, but their rather more casual observations along the coast raised the first doubts about Cook's conclusions.

A single trading ship on the coast arrived in 1785 followed by six the next year. Two fitted out in India were under the command of James Strange. When he discovered and named Queen Charlotte Sound at latitude 51° north, Strange thought that it was probably de Fonte's entrance – though it was two degrees south of the latitude given to the Río los Reyes in the printed account of de Fonte's voyage.[10] Farther north, more intensive exploration was being carried out that summer by the official discovery expedition commanded by the Comte de la Pérouse, the French answer to Cook's voyages. Significantly, its geographical instructions had been drawn up by Buache de Neuville, who in 1782 had succeeded d'Anville as the 'premier géographe du roi.'[11] Among the tasks of Pacific exploration which he was set, La Pérouse was ordered to spend three months on the northwest coast. There he was to search those long stretches of coastline between the pinpricks of the Russian, Spanish, and British sightings, in the hope of finding a waterway to the interior lakes of Canada or to Hudson Bay. The immensity of the task was soon revealed – it was, after all, to take George Vancouver three seasons to accomplish it – when La Pérouse spent almost a month exploring the inlets and channels of a single bay, Port de Français (Lituya Bay) in Alaska. From there he sailed south, mostly in rain and fog, so that, like Cook, he passed the Strait of Juan de Fuca without sighting land. The map of this part of the voyage reveals the broken nature of the coastline, with the entrances of Dixon Entrance and Cross Sound dimly appearing, but La Pérouse was in no mood for geographical speculation. As he headed for Monterey his journal entries exude scepticism and irritation: de Fonte never existed, and the idea of a passage through the continent was 'absurd,' akin to those 'pious frauds' which the Age of Reason had rejected.[12]

The 1787 season brought two major discoveries, which seemed to lend credence to both the de Fonte and de Fuca accounts. A ship commanded by George Dixon – who had sailed with Cook on his last voyage as armourer on the *Resolution* – traded along the coast between 51° and 55° north latitude. He soon realized that the 'land' was actually a group of islands, not part of the mainland at all, as Cook had assumed. In late July, in the passage inside the islands (Hecate Strait) just above latitude 53° north, the supposed position of de Fonte's Río los Reyes, floating debris 'made us conclude, that there is a large river setting out from that part of the coast.'[13] The map in Dixon's published account marked the islands as the Queen Charlotte Islands, whose position 'evidently shows that they are the Archipelago of St Lazarus, and consequently near the Straight of De Fonte.'[14] An even more intriguing discovery had just been made to the south in June as William Barkley, in the *Imperial Eagle*, sailed south from Nootka toward Cape Flattery. His wife's diary takes up the story: 'In the afternoon, to our great astonishment, we arrived off a large opening extending to the eastward, the entrance of which appeared to be about four leagues wide, and remained about that width as far as the eye could see, with a clear westerly horizon, which my husband immediately recognized as the long lost strait of Juan de Fuca, and to which he gave the name of the original discoverer.'[15] Barkley did not enter the strait, but kept south along the coast before bearing away for Macao, from where his news of the apparent confirmation of the account of the old Greek pilot reached England.

Exploration of the strait soon followed. In August 1788 the *Princess Royal*, commanded by Charles Duncan, anchored just inside the entrance off the Indian village of Claaset. Duncan's sketch of the opening was published early in 1790, with Pinnacle Rock shown near Cape Claaset (Cape Flattery), a reminder of that 'exceeding high Pinacle' which de Fuca had reported in the entrance of his strait, though on its *northern* side. Accompanying the map was a note stating that 'the Indians of Claaset said that they knew not of any land to the Eastward; and that it was Aass toopulse, which signifies a Great Sea.'[16] The following March the American trading vessel *Washington*, commanded by Robert Gray, sailed into the strait for twenty-five miles before bad weather forced it back. To the east the strait broadened to form 'a Large sea stretching to the east and no land to obstruct the view as far as the eye could reach.'[17] Other log entries showed that the *Washington*'s officers had the accounts of de Fuca and de Fonte to hand, and in May 1789 they concluded that in Clarence Strait they had discovered de Fonte's famous opening – 'we discovered that the straits of Adml. de font actually exist.'[18]

The fur-trading voyages of the late 1780s had shown that Cook's assumption of 1778 that he was sailing along the mainland coast between Nootka and Cape Edgecumbe was almost certainly wrong. As the traders pried into bays and sailed through channels which Cook had never seen, their commanders realized that the continental outline was masked by a screen of islands. After spending two seasons on the coast in 1787 and 1788 James Colnett wrote, 'It's a doubt with me if ever I have seen the Coast of America at all.'[19] Did the straits of de Fuca and de Fonte lie within this labyrinth? The most recent signs were hopeful. The Queen Charlotte Islands stretched across the latitude of de Fonte's St Lazarus Archipelago, and on the mainland there were indications of a large river. Further south de Fuca was supposed to have found a strait between 47° and 48° north latitude, and now Barkley, Duncan, and Gray had discovered an inlet only one degree off this latitude which seemed to run into a great inland sea. This surely was the *Mer de l'Ouest* of the French geographers, first conjured up by Guillaume de l'Isle almost 100 years before. On one thing the maritime traders were agreed: in the words of Robert Haswell, mate on the *Washington*, 'to survey this coast would be an allmost endless task though indispencably nesecery to finish the geography of north America trading vessels to this coast will make considerable advances toward this but it never can be thuroughly done intill it is done at some national expence whose Commanders are uninterested by commerce.'[20]

As the accounts and maps of the British traders slowly filtered back to Europe they were collated by Cook's old opponent, Alexander Dalrymple, now hydrographer to the East India Company. In 1789 and 1790 Dalrymple had published a series of maps and memoirs, arguing for a double-pronged attempt to find a waterway through or round the continent: expeditions should be sent both to Hudson Bay and to the northwest coast. Chipewyan Indian maps in the Hudson's Bay Company archives persuaded him that a strait led out of the northwest part of Hudson Bay, while his scrutiny of Hearne's journey convinced him that the polar sea sighted by the explorer lay in the 68°, not 72° north latitude, as the latter had depressingly insisted. As far as the northwest coast was concerned, Dalrymple accepted that most land sighted so far consisted of islands, as implied by the de Fuca and de Fonte narratives. These accounts were not essential to his argument, though he was inclined to think that they were true, 'however vaguely and imperfectly related.'[21] The Lake de Fonte of the 1640 'discovery,' he surmised, might well be the Great Slave Lake of the inland explorers. Cook's conviction that there was no northwest passage was dismissed with the brusque comment: 'I cannot admit of a Pope in Geography or Navigation.'[22]

The grand design behind Dalrymple's writings of this period was a proposed union of the Hudson's Bay Company and the East India Company. Such an amalgamation would join the experience of the one organization in collecting furs with the facilities of the other for selling them at Canton. Time was short, Dalrymple insisted, for while the Russians were establishing themselves at Cook's River and Prince William Sound, the Spanish were extending their settlements northwards. Dramatic confirmation of the urgency of the situation came with the Nootka Sound 'incident' in the summer of 1789, when Spanish forces seized British-owned ships and a shanty trading base at Nootka built by John Meares, a former lieutenant in the Royal Navy. At the end of 1790, after Britain and Spain had come perilously near war before reaching agreement in October, Meares' narrative of his voyages to the northwest coast was published.

Much of the bulky volume was taken up with a tendentious account of the dispute and Meares' role in it, but elsewhere Meares added his contribution to the debate over the discoveries made in the region since Cook's voyage. In the summer of 1788 Meares, in the *Felice Adventurer,* had reached the Strait of Juan de Fuca and had sent his longboat to explore it. An accompanying illustration shows the scene, with the longboat flying the British flag, though in fact Meares was operating under Portuguese colours to evade the monopoly rights of the East India Company. According to Meares, the longboat sailed thirty leagues into the strait and turned back 'with a clear horizon stretching to the East for 15 leagues more.'[23] Closer scrutiny reveals that the longboat sailed only eleven leagues into the strait, and the crew would have been unable to see more than a few miles ahead from their lowly vantage point. In the voyage of the American trader *Washington* Meares further manipulated the evidence. He first mentioned the *Washington* in July 1790, when he claimed that the vessel 'went up de Fonti's Strait and passing thro' a Sea came out at the Strait of Juan de Fuca.' In a memorial written in late July, Meares reversed the track of the vessel; he reported in his book at the end of the year that Gray had received his information about the de Fuca strait from him, and that the American had passed through the strait into a sea 'of great extent' to the eastward before returning to the Pacific through a passage farther north along the coast.[24]

By 1790, then, there were hopes that a passage to the Pacific might be found by two possible routes: the first from Hudson Bay through Hearne's sea to Bering Strait or Cook's River; the second along the rivers and lakes of the interior to Cook's River or into the great inland sea suspected to lie east of the Strait of Juan de Fuca. Cook's River was an inviting target because in June 1778 Cook had turned back before reaching the end of what is, in fact, an inlet and speculated that it might lead 'to a very extensive inland communication.'[25]

The fur traders of the North West Company had advanced rapidly into the Athabasca country in the 1780s, and the most enterprising and combative of them, Peter Pond, had reached Great Slave Lake. There he claimed to have met Indians who had seen Cook's ships on the coast, and he estimated that he was 'within six days travel of the Grand Pacific Ocean.'[26] A series of maps illustrated Pond's geographical ideas and his plan for a chain of posts stretching from the Canadian lakes to the Pacific. The most striking feature of Pond's maps was a gigantic Great Slave Lake, stretching from 124° to 136° west longitude (about 700 miles west of its true position), with a river flowing from its western end. Cook's coastal track of 1778 is marked, with less than 300 miles between

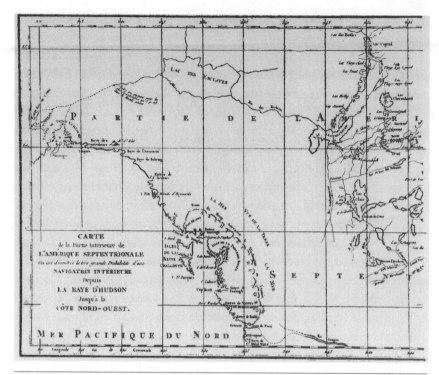

John Meares' 1790 map of the northwest coast of North America, showing Slave Lake draining into the Pacific by Cook River

the farthest point he reached in Cook's River and the open end of Pond's river running out of Great Slave Lake. The inference is clear: the two rivers were one and the same, and the fur traders were within reach of the Pacific coast. Pond was one of the last of the old fur-trade explorers, tough in body and mind, but lacking surveying skills or instruments on their arduous journeys. Pond knew the northwest better than any other white, but as one contemporary put it, his longitudes 'seemed to be guesswork and not in any respect accurate enough to be depended upon.'[27]

With information reaching him every month reporting the discovery of great lakes and rivers in the interior, identifying areas of the northwest coast as those described in the accounts of de Fuca and de Fonte, and testifying to the growing interest of foreign powers in the region, Dalrymple put pressure on both the British government and the Hudson's Bay Company for action. His gadfly tactics seem to have been effective. By the spring of 1790 William Grenville, secretary of state for home affairs, was thinking of a naval expedition to the northwest coast to establish a settlement and to explore the region between Cape Mendocino and Cook's River.[28] At the same time the Hudson's Bay Company agreed to send a sloop commanded by Charles Duncan to search the west coast of Hudson Bay for a connection to the lakes of the interior.[29] Duncan, whose appointment had been suggested by Dalrymple, accomplished nothing, while the naval expedition was delayed as the Nootka Sound crisis flared, and British forces were put on a war footing. In October 1790 Britain and Spain signed the Nootka Sound Convention, and two weeks later the Admiralty again began to prepare an expedition 'to remote parts.' It was to be commanded by George Vancouver, who had sailed with Cook on his second and third voyages.

In his instructions of March 1791 Vancouver was set two tasks: to receive restitution of the land and buildings at Nootka seized by Spain in April 1789 and to explore the northwest coast to latitude 60° north.[30] The main object of his survey, Vancouver was informed, was to discover a waterway through the continent. This was to be a passage suitable for oceanic craft rather than for the canoe-and-portage routes of the Canadian inland traders; for Vancouver was not 'to pursue any inlet or river further than it [appeared] to be navigable by vessels of such burthen as might safely navigate the pacific ocean.' Two stretches of coast were singled out for special attention. First, Vancouver was to explore 'the supposed straits of Juan de Fuca, said to be situated between 48° and 40° latitude, and to lead to an opening through which the sloop Washington is reported to have passed in 1789, and to have come out again to the northward of Nootka.' Second, he was told that there was 'the greatest probability' that Cook's River rose in one of the interior lakes, and that he should investigate this possibility. There was no mention that in 1789 Alexander Mackenzie had discovered that Pond's river out of Great Slave Lake flowed, not to the Pacific, but to the Arctic (disappointing news which had reached London in December 1790).[31] The geographical reasoning behind Vancouver's instructions was represented by a revised version of Roberts' map of 1784. The new 'improved' edition, issued in 1794 under the name of M. de la Rochette, included 'The Interesting Discoveries made by British and American Ships, since the first Publication of the Chart in 1784, Together with the Hydrographical

Materials lately procured from St Petersburg and other places.' The accounts of de Fuca and de Fonte, the theories of Buache, the arguments of Meares and Dalrymple, and the explorations of Hearne and Mackenzie, all appear here in a final summation of the theoretical geography of northwest America.

Vancouver's instructions ordered him to cooperate with any Spanish vessels he found engaged in survey work. As British ministers suspected, but could not know for sure, the Spanish at this time were exploring those stretches of the coast where the entrance of a northwest passage might lie, and where foreigners might accordingly be active.[32] The Spanish commandant responsible for seizing British vessels at Nootka in 1789 was Estéban José Martínez, who had sailed with Juan Pérez on the first Spanish voyages of discovery along the northwest coast in 1774. If his own claim is to be believed, Martínez had unavailingly urged Pérez to investigate an opening in latitude 48°20' north.[33] At Nootka, Martínez was ideally positioned to determine the existence of a strait the 'entrance of which I had seen in the distance in 1774,'[34] and which English traders were rumoured to have discovered in the previous two or three years. With a nicely ironic touch, Martínez sent José María Narvaez to investigate in Meares' vessel which he had seized at Nootka, the little *Northwest America*. Narvaez returned in July with the news that he had discovered the entrance of the Strait of Juan de Fuca, twenty-one miles wide, in the same latitude as Martínez had claimed in his journal: 'If Captain Cook had lived to the present time, there is no doubt he would have been undeceived about the existence of these straits, as all Europe will be made to see within a short time.'[35]

In October Martínez reluctantly followed orders to evacuate Nootka, and so was unable to follow up in person Navaez' discovery. At the end of the year a new viceroy, the Conde de Revilla Gigedo, reversed the evacuation decision, reoccupied Nootka, and ordered the strait to the south to be explored. This was done in a mood of weary scepticism rather than of support for Martínez's claims, characterized by Revilla Gigedo as existing in a 'sphere of dreams.'[36] In any event, it took three expeditions three years to finish this task – Quimper in 1790, Eliza in 1791, and Galiano and Valdés in 1792. In 1790 Quimper charted the north and south shores of the Fuca strait to penetrate far inside its entrance. His was a major survey, which opened to view Haro Strait, though he did not follow it into the Strait of Georgia nor explore the maze of waterways in the southeast corner of the de Fuca strait which led into Puget Sound. In 1791 Eliza sailed up the Strait of Georgia as far as latitude 50° north – that is, about halfway along the eastern side of Vancouver Island – although his charts show that he was unable to survey all the coastline in detail. In his report to the viceroy on his return, Eliza stated that he had partly explored the Canal del Rosario (the Strait of Georgia), and that 'the passage to the Atlantic Ocean, which the foreign nations search for with such diligence on this coast, cannot in my opinion, if there be one, be found in any other part; it is either, I think, by this great canal, or it is continent.'[37]

Meanwhile, the well-equipped and prestigious expedition of Alejandro Malaspina had arrived on the northwest coast for, on reaching Acapulco in March 1791 on his way to Hawai'i, Malaspina had received orders from Madrid to sail instead to latitude 60° north on the Alaskan coast and search for a passage into the Atlantic. The reason for this unexpected diversion lay in the fresh publicity given to the supposed voyage of Lorenzo Ferrer Maldonado in 1588 through the Strait of Anian, whose Pacific entrance he placed in latitude 60° north. Maldonado's 1609 report of his exploit had been rediscovered in 1781, and published in 1788 without causing much stir. Malaspina had seen the account before his expedition left Spain and seems to have displayed little faith in its veracity. All this changed when in November 1790, with interest in the northwest coast at its height following the Nootka crisis, Buache de Neuville read an enthusiastic paper on the voyage to the Académie des Sciences in Paris. The next month the Spanish minister of the navy, Antonio Valdés, sent orders to Malaspina to search for Maldonado's strait.[38]

Following their new orders, Malaspina's ships reached the Alaskan coast in late June 1791 and entered Yakutat Bay (Dixon's Port Mulgrave of 1787). Through the fog an inlet could be seen whose 'entrance and winding line toward the interior seemed to correspond to the lands of Ferrer Maldonado.'[39] The artist Tomás de Suria added that the officers believed 'that this might be the so much desired and sought-for strait.'[40] Disillusionment was swift, for the ships' launches found that the inlet ended in a bay – Puerto del Desengaño or Disenchantment Bay. Malaspina explained how events had overtaken speculation. 'It did not seem possible to admit that the supposition of the French Geographer

[Buache de Neuville] that the latitude of 60° fixed by Ferrer Maldonado, is exact. The last explorations of Captain Dixon and of our ships from San Blas greatly altered the aspect of the problem from that which Mr de Buache had visualized on examining only the voyages of Captain Cook.'[41] Passing Prince William Sound, Mount St Elias, and Bucareli Bay, the expedition found no sign of a new opening. The whole episode, Malaspina reflected later, was another example of the damage done by the splitting of geography between academic scholars and practical navigators – between 'the branch that reasons and the branch that experiments ... The first does not interfere in the experiments and the second is not authorized to contradict the reasoners. The navigators consequently exaggerate their narrations at will. The sages, with equal licence, at times adopt the findings, at times depreciate the veracity and even the existence of the navigator and finally, this chaos of mistaken ideas rather retards than favours the desired progress.'[42]

After his return to San Blas, Malaspina detached two officers, Galiano and Valdés, to carry out the third, and final, season of exploration of the Strait of Juan de Fuca in 1792. The plan to send Mourelle, veteran of the earlier voyages, to the strait was dropped, but his instructions are still extant and show the mixture of scepticism and uneasiness which affected Spanish officials at this time. He was to explore each inlet of the strait, 'until you find out if they turn back to the western sea or continue inland to Baffin Bay or Hudson's Bay, omitting no effort or time necessary for that purpose ... This examination will make your commission just so much more appreciable, inasmuch as the imaginary straits which should end in Baffin Bay and Hudson's Bay must fall in that region. I promise myself that your explorations will resolve the doubts about them, and remove the fears which such passages, if they should be discovered in the future, may occasion at our court through the general subversion of commerce.'[43] This task was conscientiously carried out by Galiano and Valdés, who encountered Vancouver's expedition while exploring the Strait of Georgia. They passed through Queen Charlotte Sound some weeks later than the British ships, with detailed charts to prove that the de Fuca strait did not connect with the seas or lakes of the east.[44]

Also in 1792 Jacinto Caamaño was sent back north to carry out yet another survey of the coast near latitude 53° north, where the English trader James Colnett had marked de Fonte's strait on a map copied by the Spanish at Nootka the previous year. Caamaño was sceptical from the beginning about Colnett's 'discovery.' After disengaging himself from the rocky, dangerous coast where Colnett's map showed the strait, he concluded that the de Fonte narrative 'seems to have no other foundation than the madness of ignorance of some one devoid of all knowledge of either navigation or geography.'[45] By the autumn of 1792, then, before Vancouver's ships had been more than a few months on the coast, the Spanish had satisfied themselves that the straits of the old accounts did not exist. Vancouver did not allow the conclusions of the Spaniards to deter him from making his own detailed surveys of the mainland coast, but, inevitably, the expedition's work was marked by a degree of scepticism and pessimism.

Vancouver's ships reached the northwest coast in April 1792, and on the 29th drew near Cape Flattery and the Strait of Juan de Fuca. That afternoon a ship was sighted flying American colours. The sight of any vessel was a novelty, for the expedition had not seen another sail for eight months, and excitement rose when the ship, the *Columbia* of Boston, was found to be commanded by Robert Gray. This was the captain who, according to Meares, had sailed through the strait of de Fuca into an inland sea, and back into the Pacific through the strait of de Fonte. It was an extraordinary coincidence that, as the expedition approached the famous strait of Fuca, it should encounter the one man who, supposedly, had sailed right through it. Disillusionment was immediate, for Gray denied making the voyage described by Meares. Lieutenant Peter Puget, who went on board the *Columbia* from Vancouver's *Discovery*, noted in his journal: 'Having now luckily seen Mr Grey he assured me, that when he commanded the Washington he had been in the Streights of De Fuca but had never proceeded more than fifteen or sixteen Leagues in an Easterly Direction up them.'[46] Gray thought that the strait was the one discovered by de Fuca, but on Vancouver's ships confidence was sadly shaken and was not restored when crew members had difficulty in picking out the famous pinnacle rock in the entrance of the strait.[47]

The ships sailed up the strait 200 years after its reputed discovery by de Fuca. On 30 April Vancouver noted that the expedition had reached a part of the strait unvisited by any other Europeans – at this point he knew nothing of the Spanish explorations of the previous two seasons

and the two Spanish vessels ahead of him in the Strait of Georgia com-
pleting the survey. The two expeditions met, amid exclamations of
mutual surprise, at the end of June, and for a time worked together. In
July Vancouver was heartened to find that a channel connected the
northern end of the Strait of Georgia with the Pacific. This confirmed
that the region around Nootka was part of a large island or archipelago
and saved Vancouver from retracing his route through the de Fuca strait.
On 9 August the ships reached the ocean through Queen Charlotte
Sound. Here they were on a part of the coast visited by several traders,
including Charles Duncan, who at this time was seeking a way through
Chesterfield Inlet in Hudson Bay to the inland sea the Natives of Claaset
had told him lay east of the de Fuca strait. The season had been well
spent, for the three months of survey work in the Strait of Juan de Fuca
and its subsidiary channels had proved that even if de Fuca had discovered the great gulf, he had never made the voyage described by Purchas.

After wintering at Hawai'i, Vancouver's ships returned in May 1793
to the northernmost point of their explorations of the previous year.
This part of the coast, from latitude 52° northward, was even more intricate than the eastern shore of the Strait of Georgia, but it was in this
region that de Fonte's Río los Reyes was supposed to enter the sea. The
same surveying procedure was followed as before, and each inlet leading
inland was traced to its head by boat parties. One such survey took
twenty-three days, and charted 700 miles of shoreline, but advanced
knowledge of the mainland coast by only sixty miles. It was during this
summer that Alexander Mackenzie reached the coast overland, but he
came down the Bella Coola to Dean Channel seven weeks after
Vancouver had been there, and the two explorers never met.

Though some on board, such as the botanist Archibald Menzies,
remained unconvinced,[48] Vancouver was adamant that the summer's
explorations had destroyed any credibility which the de Fonte account
might have had. He had surveyed the coast as far as latitude 56° north,
and had found no river which corresponded in size or location with de
Fonte's Río los Reyes. 'Unfortunately for the great ingenuity of its hypothetical projectors,' he wrote of the system of theoretical geography
based on the de Fonte account, 'our practical labours have thus far made
it totter ... should the information we had thus obtained reach Europe,
there would no longer remain a doubt as to the extent or the fallacy of

Icy Bay and Mount St. Elias, sketch by Thomas Heddington, engraved by J. Fittler

the pretended discoveries.'[49] One enthusiast in England, William Goldson, had not waited for news of Vancouver's findings before producing in 1793 his *Observations on the Passage between the Atlantic and Pacific Oceans*. The accompanying map was an example of speculative geography to end all speculative geography. It had a colossal sea of Juan de Fuca flooding most of present-day Washington State and British Columbia, an identification of de Fonte's inland geography with the discoveries of the Canadian traders, and a supposition that the Strait of Anian, sailed through by Maldonado in 1588 and by one of de Fonte's officers in 1640, was Prince William Sound.

Vancouver's third season of surveying on the northwest coast began with Cook's River, quickly found by Vancouver to be a closed inlet. If only Cook had spent one more day there, he would have realized that for himself, Vancouver wrote rather sadly – and so 'have spared the theoretical navigators, who have followed him in their closets, the task of ingeniously ascribing to this arm of the ocean ... a north-west passage.'[50] From there Prince William Sound was surveyed, not for the first time, for as well as Cook in 1778, Fidalgo had spent six weeks there in 1790. Then Lynn

Canal, Cross Sound, and the coastline back to latitude 56° north were charted. Here the expedition was closer to the lakes of the interior than at any other spot; but each arm of the sea ended in the steep range of mountains which had balked all efforts to reach inland. On 19 August 1794 the boats returned from their last survey, and an extra allowance of grog was served. Among the celebrations Vancouver wrote that 'no small portion of facetious mirth passed amongst the seamen, in consequence of our having sailed from old England on the *first of April*, for the purpose of discovering a north-west passage, by following up the discoveries of De Fuca, De Fonte, and a numerous train of hypothetical navigators.'[51]

Lacking Cook's breadth of vision, Vancouver equalled him in strength of purpose as he carried out a detailed survey of unprecedented extent. From the beginning, Vancouver was convinced that the reports of a great strait on the northwest coast were groundless – probably invented, he remarked more than once, to give credit to foreigners if a passage were ever found. This exact, meticulous explorer found his satisfaction in producing charts of such accuracy that they were used for more than a century after his death. More immediately, they enabled him to contradict and humiliate those who, in their eagerness to find a northwest passage, had dared to impugn the achievements of his old commander: 'The enthusiasm of modern closet philosophy, eager to revenge itself for the refutation of its former fallacious speculations, ventured to accuse Captain Cook of "hastily exploding" its systems.'[52] In truth the imposing figure of Cook threw a long shadow over this region, inhibiting as much as encouraging further investigation. Cook had been wrong on the location of the continental shore, but was instinctively right about the wider question of the existence of a northwest passage. It was left to Vancouver to silence the speculative geographers of Europe, for in the three seasons of wearing, grinding survey work he showed that no waterway navigable for shipping existed between the Atlantic and Pacific.

Vancouver's Survey Methods and Surveys

Andrew David

T his chapter outlines the probable survey methods used by Vancouver on the northwest coast of America, particularly during 1792, his first season on the coast. In his journal Vancouver is very reticent about his methods, apart from giving details of the astronomical observations made to determine latitude and longitude. It has therefore been necessary to draw on surrounding evidence: the methods used by Cook on his Pacific voyages; the survey instructions drawn up for Vancouver by Major James Rennell at the request of Sir Joseph Banks; the instructions issued to William Gooch by the Board of Longitude; and procedures suggested in various survey manuals known to have been on board the *Discovery*. The instruments and manuals taken by Vancouver, along with the surviving charts and drawings from the voyage, are listed in the appendices at the back of this book.

George Vancouver's first experience of hydrographic surveying came as a fifteen-year-old midshipman during Cook's second voyage to the Pacific. Although he was not one of the young gentlemen instructed in drawing by William Hodges,[1] the official artist to the expedition, Vancouver did receive valuable training from William Wales, the astronomer appointed to the *Resolution* by the Board of Longitude, one of whose subsidiary duties was to 'teach such of the Officers on board the sloop as may desire it the use of the Astronomical Instruments & the Method of finding the Longitude at sea from the Lunar Observations.'[2]

Vancouver was clearly one of these officers, acknowledging the fact by naming a prominent point on the northwest coast, Point Wales, 'after my much-esteemed friend, Mr Wales, of Christ's Hospital; to whose kind instruction, in the early part of my life, I am indebted for that information which has enabled me to traverse and delineate these lonely regions.'[3]

Two surveys signed by Vancouver survive from this voyage, one of New Caledonia and the other of South Georgia. Both are in a miscellaneous collection of charts, whose provenance suggests that they were in Cook's possession at the time of his death.[4] Only one survey by Vancouver survives from Cook's third voyage,[5] but since no logs or journals kept by him survive from this or indeed from Cook's second voyage, it is likely that any other surveys he carried out, apart from the three already mentioned, were lost with them.

Vancouver first came to prominence as a hydrographic surveyor in his own right when serving in the West Indies in the *Europa*. In late 1786, Commodore Alan Gardner, Commander-in-Chief West Indies, was instructed by the Admiralty to order all ships on the station to accurately survey any harbours visited. Accordingly, Gardner ordered Vancouver to survey Kingston Harbour, Jamaica. This Vancouver did in 1788, assisted by Joseph Whidbey, master of the *Europa*, beginning a partnership which endured throughout Vancouver's service afloat. The resulting survey,[6] drawn by Joseph Baker, who also accompanied Vancouver to the northwest coast, clearly demonstrates that Vancouver was by now a most proficient hydrographic surveyor. It also gives a good insight not only into the methods he had been taught by Cook and Wales, but also into those he adopted during the detailed harbour surveys carried out later on the northwest coast of America.

In a memoir on his chart of Kingston Harbour, Vancouver describes how he carried out his survey. First he measured a base of one statute mile, by chain, on the eastern part of the Pallisadoes, a flat area at the head of the harbour; then the 'positive situation of every point and near land-marks as well as the situation & extent of every Shoal [was] fixed by intersecting Angles taken by a Sextant & protracted on the spot, the Compass only [being] used to determine the Meridian and observe its variation.'[7]

This suggests that after Vancouver had measured his base, he then laid the framework of his survey by a rudimentary triangulation scheme plotted graphically onto his chart. From various 'triangulation' stations, probably marked by flags, other prominent marks were 'shot up' by intersecting sextant angles as described in his memoir. The coastline may have been fixed in a similar way or walked over and surveyed by a plane table. In fixing the positions of shoals, Vancouver adopted the method used in the Orkney Islands between 1744 and 1747 by Murdoch Mackenzie Senior, the first British hydrographic surveyor to use a measured base and triangulation system for surveys. Having surveyed the coastline, Mackenzie next 'sent Boats to lye at the Extremities of Rocks and Shoals, till their Positions and Dimensions were determined by the requisite Observations on Land. When a complete Map ... was made out in this Manner, I then went round the Coast in a Boat, sounded the Depth of the Water all along, and round every Rock and Shoal and thro' every Channel; marking on the corresponding Part of the Map the several Depths and Quality of the Bottom.'[8] Apparently, after establishing the positions of various rocks and shoals, Mackenzie inserted the soundings on his chart by eye, estimating the distance and bearing from the nearest danger. Vancouver may also have done the same – a not unreasonable procedure if the positions of the rocks and shoals had already been accurately determined.

In the published account of his voyage, Vancouver gives very little detail of his survey methods on the northwest coast of America. Nowhere does he mention measuring bases, for instance, though he surely must have done so during his large-scale surveys of harbours and anchorages. Cook, too, was very reticent about his methods, though Wales, in Cook's second voyage, was a little more forthcoming, mentioning in his journal that in Porto Praya, in the Cape Verde Islands, he went 'on shore and measured the length of the small island mentioned above, which is very level. I measured it both ways, and differed only ten links of the Gunters' Chain. I set the line with the Azimuth Compass both ways, whilst Capt Cook took the Angles subtended by the several points of the Bay from each station, with my Sextant from which'[9] data Wales was able to produce a creditable survey of the bay.

In Queen Charlotte Sound, Wales and William Bayley used a less exact method of measuring a base, obtaining the distance between their respective observation spots by firing guns at each station and measuring the time between seeing the flash of the explosion and hearing the report at the other station.[10] This method, most suitable for measuring bases over long distances, could well have been used on other occasions during Cook's second voyage.

Before Vancouver sailed for the northwest coast, Sir Joseph Banks, president of the Royal Society, was asked to draw up some surveying instructions for him by William Wyndham Grenville, first Baron Grenville, who, as secretary of state for home affairs, funnelled cabinet decisions on exploring expeditions to the Board of Admiralty. Banks, not feeling competent to write these himself, consulted Captain William Bligh and Major James Rennell. Bligh's contribution was much shorter, since he was then busily preparing the *Providence* for his second bread-fruit voyage; his draft is marked 'not made use of,' presumably by Banks. This, however, may not be entirely correct because, in forwarding Rennell's proposed instruction on 20 February 1791,[11] Banks apologized to Grenville for the delay, saying a great deal of time had been taken up in revising and reconsidering them. Under these circumstances Rennell probably considered at least some of Bligh's proposals in his final draft. Although it is not known whether the Admiralty ever delivered these instructions to Vancouver, they do throw further light on the survey methods Vancouver may have used during his voyage.

Earlier, Banks had received an interesting letter from Captain George Dixon, who had read in a newspaper that a vessel was being pre-pared to explore the Pacific. Dixon, who had commanded his own voy-age to the northwest coast in the *Queen Charlotte* between 1785 and 1788, advised that on this coast such a vessel 'should have two Schooners along with her of a light Draught of Water capable of being moved along with Sweeps, by which means they will be prevented from getting on Shore when the Wind Leaves them, – this being the Case 9 times out of Ten under the high Lands on that Coast and where for the most part close in Shore no Ground is to be got at 100 Fathoms, this will always intimidate the boldest Navigators in Large Ships and prevent their going Sufficiently near, by which Means they may pass considerable Inlets.'[12] It is doubtful whether Vancouver received this valuable information from his former shipmate on Cook's third voyage.

On 1 January 1790, the *Discovery* was commissioned for a voyage to the northwest coast of America under the command of Lieutenant Henry Roberts. Four days later, Roberts wrote to the Admiralty request-ing surveying instruments, including two chronometers, two sextants, an astronomical quadrant, two telescopes, a plane table, a theodolite, a chain and lines (presumably for measuring a base), two station pointers, and a portable observatory. On 14 January, he requested some additional items, 'normally allowed on similar service,' including a 16-foot cutter, two tents, and a marquee.[13] The Admiralty instructed the Navy Board to deliver these instruments to Roberts five days later,[14] except the two chronometers, which were to be supplied in due course by the Board of Longitude. When the instruments were eventually delivered to Vancouver, who took over from Roberts, the astronomical quadrant was not included, though an 18-inch instrument by Bird was eventually supplied by Ramsden, who had borrowed it from Alexander Dalrymple.[15] In addition to the sextants supplied by the Navy Board, many officers on the *Discovery* had their own, Vancouver noting that there were twelve altogether on board, the majority made by Ramsden, with others by Dollond, Troughton, Adams, and Gilbert.[16] For a full list of instruments supplied to Vancouver see Appendix 1.

On his arrival at Portsmouth, Vancouver's two chronometers were waiting for him at the Naval Academy, where they had been sent by the Board of Longitude.[17] Larcum Kendall's K3 (see Figure 1, page 73) was placed on board the *Discovery* and John Arnold's 82 on board the *Chatham.* Vancouver was particularly pleased to be entrusted with K3, 'the excellence of which had been manifested on board the Discovery during Captain Cook's last voyage, and which had lately been cleaned and put into order by its very worthy and ingenious maker, a short time before his decease.'[18] It seems strange that Vancouver was initially supplied with only two chronometers on such an important voyage and that he was not supplied with at least one chronometer watch.

William Gooch, sent out by the Admiralty in the store ship *Daedalus* to join Vancouver's expedition as its astronomer, was issued with very detailed instructions by the Board of Longitude to enable him to 'pursue the Operations necessary for Surveying the said Coast and Country.'[19] He was expected to make daily observations at sea to obtain latitude and longitude, both by lunar distances and by chronometer; to fix the positions of headlands, islands, and harbours; and to keep a daily journal of his observations. On shore he was expected to obtain latitude and longitude by similar observations and by observing eclipses of Jupiter's first satellite and occultations of fixed stars by the moon. He was also instructed to observe the range of the tide and the times of high and low water. Since Gooch was killed in Hawai'i before he could join the expedition, Vancouver presumably took charge of these instructions.

Gooch was also supplied with instruments and timekeepers by the Board of Longitude, including telescopes, sextants, theodolites, a transit instrument, a Gunter's chain, and a station pointer. 'A Hadley's quadrant, with two moveable clamps, for surveying in a boat or vessel in motion,' added at the last moment,[20] was clearly intended to be used with the station pointer. The timekeepers comprised an astronomical clock and a journeyman clock, both by Earnshaw, an alarm clock, two chronometers by Arnold (Nos. 14 and 176) and a good pocket watch with a second hand, also by Earnshaw. The pocket watch did not even survive as far as the Downs, being knocked to the deck by one of the ship's cats, Gooch excusing her since 'she is a very young Cat & perhaps its beating attracted her Notice.'[21] Thomas Earnshaw himself hastened to Portsmouth with a more expensive chronometer watch, Earnshaw 1514,[22] as a replacement.

Gooch was also provided with a set of books and charts. These included the *Nautical Almanac* for 1769 and 1774 (probably supplied for the additional articles they contained, not reprinted in subsequent editions)[23]; two sets for 1791-6; three copies of the *Tables Requisite*, presumably the second edition of 1781; and four navigation and surveying manuals. Gooch's instruments and library were taken over by Vancouver when the *Daedalus* reached Nootka in 1792. Thus, knowing that Vancouver held the four navigational and surveying manuals brought out by Gooch, gives additional insight into how he may have carried out his surveys. The full list of instruments and books supplied to Gooch is given in Appendix 2.

Vancouver's survey methods must be considered in conjunction with the instructions he received from the Admiralty shortly before he sailed. These called on him to examine the northwest coast of America between 30° and 60° north latitude to acquire 'accurate information with respect to the nature and extent of any water-communication which may tend, in any considerable degree, to facilitate an intercourse for the purposes of commerce, between the north-west coast, and the country on the opposite side of the continent.'[24] If Vancouver found any inlets or large rivers communicating with the lakes in the interior of the continent, he was to ascertain their direction and extent, but not to follow any inlet or river farther than it would appear to be navigable by any vessel likely to navigate the Pacific Ocean. The survey was to be carried out 'without too minute and particular an examination of the detail of the different parts of the coast.'[25]

For surveying harbours and sheltered anchorages such as Port Discovery in the Strait of Juan de Fuca, Vancouver likely repeated the methods he used for Kingston Harbour. First he would have measured a base on a suitable stretch of flat land by means of Gunter's chain. If the terrain was too hilly, however, he might have been forced to measure one by sound, as advocated in his surveying instructions, and a procedure he could well have witnessed Wales and Bayly use during Cook's second voyage. Next he would have built up a rudimentary triangulation scheme, as he did in Kingston Harbour, orienting the survey correctly by measuring, at one end of his base, the angle between one of his triangulation stations and the sun to obtain a true bearing, while observing magnetic variation so that magnetic bearings could be converted to true bearings.

Meanwhile the observatory would have been set up ashore, to obtain the geographical position of the observation spot, as described later, so that the resulting survey could be graduated correctly. Next the coastline and topography would be surveyed, fixing further marks on the coastline and 'shooting up' significant topographical features by intersecting angles from various triangulation stations, the intervening detail being sketched in by eye or by the plane table. The positions of rocks and the edges of shoals may have been fixed by stationing a boat over them and intersecting their positions by bearings taken from established locations on shore, as advocated by Mackenzie. However, since Vancouver had been supplied with two station pointers,[26] later augmented by the one brought out by Gooch, he may have fixed and plotted their positions by simultaneous sextant angles. This procedure was recommended in Vancouver's surveying instructions, although Rennell and Bligh were clearly unaware that a station pointer had recently been constructed to avoid the tedious business of plotting such angles graphically. Soundings too were probably fixed in the same way, though, in the vicinity of rocks and shoals, whose positions had already been fixed, some of the soundings may well have been positioned by eye. The height of the tide would also be observed during the survey, so that soundings could be reduced to a low water datum.

View of Observatory Point, Port Quadra, Straits de Fuca, watercolour by John Sykes, midshipman, able seaman, master's mate, and, from November 1794, master of the *Chatham,* on the Vancouver expedition

Off open stretches of coastline, where he could rarely land for astronomical observations, Vancouver carried out a running survey, well known to him since it had been brought to near perfection by Cook during his three Pacific voyages. It is described by John Robertson, whose manual formed part of Gooch's library, if one was not already held on board the *Discovery.* In such a survey the ship would proceed along the coast at a suitable distance offshore so that all prominent features could be easily identified. 'Ship stations' would be established from time to time from which compass bearings would be observed to prominent coastal features. Soundings would be taken at and between each 'ship station' and the distance between them measured by log-line and entered in the ship's log or the log survey book, as advocated in Vancouver's surveying instructions. A rough sketch would then be made of the coastline, as the ship sailed along the coast, and entered in the log survey book, in which all the bearings and any other relevant hydrographic information would also be noted. When observing conditions were favourable, the *Discovery's* latitude and longitude would be obtained each day at noon and plotted on the field sheet. The intervening 'ship stations' would also be plotted and their positions adjusted to fit the accepted geographical positions. Next the angles and bearings observed at the various 'ship stations' would be plotted from the log survey book, and by this means the positions of various coastal features would be established. The coastline would then be sketched in from the log survey book, and the soundings entered from the same source. Robertson described the procedure at each 'ship station' thus: 'While the vessel is in a stationary situation, take, with the azimuth compass, the bearings in degrees of such points of the coast, as form the most material projections, or hollows; write down these bearings, and make a rough sketch of the appearance of the coast, observing carefully to mark the points whose bearings were taken with letters, for the sake of reference.'[27]

Vancouver would have improved on this procedure by measuring the angles between the various coastal features by horizontal sextant angles, as mentioned in his surveying instructions and advocated by Alexander Dalrymple in 1771 in another of the survey manuals held on board the *Discovery*. In his manual Dalrymple wrote:

> Experience has fully convinced me, that Bearings, taken by Compass, cannot be safely trusted to, in making a correct Draught ... For taking Angles, the Hadley [i.e., sextant] is as much preferable to the Compass in Facility, as Exactness ... It is used with equal Facility at Mast-head as upon Deck, and therefore the sphere of Observation is by this instrument much extended. For supposing many Islands are visible from Mast-head, and only one from Deck, no useful Observations can be made by any other instrument; because Compass Bearings from Mast-head can only be taken very vaguely, and a small Error in the Bearing of a distant Object, makes a great Error in its Position; but by the Hadley the Angles may be taken at Mast-head from the one visible Object with the utmost Exactness. Besides, taking Angles from Heights, as Hills, or a Ship's Mast-head, is almost the only way of exactly describing the Extent and Figure of Shoals.[28]

To return to Robertson's procedure, the ship next had to sail in as straight a line as possible for several miles to a new 'ship station' where all the points could be observed again, the distance between the two stations being carefully measured by log-line and the courses steered between them noted. Allowing for leeway and tidal streams the position of the next 'ship station' could then be plotted. By carefully protracting the bearings and angles corrected for variation, where necessary, to obtain true bearings, the survey could now be slowly built up. Robertson also pointed out that soundings should be reduced to low water before being plotted, but this was unnecessary for many soundings obtained off the northwest coast because of the great depth of water.

Unfortunately neither Vancouver's log survey book nor the *Discovery*'s log have survived. Nevertheless, Vancouver clearly carried out his offshore surveys in very much the manner suggested by Robertson, sketching in the coastline by eye between the various prominent features 'shot up' during his survey. To avoid leaving any major gaps, Vancouver stood off the coast at dusk, returning at first light to ensure that at least one of the features seen the previous evening was still visible when he recommenced his survey the following day. Vancouver initially used a plane projection to plot his small-scale coastal surveys, but they were replotted on mercator's projection when Baker drew the final fair sheets.[29]

It is of interest to note that when George Davidson of the United States Coast Survey resurveyed the northwest coast from California to the Strait of Juan de Fuca in the 1850s, he used a procedure he called 'surveying by courses and distances,' which was in reality a running survey. His friend and chief aide, James Lawson, later explained their method:

> In this work the steamer was run at a small speed, and as close to the shore as was safe; the courses were taken by compass, and the distances by patent log, and the shore sketched as we progressed. We came to anchor each afternoon, in time to permit the erection of the observatory ... In this way, observations for time and latitude were obtained about every 40 miles, between which the running of the steamer could be readily reduced and plotted.[30]

Once Vancouver entered the Strait of Juan de Fuca, he found himself sheltered from the oceanic swell, which in the summer is from west or northwest, thus making landing and boat work much easier than on the much more exposed coast farther south. It also meant that he had to modify his survey methods accordingly. It seems that both Vancouver and the Admiralty expected that the survey would be conducted mainly from the *Discovery* and the *Chatham*. However, during his first boat expedition from Discovery Bay, Vancouver became convinced that a great deal of his survey would have to be carried out in boats because of the intricate channels encountered. This set the pattern for the remainder of his survey, the boats carrying out most of the detailed work, with the two ships moving from one convenient anchorage to another. At each anchorage the observatory was set up ashore to obtain accurate geographical positions to provide a framework for the survey.

The surveys carried out in the boats were still basically running surveys, in that they were not dependent on accurately measured bases or a regular system of triangulation. Additional survey data were, however, obtained by the surveyors' landing at prominent points along the coastline to take rounds of angles, by sextant or theodolite, to any prominent natural objects in sight and also to determine the trend of the coastline from an additional viewpoint. The surveyors would also have observed the bearings of various features as they came into line, as strongly recommended in Vancouver's surveying instructions. If the sky was not overcast, the surveyors landed at noon each day to observe the meridian altitude of the sun to obtain latitude, using an artificial horizon whenever a sea horizon was not visible. The astronomical and survey instru-

View of a Boat Encampment, Pugets Sound, Straits de Fuca, watercolour by John Sykes

ments supplied to Vancouver may, however, have been insufficient for all boat parties to be issued with one.

In the boat expeditions Vancouver and his officers may have encountered difficulties in carrying forward longitude because the two chronometers initially supplied to the expedition were box chronometers unsuitable for taking away in boats. Fortunately, this was not a major drawback: over most of the survey area the general trend of the coastline is north/south and the relatively small number of observations spots established during the survey were sufficient to avoid any major errors of longitude.

The survey of Puget Sound was relatively straightforward with enough natural features visible on both sides to conduct a satisfactory survey. Farther north this was not always the case, as Vancouver discovered during his extended boat expedition with Puget from Birch Bay in June 1792. His run from the anchorage to the vicinity of Point Roberts was probably made under sail, enabling Vancouver to establish a reasonable 'ship station' somewhere west of the point. From here a bearing taken into Point Roberts and one taken from Birch Bay enabled Vancouver to fix its position, while another bearing was taken into Point Grey, even though at a distance of over twenty miles, it was partly below the horizon. Vancouver was then forced offshore by the shoals fronting the estuary of the Fraser River. However, the following morning he was able to land on Point Grey in time to obtain a meridian altitude of the sun to fix its latitude with some accuracy, with the intersecting ray from the vicinity of Point Roberts fixing its longitude.

Vancouver next surveyed Burrard Inlet, Howe Sound, and Jervis Inlet, covering some 250 miles of coastline in just over nine days. Both Howe Sound and Jervis Inlet are almost entirely hemmed in by rugged, precipitous mountains rising abruptly from the water's edge to elevations of between 1,200 and 2,000 metres, making a detailed survey extremely difficult. In accordance with his instructions, Vancouver's principal task was to determine whether the inlets led into the interior of the continent, not to survey them in any great detail. He therefore merely followed these three inlets until he reached their ends, taking what observations he could in the prevailing wind and weather.[31] Since Vancouver's journal and Puget's account give little indication of how they surveyed these inlets, it is interesting to consider how the Spanish carried out similar surveys. When Malaspina sent Espinosa to examine Nootka Sound in 1791, his orders included specific instructions on this point: 'Since in this excursion the greatest extent of exploration is to be preferred to a scrupulous hydrographic accuracy, it will be sufficient to establish a limit to the extremities with a couple of observations of latitude and longitude.'[32]

Malaspina pointed out that by noting the turns of the channels and the time taken to sail between them, it would be easy to achieve above-average accuracy in the survey. Vancouver's survey of these inlets likely followed a similar pattern; he could not spare the time to adopt any other method. Having first established the position of the entrance to a particular inlet, Vancouver would then have proceeded up it under oars, keeping to the centre of the channel, noting his course by compass, and estimating the width of the inlet as he proceeded. To obtain the distance between turning points, he probably timed the interval his boat's crew took to row between them or perhaps obtained the boat's speed by log-line. If he was able to land at any of the turning points he would have taken a round of angles to determine the orientation of the next leg, as this would be a little more accurate than a compass bearing. Having reached the head of the inlet, if the weather was sufficiently clear to make the necessary observations, he would have obtained its latitude by observing a meridian altitude of the sun by theodolite or sextant and artificial horizon. When he reached the head of Howe Sound, for example, the weather cleared sufficiently for Vancouver to obtain an accurate latitude.[33] At the head of Jervis Inlet, where he could not wait for the weather to clear, his error of seven minutes of latitude[34] is not unexpected. There is no mention in his journal that he observed lunar distances for longitude on any of his boat expeditions.

When Vancouver joined forces with Galiano to survey the inlets near Desolation Sound, he may well have been surprised to find how well the small Spanish vessels were equipped with chronometers and surveying instruments. Malaspina had issued Galiano with two chronometers by Arnold: No. 61, a box chronometer; and No. 344, a chronometer watch.[35] In consequence, when Galiano sent Vernacci to survey Knight Inlet, he entrusted him with Arnold 344 and an artificial horizon. Thus Vernacci may have been able to obtain his longitude as well as his latitude on this occasion. Vancouver, for his part, was equipped with better boats, which had mounted swivels for protection, enabling his boat expeditions to be absent from their parent ships, *Discovery* and *Chatham*, longer than their Spanish counterparts.

In surveying the northwest coast, Vancouver relied on observation spots, generally situated several hundred miles apart, to provide a rigid framework for his survey. He obtained their latitudes by meridian altitudes of the sun and their longitudes by lunar distances. Between each observation spot he obtained further meridian altitudes of the sun, whenever possible, to establish the latitudes of prominent headlands. At each observation spot Vancouver also determined the rates of his chronometers by observing equal altitudes of the sun to enable him to carry forward his longitude between them by chronometer. Each section of his survey then had to be adjusted to fit the established positions of his observation spots and any values for latitude and longitude obtained between them. During his first season on the coast, Vancouver established observation spots in Discovery Bay, Birch Bay, and Friendly Cove. As the weather prevented Whidbey, the expedition's principal astronomical observer, from obtaining any lunar distances in Discovery Bay, Vancouver based its longitude on 220 sets of lunar distances by six different observers, taken before his arrival there and carried forward by chronometer.[36]

The accuracy of Vancouver's surveys must be considered in terms of his instructions and the constraints they placed him under. The length of coastline he eventually surveyed was so great that it was impossible for him to achieve the highest degree of accuracy, as his instructions anticipated. Nevertheless, surveyors such as Vancouver, who are experienced in carrying out accurate, large-scale surveys, are in fact also likely to conduct more accurate running surveys than those who are less experienced. In this Vancouver was brilliantly successful. It is no discredit to the man that subsequent surveyors were able to improve on his work. Nor is it surprising that he failed to find the entrance to the Columbia and Fraser rivers, though he suspected the existence of both. Similarly, his failure to find and survey Seymour and Belize inlets on the northeastern side of Queen Charlotte Sound is equally understandable.

As W. Kaye Lamb points out in his introduction to the Hakluyt Society's edition of Vancouver's *Voyage*, Vancouver's latitudes are very close to modern values, but his longitudes are not.[37] In his first season almost all Vancouver's longitudes, based principally on lunar distances, placed him farther east than their present values. His observation spots in Discovery Bay, Birch Bay, and Friendly Cove were fifteen-and-a-half minutes, nineteen minutes, and eight-and-a-half minutes, respectively, all too far to the east.[38] Vancouver also obtained some indifferent lunar distances in Desolation Sound and Menzies Bay, but discarded them in favour of longitude by chronometer based on its rate as determined on his arrival in Friendly Cove.[39] Vancouver noted that his longitude of Friendly Cove placed it 'about 20' 30" to the eastward of the longitude assigned to it by Captain Cook, and about 10' to the eastward of Senr Malaspina's observations; whence it would seem to appear, that our instruments for the longitude were erring on the eastern side.'[40] Although Vancouver would have been happy to accept the longitude 'as settled by astronomers of superior abilities,' doing so would have materially altered all the longitudes of the coast he had already surveyed. He therefore decided to retain his own longitude for Friendly Cove.

In his second season, Vancouver's lunar distances placed Restoration Cove two minutes too far to the west and Salmon Cove seven-and-a-half minutes too far east,[41] with most other longitudes for this season also too far east. In his final season, bad weather prevented Vancouver from obtaining any lunar distances at all, though he managed to obtain rates for his chronometers at the head of Cook Inlet, Port Chalmers, Port Althorp, and Port Conclusion.[42] Since their rates had now become somewhat erratic, it is hardly surprising that his longitudes placed Cook Inlet and Prince William Sound up to forty minutes and Cross Sound and Port Conclusion up to twenty minutes too far to the east.

Some of Vancouver's miscalculations in longitude can be attributed to the inherent inaccuracy of lunar distances, since an error of one minute of arc in the lunar distance (due to a mistake in either the tables, the adjustment of the sextant, the observation itself, or the calculation) leads to an error of about thirty minutes of arc or half a degree in longitude.[43] Since, in Vancouver's time, the movements of the sun and moon in the heavens could not be predicted with absolute accuracy, the *Nautical Almanac* contained unsuspected errors of some magnitude in the lunar distance tables. The magnitude of these errors was only appreciated in England when the longitudes obtained by Matthew Flinders, during his survey of Australia, were recomputed in 1811. As a result, an average of fourteen feet and, in extreme cases, of up to thirty feet had to be subtracted from the longitudes he obtained and computed in the field, based on the lunar distance tables in the *Nautical Almanac*.[44] As Flinders pointed out, 'Some sea officers who boast of their having never been out more than 5', or at most 10', may deduce from the column of corrections in the different tables [in his Appendix], that their lunar observations could not be entitled to so much confidence as they wish to suppose; since, allowing every degree of perfection to themselves and their instruments, they would probably be 12', and might be more than 30' wrong.'[45] This was something Galiano had already suspected, being convinced that errors he had experienced in lunar distances could

> be attributed almost entirely to an error in the tables with which the distances were computed. Thus, far from agreeing that longitude by lunar distances can be relied on to a quarter of a degree as had been advanced by some, one should only rely on them to the said three quarters [of a degree], accepting that in most cases the mean of various series could be within one quarter of a degree. So we told Captain Vancouver, to whom our proposition was strange because of the ideas established in England by the best astronomers, who had predetermined, as an exact method of establishing longitude, the mean of many lunar distances.[46]

Galiano based his longitude for Nootka on his observations in the San Juan Islands, where he witnessed Jupiter's first satellite emerging.[47] During his subsequent survey he made frequent observations ashore using an artificial horizon to obtain longitude by chronometer as well as latitude by meridian altitudes of the sun.[48] In partially rejecting lunar distances, Galiano was ahead of his time. Not until the 1830s did Robert FitzRoy, in his voyage on the *Beagle*, demonstrate that highly accurate longitudes could be obtained by chronometers alone. In fairness to Vancouver, however, it must be pointed out that FitzRoy carried twenty-two chronometers of a much more advanced design than the single chronometer carried on the *Discovery* during Vancouver's first season on the northwest coast.

Vancouver may have relied on lunar distances for longitude because of the poor performance of his chronometers.[49] (See the following chapter and the charts on page 81. The charts show that the rates of his four box chronometers were excessive, all of them gaining on average between fifteen and twenty seconds a day, with Arnold 176 gaining between thirty and fifty seconds.) In general, these rates increased as the voyage progressed. Earnshaw's pocket chronometer performed much better than the larger box chronometers, Vancouver describing it as an 'excellent piece of workmanship to be highly intitled to our praise'[50] and later as 'the least sensible of the change in the climate to which it was removed.'[51] Unfortunately, after first stopping on 16 April 1793, it stopped again eleven days later and could not be restarted. When it was examined by Earnshaw after the voyage in the presence of two witnesses, water was found to have gotten into the watch case and penetrated into the movement through the wind-up hole.[52]

By the end of the eighteenth century the importance of accurately drawn coastal views as aids to navigation was widely recognized. Alexander Dalrymple, hydrographer to the East India Company at the start of Vancouver's voyage, was a great advocate of such views. Because of his influence, the official account of Cook's third voyage contained six sheets of such views, one being an excellent one of the entrance to Nootka Sound. Although no official artist was appointed to his expedition, and no mention of the need to take coastal views in his instructions, Vancouver was pleased to find that 'amongst the officers and young gentlemen of the quarter-deck, some who, with little instruction, would soon be enabled to ... make faithful representations of the several head-lands, coasts, and countries, which we might discover.'[53] Three of these, John Sykes, Henry Humphrys, and Thomas Heddington lived up to Vancouver's expectation, with the result that at the end of the voyage he had over 100 drawings by these three young artists from which to select suitable coastal views to supplement his surveys.

On his return to England in 1795, Vancouver spent the next few years readying his journal for publication as the official account of the voyage. To assist him, Joseph Baker was employed 'under Vancouver's immediate inspection' preparing the various surveys for engraving, while William Alexander, who had been the official artist on Macartney's embassy to China, redrew the coastal views. Benjamin Baker, Thomas Foot, John Warner, and S.J. Neele were engaged by the Admiralty to engrave the charts, and Benjamin T. Pouncy and James Fittler were engaged to engrave the coastal views.

During the voyage Vancouver made considerable use of various Spanish and Russian surveys for parts of the coast he had been unable to examine himself. He also included their work on his engraved charts, taking particular care to differentiate between the coastline he had surveyed himself from that surveyed by various Spanish and Russian explorers. A minor exception to this is Loughborough Inlet, where Johnstone's survey shows, incorrectly, that it terminates in latitude 50°46' north.[54] At this point, the inlet changes direction sharply. Salamanca, who had also been sent to survey the inlet by Galiano, reached its true termination about five miles farther on. These last few miles of Salamanca's survey have been added onto the end of Johnstone's survey, without explanation, on Vancouver's engraved chart. A mystery also surrounds Vancouver's depiction of Nootka Sound on his engraved chart. Nootka Island appears attached to the main island despite the fact that in 1792 Bodega y Quadra presented him with a copy of Malaspina's survey of the sound, done the previous year, on which Nootka Island is clearly separated from the main island and named Isla de Mazarredo.[55] Baker incorporated Malaspina's survey on Vancouver's small-scale manuscript chart covering this area,[56] misspelling the Spanish name for Nootka Island as Y^d de Marsaredo in the process. But the same information does not appear on the engraved chart. A possible explanation may lie in a copy of a Spanish manuscript chart of Quimper's 1790 expedition,[57] forwarded from the Admiralty to Vancouver on the *Daedalus*.[58] This chart also depicts Nootka Island joined to the main island, might well have been among Vancouver's charts when Baker was working on them after the voyage, and could well be the source of this error.

As proofs of the charts and views were taken, they were sent to Vancouver for his approval. He then sent them to the Admiralty to make the final selection of plates to be included in the *Voyage*. The Admiralty in turn consulted Dalrymple, now hydrographer to the Admiralty, about the cost of engraving the various plates. Engraving the ten charts in the atlas cost £371, a saving on the estimate of £520, and engraving the six sheets of coastal views cost £206.10.[59] An atlas containing proofs of a number of these engravings, in various states, is held by the Washington State Historical Society in Tacoma, Washington, and a similar atlas is held in the DeGolyer Library, Southern Methodist University, Dallas. A proof of plate 15 – *A Survey of the Sandwich Islands* –in the Hydrographic

Office, Taunton, England,[60] has in its title the words 'Prepared by Lieu^t Jos^{ph} Baker' engraved in much larger letters than Vancouver's own name. Not surprisingly, this was rectified when the plate was finally printed.

For the greater part of the nineteenth century, Vancouver's atlas was the only reliable authority for navigating the remoter waters of British Columbia and Alaska. It was also consulted for determining the boundary in the Anglo-Russian Convention of 1825, the Oregon boundary dispute in 1846, and the San Juan Islands disagreement between the United Kingdom and the United States, which was finally settled by arbitration in 1872. More than his charts, however, the numerous names that Vancouver bestowed on the northwest coast are a lasting memorial to his work.

Vancouver's Chronometers

Alun C. Davies

W hen Cook sailed on his first voyage in 1768 he and his officers
determined longitudes by a mixture of old and new technologies. The old technology was 'dead reckoning,' essentially a blend of rule-
of-thumb measurements and expert guesswork.[1] The new technology –
more precisely, the new science – employed lunar observations, aided by
the recently calculated and freshly printed *Nautical Almanac*.[2] On Cook's
second and third voyages he continued to use dead reckoning and the
lunar observation method, augmented by the even newer technology,
the marine chronometer. A portable timekeeper capable of keeping a
close timekeeping rate under very variable and adverse conditions,[3] it
enabled longitude to be calculated more accurately and rapidly.[4]

Vancouver, so well trained by Cook, also used lunar observations
and chronometers. Sometimes he used all three methods, as checks on
each other.[5] Cook had used some of the first chronometers ever made,
including K1 and K3 (see Figure 1), copies made by Larcum Kendall of
John Harrison's famous prize-winning instrument, H4. He also took box
chronometers from the workshop of the up-and-coming young maker,
John Arnold.[6] Vancouver, too, took K3 in his *Discovery*. His expedition
also used instruments constructed by John Arnold and two timepieces
made by Thomas Earnshaw, with the former being the most eminent
representative of the next generation of great chronometer makers.[7]

By the 1830s the use of chronometers to establish longitude in navigation had become routine. The experimental stage, in which Vancouver's

voyage formed an important episode, was over. When Robert FitzRoy sailed on the *Beagle* in 1839, the use of chronometers in surveying was normal practice. In the six decades separating Cook from FitzRoy the technical and commercial aspects of chronometer manufacturing advanced steadily. Sea trials of chronometers, including the longest voyages of the ships of the East India Company, were measured in weeks or a few months. Thus the four-and-a-half years of Vancouver's expedition constituted the most sustained sea trial of chronometers up to that time. The performances of Vancouver's instruments helped influence subsequent development by highlighting technical problems and prompting improvements in construction and operation. On the commercial side, the prestige and advertising benefits arising from supplying instruments for an epic voyage were seized on by the leading chronometer firms, notably the houses of Arnold and Earnshaw, fuelling their intense commercial, technical, and personal rivalry.

Vancouver's expedition also had broader consequences for the chronometer market. It spurred the demand initially given by Cook's famous endorsement of its merits. On the supply side, output expanded and prices fell. What had once been prodigiously expensive gradually became affordable. The development costs (including prize money) of H4 exceeded £20,000; the production cost of K1 was £500 (compared with £2,700 for the entire cost of construction of the *Endeavour*), and of K2, £200. Government departments might afford these high prices, but not most ships' captains. The cost of Vancouver's instruments, as noted later, were less expensive than Cook's.

Between the eras of Cook and Vancouver, and FitzRoy, annual production increased steadily. Because of chronometers' longevity, the available stock expanded inexorably. Annual output of London's chronometer makers rose from the handful of prototypes in the 1770s, to dozens and then scores in the 1780s, to hundreds in the 1790s.[8] By the 1830s supply and demand balanced. By the 1840s excellent instruments could be bought for £40 or less.[9] The *Beagle* was supplied with off-the-shelf chronometers of tested and certified accuracy. In 1839 FitzRoy wrote in the narrative of his own distinguished voyage of discovery: '[In] a part of my own cabin twenty-two chronometers were carefully placed ... and in order to secure the constant, yet to a certain extent mechanical attendance required by a large number of chronometers, and ... to repair our instruments and keep them in order, I engaged the services of ... a private assistant.'[10]

The growing market for chronometers cannot be explained by a single episode such as Vancouver's voyage. His use of chronometers, however, raises interesting questions about how the new technology they embody relates to advancements in navigation. These connections can be explored by posing three sets of questions. First, what chronometers were taken by Vancouver? Who made them and what did they cost? Next, how were they used? How did they perform? Third, what were the commercial consequences for chronometer makers? And what general conclusions may be drawn about the nature of technological change?

Vancouver's expedition had six major timepieces. The most famous was K3 (see Figure 1), about which much is known, though less about its maker.[11] By any account, it is surely amongst the dozen most *famous* (not necessarily the best or most expensive) timepieces in the world. It was finished in 1774, went on Cook's third voyage, and undoubtedly became familiar to Midshipman Vancouver then.[12] K3 was Kendall's 'cheap' model, for which he charged the Board of Longitude £100. Unlike K1 and K2, it was not a copy or *replication* of H4, but, (as Kendall's obituary writer explained) 'when he was employed by the Board a third time he execute[d] a watch on a most simple plan, of his own invention, which may always be afforded at a moderate price.'[13] K3 lacked the refinements and embellishments of K1 and K2, but is significant for representing the first attempt to simplify the layout and lower the cost of a product of the new technology. K3's box, 'mahogany ... stuffed with wool in green cloth, the top cut out with three small circles' cost another £4 12s. 6d.[14]

K3 had spent much of the 1780s in Canadian waters, off Newfoundland, with Commodore John Elliot.[15] Its commission for Vancouver's use in 1790 is documented in the Board of Longitude's papers. Before being handed over to Vancouver it had been 'cleaned and put into order by its very worthy and ingenious maker, a short time before his decease.'[16] It was then carefully transported and placed aboard the *Discovery*. After the voyage ended in 1795 K3 was cleaned, adjusted, and returned to the Board's warehouse.[17] Its distinguished working life continued long after Vancouver's expedition, and it was taken to Australia by Flinders. It is now, of course, one of the great treasures of the National Maritime Museum at Greenwich.

Figure 1. The chronometer K3, constructed by Larcum Kendall in 1774 and employed by both Cook and Vancouver

The expedition's second major timepiece was Arnold's box chronometer, No. 82, with Broughton on the *Chatham*. It was a product of Arnold's workshop dating from the early 1780s, when he had started making batches of instruments to meet the growing demand. This may have been one of two instruments (possibly the other was K3) refurbished by Arnold in 17 November 1790. An entry in the Board's records notes a bill from Arnold for 50 guineas 'for thoroughly repairing the marine chronometers, adding to them new escapements and gold balance springs, making them go two days and a half, whereas they formerly went thirty hours, and also aligning them.'[18]

During the 1780s Arnold was certainly the most prolific chronometer maker in London. Precisely how many he made is not known, and the numbering of his instruments, like that of other makers, is not a reliable guide either to dating or to sequence of production: instruments acquired new numbers when modified or when new layouts, or calibres, were started. Sir Joseph Banks, an enthusiastic Arnold patron, suggested that the maker had produced a thousand chronometers by the early 1790s, an estimate which probably should be viewed with caution.[19]

In any event, by the time Arnold supplied chronometers for Vancouver's expedition he had been doing business with the Board of Longitude for two decades. He had done repairs for the Board[20] and, like other chronometer makers, regarded the government department as a desirable and influential customer. His best customers, however, were the East India Company's captains, and their patronage underpinned his firm's commercial prosperity in the 1780s. Through his friendship with Alexander Dalrymple, the East India Company's hydrographer, Arnold sold scores of instruments during the 1780s to the company's captains.[21]

Arnold's connection with Dalrymple was doubly important, because the hydrographer was a proponent of chronometers rather than lunar observations for determining longitude.[22] Just as Nevil Maskelyne trumpeted the merits of the lunar method,[23] so Dalrymple proselytized the chronometer. In several pamphlets he extolled the advantages of the chronometer, especially Arnold's instruments and, as we shall see, wrote instruction booklets on how to use them.[24] Vancouver and his officers were surely familiar with these. By 1790 Dalrymple was a major figure in London's horological trade, well placed to influence the selection of chronometers for Vancouver's forthcoming voyage. The choice of Arnold 82 (A82) for the *Chatham*, and Arnolds 14 and 176 to be sent with the *Daedalus*, demonstrates Dalrymple's influence and confirms the reputation of Arnold's firm.

At first the Board intended to send only two timekeepers with Vancouver, namely K3 and A82. In December 1790 Admiral Hyde Parker, on behalf of the Board of Admiralty, wrote to John Arnold to tell him that, at their Board meeting of 5 December, they had decided to send two timekeepers 'in a ship going on a voyage of discovery.' One had previously been lent to the late Vice Admiral Sir Robert Harland 'and left at his death in your hands.'[25] The other was 'to be given up immediately, within a fortnight from the date hereof; and to acquaint you if this recognition is not complied with, within a fortnight from the date hereof, I have their orders to proceed against you for the recovery of the said watches.'

These were two Arnolds (No. 14 and No. 176) brought out by the ill-fated Gooch on the *Daedalus*. The Board of Longitude's accounts with Arnold reveal that they each cost £84, and that they were delivered to the Astronomer Royal in June 1791.[26] No. 14 was 'a Marine Chronometer with a *platina* balance' – one of the balances using platinum that Arnold had been experimenting with in an attempt to compensate for temperature changes.[27]

Arnold's No. 176 is the instrument familiar to the modern city of Vancouver, as it is one of the treasures of its Maritime Museum (see Figure 2). It was one of a series of 82 made by Arnold (of which fifteen are known to survive).[28] Its great wheel had scratched on it 'cleaned and jewelled in 1791. Finished by Mr Jeffries.' The digit '1' of the serial number seems to have been engraved after the digits '76.' This was probably the original serial number, and construction of the instrument likely started in or before 1787.[29] Its balance was the sixth in the sequence of experimental balance wheels devised by Arnold. It was a 'Z' type, 'with brass cross arm and outer bimetallic semi-circular rims,' intended to improve the efficiency of the instrument.[30] Like K3, A176 had an interesting career after its voyage with Vancouver. When it was returned after Vancouver's expedition it went back into stock, and then, in 1801 (along with No. 82), was cleaned and adjusted. One axis hole for the balance was rejeweled, and it was given a new box and gimbals.[31] A176 (with K3) went to Australia with Flinders and, when it stopped, was sent home to be repaired. It accompanied Bligh to New South Wales in 1806. In 1850, Board of Longitude records indicate it was in London.[32] The Astronomer Royal ordered that it be delivered to the firm of Frodsham (successor to the firm of Arnold). Thereafter it was lost, until its reappearance in 1981 and purchase by the Vancouver Maritime Museum.

Two other instruments were also sent out with the *Daedalus*, namely, a pocket chronometer and a regulator.[33] Both were by Thomas Earnshaw, Arnold's great rival. Earnshaw himself was brilliant but irascible, and his pocket chronometer, No. 1514, displayed both its maker's genius and volatility.[34] At its best its performance was superb. But just as Earnshaw himself was capable of exaggeration (as in his vitriolic pamphlet attacks on Arnold), so No. 1514 was simultaneously exceptional in quality but

Figure 2. John Arnold's chronometer, No. 176. This chronometer was probably made in 1787 and specially refurbished for Vancouver's expedition in 1791. It was later employed by Flinders and Bligh and is now in the Vancouver Maritime Museum.

unstable in performance. For a brief period it outperformed the other instruments, but on Friday, 19 April 1793, it stopped. Vancouver recorded the incident as follows:

> On winding it up it appeared that Earnshaw's had intirely stopped ... I repeated my efforts to put it again in motion, but did not succeed; and as its cases were secured by a screw, to which there was no corresponding lever in the box that contained it, I concluded that in the event of any accident, it was Mr Earnshaw's wish that no attempt should be made to remedy it; it was therefore left for the examination and repair of its ingenious maker. I had for some time suspected that something was wrong with this excellent little watch. On its first coming on board it beat much louder than any of the others, and so continued until we quitted the Sandwich Islands, when it gradually decreased in its tone until it became weaker than any of them; from whence, I was led to conjecture, that probably too much oil had been originally applied, which was now congealed, and clogged the works.[35]

No. 1514 had a silver pair case, 'jewelled escapement and small wheel holes,' a spiral balance spring, and a 'bimetallic conpensation balance with brass wedge or segmental shaped weights.'[36] The use of jewels by Earnshaw and Arnold for their best instruments indicated craft of the highest level. Jewelled pivot holes reduced friction and wear and improved performance and reliability. Jewelling watches was a trade secret, and one reason why the Clerkenwell district of London had become the horological capital of the world in the 1790s. No. 1514 was expensive not because of the intrinsic value of its metal and jewels, but because of the cost of the labour in its construction.[37]

The sixth major timepiece taken by Vancouver was a regulator to be used whenever the portable observatory was set up. A regulator is essentially a large, plain, pendulum clock, capable of being fine-tuned literally to split-second accuracy. It had to be set up in a secure, sheltered position, for it might take several days, even a week, before its rate 'settled' to permit its use for astronomical observations.[38] Whereas Cook had taken regulators made by John Shelton,[39] Vancouver took 'an astronomical clock' by Thomas Earnshaw, one of the very few regulators he made. Those surviving are instruments of superlative quality.[40] Earnshaw's regulator for the Vancouver expedition had 'jewelled pallets and jewelled small wheel holes ... [it was] ... a capital portable month regulator in mahogany case with gridiron pendulum 9 bars.'[41] The nine bars were a temperature compensation device, a sequence of brass and steel rods whose different expansion and contraction qualities were almost mutually compensatory. Earnshaw's price for making the movement was £89 5s.[42] After the voyage the regulator was returned to the Board of Longitude. In 1828 it passed to the Royal Observatory, was sold in 1932, and is now in private hands.[43]

Earnshaw also made a journeyman clock 'in a painted case' for another £6. A journeyman clock (sometimes described as an 'assistant,' or 'follower,' or 'counter') was a secondary clock which ran for a few hours. It was synchronized with the main regulator when readings were about to be taken. Maskelyne described Shelton's original journeyman clock for Cook's observatory as 'having a pendulum swinging seconds which, after being well adjusted, would keep time very regularly for several hours. It had only a minute and second hands, and struck every minute exactly as the second hand came to sixty, which was very convenient for the counting of seconds ... I reduced the time to that of the observatory clock, by means of my watch, with the second hand.'[44] The main regulator had a relatively quiet beat. Because the portable observatory 'stood generally on the sea-shore where the roaring of the surf seldom permitted us to hear the Astronomical Clock all the time it was going,' journeyman clocks were constructed to give a very loud beat, useful when the wind was high or when there were any other noises.[45] The cost of making 'a fine and portable stand' for Earnshaw's regulator and journeyman clocks, and their packing case, came to £43. In all, the final bill for the regulator and pocket watch set back the Board £195 13s. 6d.

The stepping up or down of readings, to permit split second timing, was effected with the aid of a handful of other, minor, instruments.[46] Included with two spare watch glasses were '2 1/2 hour watch[es], 6 hour watch[es], 6 minute watches and four quarter minute [watches].' One other timekeeper worth mentioning was the alarm clock, necessary to wake up astronomers who might have dozed off in between night sightings. The alarm clock was made by Arnold and repaired by Earnshaw (or at least by someone in his workshop) at a cost of eighteen shillings.[47]

Whenever Vancouver visited a location at which the precise longitude had been previously established, he checked his instruments to determine their 'going rate.' Thus in December 1791 he set up a temporary observatory at Hawai'i, and in May 1792 at Point Discovery.[48] When the *Daedalus* arrived, it brought out with the extra chronometers (Arnold 14 and 176) and the regulator 'a new observatory,' a prefabricated unit, easy to erect and dismantle. '[It was] ten feet in diameter, in twelve frames, with a moveable roof ... Door and proper fastenings fixed on a bottom folding kerb, and packed up in cases, Delivered to Deptford Yard for the use of Mr Gooch of the *Daedalus* store ship. £20. Made by Nathan Smith, at his patent floor cloth manufactory, Knightsbridge.'[49] Vancouver's observatory was similar to one taken by Cook fourteen years earlier. Cook's has been made familiar to us in Webber's celebrated painting of Nootka Sound (1778); and John Sykes' drawing shows Vancouver's version, erected at Observatory Point, Discovery Bay.[50]

How were the chronometers used and how well did they perform? Kendall's, Arnold's, and Earnshaw's chronometers represented the finest achievements of contemporary technology.[51] They were fundamentally different from all other surveying instruments (such as compasses, telescopes, quadrants, and sextants) because they were *clockwork* devices, hand-built by artisans. Notions of quality control were hazy, and metallurgical standards were haphazard. No two instruments (not even those made in batches) performed alike. They were empiricisms.

When variations in the daily rate of gaining or losing were small, as they were in even the best of instruments, over a long voyage these inexorably cumulated into large errors. But if the variations were of known amplitude, they could be taken into account and factored into the calculations of the surveyors or navigators. Thus the importance of *rating*; that is, of determining the rate at which they were daily gaining or losing. This explains Vancouver's concern to touch locations where longitude had already been already established (Tahiti, Hawai'i, St Helena, Cape Town)[52] and also to establish new base points such as Monterey and Valparaiso.[53]

Above all, the need to determine the 'going rate' of the chronometers explains the importance of setting up the portable observatory in safe, well-guarded locations during the survey seasons. These became temporary, alternative, Greenwich meridians. If superior readings were established, longitudes could be readjusted.[54] Furthermore, in the shelter of the observatory tent, the reliability of the spring-powered chronometers could be regularly checked against the finer timekeeping precision of Earnshaw's weight-powered pendulum regulator. New going rates for chronometers could be determined, and these might be carefully checked against the hundreds of sets of lunar observations (the old technology) which Vancouver, like Cook, meticulously insisted his officers should make.[55] They could thus recalculate the time in Greenwich, half a world away.

An understanding of how a new technology works usually comes through the printed word or by 'learning by doing.' When the *Discovery* sailed from Portsmouth only Vancouver and Joseph Whidbey were experienced navigators. They passed on their knowledge and soon, 'amongst the officers and gentlemen of the quarter deck, there were several capable of ascertaining their situation in the ocean, with every degree of accuracy necessary for all important purposes of navigation.'[56] Written guidance was also available, although the celebrated textbook *Finding the longitude at sea, by Timekeepers* by William Wales, (who had sailed with Cook), giving instructions, rules, examples, and problems, appeared in

1794, too late to go with Vancouver. However, the *procedures* described in Wales' book were those developed during Cook's expeditions, in which Wales and Vancouver had both participated.[57] Vancouver and his officers would no doubt also have been familiar with booklets on how to use chronometers published by Alexander Dalrymple, including *Some Notes Useful to those who have Chronometers at Sea* (1779 or 1780)[58] and *Instructions Concerning Arnold's Chronometers or Timekeepers* (1788).[59] These were among the first of many publications, part instruction manual, part advertising pamphlet, provided by chronometer makers when they delivered their instruments.[60]

The Board of Longitude also gave Vancouver detailed instructions, similar to those addressed earlier to Cook and his officers.[61] They included relatively simple, but important, directions on how to wind the chronometer's mechanism properly and more technical details about how to use the chronometer in conjunction with the transit telescope and other instruments. Understanding an instruction booklet required the ability to read, and knowledge of how to navigate was what differentiated officers from men.

Instruction booklets were useful, but not in themselves comprehensive guides to surveying and navigation. Vancouver therefore requested that the Board send out an astronomer with the *Daedalus*, William Gooch. His untimely death left the busy Vancouver without an expert, and so he allocated surveying to the admirable Joseph Whidbey.[62] Although Whidbey at first felt rather inadequate, he was evidently a good pupil, and later he published a lucid account of how to use chronometers for navigation.[63] He worked prodigious overtime hours and felt he deserved extra pay. Subsequently both he and Vancouver petitioned the Board for a bonus.[64] The Board was sympathetic to Whidbey, allowing him £180 for 327 days' work, but turned down Vancouver's request, assuming that these responsibilities were part of his originally commissioned duties.[65]

The original chronometer records are missing. They were submitted by Vancouver to the Board after the voyage and then went back to him. They have since disappeared.[66] Fortunately, there is sufficient evidence in Vancouver's own account of the voyage for a general assessment to be made (see Figure 3).

As the charts show, the chronometers generally 'gained,' though sometimes erratically. Vancouver, like others before him, noted that the

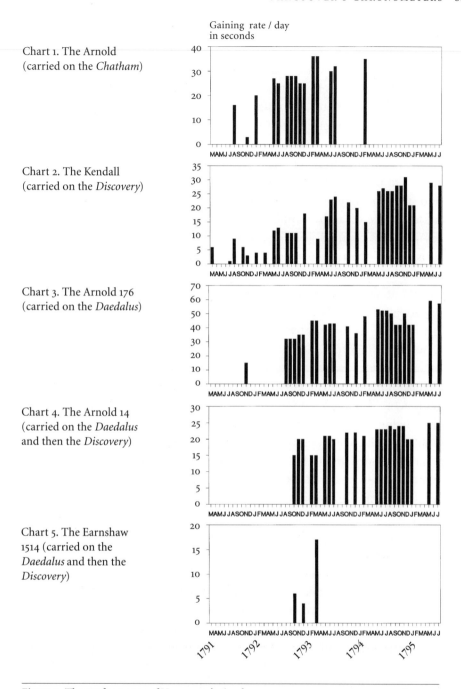

Gaining rate / day in seconds

Chart 1. The Arnold (carried on the *Chatham*)

Chart 2. The Kendall (carried on the *Discovery*)

Chart 3. The Arnold 176 (carried on the *Daedalus*)

Chart 4. The Arnold 14 (carried on the *Daedalus* and then the *Discovery*)

Chart 5. The Earnshaw 1514 (carried on the *Daedalus* and then the *Discovery*)

Figure 3. The performance of Vancouver's timekeepers

Note: In each chart the rates are rounded to the nearest second; each bar column indicates that either a new rate was determined, or an old rate confirmed, during the indicated month.

Source: extracted from entries in Vancouver, *A Voyage*, I-IV.

rate of gain was different on land and on sea, and concluded it had more to do with temperature variations than with the movement of the ships.[67] Fluctuations in the rates of going were the greatest problem confronting chronometer manufacturers before and after Arnold and Earnshaw. (The eventual resolution of this problem earned Charles-Édouard Guillaume a Nobel prize in 1920.[68]) At the time of Vancouver's voyage, few chronometer makers could spend long months at sea to record an instrument's performance, so they relied instead on navigators and surveyors like Vancouver to keep records and identify problems. The performance of a chronometer in a workshop or observatory, even if temperature changes were simulated with ovens and iceboxes, was less satisfactory than an extended sea trial, and Vancouver's experiences yielded valuable data for them.

What were the consequences for the chronometer of Vancouver's experience and what conclusions may we draw? Some have already been mentioned. Arnold and Earnshaw were well aware of the commercial benefits arising from the publicity gained by supplying chronometers for an epic voyage. Earnshaw selectively used the splendid, but brief performance of his watch (he glossed over its breakdown) in his pamphlet war with Arnold and the Board.[69] The use of Arnold's instruments, even those which performed modestly, suggested that any publicity was good publicity. The firm's commercial reputation after John Arnold's death in 1799 continued to be high, even under his less able son John Roger Arnold. A few years later Captain Meriwether Lewis was recommended to take an Arnold chronometer with him on his great land expedition.[70] Later generations of chronometer makers willingly loaned their best instruments for expeditions, because the subsequent prestige might be used in advertising.[71]

Another consequence already alluded to arose from Vancouver's observations on the performance of his instruments. Vancouver's identification of temperature changes as a likely cause of fluctuations in the rates of going was believed by his brother John to be one of the important consequences of the voyage.[72] Chronometer makers were spurred on to develop better balances. The years immediately following Vancouver's return saw a flurry of sea trials in which attempts were made to measure and control the effects of temperature changes on the instruments.[73] The question was broadened when in 1798 Samuel Varley (one of the founders of what became the Royal Institution) made the first scientific tests to see what effect magnetic forces had on chronometer performances.[74]

One possible *indirect* consequence may be seen in the attempts of the Spanish government to adopt the new technology by setting up its own chronometer-manufacturing establishment between 1792 and 1800. The Spanish had experimented with 'chronometer by longitude' in the 1770s. Admiral Mazarredo bought eight instruments from the great French maker, Louis Berthaud, and the Spanish Admiralty had purchased two of John Arnold's early models for loan to ships on scientific expeditions.[75] Malaspina bought an Arnold chronometer in 1785, which 'performed splendidly,' and then acquired three more Arnolds in the late 1780s.[76] No doubt the friendly exchanges of surveying information between Vancouver and Galiano included discussions of the merits of chronometers.[77]

The Spanish authorities were thus already fully aware of the benefits of the new technology. A chronometer workshop had been set up at the San Fernando Observatory. At considerable expense they sent their best workers to Paris and London for training and bought machinery and tools. The project failed. An epidemic wiped out their key workers and there was no equivalent in Spain of London's Clerkenwell district, with a reservoir of skilled horological artisans. In the late eighteenth century, as today, transferring a new technology was difficult.

Vancouver's experiences with chronometers remind us that technological changes usually occur in small increments, rather than in large leaps forward.[78] Outside the sometimes narrow corridors of maritime and horological history, it has perhaps been uncritically accepted that the problem of establishing longitude at sea was solved by Harrison, Kendall, and Cook. Not so. The process was slow. The chronometer only came of age after Vancouver's voyage. Above all, Vancouver's use of chronometers reminds us that new technologies do not instantly replace the old.[79] They overlap and coexist. Cook had concluded, in 1773, that the *Nautical Almanac* ought still to be used in conjunction with chronometers: 'Should the Watch be found to keep its uniform rate of going it will point out to us the greatest method of Observing the Longitude at Sea ... [and] ... by the Tables the Calculations are rendered short beyond conception and easy to the meanest capacity.'[80]

Vancouver, so admirably schooled by Cook, was wise enough to use one method to check another, and frequently used all three.[81] Neither dead reckoning nor lunar observation was abandoned when a chronometer came on board. Even with the advantage of more and cheaper chronometers a generation later, Captain Fitzroy and his officers on the *Beagle* still used the procedures for determining longitude established by Cook and developed by Vancouver. The Admiralty's instructions for the *Beagle*'s voyage noted that even 'with proper precautions and proper formulae' for determining the chronometers' rates, it would still be necessary to check them 'after long periods, and sudden changes of heat and cold,' by astronomical means.[82] Thus the *Nautical Almanac* and lunar observations – 'old' technology – long remained a crucial part of a naval officer's training. Longitude by chronometer – the 'new' technology – *was* superior, but exclusive reliance on it was risky.

A Notable Absence: The Lateness and Lameness of Russian Discovery and Exploration in the North Pacific, 1639-1803

James R. Gibson

I have to regret very much our want of knowledge of the Russian language, because the results of all our inquiries concerning the object of that power [Russia], in extending its immense empire to these distant and inhospitable shores [northwest coast], became from that cause in a great measure nugatory, vague, or contradictory. We however clearly understood, that the Russian government had little to do with these settlements; that they were solely under the direction and support of independent mercantile companies; and that port Etches, which had been established in the course of the preceding summer [as St Constantine Redoubt on Hinchinbrook Island in Prince William Sound], was then their most eastern settlement on the American coast; but I was not able to learn the number of different stations they had, though I understood from Mr Smyloff [the skipper Gerasim Izmailov, who was also one of Cook's informants on Unalaska in the fall of 1779], that the total of Russians employed between this port and Oonalashka [Unalaska], both inclusive, were about four hundred. This number, it should seem, is amply sufficient for the accomplishment of the purpose they have in view; as not the least attention whatever is paid to the cultivation of the land, or to any other object but that of collecting furs, which is principally done by the Indians, whose services they have completely secured, and whose implicit confidence they have intirely gained.

– Captain George Vancouver, 1794

Thus did Captain Vancouver learn toward the end of his meticulous coastal survey that some 400 Russian fur traders had advanced eastward from Siberia as far as Prince William Sound, just as Captain Cook had found fifteen years earlier that a similar number had progressed as far as Unalaska Island. Neither navigator likely knew, however, that the tsar's frontier settlers had reached the Pacific 150 years earlier; if they had known, they would surely have wondered why the Russians had not moved faster and farther across the rim of the North Pacific, particularly given the exceptional value of sea otter skins, the matchless hunting skills of the enserfed Aleuts, and the absence of foreign competitors until the mid-1780s (when the Russians were alerted by the publication of Cook's final voyage).[1] This chapter tries to answer that question for them.

By the early sixteenth century the 'gathering of the Russian lands,' that is, the unification of the principalities of the Eastern Slavs by Moscow, was complete, thanks to the political prowess and military might of Tsar Ivan III, sometimes called the Great for this achievement. Muscovite Russia was now free to satisfy its imperialist appetite elsewhere. The west was blocked by other great powers, and the south by the Crimean Tartars, the strongest remnant of the Golden Horde, which had kept the Eastern Slavs in thrall from the mid-thirteenth century to the midpoint of Ivan's reign. The other three leftovers, the khanates of Kazan, Astrakhan, and western Siberia, were overcome by Ivan the Terrible in the 1550s and 1580s, leaving the east clear all the way to the Pacific.

The Russians were not slow to seize this opportunity, spanning the Siberian wilderness with remarkable speed. And with good reason. The minimal relief, especially of western Siberia, presented few physiographic obstacles, and the dense network of rivers facilitated water transport in all directions. Physically, Siberia was quite similar to Muscovy, so that the Russian invaders did not have to adapt to a radically different environment. Siberia's natives were unable to offer much resistance, since their population was not large, their technology not advanced, and their stand not united; besides, the Russians employed cleverer tactics and deadlier weapons. No foreign powers opposed the Russian advance, the two in a theoretical position to do so – China and Japan – being restrained by their own ethnocentrism, isolationism, and anticommercialism. Siberia's virtual monopoly on precious sable – 'soft gold' – provided an irresistible attraction to Russian hunters and traders. And, finally, a general economic depression in the homeland between the 1570s and the 1670s, punctuated by human and natural disasters, provided an equally irresistible repellent.[2]

Thus, merely fifty-seven years after crossing the Urals and seizing the western Siberian khanate's capital of Sibir, the Russians sighted what they logically called the Eastern Ocean (more than 2,000 miles further east), when a party of thirty-one men under the Cossack Ivan Moskvitin reached the Okhotsk Sea at the mouth of the Ulya River.[3] Thus, Russians discovered the Pacific from the west a century and a quarter after it was revealed from the south by the Portuguese and from the east by the Spanish. Eight years later the *ostrog* (fort) of Okhotsk was founded some fifty miles to the north, and it remained Russia's main Pacific port for the next two hundred years. Russia was poised to play a major role, if not to take the lead, in the exploration and discovery of the North Pacific. By now the English had voluntarily left Japan, and the Spanish and Portuguese had been expelled, leaving only a few Dutch traders, who were kept under strict quarantine on the tiny artificial island of Deshima in Nagasaki Harbour. On the opposite side of the Pacific, New Spain, now more than a century old, had not yet expanded northwards into either of the Californias. The peninsularity of Baja California was not rediscovered until 1701, and San Blas, the naval station and supply base for Spanish probing of the *frontera del norte*, was not established until 1768.[4] The Manila galleons had been making their annual runs from Acapulco to the Philippines since 1564, but their purpose was strictly commercial and, remarkably, they seemed to have missed the Hawai'ian Islands.[5]

Yet Russia failed to take immediate or even imminent advantage of its early access to the North Pacific for any maritime purpose – commercial, strategic, or scientific. Nearly a century was to elapse before the Cossack Kozma Sokolov was to open a sea route from Okhotsk to Kamchatka in 1716-17 and the Dane Vitus Bering was to lead the first Russian voyages of exploration and discovery to the north and east of Kamchatka in 1725-30 and 1733-43 'to find glory for the state through art and science,' in the words of Peter the Great.[6] Russian ships (the *St Peter* and *St Paul* under Bering and Chirikov) did not cross the North Pacific until 1741, a full century after Moskvitin had entered it. The first Russian circumnavigation was not to take place until the early nineteenth century, and, although it penetrated the North Pacific, very little was left to be located and examined by then. The approximately forty Russian circumnavigations in the first half of the nineteenth century were primarily to supply and defend the Russian presence in the North Pacific, not to explore and discover.[7] Why, then, did the Russians take so long to exploit their North Pacific foothold?

One reason is to be found in what an economic geographer would call the intervening opportunity of the Amur Country to the south of the Okhotsk seaboard. Moskvitin's breakthrough did not really lead anywhere because it did not reflect the locus of Russian activity in eastern Siberia for the remainder of the 1600s, although he may have approached that locus – the Amur River – at its mouth. In the meantime other cossacks and *promyshlenniki* (freelance entrepreneurs in general and fur hunters/traders in particular) were opening and pacifying first Baikalia (Irkutsk was founded as a *zimovye* [winter camp] in 1652) and then Amuria (a fort was built at Nerchinsk, the gateway to the Amur, in 1654).

Baikalia offered superior sables and arable steppeland, as well as the prosperous Buryat natives, who not only farmed but also competed with the Russians for tribute from the Tunguses. Amuria was even more attractive, however. Native rumours credited the river basin with gold and silver, copper and lead, untapped sables, and – of almost equal importance – aboriginal grain and stock with which to provision the Russian settlements in the harsh taiga to the north. The Amur River was also seen as a convenient and navigable 'river road' from the continental interior to the world ocean – the Asian counterpart of the Great Lakes-St Lawrence and Mississippi-Ohio-Missouri waterways of North America – and as a potential trade route to China and Japan. These hopes were realized by the expeditions of Vasily Poyarkov, with 133 men, in 1643-6 and Yerofey Khabarov, with up to 150 men, in 1649-50 and again in 1650-3, with 117 men. They imposed *yasak* (fur tribute), found Native grain and beef, abundant sables and other furs, silver, lead, and iron; and they boated down the Amur to the Pacific.

Russian interest in eastern Siberia now shifted from Yakutia to Baikalia and particularly to Amuria, which became an irresistible *Belovodye* (a mythical promised land of freedom and abundance) for cossacks, promyshlenniks, peasants, traders, and adventurers. Their efforts, directed mainly from Yakutsk across the Yablonovoy and

Stanovoy ranges via right-bank tributaries of the upper Lena River, cul-
minated in founding Albazin in 1665 on the upper Amur in the heart of
Dauria, the homeland of the agricultural Daur natives. Up to 1,500
Russians of various backgrounds settled along the river.

However, in waging war, exacting tribute, and seizing land and food
in the Amur Valley the Muscovites incurred the wrath not only of its
Native inhabitants but also of their Manchu overlords. The Manchus,
who had just conquered China and established the Ching dynasty, ener-
getically and successfully resisted tsarist encroachment along the frontier
of their Manchurian homeland. Eventually the Russians were outnumbered, outsupplied, and outmanoeuvred, especially after the Manchus
suppressed a protracted rebellion in South China in 1680. Under the
terms of the Treaty of Nerchinsk of 1689, the first pact between the Celestial
Empire and a European state, Russia abandoned the Amur, including
Albazin, in return for trading rights at Kyakhta on the Mongolian frontier. The border was redrawn to follow the water divide between the Lena
(Arctic drainage) and Amur (Pacific drainage) systems. Thus, Russia lost
a potential supply base for its Pacific settlements and the fastest and
cheapest route between the Siberian interior and the Pacific Ocean.[8]

With the loss of the Amur Country, Russian attention returned to
northeastern Siberia as a fresh source of fur-bearing animals and tribute.
Yakutia, however, was already depleted of sables; in 1684 the state had
even prohibited taking sables there to avoid their extinction.[9] That left
only the Kamchatka Peninsula untapped before the North Pacific would
have to be entered and traversed in the seemingly unending search for
virgin hunting/trapping grounds. (Chukotka had already been absorbed
in mid-century, when Semon Dezhnev, by sailing through Bering Strait
from north to south in 1648, had proved that Asia and North America
were not connected.)[10] Besides, if the Russians were to utilize the ocean,
then Kamchatka, protruding nearly 1,000 miles seawards from the
Siberian mainland between the Okhotsk and Bering seas and offering
one of the world's best natural harbours at Avacha Bay, would be the log-
ical springboard.

The peninsula had become known to the Russians as early as mid-
century and was shown on Semyon Remezov's 'Godunov map' of 1667,
but its conquest was postponed until the end of the century by their pre-
occupation with Amuria. In 1696-9, within a decade after the Treaty of

Nerchinsk, Kamchatka was subjugated by an expedition of 120 men led by the Cossack Vladimir Atlasov, who counted up to 25,000 Kamchadal natives (Itelmen), contacted the Kurilian Ainus, retrieved a Japanese castaway (Denbei), and returned with 3,862 furs, nearly all sable. By 1712 Kamchatka contained 200 Russians at three forts. However, the cossacks remained mutinous from 1707 through 1717, and the Kamchadals rebellious; the latter's resistance culminated in the 'great rebellion' of 1731, when the fort of Nizhne-Kamchatsk was burned and 150 natives and 120 were Russians killed.

From the peninsula the Russians gained abundant and superior fox and sable skins. In terms of pelt size and fur thickness and glossiness Kamchatka's sables were superior to any others in Siberia. Only those of the Olyokma and Vitim basins had darker coats, and Kamchatka's were sent for sale to North China, where they were expertly dyed. So numerous were they that as late as 1740 it was said that even in the remote parts of the peninsula there were more sable than squirrel tracks along the Lena. Nevertheless, the fur-bearing animals and the tributary natives were inevitably overexploited, and tribute returns declined especially after 1720.[11]

Having occupied and depleted all of the Russian Far East, the tsar's men were now free to probe the North Pacific, with the First Kamchatka Expedition of 1725-30 under Bering and the Second Kamchatka Expedition of 1733-43 under Bering and Chirikov. Commerce was the actual purpose of both voyages, not the determination of whether Asia and North America were connected, since Peter the Great (1682-1725) already knew that they were not.[12] Bering's first venture accomplished so little that a second one had to be undertaken to locate the 'great land' (North American continent) to the east to find a fresh source of wealth for the state treasury and private entrepreneurs. And even though the second venture (which was unprecedented in scale – occupying ten years, engaging up to 2,000 members, and exploring the coast of Siberia from the Kara Sea to the Sea of Okhotsk as well as the waters to the south and east of Kamchatka) did succeed in reaching the New World, it made but brief landfalls on two islands and none on the mainland; and on the return voyage Bering lost both his ship and his life on the Commander Islands. Georg Steller, the immodest German naturalist who accompanied Bering as a mineralogist, complained bitterly – after being ordered to quit Kayak Island, where the vessels had stopped to water – that ten years had been spent preparing for twenty hours of investigation and taking fresh water from America back to Asia.[13]

The second expedition also brought back sea otter skins, which proved to be even more lucrative than sable pelts. This triggered another fur rush, propelling promyshlenniks along the Aleutian causeway to Alaska and down the northwest coast, eventually as far as New Albion where Fort Ross was founded in 1812. Not another state expedition to the North Pacific occurred until 1764-9, when Captains Pyotr Krenitsyn and Mikhail Levashov were dispatched to explore the Aleutian Islands. And it could be considered comic were it not so tragic. The venture's four ships did not manage to leave Okhotsk until the fall of 1766, soon became separated, and all four were wrecked on the Kamchatkan coast. Only in 1768 did the leaders reach the Aleutians in two makeshift vessels, returning to Kamchatka a year later. In the summer of 1770 they put to sea again, but Krenitsyn was drowned in the Kamchatka River, and Levashov returned to Okhotsk with both ships to end the expedition. It accomplished very little, principally the accurate determination of the latitude of the Aleutian chain and the insularity of Unimak Island (but not that of Kodiak Island, which was not even reached), and it lost many lives to drowning and starvation, including not only one of the leaders but also the seasoned and talented navigator Stepan Glotov.[14]

Much of the blame for these unimpressive performances lay with logistics. The North Pacific was separated from the Russian ecumene in general, and Moscow and St Petersburg in particular, by a vast space whose peculiar nature did not allow for the easy, rapid, or cheap supply of personnel and matériel. To journey overland from the imperial capital of St Petersburg to the Pacific coast was to travel some 7,000 miles – at least one-third of the way around the world at those high latitudes. This sheer distance was lengthened by marshy, wooded, or rugged terrain and long, hard winters, as well as by inept drivers and pilots and, in the words of the nineteenth-century poet Venevitinov, 'roads that facilitate delay.'[15] 'The Siberian highway is the longest and, it seems to me, the ugliest road in the whole world,' remarked Anton Chekhov in 1890 en route to Sakhalin.[16] And the 'river roads' were frozen for more than half of the year. Little wonder that, according to Russian legend, six Kamchadal girls who were sent from Bolsheretsk to St Petersburg at the command of Empress Elizabeth (1741-62) had time to become mothers before reaching Irkutsk and were visibly pregnant again before reaching the imperial court.[17]

The most difficult stretch of this overland supply line lay between Yakutsk and Okhotsk. Here the Russians had to cross the mountain wall, which served both as a drainage divide between the Arctic and the Pacific and as a transport barrier between the interior and the coast. It was breached only by the Amur River, which China had regained in 1689. So the Russians were stuck with the infamous Yakutsk-Okhotsk Track: a 750-mile obstacle course for the thousands of Yakut horses that were used annually to pack freight across the 'big bulge' of the Dzhugdzhur Range. At least half of them did not survive the journey.[18] Governor George Simpson of the Hudson's Bay Company, himself a notoriously hard driver of humans and beasts, remarked after travelling this route: 'When compared with this corner of the world, England, which is some-times said to be the hell of horses, must be contented with the secondary honour of being their purgatory. The unfortunate brutes here lie down to die, in great numbers, through famine and fatigue; and this road is more thickly strewed with their bones than any part of the plains on the Saskatchewan with those of the buffalo.'[19] In the summer of 1834 a Russian Orthodox priest, Father Gromov, vividly specified some of the route's obstacles: 'It can be said that, for our sins, on the Okhotsk Road we suffered the ten tortures, similar to the Egyptian [ten plagues in *Exodus* 7-12]. Rabid horses; quagmires, where for us the land turned into water; nocturnal darkness, often catching us en route among the thick woods; branches threatening to blind us; hunger; cold; mosquitoes; gad-flies – these are truly *biting flies*; hazardous fords across rivers; and [sad-dle] sores on the horses – the tenth punishment!'[20] And the track's eastern terminus, Okhotsk, was an inferior port, amounting to but a shallow, exposed roadstead with a navigation season of four months at most. So many vessels were wrecked on the shifting sandbars and turned into magazines that the settlement was a veritable ship museum. It was this bottleneck between Yakutsk and Okhotsk that made the Russians covet the Amur as a much easier outlet to the ocean – as a 'Mississippi of the East,' in the words of the celebrated anarchist Prince Peter Kropotkin.[21]

Thus, mounting expeditions in the North Pacific via Siberia required inordinate amounts of time, effort, and money. At the outset of his first expedition (1725-30) Bering thought that it would last three years,[22] but the difficulties of supply prolonged it to more than five, of which less than two months were spent on his voyage proper from Kamchatka. During the Second Kamchatka Expedition (1733-43), it had been assumed that Bering and Chirikov would sail from the peninsula after four years,[23] but by then Bering had gone no farther than Yakutsk, and they did not sail out of Petropavlovsk until 1741. The expedition took twice as long as had been expected and cost the treasury at least one and one-half and perhaps more than two million rubles.[24] This staggering expense discouraged additional state probes in the North Pacific for a couple of decades.[25] Not until 1764 was the next one – the Krenitsyn-Levashov expedition – mounted. It likewise took too long, cost too much (112,469 rubles)[26] and gained too little, again because of problematical logistics. Even the more successful 'geographical and astronomical expedition to the northern parts of Russia' in 1785-94, provoked by Cook's third voyage and commanded by one of Cook's officers, Joseph Billings, achieved only 'modest' results after three years and did not sail the North Pacific until 1789.[27]

Russian exploration and discovery in the North Pacific were also hampered by what might be termed Russia's continental as opposed to its maritime nature. Russia was basically a land power, not a sea power, for two good reasons: lack of opportunity and lack of necessity. Russia had little opportunity to develop a trading, fighting, or fishing fleet because of limited access to the ocean. To the north the pack ice of what the Russians called the Icy Sea (Arctic Ocean) restricted shipping to cabotage in the short ice-free period, although the North Atlantic Drift (an extension of the Gulf Stream) did keep Murmansk open year-round and, as far as the Kara Gates, did lengthen the navigation season. To the south lofty ranges and plateaus, plus Ottoman Turkey, Persia, and British India, blocked access to the Indian Ocean. To the west access to the ocean lay along either side of the great isthmus beginning between the Baltic and Black seas and terminating in the peninsulas and islands of Europe. In either case, however, access was indirect and insecure, the outlets of both inland seas – the sound and the straits – being controlled by foreign powers. Finally, to the east the Pacific's utility was constrained by both distance and season.

Moreover, where the Russian land mass met the open sea, the country was blessed with few superior natural harbours, that is, harbours with plenty of room, depth, and shelter for sailing vessels. The fiord of Murmansk and the calderas of Petropavlovsk and Vladivostok were exceptions, but Petropavlovsk and Vladivostok in particular were so far removed from the ecumene as to be of little service. Furthermore, Russia had few peninsulas like Iberia that jutted far seaward and few embayments like Hudson Bay that reached far inland – thereby further diminishing maritime opportunity. Several arterial rivers, such as the Ob, Yenisey, and Lena, did run far inland, but, unlike the Amazon and Platte, most flowed into the virtual dead-ends of the Caspian and Aral seas. The Russian Empire was the very embodiment of the continental; for every mile of coastline there were 800 square miles of territory, compared with ratios of 1:110 for France and 1:12 for the British Isles. Worse, most Russian coastline was frozen for much of the year, because of the high latitude, low salinity, and shallowness. All of this helps to explain, incidentally, why the Russian Empire was, with the solitary and temporary exception of Alaska, a continental, contiguous rather than a maritime, scattered enterprise. Russia expanded overland, mostly across the northeastern quadrant of the Old World, not overseas to the New World, and Russians therefore had no occasion to sail the oceans to discover, explore, and colonize new lands.[28]

The lack of necessity was as compelling as the lack of opportunity. The Russian Empire was so large and so varied – physically and culturally – that, much like the Celestial Empire, it enjoyed a very high degree of self-sufficiency or, as an economist might call it, import substitution. Indeed, during the Stalin period (1928-53) national and regional autarky was a prime objective and was substantially achieved. The point is this: because Russia could meet most of its needs domestically, there was little need for foreign trade or, consequently, for a merchant marine, a navy, or, for that matter, a fishing fleet, given the abundance of river and lake fish. The few imports were chiefly technicians and manufactures, owing to Russian educational and industrial backwardness.

Hence the overwhelmingly continental cast of Russia. Not surprisingly, most Russian expeditions of exploration and discovery operated overland, not overseas. Of the 192 expeditions sponsored by the Academy of Sciences in the eighteenth and nineteenth centuries, perhaps 18 (less than 10 per cent) could be classified as maritime.[29] Russia's continentality was even regarded as an advantage in the imperial contest with the maritime colonial powers of Western Europe. Witness the geographer Ivan Kirilov, the author of the first *Atlas of the Russian Empire* (it was begun in 1726, and twelve of the projected 360 maps were published in 1734) and of the first comprehensive geography of Russia (*The Flourishing Condition of the All-Russian State*, initiated in 1720 and completed in 1727 but not published until 1831).[30] Kirilov was also the chief secretary of the Senate and, according to the historian Gerhard Müller, the 'primary driving force' behind the Second Kamchatka Expedition. He stressed in 1733 that continental Russia was better situated to take advantage of trade in the Far East: 'Russia has been especially endowed by God for the development of this new eastern commerce: natural canals, that is, great rivers, run right across Siberia, and boats with goods can ply them, and only in three places are there short portages on this overland route.' He added: 'Here we have a great advantage over Europeans who sail to the East and West Indies: it is not necessary [for us] to cross the Equator and to suffer the intense heat of the sun; also, we will not come to fear Algerian or other pirates, and, above all, in going to foreign ports they [Europeans] spend all they have, whereas with us all that goes to benefit our subjects.'[31]

Nevertheless, Kirilov advocated the overseas supply of the Second Kamchatka Expedition by a naval fleet. But, he emphasized, such a round-the-world expedition would safeguard Russia's border and trade in the Far East, not promote exploration and discovery. This strategy had been proposed in 1732 by both Count Nikolay Golovin, president of the Admiralty, and Vice-Admiral Thomas Saunders. Golovin asserted that two frigates and one supply ship with 300 men, sailing from Kronstadt via Cape Horn, would take no more than a year to reach Kamchatka, whereas supplying the Bering-Chirikov expedition overland would take at least six years. He also summarized the venture's aim: 'To seek new lands and a passage to America and to the Japanese islands and to describe the Siberian coast from the Ob River to Okhotsk'. He stressed that the main advantage of such a voyage (which, if successful, should be repeated annually by two frigates) would be to improve the stagnant Russian fleet and to train Russian naval officers and crews, as well to open trade with various countries, particularly Japan. Saunders suggested two packet boats with fifty-one men be dispatched via Cape

Horn; he contended that they would reach Kamchatka in only eight to ten months, whereas overland supply would take at least four years. Like Golovin, he emphasized that such a voyage would not only supply the Second Kamchatka Expedition faster but also protect the Russian Far East, train Russian sailors, and open trade, especially with Japan. In addition, Saunders, like Kirilov, pointed out that continental Russia enjoyed more secure imperial links than did the maritime powers of Western Europe, whose oceanic colonial connections were vulnerable to disruption by rivals and pirates as well as by navigational hazards.[32]

Both proposals, however, were rejected. Russia was unable or unwilling to organize a round-the-world voyage until the end of the century. It took Cook's third voyage, which penetrated the waters of Russian America and the Russian Far East, to alarm St Petersburg into action. In 1786 Peter Soimonov, personal secretary to Catherine II (the Great), proposed that three to four frigates be sent to the North Pacific to protect Russian settlements and activities there against British encroachment. He submitted his proposal to the Ministry of Commerce, which concurred and ordered the dispatch of five ships, 'armed in the manner of those used by the English Captain Cook and other navigators for similar discoveries.' Captain Grigory Mulovsky, an educated and seasoned officer of twenty-nine, was appointed commander of the flotilla, comprising the *Kolmogor* (600 tons), *Solovki* (530 tons), *Sokol* (450 tons), *Turukhan* (450 tons), and *Smely*. The expedition's principal objective was 'the defence of our rights to the lands discovered by Russian seafarers.' In addition, it was to explore, establish trade with Japan, and deliver ships and goods to the Russian Far East. The ships were to depart in late 1787 and proceed via the Cape of Good Hope to the Hawai'ian Islands. From there, two vessels under Mulovsky were to sail to Nootka Sound and then northwards to discover and claim any unoccupied coastland. Another two vessels were to sail to the Kuriles, Sakhalin, and the mouth of the Amur to explore, and the *Smely* was to sail directly to Petropavlovsk with freight. By the fall of 1787 the expedition was ready to sail; however, war broke out first with Turkey and then with Sweden, and the ships and crews were transferred instead to the Mediterranean and Baltic theatres, where Mulovsky was killed in action in July 1788.[33] The first Russian circumnavigation had to wait another fifteen years and the next century.

Another reason for the delay in enhancing Russia's position in the

North Pacific was its backwardness in crafts and fields essential to the success of exploration and discovery, continental or maritime – endeavours such as shipbuilding and navigation, medicine and nutrition, mapping and printing. Culturally, Russia was Europe's stepchild. European intellectual currents like the Renaissance, Reformation, and Enlightenment reached the country late and lame, or not at all, impeded by sheer distance, the Cyrillic script, Russian Orthodoxy, Russian xenophobia, and even Russian autocracy. Latin, and everything written in it, was for centuries deemed the tool of the devil and the enemy of Russian Orthodoxy, whose Byzantine antirationalism was intrinsically incompatible with scientific inquiry. Having been invaded so frequently by steppe nomads and European armies, Russia developed a garrison mentality, inferiority complex, and paranoid distrust of the outside world, including its scientific ideas. The guardians of official ideology, particularly after the mid-point of Catherine II's reign (1762-96), were ambivalent toward science: on the one hand, they respected it as a means of achieving practical results, but on the other they feared it as a competing ideology. Indeed, science did not flourish in Russia until the 1860s, and until then was dominated by foreign scholars.

The painfully slow acceptance of scientific ideas arose, too, from the absence of a leisure class of intellectuals who could pursue scientific work free of church control, the absence of secular schools, and the devotion of the limited printing facilities to the publication of government documents and religious literature. The widespread antipathy to formal education and scientific inquiry was scarcely weakened even in the eighteenth century by Peter the Great's enthusiasm for scientific education or by Catherine the Great's ambitious plan for a public school system. It was Peter who abruptly and forcibly began wresting control of education from the church. His own intellectual awakening was derived from foreign friends of his youth, and stimulated by his 'Grand Embassy' to Western Europe and his association with the German philosopher and mathematician Gottfried von Leibniz. The 'carpenter tsar' saw that the development of the sciences and trades in his country would earn his subjects respect and honour abroad and refute the widespread belief that they were inhabitants of what Elizabethan England had regarded as a 'rude and barbarous kingdom.'[34]

Peter was especially interested in geographical expeditions because of his pragmatic attitude toward science as a powerful means of achieving a more bountiful, more rational exploitation of Russia's natural resources. Yet it was not until 1745 that Russians replaced the *chertyozhi* (crude sketch maps not drawn to scale and without geodetic latitude and longitude) and compiled a map of their country based upon the astronomical determination of longitude. Peter did found a navigation school in 1701 in Moscow and a naval academy (stressing shipbuilding) in 1715 in St Petersburg, but they had few pupils, who had even fewer prospects of jobs. Hydrographic science did not develop until the early 1700s, when Russia acquired a navy (1696), an admiralty (1700), and frontage on both the Black Sea (1700) and especially the Baltic Sea (1721).

Peter's dream of Russian naval power was not realized, however; in 1734, nine years after his death, there were only fifteen seaworthy armed vessels, with no officers to command them.[35] The sextant, invented by John Hadley in 1731, did not reach Russia until 1757, whereupon it was rejected as too complex and too costly; it was not manufactured in Russia until the end of the century, when John Harrison's chronometer (invented in 1735) was finally introduced.[36] Thus, when the *Resolution* and *Discovery* put into Petropavlovsk in the spring of 1779 following Cook's fatal winter in the Sandwich (Hawai'ian) Islands, the Russian commandant, Major Magnus von Behm, was amazed that the British expedition had been able to operate without more crew and more sickness. Surgeon David Samwell reported:

> The Major often expressed his Surprize that all our people should look so well after having been out near three Years, and said that from our Appearance he should have supposed that we had but just left England, nor was he less astonished to hear that we had lost but such a small Number of Men by sickness, telling us that the Russians send their small Sloops with about 60 Men in them on a Summer's Cruise to the Coast of America and the adjacent Isles & that it often happens that not more than 20 or 30 of them return home alive, the rest dying of the Scurvy & other Disorders; & he was somewhat amazed to find that we carried only 112 men in the Resolution [500 tons] but 70 in the Discovery [300 tons], for the Russian Sloops of one Mast and ab^t 70 ton Burden generally carry sixty Hands.[37]

Unbeknownst to Samwell, these Russian sloops represented a

marked improvement over the crude vessels and rough crews that had begun plying the sea otter trade eastward from Okhotsk along the Aleutian Islands less than forty years earlier in the wake of Bering's and Chirikov's findings. The vessels were clumsy and flimsy – short and wide, single-decked and single-masted, and high-sided and flat-bottomed, with wooden anchors and hide sails. They were called *shitiki* ('sewn ones'), because the unseasoned and unplaned sideboards were bound to the timbers with leather thongs, willow osiers, or even whalebone and chinked with moss. Not until 1757 did the Russians begin using *gvozdenniki* ('nailed ones'), that is, barks with ribs and nails or pegs. They averaged only two knots or so and carried no more than eighteen tons. The crew were *morekhody*, that is, 'seafarers,' not able sailors. Up to half were Kamchadals, whose marine tradition was slight; the rest were Russian peasants and townsmen, some of whom only had experience in boating along rivers or coasts. For food they relied upon Steller's sea cow (at least until it was exterminated by 1768), and they lacked instruments and charts. The consequences were predictable. Accident, disease, and warfare took the lives of one-quarter to one-third of the crewmen.[38] Captain Adam von Krusenstern, the commander of the first Russian voyage around the world in 1803-6 on the *Nadezhda* and *Neva*, wrote that usually one of three such ships was lost every year because of 'the wretched construction of the vessels; the ignorance of most of their commanders; and the navigation of the stormy eastern ocean, which throughout the year was attended with danger to vessels of this description.'[39]

But Von Krusenstern himself and his voyage illustrated the Russian problem. He and Captain Yury Nevelskoy of the *Neva* had to apprentice six years (1793-9) in the British navy to refine their naval skills. Their two vessels, the sloops *Leander*, 450 tons and three years old, and *Thames*, 370 tons and fifteen months old, were bought in London for £17,000 plus £5,000 for repairs. Von Krusenstern and Nevelskoy completed their round-the-world trip nearly 300 years after Ferdinand Magellan's circumnavigation for Spain and fifteen years after Robert Gray's for the young United States. They failed, incidentally, to achieve two of the expedition's main goals – to establish relations with Japan and to secure trading rights at Canton, where both ships narrowly missed seizure. By now, of course, the North Pacific, especially the eastern side, had already been well probed; even the Sea of Japan stretch of the western side had already been investigated in 1797 by Captain William Broughton, late of the Vancouver expedition. Only the configuration and alignment of Sakhalin and the Amur's mouth remained to be clarified, and the Russians did not get around to doing that for another half century.

Russian neglect of the North Pacific stemmed, too, from its low rank in St Petersburg's order of foreign policy priorities. Russia's strategic interests were, of course, focused on its main rivals for national survival and economic development. Those rivals were initially steppe nomads and subsequently European states such as Lithuania, Sweden, Poland, and Ottoman Turkey that tried to prevent Muscovy from expanding its borders westwards to the Baltic Sea and southwards to the Black Sea. To the east there was no real threat and therefore not much concern. Siberia's aboriginals – not numerous, not united, not advanced – were easily suppressed and eventually outnumbered by loyal Russian colonists. Finally, no other power expressed much interest in Siberia. The two that could have posed a threat – Japan and China – remained aloof, despite the accession of powerful regimes (the Tokugawa Shogunate in 1604 and the Manchu, or Ching, dynasty in 1644) just as Russia was in the midst of its push to the east. Both ethnocentric Oriental states preferred to remain isolated and unsullied.

Even in the far North Pacific Russia's eastward advance went unchallenged for a generation – and may well have gone unchallenged much longer if the Russians had not taken so long to enter and cross the Eastern Ocean. By the 1770s, however, the Spanish activity had reached far enough north for Madrid to become alarmed by the Russian push toward its weakly defended Californias. The result was a series of voyages, beginning in 1774, from San Blas up the northwest coast to check the Russian thrust and to seek the elusive northwest passage. Almost simultaneously (1778-9) Cook's third expedition arrived on the same chimerical quest. He, however, found something else of equal or greater value – both an abundant and cheap source of, and an enormous and lucrative market for, sea otter furs, which proved even more valuable than sable pelts. First British and then American traders came to the scene, and further Russian expansion was finally blocked.

In the face of such strong commercial competition and the stout resistance of the northwest coast Indians, who offered stiffer opposition than did the Siberian Natives, Russia faltered and, of course, eventually

Port Dick, near Cook's Inlet, sketch by Henry Humphreys, engraved by B.T. Pouncy

withdrew in 1867. Peter the Great's successors lacked his imperialist vision and stomach, at least until Catherine the Great, but even she was cool to Pacific power plays, mainly because Russia, not its rivals, was shorthanded there. Thus, in reply to a request by two Russian merchants for a loan, some soldiers, and a monopoly to safeguard their business in the Gulf of Alaska, the empress wrote: 'Much expansion in the Pacific Ocean will not bring concrete benefits. To trade is one thing, to take possession is quite another.' She also feared any overseas colony would eventually be lost through independence, adding: 'The example of the American settlements [Thirteen Colonies] is not very flattering and, moreover, not advantageous to the motherland.'[40] Russia was already overextended and overexposed in the Russian Far East, let alone in Russian America, with its several hundred promyshlenniks scattered over far-flung islands and coasts halfway around the world without the protection of an army or navy. Furthermore, the foreign threat in the North Pacific materialized at the very time when Russia's western frontier, its most sensitive, was unstable. War with Turkey in 1768-74 and 1787-91 and with Sweden in 1788-90, the hostility of England, France, and Prussia, and Polish unrest and partition preoccupied St Petersburg. Peter the Great had solved one of the three problems of Russian foreign policy, the Swedish one; Catherine the Great solved the remaining two, the Polish and Turkish problems, thereby gaining Courland, Lithuania, Belorussia, the Ukraine, and the Crimea and finally suppressing the Crimean Tartars. Given these struggles, Russia could not risk a firm commitment in the North Pacific. For this very reason, of course, the Mulovsky expedition had to be postponed until 1801.

Finally, Russia did not appear to loom very large in the North Pacific because it did not publicize its presence. What it did accomplish there was underappreciated, particularly abroad. In this respect the Russian voyages resembled those of the Spanish, which, in the words of Archibald Menzies, Captain Vancouver's surgeon-botanist, were marked by an 'odium of indolence & secrecy.'[41] The several voyages ordered by Peter the Great to probe Far Eastern waters in the 1710s and 1720s – the abortive Great Kamchatka Detail of Yelchin of 1716-18, the Yevreinov-Luzhin voyage of 1719-21, and the Shestakov-Pavlutsy-Fyodorov-Gvozdev venture of 1727-32 – were officially declared 'secret.' Indeed, the commanders of the Kamchatka expeditions, Bering and Chirikov, were instructed to tell outsiders that they were seeking the Strait of Anian, not new hunting and trading grounds on the American mainland. This subterfuge was so successful that it is still cited in the literature as the actual purpose. Notice of the First Kamchatka Expedition was not published outside Russia until 1735 (five years after it ended) and even then only as an appendix to a description of China by the French Jesuit Jean Du Halde. Krenitsyn was ordered 'to maintain the utmost secrecy' during his expedition with Levashov to the Aleutian Islands in 1764-9. At first not even the Senate was informed of it and, to mislead outsiders, the venture was officially titled 'An Expedition to Inventory the Forests along the Kama and Belaya Rivers [in northeastern European Russia].' Its existence did not become known to readers both inside and outside Russia until Coxe's *Russian Discoveries* was published in 1780.[42] The same publication gave Western readers their first knowledge of the post-1741 Russian fur-trading voyages along the Aleutians.

This seeming paranoia arose from two concerns. One was the fear that imperial rivals might learn of the lucrative fur rush by promyshlen-niks down the Kuriles and across the Aleutians, intercede, and block further progress – which is exactly what happened eventually. In the meantime, however, thanks to their policy of secrecy, the Russians had the maritime fur trade all to themselves for nearly half a century – including the most valuable colour phases of the sea otter, the Kamchatkan-Kurilian and the Aleutian, and the most adept sea otter hunters, the Aleuts and the Konyagas (Kodiak Eskimos). Both business and government reaped a rich harvest of golden fleece. From 1743 to 1800 at least forty-two private companies in 101 voyages to the 'Eastern Islands' collected up to 10,000,000 rubles worth of furs, mostly sea otter (as much as 190,000) but also fur seal skins, and usually realized profits of 100-200 and sometimes 500-700 per cent.[43] The state gained both taxes (10 per cent) and duties from this catch, fur tribute from the islanders, and a duty of 20-25 per cent when the sea otter skins were exchanged at Kyakhta on the Mongolian frontier for Chinese goods in the early 1770s (for an annual revenue of 550,000 rubles).[44] When the Russian monopoly of the sea otter trade was finally broken by Cook's compatriots in the middle 1780s, the price of skins at Kyakhta had to fall to meet the British (and subsequent American) competition at Canton.[45]

The other cause for concern was the strategic vulnerability of the Russian presence in the North Pacific. The Russian government was well aware that its subjects there were weakly defended, with no army or navy present or even nearby. The less that foreign powers knew of this weakness, the better, otherwise they would take advantage of it. This is exactly what the Americans in particular did on the northwest coast from the middle 1790s, when they poached and smuggled under the very noses of the Russians, who were helpless to prevent them. So weak were they militarily that Russian America's capital of New Archangel (Sitka) was captured and destroyed in 1804 by the Tlingit Indians (using American and British military aid) and besieged by the same Indians as late as 1855. Indeed, during the Crimean War (1853-6) the Russian government felt constrained to negotiate a neutrality agreement with the British government putting the exposed territory and shipping of the Russian-American Company off limits. This vulnerability, incidentally, was to be used in the mid-1860s as a forceful argument by Russian proponents of the sale of the Alaskan colony to the United States. With the sale, Russia withdrew to the Asian side of the Pacific and concentrated its imperial attention on western Turkestan and Amuria, which were economically more promising, logistically less problematical, and militarily less vulnerable. Its sole attempt at maritime expansion was thereby terminated.

Nootka Sound and the Beginnings of
Britain's Imperialism of Free Trade

Alan Frost

In 1786, the British government of William Pitt the Younger claimed half
a continent when it decided to establish a convict colony at Botany
Bay, Australia. In 1790, it used the Nootka Sound dispute to establish
British control over half a continent bordering the northeastern Pacific.
How are these moves best seen? – as fits of absence of mind? as reactions
only to pressing domestic circumstances? – or as parts of a coherent
imperial policy?

A good many historians – most recently, David Mackay and Mollie
Gillen – have argued that the Pitt Administration had little imperial
capacity. In Mackay's words,

> It requires some gifts of imagination to embody the foundation of the
> New South Wales colony into the substance of some wider imperial
> purpose ... Those who put the foundation of the settlement in the con-
> text of a 'swing to the east,' and those who see its establishment as part
> of some great commercial endeavour, greatly overestimate the policy-
> forming resources and enterprise of the metropolitan government.
> They assume a capacity for long-term planning which did not exist.
> They assume the existence of a philosophy of empire without specify-
> ing exactly where such a philosophy might reside or how it might be
> expressed. In this way the New South Wales example poses the ques-
> tion of how well adapted the government was at this time to view any
> imperial question in a wider context of direction and purpose.[1]

The Nootka Sound crisis in fact provides rich materials for the determination of these questions. This 1790 crisis arose from a combination of general and particular circumstances. There was Spain's claim to the exclusive right to navigate in and trade about the Pacific Ocean; and there was Britain's desire to overthrow this claim, thereby opening an extensive commerce, particularly with Spanish America. There was Chinese disinterest in European goods, which made it necessary for the English East India Company to purchase tea with bullion; and there was the fact that some of Cook's crew had traded trifles for sea otter pelts with the Indians of what is now British Columbia, most of which they subsequently sold to a Russian merchant for up to £7 each, and the remainder at Canton, for up to £15.

The publication of the official narrative of Cook's third voyage in 1784 alerted Europe to these commercial possibilities, and a host of adventurers were soon attempting their realization. The nation's circumstances in the aftermath of the wars of 1776-83 led the members of the Pitt Administration to see both trades as being in the national interest.[2] On the one hand, Britain's 'Southern' whalers were eager to extend their range of operation so as to increase their catch; and the American whalers, who had remained loyal, had lost their New England bases, so that an important and lucrative industry was in limbo. On the other hand, if sea otter pelts might be had cheaply on the northwest coast of North America and sold dearly in China, the pressure on the East India Company to find bullion might be lessened – a development that would greatly facilitate Pitt's plan to expand revenue by so reducing the duty on tea as to make smuggling uneconomic.

Accordingly, in 1785-6 the Administration persuaded the East India Company and the South Sea Company to license the Southern whalers to hunt east of the Cape of Good Hope and west of Cape Horn. The Administration also persuaded a group of merchants headed by Richard Etches, and encouraged by Sir Joseph Banks, to make an experimental voyage to Nootka Sound to develop a fur trade with Japan, Korea, and China.[3] Forming themselves into the King George's Sound Company, Etches and his partners equipped two ships captained by Nathaniel Portlock and George Dixon, which departed in late August 1785. Sailing via the Falkland Islands and Cape Horn, these ships reached the northwest coast of North America in July 1786 and, after wintering at the

Hawai'ian Islands, returned there in 1787. The company also sent out two more vessels in 1786 under the command of James Colnett, which traded on the northwest coast in the summers of 1787 and 1788.

This officially sanctioned venture had some severe competition. James Hanna mounted two voyages, sailing from Canton in 1785 and 1786. At the end of 1785 James Strange took two vessels out from Bombay, which reached the northwest coast in June 1786. Simultaneously, John Meares and William Tipping took two ships out of Calcutta. Progressively, other would-be traders also appeared – William Bolts and his sometime colleagues on the *Imperial Eagle*, which arrived in 1787; and New England merchants, who sent out two vessels under John Kendrick in September 1787, which reached the coast twelve months later. Meares reappeared, now sailing out of Macau under a Portuguese flag. Spanish traders from the Philippines and Russian merchants from Kamchatka materialized as well.

These ventures had mixed results. Some of the early ones were very successful, while others, such as Tipping's, were disastrous. In general, the trade did not realize expectations. The Canton market was soon glutted, and the traders failed to open new markets in Japan and Korea. Limited demand and falling prices were not, however, the only impediments. It was soon apparent that trade with the Indians might be more efficiently conducted if there were permanent coastal settlements. The Etches group had anticipated this, but Portlock and Dixon failed to follow their instructions to establish factories. Also quickly apparent was the need to have an intermediate base for reprovisioning ships and refreshing crews. The fur traders developed the habit of wintering at the Hawai'ian Islands, which gave rise to the idea that the government should form a colony there.[4] At the same time, the whalers realized the need for a base on the southern edge of the Pacific and accordingly proposed the island of Juan Fernandez and mounted the *Emilia*'s exploratory voyage around Cape Horn.[5]

The Pitt Administration responded to the whalers' need by beginning to organize a surveying voyage by the sloop *Discovery* of islands in the South Atlantic and sections of the southern coasts of Africa not occupied by other European powers. The fur traders moved to solve their logistical problems by themselves. First, John Meares set about establishing a factory at Nootka Sound. Sailing from Macau with two vessels carrying Chinese smiths and carpenters, he reached Friendly Cove in May 1788. He obtained a site from Chief Maquinna, fortified it, erected a rudimentary shed, and began boat-building.[6] In early 1789 Meares and his backers and the Etches party joined forces so as to pursue the fur trade in a more orderly fashion. The Etches' captain, James Colnett, was given overall command of the combined group's five vessels. When he sailed from Canton to renew the trade in April 1789, Colnett did so with orders to consolidate Meares' beginning at Friendly Cove. The proposed factory was to be 'a solid establishment, and not one that is to be abandon'd at pleasure.'[7] To that end, Colnett took with him twenty-nine Chinese artificers and building materials, and a small vessel in frame.

By this time, however, the Spanish had begun measures to assert both their general claim to a monopoly of European activity in the South Atlantic and the entire Pacific Ocean, and their specific claim to the northwest coast of North America. In 1788, Madrid began mounting a scientific expedition to rival those of Cook, in the belief that 'a carefully planned expedition with navigators and scientists of the highest calibre could do much to explore, examine, and knit together Madrid's far-flung empire, report on problems and possible reforms, and counter the efforts of rivals to obtain colonial possessions at Spain's expense.'[8] Led by Alejandro Malaspina in two corvettes of 306 tons each, this expedition left Cádiz at the end of July 1789, but its extensive itinerary meant that it did not reach the northwest American coast until June 1791 (or Port Jackson until March 1793). In the meantime, in accordance with royal orders, the viceroy of Mexico despatched a force of two vessels under the command of Estéban Martínez to examine the coast as far north as Alaska for signs of the presence of other European nations and to take possession of sites suitable for settlement. Martínez found that the Russians had trading camps at a number of places, and that the governor of Kamchatka intended to establish a fortified factory at Nootka Sound.[9] From them, too, Martínez learned of the activities of British and American traders. On his return to San Blas, he urged the viceroy to establish a base at Nootka Sound, from which these encroachments might be resisted. Accordingly, the viceroy sent Martínez north again in the spring of 1789.

On arriving at Nootka Sound on 2 July 1789, Colnett found that Martínez had already seized two of his group's vessels, while leaving American ones untouched. When Colnett argued with Martínez about personal and national rights, Martínez seized Colnett's *Argonaut* as well. He then seized a fourth ship, sending it and the *Argonaut*, with their crew imprisoned, to San Blas, where a number of the British sailors died. As he waited to be resupplied, Martínez used the Chinese labourers to begin establishing a base.

These actions in the North Pacific were paralleled by some on the coast of Patagonia, where in April 1789 a Spanish commodore ordered away the *Sappho* and *Elizabeth and Margaret*, two whaling ships which had called into Port Desire to wood and water. The British captains maintained that they did not understand Spanish sovereignty to extend over this 'desert' coast; the Spanish officer replied that indeed it did, as well as over the ocean adjacent, and that his orders were to see that no foreign ships frequented the one or the other. The stage was set for international conflict.

John Meares, who had stayed at Macau, learned about the events at Nootka when the American vessel *Columbia* reached Canton in November 1789; he immediately took ship for London. Meanwhile, a new viceroy of Mexico reported them to his Court, in dispatches which reached Madrid at the very end of the year. These dispatches (and perhaps also private communications between Mexico and Madrid) were sent by the chargé d'affaires in Madrid, Anthony Merry, to London on 21 January 1790, and were the first news received by the Pitt Administration. Although Merry's first account was somewhat garbled, it conveyed the essentials.[10] Three days later, Merry was able to forward a translation of a purloined letter which, except for identifying Meares' vessel as a Portuguese one, reported the affair accurately.[11]

In advance of instructions from London, Merry raised the matter tentatively with the Spanish foreign minister, Floridablanca, on 14 or 15 January. Floridablanca declined to discuss it in any detail, indicating instead that he was instructing his ambassador in England to represent Spain's position to the British government.[12] The Pitt Administration received Merry's second dispatch with its translation at the end of January; and the Marquis del Campo gave a Note to the Duke of Leeds, the British foreign secretary, on 10 February.[13] These opening exchanges were certainly friendly enough, with Merry reporting on 28 January that Floridablanca was expressing 'the strongest desire to see the harmony and friendly correspondence which at present so happily subsist between the two Courts improved as far as possible.'[14] Del Campo's letter was similarly conciliatory. Nonetheless, even at this early stage, both sides well knew what the great issues were: for the Spanish, a last attempt to assert that right, granted by the Pope (1493) and enshrined in the Treaty of Tordesillas (1494), to an exclusive navigation of the southwestern Atlantic Ocean and the entire Pacific Ocean, and possession of the southern and western coasts of the Americas; and for the British, the assertion of the right to navigate in the Pacific, to trade about its shores, and to establish sovereignty over areas not actually settled by Spain.

After his first tentative discussion with Floridablanca Merry expressed disappointment that the Spanish foreign minister did not bring up the subject of rights at their second meeting.[15] Yet these were certainly foremost in the minds of the ministers of both countries. On 2 February, Leeds advised Merry that, if the subject arose, to be 'extremely guarded in what you may have occasion to say...; as it is a matter of equal delicacy & importance in which you should be very cautious of giving even a hint which may be construed into dereliction of our right to visit for the purposes of trade, or to make a settlement in the District in question.'[16] And when he represented Spain's position to Leeds, del Campo asserted that as Spain had already, by discovery and occupation, established its claim to Nootka Sound, the British activities were clearly inimical to good relations, and would they please discontinue them.[17]

Two weeks later, the British cabinet responded to the Spanish note 'with a high hand.'[18] On 26 February, in a reply to which Pitt contributed significantly, the Administration informed del Campo that Britain expected Spain to restore completely the seized boats and property, and to compensate the traders for their losses, before any negotiations over respective rights on the northwest American coast.[19] This unyielding stance 'astonished' the Spanish, who took it as evidence of Britain's wanting armed conflict and quietly set about warning viceroys and colonial governors, commissioning warships, and seeking support from European allies.[20]

The Pitt Administration responded to the first news of the events at Nootka Sound much more rapidly and vigorously than historians have hitherto allowed. While the cabinet ministers' initial discussions were evidently not recorded in any detail, their substance is reflected in Leeds' dispatch of 2 February to Merry: Britain had a 'complete right' to 'visit for the purposes of trade, or to make a settlement in, the district in question,' and it would assert this right 'with a proper degree of vigour, should circumstances make such an exertion necessary.' Relevant to such exertion would be the naval force Spain might assemble on the northwest coast. Leeds accordingly asked Merry to discover this, including the size and force of 'the Ships which sailed a few months ago for California under the command of M. Malaspina.'[21]

At this point, the ministers had three paramount concerns: first, to establish Britain's right to sovereignty of Nootka Sound in particular, and of the northwest coast in general; second, to protect those nationals already on this coast, or about to venture to it, so that they might trade for furs unimpeded by Spanish actions; and third, to reserve for Britain the supposed passage from Hudson's Bay to the Pacific Ocean, the long-sought, convenient route from northern Europe to Asia.

The first concern presented the Pitt Administration with considerable difficulties. As was usual in such disputes, Spain based its claim to exclusive possession of the northwest coast, in the first instance, on ancient, general dispensations; but it also invoked the precepts of first discovery, symbolic acts of possession, and effective occupation, the first two deriving from the voyages of Pérez and Martínez to latitude 55° north in 1774, of de Hezeta and Bodega y Quadra in 1775 (when the latter reached latitude 58° north), and of Arteaga and Quadra to Alaska in 1779, and the third deriving from Martínez's colonizing in 1789.[22] Put so strongly in terms of the well-established conventions for possessing 'waste' or 'desert' lands, the Spanish claim carried a good deal of force. As recently as three years before, the Pitt Administration itself had established Britain's right to New South Wales under international law by following up Cook's first European discovery of its eastern coast and his acts of symbolic possession with occupation.[23] How could it now deny the validity of another claim so similarly based?

The first step in countering the Spanish claims was to check on their accuracy. Here, the Home Office undersecretary, Evan Nepean, turned to Sir Joseph Banks for help. Banks, perusing the translation of Francisco Mourelle's account of the 1775 voyage published by Daines Barrington,[24] decided that, as the commanders had claimed a number of harbours on the northwest coast individually, the Spanish 'did not then consider themselves as intitled to the Whole Coast'; and that Mourelle's not recording a stop at, or even mentioning, 'San Lorenzo' harbour (i.e., Nootka Sound) suggested that the Spanish had not discovered it before Cook did.[25]

Although this was comforting advice, the British stance was distinctly weak under international law. Cook may have been the first European discoverer of Nootka Sound, but Britain had not followed up his discovery with effective occupation. Without this second circumstance, the British claim that their nationals should be able to trade freely in the area was unconvincing and would only become robust with regular settlement sanctioned by authority and bringing with it the rule of British law.

Settlement would also go far to removing the second concern. To facilitate trade, the Etches group had intended to establish two factories, and had therefore shipped 'every description of stores, Provisions, Merchandise, Implements of husbandry &c &c for such purpose ... with Forty extra Officers and Settlers.' When they learned of Portlock and Dixon's failure, Etches had importuned Banks to persuade the government to establish a small convict colony modelled after Botany Bay. If this were done, he thought, his people might trade up and down the coast in small boats, sending out a ship 'annually with Stores and provisions, and to take their produce to Markett.'[26] In the autumn of 1789, Alexander Dalrymple had also advised such a settlement.[27] Now, in light of the events at Nootka, the Administration saw with Dalrymple that, as well as assisting the British fur traders, settlement would also be a means 'for preventing the Spanish from engrossing that very valuable branch of Commerce which has lately been carried on between Adventurers from this Country and the Natives.'[28] Furthermore, the troops and armed ships would discourage the Spanish from repeating their recent actions.

Settlement was also relevant to the third concern. The British had been seeking a convenient northwest passage from the Atlantic to Asia for 250 years. Discovering this passage had been the major goal of Cook's third voyage and, although he had failed to find it, several fur traders had reported locating the strait's vent to the Pacific and explorers of Canada's west had deduced its existence from other evidence.[29] It was vital that Britain not be preempted in obtaining possession of this passage, a threat raised by Malaspina's expedition with instructions to survey the northwest coast in detail.[30] Making a settlement at or near the strait's western entrance would ensure that it became a British waterway.

Under the direction of Lord Mulgrave – Banks' friend, a former lord commissioner of the Admiralty and now the member of the India Board responsible for strategic planning – the Administration developed a far-reaching and intricate plan for settlement. In explaining it to the Admiralty in early February, Evan Nepean briefly described events at Nootka, then asserted that 'His Majesty has judged it highly expedient that measures should instantly be taken for affording protection to such of His ... Subjects as may have already proceeded to that part of the American Continent.' As the 'utmost degree of secrecy' was required, Nepean continued, it was the ministry's intention to use the *Gorgon*, the 44-gun frigate, then preparing to sail for New South Wales *en flute*, with guns on upper deck only. After landing the supplies intended for the colony and the troops of the newly formed New South Wales Corps at Sydney, the ship was to have its lower-deck guns remounted, and then cross the Pacific. Mentioning that Malaspina had also sailed in two ships for the northwest coast, Nepean pointed out that they could not know for certain the combined naval force of the Spanish there, but that it appeared to be (in the context of a very distant colonial situation) substantial. Accordingly, the ministry also intended to send the *Discovery*, the 10-gun sloop then fitting out for surveying the South Atlantic, with the *Gorgon*. One advantage of using these vessels was that their departure would not arouse suspicion.

If, however, the *Vestal*, the 28-gun frigate sent on a special mission to the East in August 1789 and now likely ready to return, was intercepted at the Cape of Good Hope, then it might sail in place of the *Discovery*, which would then proceed on its original mission. Alternatively, if the *Vestal* had already passed the Cape, the *Discovery* would sail with the *Gorgon* to New South Wales to be replaced by the 26-gun *Sirius*, if fit for a lengthy passage. The governor of New South Wales, Captain Arthur Phillip, would provide enough men to fill the complements of the vessels and a party of marines. As it was the intention of the king, George III, that the expedition should form a permanent settlement on the northwest coast, Phillip would also provide workers with the requisite skills.

As the pair of ships (whatever the final combination) would be too large for inshore survey, the Admiralty was also to prepare a suitable small vessel 'with all possible expedition,' to be commanded by an officer skilled in the business. As the *Gorgon* and *Discovery* might be ready to sail by late February, the survey vessel would have to follow. With a seven-month voyage to New South Wales, they would then (in September) be too late to reach Nootka Sound at a suitable time. Phillip should see them refitted and send them to Tahiti, where they might refresh before going on to the northwest coast in the spring of 1791. If any Spanish naval ships were encountered there, the officer leading the expedition was to 'demand immediate satisfaction, and in case of refusal, to use his best endeavours to obtain it, even by seizing on such Ships or Vessels as may have been engaged in such Hostile proceedings, His Majesty being determined to support his right to a free and uninterrupted intercourse with that part of the Coast, which, from prior discovery and other circumstances may well be justified.' Such action must, however, be contingent upon the accuracy of the information which the Administration presently had. If the commanding officer should, on examination, find that this was 'ill-founded,' he was 'particularly enjoined not to molest or disturb in any degree the subjects of His Catholic Majesty or those of any other Nation, who shall be engaged in Trading with the Inhabitants of that Coast.'[31]

Evidently, immediately after Nepean prepared this letter, in order to make the British expedition the equal of the known Spanish forces on the northwest coast, Mulgrave planned to dispatch a frigate from the India squadron to rendezvous with the other vessels at Tahiti. In doing so, he also compiled 'Heads of Instructions for an Expedition to NW.ᵗ Coast of America,' listing the necessary steps for it to proceed.[32] As was common with eighteenth-century secret expeditions, it was to sail under the orders of a secretary of state rather than orders of the Admiralty. Therefore, Commodore Sir William Cornwallis in the East Indies, Governor Phillip in New South Wales (who in his naval capacity would hold the rank of commodore), and the captain of the three ships needed to be directed to follow the authority of the secretary of state rather than that to which they were usually subject. Detailed instructions needed to be drawn up for the commodores and the commanders of all three ships.

As the planning proceeded in the office of the home secretary, William Grenville, Evan Nepean effectively furthered it, with the requests he drafted going out over Grenville's signature. On 9 February, Grenville asked the Admiralty to direct Commodore Cornwallis to follow the secretary of state's orders, which the Admiralty did on 25 February.[33] The next month, Nepean drafted a similar request concerning Phillip, which seems not to have been sent from the Home Office.[34]

Through March, Nepean progressively drew up the requisite instructions for these actors in the intended far-flung drama. Those for Roberts, the commander of the *Discovery,* announced that as 'the execution of the Service for which the Ship you command was originally designed, shall be postponed,' and as 'she shall be employed on a particular service in a more distant part of the world,' he was 'to make the best of your way to Port Jackson on the Coast of New South Wales, and on your arrival there deliver the inclosed Packet to Governor Phillip,' and thereafter to follow Phillip's orders.[35] The instructions for Harvey, the commander of the *Gorgon,* if actually drafted, have yet to be found. Those to Phillip exist in two drafts. The earlier one, which Nepean must have prepared before 15 March, bears extensive emendations by Mulgrave, which Nepean incorporated into the later one. These instructions add that Governor Phillip was to provide a colonizing party of perhaps thirty persons, half of them marines, and including a 'discreet Subaltern Officer, who is to be entrusted with the temporary Superintendance of the New Settlement.' It should also include 'two or three of the most intelligent of the Overseers who have lately been sent out' [i.e., on the *Guardian*], 'a Storekeeper, and any other persons who may be desirous of accompanying them; together with a few of the most deserving of the Convicts, to whom you may offer a remission of a part of their Service as an inducement to go.' Roberts would give Phillip the instructions for the captain of the frigate to be sent from the East Indies. Phillip in turn was to pass them on to the commanders of the *Gorgon* and the *Discovery* as he sent them on to Hawai'i, now the Pacific rendezvous. However, news of the mutiny on the *Bounty* was brought by Captain William Bligh in person on Monday 15 March, causing Mulgrave to add that, on his way down to Port Jackson again, the captain of the *Gorgon* was to search for the mutineers in the Society and Friendly islands. If the *Bounty* were recovered, Phillip might use her as he saw fit.[36]

At the end of March, Nepean prepared the instructions for Commodore Cornwallis and the captain of the frigate he was to dispatch. To Cornwallis, Nepean reiterated the details and stressed the need for secrecy.[37] After rendezvousing at Hawai'i, the captain of the frigate was to take the expedition up to the northwest coast 'as early in the

Spring as circumstances will allow.' He was to go first to Queen Charlotte Sound (latitude 51° north), where, 'according to the late discoveries, Charts of which are herewith inclosed, there is reason to believe that there is a considerable River or Navigable inlet into the interior Country.' If initial investigation pointed to this being so, he was to disembark the settlers. He was then to survey 'the whole of the Coast Northward from the Latitude of 51 degrees, to Cook's River, which is in the Latitude of 60 degrees; and South from the Latitude of 49 degrees, to Cape Mendocino in the Latitude of 40 degrees, carefully examining such Rivers or inlets within the said limits, as you shall judge likely to afford a communication with the interior part of the Continent, and with the lakes already known in that part of the world.' If this survey revealed a more eligible waterway, he might relocate the settlement accordingly. As 'the discovery of any water communication with the interior Country ... [was] so material an object of this expedition,' two complementary overland probes would be mounted, one from Hudson House, the other from Lake Athabasca. He might encounter these parties and therefore utilize their knowledge. In his proceedings, he was to maintain friendly relations with the Natives and was to negotiate with any who appeared to hold sovereignty the grant or purchase of the land needed for the settlement. At the end of the summer, he was to send the *Gorgon* south to Port Jackson and was himself to winter the other ships at Hawai'i, so as to be able to return to complete his survey in the summer of 1792. He was not to frequent any harbour where other Europeans had settled. If he encountered the Spanish, he was to demand immediate restitution of the captured British ships and goods. If attacks were made on his or the fur traders' ships, or on the settlement, he was to resist, 'to the utmost,' and 'to endeavour to destroy or capture the Vessels making such attack.'[38]

A good deal of the difficulty in assessing the Pitt Administration's imperial capacity arises from the fact that, for a variety of reasons, many projects mooted or planned, at least in preliminaries, either did not eventuate or quickly foundered. Lack of success seems to indicate incompetence or lack of commitment; failure even to mount the project seems to show that it was always a phantasm in the minds of its deluged projectors and the incompetent ministers who entertained it. Such stances are not always correct; and when they are not, they seriously distort our understanding of how the Pitt Administration saw the world and, consequently, what its major concerns were. Although the expedition to discover and settle the northwest coast did not proceed as planned in the early months of 1790, the Administration was undoubtedly serious about it. On 8 February, the Admiralty requested the port admiral at Portsmouth to see that the *Gorgon* carried its guns in the hold.[39] By the end of this month, both it and the *Discovery* were on the point of sailing, when a typhus epidemic swept through the troops on board. It was 11 April before the ship was ready again. As the Administration waited for the surgeons to stop the infection, Banks sought Archibald Menzies' advice on the most effective trading goods at Hawai'i and on the northwest coast.[40] The Home Office passed Banks' list on to the Admiralty on 12 April, asking that some £6,800 worth be purchased. On 27 April, the Home Office asked the East India Company to ship twenty tons of these goods on the *Foulis*, then ready to sail for India, for loading into the frigate Commodore Cornwallis was to dispatch. In these weeks, too, Dalrymple and Nepean arranged for the Hudson's Bay Company to mount the overland expeditions under Charles Duncan and George Dixon.[41] By late April, the *Gorgon, Discovery*, and *Foulis* were within a day or two of sailing, when the Administration suddenly called off the expedition.

Calling off the expedition of discovery and settlement followed on the arrival in London of John Meares, whose account of events at Nootka Sound created, as it were, a new dispensation. A principal purpose of the proposed expedition had been to establish Britain's right of possession by effective occupation – that is, by purchasing land and forming a regular settlement on it. Meares reported that this had already been achieved. First, Meares asserted that he had purchased land at Nootka Sound, had fortified it, and had built a house on it, over which he had flown the British flag. Second, he had negotiated with the Nootka and other Indians the exclusive right to trade. Third, and most significant, Chief Maquinna and his people had acknowledged – indeed, *requested* – British overlordship.[42]

As Meares was a naval officer, the politicians believed that he had acted not merely in a private capacity, but also in the name of the sovereign. Indeed, Meares was explicit that this had been so: he was 'Lieutenant in his Majesty's Navy,' he had 'hoisted British colours,' and one of his officers had taken possession of an area of land 'in the King's name.' Leeds indicated the ministers' acceptance of this perspective when on 4 May he instructed Merry to represent, not only Britain's continuing implacable opposition to Spain's claim of general sovereignty, but also that 'the Soil at Nootka, and in some other Parts of the Coast, particularly in a Strait in or about the Latitude of [48 Degs. 30 Minutes,] had, previous to [Martínez's actions], been purchased of the Natives, by a British Subject, and the British Flag hoisted thereon.'[43] Martínez had attacked a British settlement on purchased land (an arrangement, moreover, buttressed by treaty and acknowledgment of sovereignty) and imprisoned British subjects going about their lawful business. The case was clear: the Spanish had transgressed Britain's properly established rights on the northwest coast. The British government, Leeds instructed Merry on 4 May, 'could never in any shape accede to those claims of exclusive sovereignty, commerce and navigation' made by the Spanish. British subjects had 'an unquestionable Right to a free and undisturbed Enjoyment of the Benefits of Commerce, Navigation and Fishery, and also to the Possession of such Establishments, as they may form, with the Consent of the Natives, in Places unoccupied by other European nations.'[44] If Spain would not concede, then the circumstances justified war.

On 30 April the British cabinet ministers decided to force the issue in Europe.[45] The next day, Grenville warned the lords commissioners of the Admiralty of the likelihood of war, asking them to fit forty line-of-battle ships for sea.[46] According to the historian who has made the closest study of Britain's naval circumstances then, 'because of Pitt's financial generosity since 1783, and the indefatigable work of Sir Charles Middleton, Comptroller of the Navy Board 1776-90, the navy was in the best peacetime condition of the century, with about 93 battleships in good repair,' so that the Navy Board was able to attend expeditiously to this request.[47] On 3 May, the King and cabinet authorized a 'hot' press to man the ships, which began the next day.[48]

As these home preparations proceeded, the Administration warned its officers on colonial stations, with the Admiralty sending circular letters to the commodores in the Mediterranean, Jamaica, and the Leeward Islands and Canada on 2 May; and with Grenville informing the Lord Lieutenant of Ireland on 3 May, and the superintendent of the timber-cutters on the Mosquito Shore on 15 May.[49] As part of this alert, Nepean wrote to James Mario Matra on 1 May. As consul at Tangier, Matra would have the task, crucial to the successful operation of the Mediterranean squadron during war with Spain, of keeping Gibraltar supplied with food. On 4 May, Nepean sent Matra a copy of Dr Johnson's *Dictionary*, to be used for deciphering and ciphering dispatches.[50]

On 7 and 8 May, the India Board and the Secret Court of Directors of the East India Company prepared circular warnings for the company's three presidencies and for its officers in Canton. On 10 May the company warned the Administration of the danger to its China ships should war occur. The next day, the India Board (Pitt, Dundas, and Grenville) decided that two warships should be sent to escort the company's ships from China into the Indian Ocean, and drew up a sailing plan. The company then forwarded this information to India and China; Grenville asked the Admiralty to supply the warships, and the India Board wrote to the governor-general of India, Lord Cornwallis, at Calcutta.[51]

The Administration followed up these warnings by organizing ship and troop reinforcements for the colonial stations. On 6 and 8 May, Grenville requested the Admiralty to transport four regiments to the West Indies; on 15 May, he asked for artillery and 1000 muskets be sent to Honduras; on 17 May, for shipping to carry troops to Gibraltar; and on 29 July, for the two warships to be sent to China.[52] All the while, Nepean had monitored Spain's naval preparations, continuing to receive and digest intelligence from various sources. Now he added to the range of information by having the Admiralty send out spying vessels to Cádiz, Ferrol, and Cartagena. By June, Nepean knew accurately week by week of the preparation and disposition of the Spanish fleet.[53] In late June, to demonstrate Britain's preparedness publicly, the Administration ordered Admiral Barrington to take the squadron of twenty line-of-battle ships assembled at Spithead to Torbay, where he arrived on 6 July. Two days later, that superior war commander Earl Howe took charge of this force, increased to thirty-one battleships by the end of the month.[54]

A prospect of a peaceful resolution briefly appeared. In an attempt to mobilize European opinion against Britain, Spain had, on 13 June, sent a circular to all governments justifying its claims on the basis of treaties going back over 200 years. When this did not bring forth any willing allies, it had begun to waiver, disavowing Martínez's seizure of the fur traders' vessels and offering compensation, with both nations agreeing to settle the matter of their respective 'rights' in further negotiations.[55]

However, despite a formal agreement in Madrid on 24 July, both nations continued preparations for war. The Spanish fleet of twenty-six-line-of-battle ships and attendant frigates put out from Cádiz on 20 July and slowly made its way up the Atlantic. On 10 August, Howe took the British fleet to sea, to patrol in the Bay of Biscay west of Cape Ushant, with orders to turn back the Spanish fleet if he encountered it.[56] Simultaneously, Captain John Blankett set out for China in the 50-gun *Leopard* and the 32-gun *Thames*.[57]

Now, too, the potential theatre of war widened even more, with the British receiving indications that Sweden might join with Russia and both take Spain's part. Such a move would threaten Britain's supply of naval materials from the countries about the Baltic, a supply indispensable to the successful operation of the fleet. Nepean accordingly began to compile information about the Swedish fleet, in mid-August sending Captains Henry Roberts and James Lawford to spy on it. The reports he then received were so alarming that in early September the Administration requested the Admiralty to assemble a powerful squadron in the Downs. When, on 7 September, firm news of Sweden's peaceful intent arrived, the fifteen line-of-battle ships already there were ordered to join Howe's fleet.[58]

Both nations kept up such preparations in the next months, with the Admiralty and the Navy Board continuing to bring ships into commission and to man them, and Nepean continuing to receive and sort intelligence. In September, the Admiralty sent a ship to watch the French squadron at Brest, and Nepean received Blankett's account of the Spanish fleet, met as he proceeded down the Atlantic.[59] Then Alleyne Fitzherbert, ambassador extraordinary to Madrid, reported that the Spanish were sending a squadron with troop reinforcements to Havana, information which led the British to order more troops and ships to the West Indies.[60]

By this time, given the success of their mobilization and given Spain's singular failure in finding allies, the British had become extremely confident about the outcome of any war. On 13 October, the British ambassador presented the Spanish court with an ultimatum: it had ten days to accept British terms, or the nations would be at war.[61] Simultaneously, the Administration ordered Howe to take the fleet to sea, now augmented to forty-three line-of-battle ships and ten frigates.[62] Because he knew full well that the most likely consequence was battle,

Howe insisted on settling every last detail of his ships' fitting. This meticulousness meant that the British fleet was still in port when the Administration received the news that Spain had given in and conceded British demands. On 4 November, the Pitt Administration ordered a halt to its preparations for war.[63]

From the moment they had news of events at Nootka Sound, Pitt and his principal advisers had much more in view than gaining some acres at Nootka Sound and engrossing the fur trade. Central to their intentions was obtaining for British manufacturers access to the vast markets of Spanish America. On 14 February Pitt held a 'long conference' with the patriot Francisco de Miranda, in the course of which Miranda elaborated his visionary plans for revolutionizing Spanish America; for creating an autonomous government to hold sway over all of South America (except Brazil and Guiana), over Mexico, and over North America westwards from the Mississippi to 45° north latitude; and for forging commercial links between this vast domain and Britain. According to Miranda, Pitt asked him 'to write down ... all the purport of our Conversation, adding a statement of the whole produces of South America, the Exports and imports from Spain, the military and naval forces in both countrys, their populations, etc.' This Miranda did on 5 March.[64]

Political change of such magnitude was then inconceivable except as a consequence of general war, which from the end of April became likely. In early May, sketching schemes for expeditions against Spain's colonies from both the west and east, Mulgrave presented four options to the India Board:

(1) sending the East India squadron to attack Manila (where operations should be completed by January 1791), then across the Pacific via the Hawai'ian Islands to the west coast of America;
(2) the squadron taking the same path across the Pacific, but bypassing Manila;
(3) the squadron sailing south, refreshing at New Holland (Australia) or New Zealand before crossing the Pacific;
(4) a squadron sailing from England via Brazil and round the Horn.[65]

Mulgrave's suggestions either followed from, or ran parallel to, advice offered by Miranda, who saw Pitt and Grenville on 6 May,[66] and Major-General Sir Archibald Campbell, who had been meditating such an attack from the early 1780s. Campbell, who now joined the India Board, was immediately busily seeking further advice. William Dalrymple, who had proposed an expedition from India across the Pacific in 1780, now asserted that this was the 'perfect move';[67] and James Creassy, who had travelled widely in Spanish America, reiterated his older scheme of an expedition round Cape Horn, and another via the West Indies, 'to establish *and forever secure to Great Britain* a Communication across the Isthmus of Panama,' thus dividing Spain's American empire. 'By once getting a superior Naval power in the South Seas, and securing a safe conveyance across this important passage,' Creassy maintained, the British 'would become masters of the Spanish wealth' and 'the keepers of the Keys of their treasure.'[68]

The India Board quickly settled on the first option outlined by Mulgrave, telling the governor-general, Lord Cornwallis, on 21 May that he was to facilitate any attack 'against any of the Spanish Possessions.' On 5 June, the Board told Lord Cornwallis and his brother, Commodore Cornwallis, that Manila was to be attacked in January, and that Blankett's ships would join the squadron there after they had seen the China ships safely into the Bay of Bengal. The augmented squadron would then cross the Pacific. Another dispatch to this effect followed on 16 June.[69] This thrust across the Pacific was to be made in conjunction with another from the West Indies across Central America, to be completed by early April 1791 before the onset of the wet season. The force for this assault would come from England and be augmented in the West Indies by black soldiers and irregulars from the timber-cutters on the Mosquito Shore.[70]

Campbell assumed particular responsibility for planning these schemes. In July he asserted to Pitt that

> Spain is no where more vulnerable than in her Colonies abroad. The Philippine Islands, Mexico, and South America afford to the British Nation, Objects of serious Importance for Military Enterprise.

> The Philippine Islands are to be attacked with most Effect from the Presidency of Fort St George in the East Indies. Mexico and the Western Coast of South America from the Island of Jamaica in the West Indies. If the West Indian Army could be supported with a Squadron in the South Seas, and with a Military Force from the East Indies, across

the Pacific Ocean, their Operations could not fail to meet with complete success.[71]

The Administration continued to plan this dual attack right up to the moment that Spain gave way. In August, Miranda composed a proclamation to be read to the liberated populations, announcing the interim government.[72] Campbell wrote further to Pitt about both expeditions on 18, 26, and 28 October, reinforcing his own views with those of Robert White, who had urged an attack from the West Indies government during the previous war.[73] On 29 October, William Popham, who had participated in the capture of Manila in 1762, also supported the idea of an attack across the Pacific.[74] At this time, too, Grenville requested the Admiralty to ship additional regiments to the West Indies and to instruct Admiral Laforey to cooperate with General Matthews in the Leeward Islands 'in any operations which he may judge it adviseable to undertake against the Spanish possessions in those Seas'; and the Administration looked about for persons with knowledge of the Spanish ports and coasts.[75] Then, giving rise to another of those historical disjunctions, the Administration abruptly ceased this planning when Britain and Spain agreed to terms.

In the space of seven months, the Pitt Administration had readied some forty-three line-of-battle ships and almost the whole of its fleet of frigates for sea, and had increased the number of its enlisted sailors from 17,300 to 55,000 and its marines from 3,700 to 5,300.[76] It had prepared for action in Europe, the West and East Indies, the China seas, and along the coasts of South and North America. The speed, scale, and global range of these preparations would be impressive even in the twentieth century, when means of communication and modes of transportation are light years ahead of eighteenth-century horses, coaches, and sailing ships. Spain's humiliating acquiescence in late October is the most powerful indicator of the Pitt Administration's bureaucratic and naval competence. To put it bluntly, no other European power had either the resources or the administrative machinery to match the British. This same point can also be made for their much-maligned planting of a colony 12,000 miles away (Botany Bay), as Roger Knight has argued.[77]

Next, it is clear that this exercise of massive imperial power was called forth by considerations of international trade. As Pitt told Parliament in the middle of the crisis, the Spanish claim to 'exclusive sovereignty, navigation and commerce' in and about the Pacific Ocean, if accepted, would 'deprive this country of the means of extending its navigation and fishery in the southern ocean, and would go toward excluding his majesty's subjects from an infant trade, the future extension of which could not but be essentially beneficial to the commercial interests of Great Britain.'[78] As this comment indicates, it was not only whaling and the fur trade that Pitt had in mind. What his Administration strove for from the beginning of the crisis were the means of establishing a massive triangular exchange of European, American, and Asian goods, with the Pacific Ocean as the arena of interchange and the independent traders as its agents. As Pitt supporter, and soon-to-be Home secretary, Henry Dundas observed after the convention had been signed, the Administration had been contending, not 'for a few miles, but a large world.'[79]

The favourable resolution of the crisis removed one of the largest difficulties in the way of this grand scheme, that of Spanish exclusivity. It also laid the way for opening the Spanish-American markets. Even so, other obstacles remained in late 1790, which the Administration then sought to remove. With Vancouver's voyage, it renewed the search for the elusive northwest passage. With Lord Macartney's embassy to China, a sequel to that undertaken by Colonel Cathcart in 1787, it sought to open the markets of China and northern Asia.[80] And it reopened negotiations with the East India Company to free the whalers and fur traders from geographical restraints on operating in the Indian and Pacific oceans.

What linked all these steps, and gave considerable coherence to British imperialism in the last decades of the eighteenth century, was the emerging ideology of free trade, particularly as enunciated by Adam Smith. Announcing grandly that 'the discovery of America, and that of a passage to the East Indies by the Cape of Good Hope, are the two greatest and most important events recorded in the history of mankind,' in Volume II of *The Wealth of Nations* (1776) Smith argued powerfully that it was not from gold and silver (or any other 'rude' product), but rather from creating markets for manufacturers that European powers had derived wealth from their colonizing ventures in the Americas; and that monopolies of or restrictions on trade were inimical to exploiting the full potential of these markets. 'If the manufactures of Great Britain ... have been advanced ... by the colony trade, it has not been by means of the monopoly of that trade, but in spite of the monopoly,' he wrote at one point; and at another, that if Britain were to relinquish dominion over her colonies, she 'might settle with them such a treaty of commerce as would effectually secure her a free trade, more advantageous to the great body of the people ... than the monopoly which she at present enjoys.'[81]

Smith saw the retarding hand of restriction even more evident in the European nations' commerce with Asia. Here was not only the 'external' monopoly of mercantilist practice, whereby the metropolitan powers limited trade with their colonies to their subjects and shipping, but also the 'internal' one of trade usually being the prerogative of a chartered company enjoying a monopoly. Seaborne geographical discovery, Smith summed up, had opened 'two new worlds ... each of them much greater and more extensive than the old one' to European industry; with the freeing of trade, European nations might become the manufacturers and carriers for the rest of the globe, to the vast augmentation of their wealth.[82]

By the mid-1780s, Pitt and Dundas (and even, to some degree, Lord Hawkesbury, president of the board of trade) were converts to these doctrines. In November 1786, Dundas told Lord Sydney, the secretary of state: 'Nothing can be greater insanity than our being jealous of, or adverse to other Nations trading to our Asiatick possessions.'[83] This idea of opening British settlements about Asia to *all* trading nations underlay each of the major steps taken by the Pitt Administration to create a vast commercial network based on the Pacific. In 1787, in a draft set of Colonel Cathcart's instructions for his embassy to China, Dundas announced that he was to tell the Chinese court that 'our views are purely commercial[,] not having even a Wish for Territory'; and that 'should a new Establishment be conceded,' he was to 'endeavour to obtain free Permission of Ingress and Regress for Ships of all Nations, upon paying certain settled Duties, if so required by the Chinese Government.'[84]

In 1788 Governor Phillip also had this expectation for Botany Bay, the convict colony he was busily establishing on the southwestern edge of the Pacific. 'This Country,' he wrote to Lord Lansdowne (formerly Lord Shelburne – first minister 1782-3) on 3 July 'will hereafter be a most Valuable acquisition to great Brittain from its situation.'[85] 'When this Colony is the Seat of Empire,' he wrote to Admiral Charles Middleton three days later, Port Jackson would offer 'room for Ships of all Nations.'[86] The notion that the northwest American coast should be open to all European nations informed the 1790 negotiations with

Spain.[87] We may reasonably adduce that Pitt and his colleagues also viewed opening trade with Spain's colonies in this light, for when Dundas advised Pitt of the desirability of capturing the River Plate area in 1800, he cautioned:

> Even if you were not able to keep it, the Possession of it at the time of negotiation, would enable you to treat for and insist on the freedom of the South American trade. No other nations, not France itself, would have an interest to resist such a plan, and if it was not too large a field to enter upon at present, I think it could be demonstrated, that if the South American market was to be opened, it would be worth while for Great Britain to remove all commercial jealousies, and put an end to all pretences for colonial advantage ... by agreeing that the Colonies of all the nations in Europe should be open to the commerce of all.[88]

Events then conspired to see that the Pitt Administration never did bring its grand scheme to fruition. As Vancouver learned, the fabled northwest passage did not exist. The East India Company fought tenaciously to limit the activities of the independent traders; and its view prevailed, at least in 1791-2. In 1793, when Pitt and Dundas had thought greatly to diminish its monopoly, Britain was at war with Revolutionary France, and the move seemed impolitic. In the end, not until 1813 did another Administration carry out the mooted reduction. Still, in the intervening twenty years, the southern whalers conducted an unremitting campaign to have the geographical limits to their operations abolished. This was a campaign which they progressively won. In 1798 they obtained permission to hunt in the waters off New South Wales; from 1802 onwards, they no longer had to be licensed to operate in the Pacific, were able to exit via Torres Strait, and could sail among the eastern islands of Indonesia; in 1811, they were allowed to go as far north as the southern Philippines, to New South Wales, to Africa, and to the myriad islands in between.

The beginning of Britain's imperialism (in the form of free trade) can, then, be located in the policies of Pitt, Dundas, Mulgrave, and Hawkesbury; in the colonization of New South Wales and in the exploration of the northwest American coast; in the encouragement of the southern whalers and the Nootka Sound fur traders and in their incursions into the monopolies of the East India and South Sea companies; in the 1790 convention with Spain; and in both embassies to China. It will be one of the very considerable ironies of history if, in the twenty-first century, the Pacific Rim becomes central to the world economy, the position that Pitt and his colleagues sought for it 200 years ago.

Seduction before Sovereignty: Spanish Efforts to Manipulate the Natives in Their Claims to the Northwest Coast

Christon I. Archer

Solo el filósofo podría acaso encontrar en estos parages materia de contemplación, á vista de un suelo y de unas gentes tan vecinas al estado primativo del mundo, como distantes de la civilidad europea, que ni aprecían ni codicían.

– Dionisio Alcala Galiano[1]

They [the Spanish] it should seem, are a nation designed by Providence to be a scourge to every tribe of Indians they come near, by one means or another.

– Nathaniel Portlock[2]

Stretched thin to control an enormous North American continental and coastal frontier, Spain was slow to explore, exploit, and to consider settling the North Pacific littoral. By the latter eighteenth century, the flimsy claims to sovereignty of prior discovery and archaic exclusion laws beginning with the 1493 Papal Bull of Alexander VI were insufficient to deter Britain, the United States, France, and other nations. Spanish exploratory voyages in 1774, 1775, and 1779 solved many mysteries about the North American coastline, but raised new questions about how the Native populations should be approached. In 1774, for example, Viceroy Antonio María de Bucareli rejected the idea of garrisoning Spanish vessels with tough frontier soldiers used to maintain order in the new California presidios and elsewhere on the northern frontier. Bucareli reminded the commander of an expedition to the northwest coast, Ensign Juan Pérez, that the purpose of his voyage was to discover unknown lands and not to fight the indigenous inhabitants.[3] Given the nature of Mexican frontier institutions and the role in Alta California of the Franciscan friars of the Colegio de San Fernando based in Mexico City, Pérez and his successors probably assumed that exploring and entrenching sovereignty on the northwest coast would extend existing frontier institutions. The friars pacified nomadic bands, converted them to Christianity, and sought to alter them to a sedentary lifestyle as hard-working agrarians. Since compulsion and punishment underlay the disciplinary regimen, close cooperation was necessary between the missionaries and small garrisons of presidial troops.[4]

Despite the limited human and financial resources available and unlike the other nations active in the North Pacific during the eighteenth century (except Russia in Alaska), Spain kept alive the dream of carrying the Holy Gospel to the Natives 'with the Spiritual Conquest that will lift them from the shadows of idolatry in which they live, and teach them the road to eternal salvation.'[5] In the 1774 expedition two friars of the Colegio de San Fernando, Juan Crespi and Thomas de la Peña,[6] collected ethnological data and kept journals of their observations.[7] Beyond customs and lifestyle, Viceroy Bucareli wanted information about Native religions, governance, methods of taxation, and their views on the ownership of property and possessions. Adding an element of the bizarre, Pérez was to question the Natives to see if they could identify samples of pepper, cloves, nutmeg, and other spices unavailable at higher latitudes along the North American coastline.[8] The viceroy concluded his instructions with an invocation that nothing was to be taken from the Natives without payment, and that everything possible was to be done to instill a good impression of the Spanish visitors to pave the way for later colonizers.[9] Pérez received four cases of beads and other assorted trinkets to be used as gifts, with the instruction that distribution should be weighted to favour the Native leader or leaders. The Spanish were to avoid violence at all cost, except in defense of their own lives, and under no circumstances were they to engage in hostilities to confiscate Native lands.[10] With this instruction, Viceroy Bucareli established guidelines that recurred in the viceregal orders issued to all subsequent Spanish explorers of the northwest coast.[11] For the duration of their presence, the Spanish sought to adapt and to modify Mexican frontier institutions designed to pacify and to settle Native populations.

The Spanish expeditions produced a wealth of descriptive journals and significant collections of artifacts from Tlingit, Haida, Nootka, and other Native cultures from Northern California to Cook Inlet in Alaska. During the 1770s, the Spanish, from the marine explorers and friars to King Carlos III and his court, admired the high level of artistry and technical achievements of the northwest coast cultures. Indeed, comparing the apparently less developed societies of California with those of the north revealed numerous differences that might hinder attempts at meaningful sovereignty. The northern Natives possessed some copper and iron weapons and sophisticated armour, and the warriors showed off ugly scars as badges to underscore their martial tendencies. They were almost equally aggressive in initiating commercial exchanges that would bring them iron, copper, knives, and, later, muskets and ammunition.

The Spanish marvelled at the beautifully engineered sea-going canoes and developed maritime traditions that denoted much higher civilizations than they had anticipated. In the Queen Charlotte Islands Pérez collected Chilkat cloaks of outstanding technical quality woven in black and white checkerboard squares and trimmed with fine sea otter skin. Off Nootka Sound, before a sudden change in the weather compelled Pérez to forgo a landing to take possession, some Natives paddled out to trade fish, sea otter pelts, and wolf skins for Monterey abalone shells.[12] Later in Madrid, Julián de Arriaga, the minister of the Indies, provoked something of a sensation among members of the royal court and assembled foreign diplomats when he displayed the two Haida cloaks and other northwest coast artifacts. Arriaga informed Viceroy Bucareli, 'If these cloaks are woven by Indians of the country, that nation is more cultivated and civilized than all others discovered until now in America.'[13]

Although Pérez enjoyed amicable relations with the Haida and Nootka, in the following year Juan Francisco de la Bodega y Quadra, captain of the schooner *Sonora* escorting the frigate *Santiago* commanded by Lieutenant Bruno de Hezeta, lost six armed sailors sent ashore to obtain water and firewood near Point Grenville on the Washington coast.[14] Accustomed to friendly receptions from Natives further south, Quadra misinterpreted outward signs of friendship, offers of fish, commercial exchanges, dancing, and the presence of women accompanying the men visiting alongside the *Sonora*. When the longboat landed, 300 heavily armed and armoured Natives rushed from the undergrowth to massacre the crew as they struggled through the surf. In the turmoil, horrified observers on board sighted only one powder flash from a musket or pistol. Lacking another boat to rescue possible survivors seen swimming in the frigid water, Quadra and his men fired swivel guns and muskets, but they were much too far out of range to halt the attack.

When Quadra set sail to seek assistance from the *Santiago*, the Natives surrounded his ship with nine large canoes, some carrying as many as thirty armed warriors. In one canoe, nine men assumed to be chiefs, dressed in hide armour and heavily armed, tried to deceive the Spanish with new invitations to visit their village. Although only Quadra, his first officer Francisco Antonio Mourelle, and one sailor were healthy enough to repel an assault, they prepared cartridges and attempted to lure the Natives closer with offers of beads, handkerchiefs, and other gifts. Emboldened by the few defenders remaining, the chiefs brandished their bows and closed in to board *Sonora* at the bow. Just as they did so, Quadra and Mourelle opened fire with two swivel guns loaded with grapeshot and three muskets, mutilating or killing six of the nine attackers. Stunned, the survivors escaped out of musket range, covered their fallen comrades with skins and, after some highly animated consultations, fled to shore. Both Quadra and Mourelle reported that the main force of Natives in the canoe flotilla failed to assist the chiefs during the first fusillade or later to contemplate a second attack.[15]

Furious at what they viewed as the deceitful massacre of their crew, Quadra and Mourelle requested the longboat from the *Santiago* to search for possible survivors and try to obliterate the Native village.[16] Hezeta convened a junta of officers from both ships in which he argued against retribution, pointing out the impossibility of surprising the Natives, who would simply flee into the woods and then ambush the landing party once it was beyond the protection of the ship's guns. In seeking revenge, the Spanish might suffer additional casualties that they could ill afford given the inroads of scurvy among the crews. Moreover, both ships were anchored downwind from the village, and several days might be wasted to beat back into position. During this time, the Natives would have ample time to prepare their defenses. Finally, Hezeta reminded his officers about Article 23 of their viceregal instructions that forbade violence except in defense of Spanish lives.[17] Quadra and Mourelle argued strongly in favour of retribution, pointing out that possible survivors of the boat crew would have no refuge except among the 'savages.' Moreover, these duplicitous Natives deserved exemplary punishment so that subsequent Spanish visitors would not receive similar treatment at their hands. Finally, Hezeta, Juan Pérez (who was serving aboard *Santiago*), and other officers voted to reject Quadra and Mourelle's suggestion.[18]

Although the two vessels separated and only Quadra and the *Sonora* reached Alaskan waters, both crews experienced other northwest coast Native bellicosity as well as their enthusiasm for trade. On 18 August 1775, at Puerto de los Remedios on Kruzof Island, Quadra landed an armed party to erect a cross, engrave another on a large boulder, and take formal possession of the land for Spain under the detailed formula given in Bucareli's instructions. Nearby some Natives watched the ceremony from a well-built fortification surrounded by a palisade of posts dug into the earth. When the landing party returned to the ship, the Natives took down the cross and erected it in front of their fort. Later, when Quadra sent a boat to obtain water, the Natives demanded payment and refused to be pacified with trifles such as beads and pieces of cloth. Seeing that the Spanish would not give more, they dashed back to their fort, put on their armour, and returned brandishing long, flint-tipped spears. Quadra ordered a careful withdrawal which took place without hostilities.[19]

Further south aboard *Santiago*, Hezeta purchased a well-made canoe and some sea otter pelts from some Natives who initiated trade offshore at Clayoquot or Barkley sounds on Vancouver Island. Describing them as deceitful, Hezeta, after many delays, threatened the Native traders with firearms to make them conclude their complex negotiations. Turning for Mexico because of severe scurvy among the crew near where the sailors from the *Sonora* had been killed, Hezeta encountered a canoe with ten Natives who wanted to trade fish and furs. When some sailors claimed to recognize participants in the earlier massacre, Hezeta decided to capture hostages and to see whether he could exchange them for possible Spanish survivors. He permitted trade to continue, but failed to lure any of the Natives on board. Finally losing patience, he ordered a crew member to throw a heavy iron grapple into the canoe. It struck and injured one of the paddlers, but he recovered sufficiently to cast the grapple out of the canoe. The Natives fled upwind precipitously – hastened by musket volleys fired into the air over their heads – and escaped toward shore.[20]

If these experiences were not sufficient warning that the northwest coast peoples were quite different than the more pacific and pliable California Natives, the 1779 voyage of Lieutenants Ignacio de Arteaga and Quadra with the frigates *Princesa* and *Favorita* clarified any remaining misunderstandings. Sailing north to Bucareli Sound on Prince of Wales Island, the Spanish for fifty-eight days conducted a detailed reconnaissance and treated with the fierce Tlingits, who showed them almost no respect. Indeed the adventure-packed longboat explorations and other incidents left the Spanish with no illusions that the Natives perceived them as unwelcome intruders. They admired the Tlingit double-ended, bayonet-like iron knives and well-designed rod- and slat-armour made like European corsets that Ensign José de Cañizares described as 'similar to the breastplate and back-plate used by the Ancients.'[21] The Natives covered their armour with beautiful hide mantles to deflect arrows, protected their throats with gorgets, and wore sturdy helmets carved to represent wild animals. The men tied back their hair in a neat tail like 'the most polished soldiers,' but left their genitals uncovered to the consternation of the prudish Spanish observers.[22] During the longboat explorations, Francisco Mourelle visited two temporarily abandoned fortified villages situated on a high bluff and a rocky islet that were surrounded by cliffs and accessible only by wooden ladders. Climbing up to investigate, the Spanish found the ground so broken that wooden catwalks were the only means to connect the houses.[23] Juan Pantoja reported that one slip would result inevitably in a disastrous fall and instant death.

The Tlingits treated the Spanish with very little regard. They pilfered tools, utensils, and clothing, and sought any iron objects, including fixtures attached to the ships, such as the rudder pintles, or the nails from the cross erected ashore by the friars. Despite the vigilance of the sailors, they stole cooking utensils, ramrods, and even the quoin or wedge used to elevate the barrel of a swivel gun.[24] During the longboat expeditions, the Natives sometimes reacted negatively when the Spanish tried to set up camps ashore. On one occasion, a band sent a canoe flotilla with many men, women, and children with their house boards and household furniture to dispute control of the exact spot occupied by the Spanish.

They left no doubt about sovereignty or specific ownership of the land. In these provocative incidents, the warriors donned their slat and hide armour, tested their arrows on their canoes, and brandished their long lances. Although Pantoja noted that grapeshot fired by the swivel guns could have mowed down large numbers, the Spanish exercised restraint.

At first, the Tlingits belittled Spanish weapons that appeared only to create havoc by making loud noises, whereas their own daggers and spears 'wounded the heart and killed.'[25] A demonstration of swivel gun fire against an empty canoe, a fusillade of musketry that splintered a wooden tub, and bullets fired across the surface of the water curbed some aggression, but did nothing to deter thefts or the Native insistence upon exerting sovereignty. Even at the frigate anchorage, the Natives assembled a temporary encampment of over 1,000 people. Arriving in various craft, including great canoes capable of conveying as many as thirty people, they made obvious signs that they had ownership and that the Spanish must depart.

For several weeks, the Spanish endured thefts and other incidents until the emboldened Tlingits captured two sailors from the *Favorita* who were ashore on a washing detail. In response, Arteaga fired a deafening broadside from both frigates over the heads of the Natives. Terrified, many upset their canoes and one Tlingit man died in the water of a bullet wound. The Spanish rescued nineteen hostages and dispatched four longboats armed with swivel guns to the Native encampment. Even though they now recognized the superiority of firearms, the warriors appeared in their armour, brandished their spears, and fired off volleys of arrows that landed in the water short of the boats. Negotiations eventually terminated the standoff and allowed a prisoner exchange. During this incident, the Spanish learned about the fragmented tribal and band divisions of the northwest coast. One Spanish prisoner was held by a clan that did not have hostages aboard the ships. These people showed little concern about the Native hostages and resisted the advice of other Natives to return their captive. Pantoja stated that the kidnappers hesitated several times before finally deciding to return their prisoner. Without the siege of their encampment by the armed longboats, he doubted whether the unfortunate sailor ever would have been returned.[26]

Despite their bellicosity, the Spanish praised the artistry and advanced technical skills of the Tlingits, all admiring the Native textiles, woven mats, wood carvings, jewellery, fishing equipment, and the whistles or fifes which they played like flutes. Mourelle described their bows and arrows as being so beautifully finished that they compared favourably with the finest European musical instruments. However, the naval officers were less successful in moving beyond mere observation to collect data on complex subjects such as religion or systems of government. They achieved almost no progress in trying to compile vocabularies or to decipher the Native language. Mourelle noted that the Spanish officers could not even write the names pronounced by the Natives or reproduce the answers to simple questions asked about objects. He stated that the movement of the tongue against the palate and the excessive use of diphthongs made pronunciation exceptionally difficult. This was even more marked with the women, who had lost much of the use of their lips through wearing the disfiguring labret.[27] Quadra described the language at Bucareli Sound as 'very guttural,' and at Prince William Sound he went even further to declare that the Native tongue 'seemed a confused gibberish without connection with any other language.'[28] The absence of trained scientists assigned to the early Spanish expeditions to the northwest coast cost opportunities for more thorough observations in various different fields from ethnology to botany.

The failure of oral communication with the Tlingits left little expectation for better relations in the future. Although only one Native man at Bucareli Sound perished from gunshot wounds inflicted during the major hostage incident, the Spanish whipped two others and completely lost patience with a people who were in every respect just as haughty and aggressive as Europeans. On the other hand, the Natives presented a possible solution to the communications barrier when they offered to exchange children for pieces of iron and cloth. At first, the officers expressed mere curiosity when some Natives appeared to put a price on a boy, and negotiations produced no agreement. Later, a man believed to be the father of a very ugly seven- to nine-year-old girl offered her to the *Princesa* in exchange for a coarse cloth coat and two barrel hoops.[29] The ships' chaplains begged Arteaga to permit the transaction 'to remove her from an unhappy fate.' A more attractive, but much younger, girl of only three to four years, so ill that she was considered close to death, was also sold to the same officers.[30] Mourelle concluded, incorrectly, that the

Natives lusted so much for iron and cloth that they were willing to sell off their own children. In a later journal entry, however, he recognized the truth when he observed that healthy children who came in the Native canoes were never placed on sale. When the Spanish offered to purchase these children, the Tlingits scoffed at such preposterous ideas.[31] As later experience confirmed, the children offered for sale were either prisoners of war or expendable outcasts from their own societies. The boatswains of the *Favorita* bought two boys aged four to six years who were named Manuel and Antonio after their purchasers. Quadra went along with these negotiations because he felt that the children could be trained as informants and interpreters for later expeditions.

When the opportunity arose, Quadra purchased a 'lively and vivacious'[32] nine- or ten-year-old boy whom he named Juan Francisco after himself. A great favourite among the sailors, this boy warned the Spanish about possible Native treachery, even going so far as to take the marine guards to the arms chest, encouraging them to fire on nearby canoes. By signs he indicated which Tlingits were friendly and should be protected. Of the lowest status in their own societies, these children relished their new situations so much that they could be disciplined simply by the threat of being returned to their people. They warned of possible surprise night assaults against the ships and gave other warnings which kept the Spanish constantly at full alert.[33]

Unfortunately, the Tlingit children did not live to become interpreters and guides in subsequent voyages. Both girls aboard the *Princesa* died during the voyage and the boys Manuel and Antonio succumbed to disease at San Blas. Juan Francisco, baptized at the Mexican town of Tepic, survived under Quadra's care and in 1783 accompanied his master on a voyage to Peru.[34] At the same time, José de Gálvez, the minister of the Indies, expressed strong reservations against any traffic in Native children. After examining the matter, he ordered Juan Francisco assigned to the Commissary of San Blas, Juan Francisco Domínguez, who was to ensure that the Tlingit boy received a proper education. If he wished, Juan Francisco might be permitted to join a future voyage of exploration so that he could be seen by his own people, but he was not to be returned to them, as King Carlos III wanted him to complete his studies in Mexico.[35] That the Spanish king, the minister of the Indies, and the Mexican viceroy devoted so much attention to the fate of a single Tlingit boy is most interesting. Probably aware of the Pacific islanders and other indigenous people paraded as curiosities in London and Paris, the Spanish authorities had no wish to be blackened by the reputation of having started a trade in Native children who might end up in some form of permanent servitude. After 1789, this undercurrent of official disquiet grew as larger numbers of northwest Native children turned up in Mexico.

In 1788, when Spain finally got around to dispatching a new expedition commanded by Esteban José Martínez to verify recurring rumours of Russian expansion toward California, the North Pacific was no longer an unknown frontier. The posthumous publication in 1784 of Captain James Cook's journal expedition, including the account of his visit to the coast in 1778, convinced the world that Britain enjoyed the best claim to the northwest coast. In addition, Cook and his officers publicized the potential wealth to be made in a trans-Pacific trade to China in sea otter pelts. Martínez sailed north with orders that included copies of the 1773 (Pérez) and 1779 (Arteaga) instructions and journals, now supplemented with copies of Cook's charts and vocabularies of Native languages. Florez improved the gifts to be given to Native leaders – including swords, machetes, axes, knives, and perforated coins for jewellery – that would advertise the Spanish presence. In addition, Martínez conveyed trade goods, including iron nails, mirrors, glass beads, and textiles. Native chiefs were to be informed that Spanish ships would return annually to present gifts and to engage in commerce. Viceroy Florez recommended that Martínez should recruit one or two Natives of each different language for training in Mexico if they would go voluntarily or purchase them if the chiefs were willing to sell their compatriots into the Spanish service. Like Arteaga and Quadra, Florez believed that Natives could become emissaries and interpreters for subsequent Spanish expeditions.[36]

Commanding the frigate *Princesa* and the packet *San Carlos* under Gonzalo López de Haro, Martínez sailed north to Montague Island off Prince William Sound. For the first time, the Spanish discovered a well-constructed house with windows that suggested a Russian presence and obvious evidence of other visitors. On hearing the boatswain's whistle, the Natives shouted in English, 'All hands ahoy,' and they used words such as 'plenty' and 'yes.' They were able to recall the names of Cook's ships and mentioned others that Martínez thought might be French, since one 'savage' possessed a blue coat and all men and women wore iron and glass beads of European manufacture.[37] Although the Spanish officers recorded details on the Native culture, they made little headway with the language and recognized only a few words from Cook's vocabulary. When they read words, the Natives kept on talking as if they had not understood anything.[38] Sailing westward, López de Haro visited the Russian post at Three Saints Bay on Kodiak Island commanded by Eustrate Delarov, while Martínez continued to Trinity Island where the Natives showed him tribute tax receipts. He took these and replaced them with new papers on which he wrote in Spanish: 'This individual has presented me with a slip of paper dated 1786.' Under that he added, 'The Spanish expedition belongs to His Catholic Majesty, the King of Spain, Don Carlos III, God keep him, that anchored on this island on June 27th of the year 1788. The commander is Esteban José Martínez.' Although the Natives did not comprehend the exchange, they informed the Spanish that the Russians whipped them if they did not produce their quota of pelts.[39] Martínez continued westward to Unalaska Island before returning to Mexico.

Not only did the 1788 expedition convince Spaniards such as Martínez about the potential of North Pacific frontier peoples and resources, but it acquired details from the Russians about British fur-trading activities at Nootka Sound and to the north. Even before he returned to San Blas, Martínez prepared reports pressing Viceroy Florez to initiate a rapid Spanish naval thrust in 1789 to anticipate a rumoured Russian plan to occupy Nootka Sound and to close the region to the British fur traders. At the same time, knowledge of the methods employed by the Russians strengthened Martínez's views that Spain might be able to occupy the North American coastline as far north as Prince William Sound or Cook Inlet. The scene was set for the Spanish occupation of Nootka Sound and for the events that precipitated the clash between Martínez, the fur traders, and the Natives.

Dreamer, schemer, patriot, visionary, and rogue, Martínez was hardly the level-headed diplomat to negotiate Spain's relations with European nations or Native cultures on the northwest coast. Indeed, his wild mood swings, temper tantrums, drinking bouts, and abuses of his junior officers made Viceroy Florez cringe at sending such an officer to uphold Spanish sovereignty.[40] Although several well-trained, clear-sighted naval officers, including Quadra, were on their way to Mexico

Cheslakee's Village in Johnstone's Strait, sketch by John Sykes, engraved by J. Landseer

with the new viceroy, Conde de Revilla Gigedo, Martínez sailed long before they arrived. Jealous of Spanish sovereignty and anxious to emulate Russian and British successes, Martínez conceived plans to create a new Spanish Pacific empire in which the Native peoples were to play a significant role. In setting his grandiose schemes in motion, Martínez gained the attention of the Spanish king, tweaked the tail of the British lion, came close to setting off a disastrous naval war, and set the pattern for Spain's short-lived occupation of Nootka Sound. Before the end of 1789, Ensign Martínez was famous or infamous in Madrid, London, and Canton, as well as in the Native villages of Nootka Sound. Because of Martínez, Spain found itself embroiled in commitments to establish its sovereignty over the northwest coast and to create ad hoc relations with the Natives that were quite different from previous Spanish policies. For the Natives, living in balance with their marine environment, the arrival of so many Europeans spelled the beginning of disasters that even now have not been fully played out. The empty bays, beaches, estuaries, and creek mouths of today's Nootka or Clayoquot sounds have few reminders of the village sites and camps and of the dynamic and complex culture of 1789.

Even without the factor of Martínez, the 1789 expedition, organized in great haste, lacked adequate planning. Viceroy Florez believed that if the Russians preceded Spain to Nootka Sound, they would dispute the legitimacy of sovereign claims based upon the 1774, 1775, and 1779 expeditions. Florez feared Russian domination of commerce, as well as methods used in subjecting 'barbarian Indians' that would be implanted close to the Spanish missions of California. With the evidence of British activities and recent reports concerning the arrival in the Pacific of the American ship *Columbia* and its escort *Washington*, Florez wished to instill the impression that Spain's occupation of Nootka Sound began in 1774 with the Pérez expedition.[41] The question was how to confirm Spanish precedence. The answer appeared to lie with the evidence of the Natives. Florez knew from reading Cook's journal that in 1778 the English purchased two silver spoons suspended from the neck of a Native as ornamentation which they identified as Spanish-made.[42] Martínez now claimed that the spoons had been stolen from him during the pause offshore at Nootka Sound in 1774. Although it is quite clear from Martínez's own journal and other documents that the Natives who approached the *Santiago* traded from their canoes and did not actually board it,[43] by adopting this fiction to prove their prior claims to sovereignty, the Spanish needed supporting testimony from the Native observers. In any event, if Russian or other foreign ships arrived at Nootka Sound in 1789, Viceroy Florez wanted it occupied by a squad of troops, a fort, several missionaries, and sufficient livestock to feed the garrison. Four Francis-can friars of the Colegio de San Fernando – Padres Severo Patero, Lorenzo Socies, José Espi, and Francisco Miguel Sánchez – were to introduce the Natives to the Holy Gospel.[44] Until the Spanish Crown approved all of these measures, Florez made certain to describe the initiative to occupy Nootka Sound as temporary. By arresting the British fur traders, Martínez made all of this much more complex.

As soon as the *Princesa* and *San Carlos* arrived at Yuquot (Friendly Cove) on 5 May 1789, the Spanish found that the presence of foreign competitors greatly complicated their relations with the Natives. Chief Maquinna's people welcomed Martínez's expedition as simply one more commercial arrival at the busy fur-trading entrepot. The American vessels *Columbia* and *Washington* had wintered over at Nootka Sound, and in 1789, a Portuguese ship with a British crew, the *Iphigenia Nubiana*, had preceded the Spanish. Other foreign ships arrived shortly to contest

Spain's sovereignty. The first Natives to visit the *Princesa* offshore possessed European fishing lines, iron hooks, and English knives with bone handles, and they wore copper, brass, and iron bracelets. Chief Maquinna went out to welcome Martínez in a large canoe paddled by eighteen men. He produced a wooden box containing sea otter pelts that he offered to exchange for a Spanish musket. Prohibited by superior orders from trafficking in firearms, Martínez refused.[45] Before long, however, the Spanish ship was surrounded by sixty canoes.

Ashore at the Yuquot village, the officers and four Franciscan missionaries attended a Native ceremony to recognize Maquinna's principal son, and the chief sang a song repeating Martínez's name. In his journal, Martínez noted that with the English fur traders present, Maquinna produced some Monterey abalone shells obtained in 1774 during the first Spanish visit. The chief went on to declare that the man who stole the silver spoons had died some time before.[46] Maquinna was said to recall an incident during the Pérez visit when Martínez threw an abalone shell from the ship that struck and slightly injured his brother. Given the potential significance of this information, one would expect that some other observers present might have mentioned Maquinna's revelations. But Padre Sánchez, who attended the same celebration, made no reference in his journal to Maquinna's statements – if, for that matter, the Spanish could have understood any of this complexity in the Native language. More likely, Martínez planted words in Maquinna's mouth to bolster Spain's claim to precedence and sovereignty.

This use or misuse of Native evidence, whether they actually uttered the remarks attributed to them, became a major feature woven into the complex relationships and diplomacy of Nootka Sound. Indeed, much of the information that ended up in the historical record – especially concerning the Native culture – must be questioned. From the beginning, the American fur traders acted as intermediaries between the Spanish and the Nootka people. Despite limited communications with the Natives through the winter months, John Kendrick, Robert Gray, and Joseph Ingraham presented themselves as understanding the Native language so well that they could converse familiarly and assist the Spanish with translations. Ingraham provided evidence that strengthened Martínez's claim to sovereignty based upon the 1774 offshore visit. According to his written testimony, the Natives spoke of a ship that had anchored near the rocks at the eastern side of the sound for four days some forty months before Captain Cook. The mystery vessel was said to be copper-sheathed with a copper or yellow-gilt figurehead. The officers appeared in blue, lace-trimmed coats, and many of the sailors wore bandannas tied about their heads. Although the Natives admitted that they had been frightened, a few approached the mystery ship where, in exchange for fish and items of their clothing, they received large mother-of-pearl shells and knives with crooked blades.[47] Declaring himself to Martínez as 'your most sincere friend and most humble servant,' Ingraham concluded: 'From every circumstance I was led to believe at the time this must have been a Spanish ship which immediately accounted to me for the two spoons Capt. Cook found among the Natives but your arrival [in 1789] is a key to everything and clears the conjecture beyond a doubt as you was an officer in the same ship.'[48] If this authentication was not conclusive, the Spanish and Americans tested the Natives by showing them national flags and asking which was first seen at Nootka Sound. As might be expected, they chose the Spanish banner and coat of arms.

Ordered later to evaluate the evidence of the silver spoons, Francisco Mourelle concluded that the inhabitants of Nootka Sound could not have referred to the 1774 expedition of the *Santiago*. Pérez paused offshore for only twelve hours and not four days, and as no Natives actually boarded the ship, they could not have stolen Martínez's silver table spoons. Furthermore, Mourelle argued that only the captain and one military officer aboard might possibly have worn their blue coats, but in all of his lengthy experience as a naval officer serving the northwest coast expeditions, he had never seen a captain wear his formal dress. In some respects the Native testimony appeared to fit the 1775 expedition of Hezeta and Quadra better than that of 1774. At Point Grenville on the Washington coast, where the Natives massacred the boat crew, Quadra's servant had lost two spoons that slipped through the scuppers while they were being cleaned. Mourelle wondered whether at that time Hezeta might have donned his dress uniform for a possession-staking ceremony ashore.[49] Mourelle did not even bother to explain how the spoons lost overboard could have ended up in Native hands or travelled a considerable distance along the coast to reappear three years later at Nootka Sound.

Without accepting a series of miraculous coincidences, it seems obvious that Martínez cooked up evidence involving the Natives to enhance the case for Spanish sovereignty. Moreover, on all substantive and theoretical matters concerning the Native culture, religion, and beliefs, one might question how well Ingraham or the other fur traders really comprehended the Native language. Martínez knew that he would have difficulty establishing the Spanish position to thwart the British fur traders and possibly a Russian naval expedition. He needed friends like Kendrick and Ingraham who, as American participants in the fur trade, viewed Spain as the least objectionable power to claim sovereignty. Known for unpredictable behaviour during the 1788 expedition, Martínez worked under even more intense pressure during June and July 1789, as he grappled with maintaining Spanish sovereignty against what appeared at first to be an official British effort to establish a settlement. When he arrested the British fur traders, James Colnett of the *Argonaut* and Thomas Hudson of the *Princess Royal*, dispatching them with their ships and crews as prisoners to San Blas,[50] Martínez had to find the means to justify his aggressive actions on behalf of Spain. A low-ranking ensign without good patronage connections in the navy, he must have known that he had taken initiatives that might well damage his naval career.

Martínez had to make the northwest coast appear to be a truly valuable Spanish possession – one worthy of defending by military force. In July he informed Viceroy Florez that in 1774 he had sighted the Strait of Juan de Fuca, but did not record the fact in his official journal because Pérez had not wished to approach the coast. According to rumours circulating in 1789 among the fur traders, the strait opened to the fabled Northwest Passage through the continent to a terminus near New Orleans or the Mississippi River.[51] If this were not sufficient incentive for a Spanish presence, Martínez envisaged a chain of Spanish missions operated by a private joint-stock company somewhat on the model of Russian Alaska; a shipbuilding industry that would employ Native workers from Nootka to California; Spanish dominance of the trans-Pacific fur trade to China; and the conquest of the Hawai'ian Islands.[52] Although some Spanish authorities viewed Martínez as a megalomaniac, apocryphal voyager, or crank,[53] none of these grandiose projects could be dismissed out of hand by the Spanish Crown for several years. What might, under other circumstances, have been a single expedition in 1789 to establish that foreign involvement and the sea otter trade made sovereignty impossible, now became a much more complex Spanish presence at

Nootka Sound. The post at Yuquot occupied Maquinna's best summer village site. This, and the emergence of Nootka Sound as a haven for explorers, international fur traders, diplomatic missions to decide sovereignty, and scientific voyages, exerted a growing impact upon the Native culture.

Despite the importance of their mission to attract the Native population to Christianity and subjection to the Spanish Crown, the four Franciscans who accompanied Martínez did not even manage to begin their ministry. Instead of preaching in the twenty-two summer villages and encampments of the Nootka Sound region, they spent almost all of their time bemoaning their situation and, being vexed that, in such a rocky and sterile place beset by constant rainfall, there was no land suitable for cultivation. The friars gave up any hope of establishing the Holy Gospel among the 'savages.'[54] Moreover, the Natives had become accustomed to trading with many different vessels and favoured the English too much. Quite content to leave the Natives in a barbarous state, the fur traders exchanged pieces of copper, trifles, hogs, and other items for sea otter pelts.[55]

Accustomed to the much easier proselytizing in California and indoctrinated by the belief that any successful mission must be sustained by agricultural production, the friars perceived little prospect of attaining a spiritual conquest or in coalescing the various bands into a settled community. Padre Severo Patero informed Viceroy Florez: 'It is very painful for me to have to tell you that we have not been able to preach the gospel.' He blamed the rugged terrain and absence of agricultural potential, noting that in most other pagan territories of the Americas, the inhabitants fed themselves from various grains on their lands. At Nootka Sound, however, the Native population knew no seed other than the fish which they followed from one location to another. He stated that in only two months the people of Yuquot occupied three different locations – each one quite distant from the other.[56]

Beyond the depressing reality of Native tribes that could not be reduced to mission life through methods employed elsewhere in frontier Mexico, the friars lacked opportunities to observe and to gather information about Nootka culture. On 14 May, only about ten days after Martínez's arrival, Maquinna's group dismantled their village at Yuquot and set up a camp on the open ocean beach about five kilometres away. They left behind their house frames with the carved figures called *klummas* that served as posts to support the heavy joists. Although Captain

Cook speculated that these figures might be representations of gods, with the departure of Maquinna's people, the friars expressed surprise to see the figures abandoned to the climate and Spanish sailors who chopped them up for firewood. The Natives manifested little outward anger about the destruction of these figures which they were also quite willing to sell, but complained loudly when the Spanish appropriated house boards left behind. Indeed, the removal of lumber from Native dwellings became a chronic source of dispute between the Spanish garrison and the Nootka bands.[57]

On 7 June, the Spanish received a visit by Chief Wickaninish of Clayoquot Sound to the south, who had been raiding along the coast. Commanding a flotilla led by four great war canoes, Wickaninish and two other leaders offered to sell some captured prisoners of war and pillaged sea otter pelts. Although Martínez was anxious to trade, the Natives would accept only abalone shells or copper sheets, refusing beads, cloth, and blankets unless offered as gifts.[58] Wickaninish departed at dusk, but the Spanish fired a cannon later that night to frighten off some Natives who were seen in the distance and thought to be plotting a robbery or some other misdeed. On 17 June, Chiefs Maquinna and Callicum visited with eight canoes to reiterate their grievances against Spanish sailors who raided nearby villages to strip planks and other items from their houses.[59] On 25 August, Maquinna and his people paddled past Yuquot with their house boards and other utensils lashed across their canoes, on their way to Tahsis where they said they would pass the winter.[60] Other than these occasional visits and during local reconnaissance explorations, neither the friars nor the naval officers had good opportunities to observe the Native culture.

As a result of limited contacts, the Spanish depended heavily upon fur traders such as Kendrick and Ingraham for important elements of their ethnological data. Ingraham informed Martínez that the Americans had established that the Natives were cannibals both from Captain Cook's evidence and from their own confirmation when they 'owned without hesitation they not only eat their enemies but bought men for the purpose of eating.'[61] Native vendors had presented human remains to the Americans for sale, including one perfect three-year-old child's hand that appeared to have been grilled. Captain Kendrick added repulsive detail explaining to Pilot José Tobar y Tamiriz that the Natives kept young male and female prisoners of war, whom they butchered and sold in pieces.[62] As might be expected, the friars who gathered much of their information on the Natives from the Americans expressed revulsion at this information. Padre Sánchez anguished: 'These brutes eat boys and girls captured in wars,' and went on to explain that this was most often done in winter when there were shortages of fish.[63] Although he possessed no first-hand evidence, Padre Lorenzo Socies added that he heard Chief Maquinna actually fattened boy prisoners before he fell upon them at a ceremony in which his people formed a circle enclosing the potential victims. Assuming an enraged countenance, Maquinna grabbed a victim, slashed open the belly with a single blow, cut off the arms, and feasted on the raw flesh.[64]

As appalling rumours spread, neither the friars nor the officers stopped to consider that they had witnessed absolutely none of the reported cruelties described by the American and British fur traders. Since they found the Natives quite different in person than they had been depicted, the friars concluded that the fur traders condemnation of cannibalism must have compelled Maquinna and other chiefs to conceal their ancient barbaric rites. In a later evaluation of the mission to Nootka Sound, Padre Manuel de Trujillo concluded correctly that the Franciscans had been influenced too much by American and English gossip.[65] Isolated in their post, the naval personnel and the tremulous Franciscans became the victims and then the agents of exaggerated stories. Captain Kendrick offered his services to create a program to ransom children. He helped Martínez to purchase a five- or six-year-old boy handed over to the friars for conversion and language training.[66] Lacking copper sheets, the currency of northwest coast commerce, the Spanish suspended their own prohibitions against selling muskets, most prized by the Natives. The apparent compulsion of the Spanish to buy children surprised and confused the Natives, who asked if their purpose was to eat them.[67] Clearly, all of these misunderstandings had the negative impact of actually stimulating the trade in children. By 25 July, the feast day of the Apostle St James, patron saint of Spain, Padre Severo Patero baptized the first Native converts – who were all boys. Later, Martínez purchased an eight-year-old girl from Wickaninish for a copper frying pan and a pot.[68]

The Spanish project to establish a mission began without the essential presence of proselytes, except the purchased children. The tales of the fur traders concerning cannibal feasts and other Native cruelties kept the friars safely restricted to the post. Unfortunately, Martínez provoked a damaging incident that confirmed the Natives' desire to keep well clear of the Spanish. With the arrest of the expedition of James Colnett and Thomas Hudson, their friend and trading associate Chief Callicum went to Yuquot to complain about the detentions. According to Martínez's own account, Callicum paddled about Friendly Cove yelling, 'pe-shak, Martínez cap-sil' or 'Martínez is a bad man and thief.'[69] Martínez attempted to negotiate with Callicum, but the chief was egged on by the British prisoners who apparently considered the scene entertaining. Before long, Martínez's hair-trigger temper snapped and he fired a musket in Callicum's general direction. Whether this shot killed the chief as some Spanish observers stated, or Martínez misfired and a nearby marine guard took more accurate aim, the result was tragic.[70] Callicum died and the Spanish plans to befriend the Natives were in tatters. Not only could the fur traders who wanted the meddlesome Spanish off the coast convince the Natives of Martínez's cruelty, but the British also used the incident in the propaganda war for sovereignty to renew negative Black Legend perceptions about the Spanish character and to trumpet Callicum's death as yet another bloodthirsty Spanish atrocity.[71]

By October, after six months at Nootka Sound, Martínez realized that orders to winter in the north would not be forthcoming. Implementing Viceroy Florez's prior instructions to withdraw, much to the shock of his replacement, Viceroy Conde de Revilla Gigedo, who had received an urgent royal order to sustain the Nootka post, Martínez arrived back at San Blas on 6 December 1789. Whereas Revilla Gigedo had intended to relieve Martínez and to replace him with a more senior naval officer, now he had to restore the northern post from scratch. Martínez did not appeal at all to Revilla Gigedo, who described his actions in capturing the British vessels and crews as 'imprudent, inopportune, and poorly founded.'[72] Revilla Gigedo appointed Lieutenants Francisco de Eliza and Salvador Fidalgo and Ensign Manuel Quimper, all of whom had accompanied him from Spain, to reoccupy and to fortify Yuquot as soon as possible in 1790.[73]

Although these naval officers received explicit instructions to submit detailed reports on the Native civilization,[74] the idea of establishing missions on the California frontier model ceased to have major significance.

Following Revilla Gigedo's own inclinations, the Spanish naval officers on the northern frontier were to reflect modern Enlightenment themes: to observe and to record their findings; to act as scientists; to be pragmatic in their approaches to the Natives of the northwest coast; and to endure foreigners.[75] Although Martínez accompanied the 1790 expedition as second in command, no longer was he able to promote his vision of a chain of missions, a fur-trading empire, new industries, and the means to achieve trans-Pacific dominion for Spain.

It was evident from Eliza's arrival at Yuquot on 5 April 1790 that killing Chief Callicum and the reoccupation of the Yuquot site caused the Natives considerable trepidation. In the months since the departure of Martínez, the British and American fur traders had warned Maquinna of impending dangers should the Spanish return to Nootka Sound. Indeed, when they were told of Spanish ships offshore, Maquinna's people had abandoned Yuquot only twenty-four hours before the twenty-gun frigate *Concepción* anchored in the port.[76] Eliza found a large palisade extending into the water from the beach that the Natives used to trap herring for their winter provisions, but there was neither a village nor a temporary encampment on the site. The following day, a few canoes arrived to barter fish, but all Natives were quite apprehensive at first.[77] Eliza made every effort to dispel their fears – handing out biscuit, abalone shells, pieces of copper, and other gifts, but for some weeks he could not overcome their worry that Martínez had returned to do them harm.

Where Chief Maquinna was remained a mystery until the beginning of June when Ensign Manuel Quimper touched at Clayoquot Sound on his way to explore the Strait of Juan de Fuca. Chief Wickaninish and his brother Tutuciaticatz boarded the *Princesa Real* (Princess Royal) and dispatched twenty canoes to tow the vessel to safe anchorage. From dawn to dark, a multitude of canoes filled with men and women of all ages surrounded the vessel demanding *pa-chito* ('gifts') and yelling *pe-shak* ('bad') when none appeared. They made it clear that when other ships entered port, everyone received presents. Feeling some desperation, Quimper ordered his caulker to cut up two large copper sheets from a shipment that the viceroy had sent paid on behalf of the Mexican treasury to test the market in sea otter pelts.[78]

Ashore in Wickaninish's village of over a thousand inhabitants, Quimper found Chief Maquinna who explained that for fear of Martínez, he had suffered involuntary exile from his own lands. Quimper explained that Martínez was no longer chief and that Eliza would be pleased to see him. Unconvinced, Maquinna asked the sailors if Martínez commanded the frigate at Yuquot. Receiving the same answer, he embraced Quimper, saying *amigo* ('friend'), *amar a Díos* ('love of God'), and other Spanish words.[79] Quimper traded Mexican copper sheets for twenty fine sea otter pelts. Maquinna asked for a sail for his canoe so that he could visit Eliza, and Wickaninish made the same request. Knowing the importance of friendship with both chiefs, Quimper acceded. Wickaninish, who dealt with so many foreign fur traders, responded with six sea otter pelts – offering a better price than Quimper had obtained previously for the copper sheets. The chiefs warned Quimper not to sail further into the Strait of Juan de Fuca with such a small vessel because the chief there, named Tatoosh, was evil, having recently murdered two captains of fur-trading ships. They recommended that Quimper return to his country to bring back a cargo of copper and abalone shells to trade at Nootka and Clayoquot sounds.[80]

Although Eliza's primary concern during 1790 was to construct facilities and a gun battery at Yuquot to protect against possible European aggression, he took steps to improve relations with the Natives. What developed for the five years of Spanish occupation was a relationship based upon mutual advantage and continuing suspicions. On the one hand, the Natives continued to be key witnesses in Spain's case for sovereignty against Britain. Viceroy Revilla Gigedo instructed all of the Spanish naval officers to gather detailed information on all aspects of the Native culture. Eliza issued orders to his garrison, urging it to attract the Natives to Yuquot to learn to exchange their barbarous customs for those of civilization. Captain Pedro de Alberni, commander of the Volunteer Company of Catalonia garrisoned at Nootka, composed a song in honour of Chief Maquinna that helped to restore friendly relations.[81] Eliza reported that the chiefs of Nootka and Clayoquot sounds soon gained confidence to visit the post and that they ate and slept in his quarters 'with too much frequency.'[82] In 1792, he informed Revilla Gigedo that the Natives had become so civilized that over a short period few would remain who had not converted to the Catholic faith. Once they overcame their continuing resistance to living in permanent residences near the Spanish garrison at Yuquot, Eliza was certain that they could be gov-

erned by the rule of law. He saw no reason why they should have the
slightest complaint against the Spanish.[83]

Notwithstanding Eliza's optimism, on the other hand, the disruptive
presence of the Spanish garrison at Nootka Sound continued to provoke
numerous incidents. Eliza and his successors in command could not
help but recognize the irritations and dislocations caused by their occupation of the Yuquot summer village that reduced Native access to the
strategic fisheries. Eliza reported that Maquinna's people 'do not cease in
coming to question me daily about when we will leave.'[84] Even with amicable relations restored in 1790, Natives who ferried soldiers and
mariners back and forth from the ships to shore on one occasion kidnapped a sailor and took him to their village. Eliza had to request inter-
vention from the chiefs at Clayoquot to obtain his release. In June 1790,
garrison troops killed five Hesquiat Natives from Estevan Point who
came at night to steal iron barrel hoops.[85] Jacinto Caamaño reported that
on two occasions launches armed with light artillery and troops were
driven from Native settlements. In the first instance, the Spanish sought
to cut grass for thatching their buildings. In the second, they attempted
to appropriate boards from Native dwellings. The inhabitants defended
their property tenaciously by firing swarms of arrows, but withdrew
under the fire of muskets and swivel guns after one man was killed.
Caamaño could not imagine why they behaved so negatively; in his view,
it was indispensable that the Spanish garrison meet the needs of construction and the Natives could make more planks easily. He argued that
expropriating house boards by force was, in fact, a legitimate purchase
and not outright robbery, as the soldiers and sailors left copper sheets in
payment. In Caamaño's less-than-balanced opinion, his troops had
treated the Natives with prudence and Christian conscience.[86]

Like the Franciscans before him, Caamaño concluded that the
mobile lifestyle of the Native population and the lack of agricultural land
made religious conversion and effective governance impossible. Although
provisions for the Native converts could be shipped northward from
California, leakage, putrefaction, and damage by rats made commerce of
this sort much too costly. Even the small Spanish garrison was not fully
supplied and sometimes had to endure rigorous rationing. In Caamaño's
view the best way to control the Natives was to instil terror in them so as
to prevent their depraved designs. He warned against carelessness or

misplaced confidence and cited the mysterious deaths, in October 1790, of Captain Hudson and six crew members of the *Argonaut* who drowned in a boat accident off Estevan Point on their way to Nootka from Clayoquot Sound. Although there was no evidence of foul play, Caamaño stated that these men had obviously died at the hands of the Hesquiats at Estevan Point – murdered as they struggled ashore after the long swim from their wreck.[87]

Most of the naval officers who served at Nootka Sound accepted earlier reports that the Natives practised cannibalism. Salvador Fidalgo had his suspicions confirmed when he was offered a preserved child's hand in barter for abalone shells. Horrified, Fidalgo ordered the seller away from the side of his ship.[88] Eliza noted, almost casually, in a discussion of Native food preparation and dining habits that some slaves were fattened to be butchered during famines or at ceremonial events such as the seasonal observance of the killing of the first whale.[89] Like his predecessors, Eliza sanctioned the purchase of Native children for copper sheets and abalone shells – assembling eight boys and seven girls whom he turned over to officers and crew members willing to look after their education and upbringing. He also realized that the children sold in this manner were prisoners of war destined for slavery, but was certain that some of the younger ones ended up as the victims at Maquinna's cannibal feasts. He lectured the chiefs about the evils of cannibalism and human sacrifice, threatening great violence if these practices continued. Caamaño appears to have gathered his stories about cannibalism from Native informants corroborated by the English sailors aboard the *Argonaut,* who repeated the tales of Maquinna bashing in children's skulls and 'making fearsome gestures and grimaces' as he gobbled the warm flesh. When Maquinna brought a girl for sale, Caamaño paid for her with a sheet of government copper – convinced that he had saved her from a brutal end. He rejected Maquinna's denial of cannibalism and his quite plausible explanation that these stories were nothing more than slander directed against him by the people of unfriendly bands. Like Fidalgo, Caamaño had seen the arms and bones of children offered for sale. He informed Maquinna that if the Spanish heard of renewed cannibalism, his village would be burned to the ground and everyone in it put to the sword.[90]

The Spanish naval officers' relations with Native people moved away from the previous emphasis on future proselytization. Although Viceroy

Revilla Gigedo hounded his officers to prepare detailed ethnological reports,[91] he expressed concern that they were overly prodigal in developing diplomacy based upon gifts to Native chiefs of the copper sheets provided by the royal exchequer to test the potential of the sea otter fur trade. The viceroy noted that Eliza had given Chief Maquinna five copper sheets for investigating the death of Hudson and his crew members off Estevan Point. Although at first the Hesquiats refused to mention salvage, Maquinna convinced them to show him some pantaloons and stockings that had been cut off the drowned sailors.[92] In these delicate negotiations or during Quimper's diplomacy at Clayoquot where he cut up copper sheets as gifts to compete against the fur traders, Revilla Gigedo simply could not comprehend the difficulties for the small Spanish garrison in a region dominated by the European-Native trade. The cases of scrap iron, trinkets, baubles, and glass beads provided to Eliza and other commanders at Yuquot lacked meaningful value among the Native chiefs, who wanted copper sheets, muskets, munitions, textiles, and manufactured goods. By 1791, even the much celebrated California abalone shells had become so plentiful that they were losing their commercial appeal.[93]

In many respects, the Natives maintained their distance and controlled their relationships with the Spanish garrison. Continuous incidents provoked by minor thefts, misunderstandings, or dire warnings by the Spanish directed against imagined cannibal practices caused the bands to leave the post in isolation for lengthy periods. In addition, rivalries among the different Nootka bands provoked mistrust, suspicions, and rumours. At the beginning of the two-week visit by Alejandro Malaspina's scientific expedition during August 1791, generous gift-giving was needed to overcome Native fears and to convince them to board the *Atrevida* and *Descubierta*.[94] Tlupananutl, the first Nootka chief to present himself, denigrated Maquinna, who he claimed was plotting to expel the Spanish from Yuquot. Notwithstanding the interpretation skills of Captain Pedro Alberni, one must suspect that literary elements and some fiction crept into Tlupananutl's speech as recorded by the expedition artist Tomás de Suria.[95] Maquinna appeared nervous when he visited Yuquot to sell children aboard the *Concepción*. During a launch expedition to explore Nootka Sound, Malaspina's officers learned that the Spanish raids to obtain house boards and other supplies had left

highly strained relations. When the boats appeared, Tlupananutl's people fled from their village into the woods. At Tahsis, until lavish gifts
proclaimed the friendly motives for the visit, Maquinna organized a
force of 400 men to obstruct a landing. Later, as if to publicize his developing military strength, he showed off an arms chest containing fifteen
muskets.[96]

Suspicious about gossip and rumours that circulated in the narrow
world of the Spanish post, Malaspina and his officers were more scientific in their ethnography. On the matter of cannibalism that continued
to sour relations between the Nootka chiefs and Spanish naval officers,
Suría questioned a Native boy named Primo who explained that, as a
prisoner of war, he had been destined to be eaten or sacrificed by Maquinna
or another of the many cannibal chiefs.[97] Primo's story referring to a
blindfolded Maquinna groping to select a child victim originated with
Meares and other fur traders. Although they had become a permanent feature at Spanish Yuquot, Malaspina's officers found such stories implausi-
ble. Children such as Primo learned about their narrow escapes with
death from their Spanish masters and could not provide any details
describing the Native ceremonies. Maquinna was consistent in his
denials of cannibalism and no one could produce an eyewitness account.
When questioned, a young Native named Nanikius who had learned some
Spanish, responded affirmatively to questions about cannibalism, but
when he comprehended the exact meaning, he changed his reply and
manifested his repugnance at the idea. Another Native informant, Natzape,
described the bones, preserved hands, and other body parts offered in
trade as battlefield trophies, and he expressed revulsion at the thought of
actually consuming human flesh.[98] At more or less the same date, however, the acting commandant of the post, Lieutenant Ramón Saavedra
heard rumours from some other Natives that, owing to a shortage of
salmon, Natzape had gone north to kidnap Nushatlet boys for food.[99]

If cannibalism was a myth, the trade in so many Native children
became unnecessary or even repugnant. During their visit, Malaspina's
officers found twenty-two children[100] aboard the Spanish ships and at
the post, and the Natives regularly produced more for sale. Without the
danger of cannibalism or the motive to educate converted Natives as
agents in a future mission, purchasing children was extremely difficult to
justify. With the growing pressure by the Natives for muskets, powder,

and lead, it was obvious that raids by stronger tribes against their weaker neighbours might be organized simply to produce captives for the Spanish trade. Although the evidence of increased warfare is sparse, there are indications that the stronger Nootka and Clayoquot bands stepped up raids against the Hesquiats, who resided between them, and against the Nushatlets to the north.[101] The only remaining grounds for justifying the purchase of Natives was to redeem them from slavery in their own society. In 1792, Quadra granted permission for officers of the warship *Santa Gertrudis* to ransom slaves – including a twelve-year-old boy and a woman with a baby at her breast.[102] As in the past, senior members of the Spanish government expressed concerns about the traffic in northwest coast Natives and ordered investigations to ensure that they were converted to Christianity, educated, and given proper treatment in Mexico.[103]

Despite the Spanish view that their presence at Nootka Sound was benign or even positive for the Native inhabitants, the occupation of Yuquot continued to cause stresses for the bands of the region. During the spring and summer months of 1791, Maquinna asked almost every Spanish officer he encountered when they would depart from his summer village site.[104] In June, he informed Saavedra that, although his present village up the sound was the best after Yuquot, it was unhealthy and a poor place for fishing and gathering food. To illustrate his point, Maquinna exposed his emaciated body and stated that the inferior village location explained why he was so thin. Saavedra took the opportunity to invite Maquinna and his people to settle alongside the Spanish garrison at Yuquot, but the chief declined, stating that while he trusted the *taises* ('officers'), the other Spanish would violate the Native women. By August, illness and shortages of fish compelled Maquinna to move his village early to the winter site at Tahsis. At the Spanish base, the arrival of adult Natives seeking refuge and other incidents suggested an increase in armed raids among the bands and other quarrels. Unsure whether the Spanish had kidnapped Native people who moved to the post, Maquinna expressed renewed apprehensions about visiting Yuquot.[105]

This was an inauspicious beginning for the negotiations of 1792 between Bodega y Quadra and George Vancouver. Like Martínez before him at Nootka Sound, Quadra depended in part upon Native testimony to challenge British claims that John Meares bought lands from the

Natives at Yuquot and constructed a substantial building. A consummate diplomat, Quadra convinced all visitors to Nootka Sound that he had introduced 'a system of humanity'[106] in his relations with the Natives. Notwithstanding previous mistrust by Maquinna, incidents such as the unsolved murder of a Spanish servant boy at Yuquot,[107] or the reprisal massacre by Salvador Fidalgo of innocent Makah Nootkas to the south at the Spanish settlement of Nuñez Gaona (Neah Bay) in the Strait of Juan de Fuca,[108] Quadra made seduction and good treatment of the Natives and the foreign fur traders into key elements in building the Spanish claim to sovereignty. Cayetano Valdés, commander of the schooner *Mexicana*, expressed surprise at the remarkable improvement in Maquinna's confidence in the few months since Malaspina's visit in the previous year.[109]

Indeed, the 1792 journals and logs reflect Quadra's adoption of Eliza's approach, which was to open his own residence to the Native chiefs and to offer gifts of copper sheets and other trade goods 'to domesticate the Indians.'[110] Quadra granted Maquinna special preference above other chiefs, invited him to eat at his table where the Spanish commander served him, and presented him with special gifts, including a showy, tin plate-mail suit of armour. Quadra's banquets were famous among visitors to Nootka Sound, who unanimously praised his lavish hospitality.[111] Unlike previous Spanish commanders, who expected the chiefs to visit at Yuquot, Quadra went to pay his respects to Maquinna at Marvinas, Kupti, and other places where the Natives performed dances and sang songs accompanied to rhythms beat out by their lances and muskets. At Kupti Quadra witnessed the ceremonial entry of Maquinna's daughter into puberty and the Spanish sailors participated in wrestling games with the Natives. Later, Quadra invited Captain Vancouver and his officers to visit Maquinna at Tahsis, where the inhabitants made warlike motions dressed in a wild assortment of trade garments. Edward Bell was surprised when Maquinna's brother appeared in the ridiculous suit of armour which, he noted, 'very likely was often the property of Hamlet's Ghost.'[112] In his general enthusiasm for the northwest coast, Quadra adopted some of Martínez's plans to promote the fur trade, noting that the proximity of the copper mines and textile factories of New Spain would allow Spanish and Mexican merchants a significant advantage over those of other nations.[113]

Although Maquinna supported the Spanish position on sovereignty and rejected Meares' claim that the chief had sold land to the British trader, he always maintained the central preeminence of Native owner-ship. Quadra had ulterior motives for according his friendship and invi-tations to the Nootka chief to sit beside him at dinner. Maquinna exercised his own diplomatic talents among the European captains and officers, manipulating his knife, fork, spoon, and wine glass effectively at the commandant's dining table.[114] Unfortunately, the invitations ended with the completion of the negotiations with Vancouver and the reduced need by the Spanish for Native support. By buying off the chiefs with rich gifts and attention, Quadra impressed all British observers and visit-ing fur traders with his gentility and diplomacy. Some, such as Edward Bell and Jacinto Caamaño, his own subordinate, thought Quadra too soft in his Native policies. Caamaño felt that Quadra bought Native friendship with gifts – 'the only means of gaining their support.' Bell warned: 'The man that would profess himself your warm friend today would cut your throat and dine off you tomorrow.'[115] Caamaño echoed his British colleague when he stated, 'the perverse inclinations and hatred of the Indians for all foreigners are manifested whenever a secure occasion becomes available.'[116]

With the departure of Quadra and his flotilla, the attention, flattery, and good manners directed toward the Nootka chiefs terminated abruptly. Unable to agree on the implementation of the Nootka Sound conventions, both sides sailed away to consult their governments. For Maquinna, Tlupananutl, and other chiefs, the replacement of Quadra with Lieutenant Salvador Fidalgo ended the warm welcome at Yuquot, the invitations to dinner, and all the other courtesies. Fidalgo com-plained that the chiefs constantly asked him for gifts and reminded him that Commander Quadra, the English, the Americans, and others had given them presents whereas he gave them nothing.[117]

During the last years until the final settlement of the diplomatic issues with Britain in 1795, the Spanish post at Yuquot made little impression upon the Native world. There were no further scientific visits and Spanish naval officers suspended their efforts to study Nootka soci-ety or to collect ethnographic data. In many respects, the small Spanish garrison at Yuquot became the hostage of Native activities and of the rivalries among the different Nootka tribes. The commanders prohibited

Village of Friendly Indians at the Entrance of Bute's Canal, sketch by T. Heddington, engraved by J. Landseer

unauthorized movements by members of the garrison beyond the harbour entrance, and, to prevent incidents, all official delegations to Native settlements were to be commanded by officers.[118] A few Natives intruded occasionally to frighten the Spanish shepherds and to mock the guards who fired muskets to drive them away. In 1793, the Spanish commander, Lieutenant Ramón Saavedra, declared that he feared Native treachery if his men operated beyond the effective artillery range of the fort. The Mexican mestizo soldiers of the Infantry Company of San Blas garrisoned at Yuquot suffered from the climate without adequate uniforms, boots, or heavy clothing. Dressed like many of the northwest coast Natives in cast-off great coats, assorted uniform parts, and other garments, the differences in appearance must have been minimal.[119] In November 1793, Chief Tlupananutl sought unsuccessfully to borrow a longboat to secure a beached whale in his territory. Since his people had suffered food shortages, he took the precaution of asking the Spanish priest to celebrate a Mass to bring fish.[120] In February 1794, an incident occurred when Chief Guacatlazapé, brother-in-law of Maquinna, clubbed a Native man to punish him for selling herring without permission. In the aftermath, the Spanish expected further violence and fired a cannon that caused several terrified Natives to overturn their canoes. Hostages were taken, including Maquinna's eldest daughter, but they were soon released. Demanding proper negotiations to settle the incident, Saavedra closed Yuquot to fishing, but the Natives paid no attention and carried on as though nothing had happened.

To enforce his jurisdiction at least within the bay, Saavedra dispatched a longboat armed with swivel guns to expel the Native fishermen. When they came back each time the boat returned to shore, Saavedra ordered two heavy guns with solid shot to be fired over their heads. This worked the first time, but the Natives soon reappeared and fished anyway despite occasional cannon balls passing over their heads. Once again, Saavedra embarked in a longboat and drove the Natives away with swivel gunfire. When questioned, the fishermen protested that they were from Tlupananutl's village and that they had no part in the original incident provoked by some of Maquinna's people. Although these incidents heightened mistrust, Saavedra solved the problem by lecturing Chief Chicomasia, another brother-in-law to Maquinna, on safer methods of disciplining petty offenders. He recommended whipping rather than brutal beatings that caused severe contusions, broken limbs, and dislocated bones. In the end, Saavedra dispatched a boat with a dragnet to fill Native requirements for herring.[121] By the beginning of March, the Natives arrived at Yuquot Cove to construct their usual palisades designed to trap herring. They set up temporary plank shelters and pursued their activities as if the Spanish did not exist.

If Quadra manipulated Maquinna to bolster Spanish claims to sovereignty, the Nootka chief proved himself equally adept at using the Spanish to strengthen his own diplomatic position. The traditional role of the Nootka Sound bands as brokers in regional commerce had been eroded by the number of British-, American-, and Portuguese-registry fur-trading vessels that dealt directly with the producers of sea otter pelts and disrupted Native trading patterns. Between June 1793 and June 1794, seventeen foreign vessels called at Nootka Sound.[122] In March 1794, Maquinna arrived at the Spanish post with two visiting Nuchatlet chiefs whom he wished to impress. Saavedra offered them tea, brandy, and bread and prepared to give each of them some knives and ten abalone shells. Maquinna intervened to whisper instructions that two shells would be sufficient. He did not want the Spanish to damage his own business with the Nuchatlets who had come to trade sea otter pelts for abalone shells and copper. Maquinna made a great show of affection – often saying *te quiero* ('I love you')[123] and other expressions of endearment to the Spanish – not at all unlike Quadra's behaviour in 1792 to impress the British and other visitors. As Saavedra understood and appreciated, Maquinna's ploy was to show off a special relationship and friendship with the Spanish that might serve his political and commercial interests.

Given the weakness of the garrison, Saavedra must have been concerned when, on 19 March, Maquinna requested permission to set up a temporary village alongside the Spanish post. In previous years, the friars would have considered this a major victory in their schemes to proselytize. In 1794, however, Saavedra's first thought was to place Maquinna to one side of the settlement, where his house would be situated under the guns of the anchored Spanish ship. Over the next few days, Guacatlazapé, Chicomasia, Natzapi, and other chiefs arrived to build houses – some of which were more permanent post-and-beam dwellings capable of housing large numbers. Maquinna's change of heart about accepting proximity to the Spanish resulted from his greater fear of an all-out war against his people by Chief Wickaninish of Clayoquot. He was said to have purchased as many as 400 muskets and, more recently, two light artillery pieces and ten cartridges from an American fur trader who wintered at Clayoquot. Other Americans, such as John Kendrick, had been selling muskets since 1791, but the Natives complained that the barrels of all but twenty of these had blown out.[124] Wickaninish's anger was said to originate because Maquinna held one of his daughters captive when the husband selected for her turned out to be too young for marriage. However, when Wickaninish sent a canoe with a gift of six sea otter pelts, Maquinna realized that whole affair was nothing more than a lie spread by the wicked Hesquiats. Aware that there was a trade in sex between women of his band and members of the garrison, Maquinna packed up his village quickly and moved. Later that summer, Wickaninish, allied with Guacatlasapé of Nootka Sound, launched a secret night attack against a sleeping Hesquiat village. Sneaking ashore from twenty-nine canoes, the Clayoquots and their allies murdered and decapitated seventy people and carried off many children as their captives.[125]

Aware that with the publication of George Vancouver's journal, the world probably would credit Britain for discoveries on the northwest coast,[126] at least some of the Spanish naval officers recognized that their own efforts would be forgotten. The maritime fur trade, which was the only major commercial attraction of the coast, appeared limited by the over-hunting of the sea otter, by the pressure of competition by too many fur traders who inflated the value of furs, and by reduced access or low prices in the Canton market. Although Mexicans might have been able to compete by offering lower prices for copper, textiles, and marketing by way of the Manila galleons, Martínez, Malaspina, and Quadra failed to stimulate significant interest in the merchant guild of Mexico City.[127] Without some other impetus beyond the general claims to sovereignty, the agents of the Spanish state and the missionary friars remained little more than temporary intruders among the Native peoples of Nootka Sound and elsewhere on the northwest coast. Lack of arable land and the Native way of life, which was based upon an annual round to harvest the rich marine and land environment, made the coastal tribes impervious to the promise of a stable food supply in exchange for permanent residency in a mission community. In the eighteenth century, the Franciscan model from California simply did not apply on the northwest coast. Although some naval officers who served at Nootka Sound were effective diplomats, scientists, and observers, their relations with the Natives were intended to produce short-term political gains rather than to pave the way for future settlement. The Spanish regime lacked the motivation or the population to maintain its sovereign claims to the coastline and ocean north of California. Other than the northwest coast Natives sent to Mexico and perhaps a few mestizos born at Nootka Sound, the Spanish efforts left little impact upon the Native societies. As for sovereignty, on 27 March 1795, Brigadier José Manuel Alava for Spain and Lieutenant Thomas Pearce for Britain read their declarations and counter-declarations to implement the Nootka Sound conventions, raised and lowered their national flags, and both sides abandoned Yuquot. Even before the ship left the harbour, Maquinna's people were hard at work erecting house posts for their summer village.

Dangerous Liaisons: Maquinna, Quadra, and Vancouver in Nootka Sound, 1790-5

Yvonne Marshall

When European explorers and traders first came to the west coast of Vancouver Island in the closing decades of the eighteenth century, they recognized that a common language and culture united the inhabitants of the northwest tip of Washington State with people living as far north as Brooks Peninsula near the northern tip of Vancouver Island (see map, page 161). Although the inhabitants of this windswept coast used no common name, choosing instead to identify themselves as belonging to smaller sovereign groups whose names indicated their various places of origin and residence, they did recognize through their marriages, potlatch ceremonies, and trade a wider west coast cultural community. In that community lay the roots of their contemporary political unification and the modern Nuu-chah-nulth Tribal Council. This chapter illustrates how the council's formation was presaged in the earliest contacts of the Nuu-chah-nulth peoples with European newcomers by examining a cameo moment in the history of the west coast – the summer of 1792.

By 1787, two years after the maritime fur trade had begun, trade along the west coast of Vancouver Island was controlled by three large trading blocks, each dominated by a single powerful chief.[1] In the south was Chief Tatoosh, whose main village was on Tatoosh Island at the entrance to the Strait of Juan de Fuca. Less is known about Tatoosh than the other trading chiefs, but he seems to have been somewhat unpredictable in his dealings with Europeans. At times he could be 'surly and forbidding,'[2] but if it suited his purpose he could also be charming. An instance of this charm occurred when he wanted to look over the two Spanish ships, *Sutil* and *Mexicana*, possibly with the intention of helping the Clayoquot chief, Wickaninish, realize a plan to obtain and learn to operate a European trading vessel.[3]

Further north was Chief Wickaninish himself, a man of mature years and a corpulence indicative of his wealth.[4] From his villages in southern Clayoquot Sound Wickaninish dominated the central coast from Hesquiat Harbour to Barkley Sound, an area exceptionally rich in whales, sea otters, and other open-sea resources. The superior wealth of the Clayoquot people, especially compared with that of the people of Nootka Sound, was noticed immediately by Meares[5] and remarked upon by many later European visitors. Wickaninish, his brothers, and other family members exercised such complete control that the Clayoquot group could be said to comprise an oligarchy. The most striking expression of their authority was that Wickaninish or one of his brothers managed all interaction with visiting Europeans. Even Wickaninish's close associate, Captain Hanna, chief of the powerful Ahousaht group, was not usually permitted to trade directly with European ships.[6]

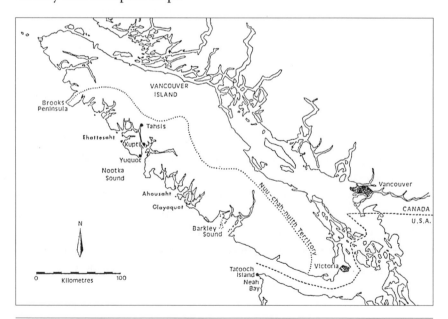

Vancouver Island

Wickaninish wanted European trade, but only on his terms. Given the richness of the Clayoquot Sound, his strong hold on political power within the Clayoquot group, and his domination of trade with Europeans throughout Clayoquot and Barkley sounds, he was certainly in a position to dictate terms. But he may have been planning to manage without the Europeans altogether. During the winter of 1790-1 Wickaninish unsuccessfully attempted to seize the English vessel *Argonaut,* and the following winter made another unsuccessful attempt on the *Columbia* and *Adventure.*[7] Historians have generally assumed that Wickaninish wanted these ships and their armaments to wage war on other Native groups. However, as Nuu-chah-nulth warfare consisted largely of surprise night attacks and other trickery, it is difficult to see how a European ship would have been useful. Certainly they were not used to any extent during the widespread wars which raged among the Nuu-chah-nulth in the nineteenth century.[8] Possibly Wickaninish wanted to capture these vessels to take furs directly to Canton, which would also explain Tatoosh's intense interest in the *Sutil* and *Mexicana* as part of this plan.

The most northern of the three chiefs was Maquinna, a young man in his thirties whose home was in Nootka Sound.[9] Because there were few sea otter in Nootka Sound, Maquinna collected furs from the groups living along the coast north to Brooks Peninsula and from the Nimpkish of eastern Vancouver Island via an overland trail which began at Tahsis, his winter village. In contrast to Wickaninish, Maquinna was the first-ranked chief of a political collectivity of at least seven component groups whose chiefs all held positions of rank and authority. As power was shared by all component groups, this collectivity can be characterized as a confederacy. Maquinna usually conducted trade with the Europeans with the help of Callicum, a man in his fifties,[10] who, as head of the second-ranked component group, was the second ranking chief of the collectivity. The two chiefs, therefore, belonged to separate lineages and no evidence exists that they were directly related. If both Maquinna and Callicum were absent from Yuquot when European vessels were present, then Hannape, chief of an Ehattesaht group allied with the collectivity through his daughter's marriage to Maquinna, would take charge.[11]

Given the poor fur resources available in the Nootka Sound area and the more consensual nature of his political power, Maquinna wisely chose to draw trading vessels to Nootka Sound by providing them with a safe, hospitable environment in which to trade and reprovision.[12] Even after Don Estevan Martínez murdered Chief Callicum at Yuquot in 1789,[13] Maquinna maintained this policy, although the Spanish would not again enjoy the full trust and confidence of the Nootka Sound people until 1792.

Wickaninish, and to a lesser extent Tatoosh, were portrayed by European visitors as leaders with great power who tended toward direct action. In comparison, Maquinna was seen as less powerful and less wealthy, but nevertheless a leader of considerable social standing more inclined to diplomacy. It is therefore interesting that despite Wickaninish's widely reported superiority in power and wealth, John Meares found that Wickaninish was 'not considered as equal in rank to Maquilla [Maquinna].'[14] Thus it appears that, by the late eighteenth century, Nuu-chah-nulth society placed a higher social value on political consensus than on instrumental authority. Chiefs who operated by consensus and diplomacy were more highly regarded than leaders who exercised instrumental authority, however powerful.

Furthermore, because the three leading chiefs and their closest associates were all related by marriage, as described later, they could each call upon the others to act as allies. Maquinna's membership in this network of alliances combined with his very high rank and social status meant that, although he held no formal position of overall authority, in practice his influence could amount to that of an umbrella chief. This informal influence was to be both strengthened and tested by the events of the summer of 1792.

On 29 April 1792 Captain Juan Francisco de la Bodega y Quadra,[15] commandant of the San Blas naval station in California, arrived at Yuquot to take charge of the Spanish establishment and to meet with Captain George Vancouver, representative of the British Crown, to carry out the terms of the Nootka conventions. Maquinna understood that the new arrival was a person of exceptionally senior rank and, eschewing the reticence he had displayed since the murder of Callicum in 1789, was at Yuquot within hours to welcome Quadra and proclaim friendship.[16] Quadra responded in kind. His attitude and behaviour toward the people of Nootka Sound were unusually respectful.[17] Not only did he strive to carry out his stated policy of treating the 'Indians as men ... and not as though they were of inferior stock,'[18] but also, having identified Maquinna as the highest ranking chief, he then treated him as he would

Friendly Cove, Nootka Sound ... , sketch by Henry Humphreys, engraved by J. Heath

any other head of state. 'I constantly treat Macquina as a friend singling him out from the rest with the clearest demonstrations of appreciation, he always occupies the first place when he dines at my table, I myself take the trouble of waiting on him, of serving him with as much as he likes, and he makes a lot of my friendship and much appreciates my visits to his rancherias.'[19]

Such overt European recognition of Maquinna's high rank was to affect the internal politics of both Nootka Sound and the wider west coast community. Of even greater significance for local politics were the demonstrations of respect implied by Quadra's policy of open hospitality. Quadra had understood that an important part of his task at Nootka would be to receive state representatives 'with appropriate dignity and formality.' Before he left San Blas he stocked up with foodstuffs suitable for entertaining and packed his personal silver dinner service.[20] These civilized accoutrements, complemented by Quadra's considerable personal charm, were a source of both astonishment and delight to the Natives, who were among the steadiest, and possibly the most appreciative, recipients of Quadra's hospitality. Not only did the chiefs commonly eat at Quadra's table while the lower ranks were served 'a plate of kidney beans, as they preferred eating these to anything else,' but also the people of Nootka Sound 'filled the house of the commandant day and night.'[21] When paying an extended visit, Maquinna would sleep in Quadra's bedroom, whereas Quiocomasia and Nanaquius, two chiefs of lesser rank, would sleep in the bedroom of the Spanish botanist Mozino.[22]

Quadra's hospitality, especially the importance he attached to rituals involving the serving of food, the attention he paid to placing people at his table according to rank, and his policy of housing high-ranking guests in his own quarters, again placing them according to rank, closely paralleled local notions of appropriate chiefly behaviour. Paramount among Nuu-chah-nulth chiefly virtues was hospitality, in particular lavish generosity with food.[23] In west coast society of the late eighteenth century, chiefly rank was widely reported to be hereditary.[24] However, the detailed account left by John Jewitt, held captive by Maquinna from 1803 to 1805, makes it clear that a chief's inherited rank had to be validated by giving a potlatch, and his status had to be constantly 'kept up' by giving feasts for both commoners and other chiefs and through other displays of hospitality and generosity.[25] The status of a chief was closely tied to his ability to fulfil the expectations of chiefly office. In a manner unique among the European visitors to the west coast but comparable to the practice of a local chief, similarly, Quadra, by his hospitable and generous actions, demonstrated to the people of Nootka Sound the correctness and appropriateness of his exalted rank.

Over the summer Maquinna and Quadra's mutual respect deepened into friendship. By the time the *Sutil* and *Mexicana* arrived in Nootka Sound in May, Maquinna had come to live intimately with the Spanish, eating every day at Quadra's table usually accompanied by his brother Quatlazape.[26] Maquinna returned Quadra's hospitality with regular invitations to attend ceremonies at his villages. The first of these was given specifically in honour of Quadra. Later, Quadra visited Maquinna at the village of Mawun and attended the puberty ceremonies for Maquinna's daughter Apenas in the village of Kupti.[27] Also in accordance with chiefly protocol Maquinna supplied the Spanish settlement with fish 'without seeking to receive any kind of return.'[28] Such behaviour was in strong contrast to the strictly commercial nature of most transactions in the maritime fur trade between Natives and Europeans.

Maquinna's position of favour with Quadra did not go uncontested by other chiefs, particularly Tlupananutl, chief of the central Nootka

Sound and Tlupana Inlet groups, and Quiocomasia, who had recently succeeded his father Hannape as chief of an Ehattesaht group. Both groups were allied with Maquinna by marriage but were not part of his collectivity. They were not, therefore, formally positioned with respect to Maquinna and other chiefs within his confederacy, but their status and authority were widely regarded as inferior to Maquinna's. Tlupananutl and Quiocomasia sought to challenge Maquinna's superior status by seeking greater recognition from the Spanish. They did so by extending the local potlatch and feasting ceremonies to include the Spanish, as though they were simply another resident group. This was quite different from the common practice of inviting Europeans to attend scheduled ceremonies as observers. Reports of speeches given by chiefs at pot-latches in Nootka Sound during 1792 indicate that some ceremonies, at least, were specifically directed toward the Spanish. Tlupananutl and Quiocomasia probably chose this avenue because Quadra behaved so much in accord with other local customs. Their efforts were sufficiently vociferous as to lead one Spanish officer to remark with ill-concealed exasperation that 'vaunting each above the other is the main topic of conversation among the "taises" or chiefs.'[29]

Hannape and his four sons made a very favourable impression on Quadra and other visitors. They were frequently praised by Europeans for their facility in speaking both Spanish and English and for their abil-ity to explain Native culture and comprehend that of the Europeans.[30] Nanaquius in particular became 'a very great favourite with Sr Quadra and all his officers.'[31] Quiocomasia, the newly appointed chief of about twenty years of age,[32] gave at least one ceremony in honour of Quadra,[33] and invited the crews of the *Sutil* and *Mexicana* to attend a 'dance' at the village of Mawun. During the celebrations Quiocomasia made a speech in which he highlighted his recent marriage to the daughter of a Nimpkish chief then promoted himself as a *tais* of both Nootka and Nimpkish and 'proceeded to explain to us how entirely superior he was to Macuina [Maquinna].'[34] In exactly the same way that a Nuu-chah-nulth chief would today thank high-ranking witnesses at a potlatch by distributing gifts, Quiocomasia then 'placed himself at some distance in front of our people, and naming each one of us individually in a loud voice, caused us to be given otter skins.'[35] Quadra, however, remained unmoved by Quiocomasia's appeals.

Tlupananutl, a very elderly man of possibly ninety,[36] also sought to challenge Maquinna. The previous year he had tried to turn the Alberni against Maquinna, and he now continued these machinations[37] by feasting the Spanish, bringing them gifts of food, and generally placing his chiefly services at their disposal.[38] He gave a feast for Quadra followed by an exhibition on the water in his large display canoe.[39] Again these claims went unacknowledged by Quadra, and Tlupananutl continued to sit at Quadra's table in the less favourable place opposite Maquinna.[40]

No chiefs from within Maquinna's confederacy hosted such ceremonies, confirming that their relative ranks were firmly entrenched, whereas the relative statuses of chiefs within Nootka Sound but outside the confederacy were not so rigidly fixed that the chiefs did not attempt to contest and change them. Given the way events transpired, however, even these less formal relative positions must have been well established. Maquinna confirmed this situation in a speech he delivered later that summer when Quadra and Vancouver visited him at Tahsis. Vancouver reported that when Maquinna spoke of the honour that their visit showed for his social position he referred only to his superiority to Wickaninish, making no mention of either Tlupananutl or Quiocomasia.[41] Thus Maquinna demonstrated his indifference to their rival claims to equal or superior status. By contrast, he gave considerable attention to emphasising his high status relative to Wickaninish which suggests not only that such a claim was open to dispute, but also that the actions of the European diplomats were of some consequence in this matter.

While the peaceful machinations of international state relations were proceeding at Yuquot, the southern chiefs had become embroiled in bitter conflicts with the Europeans. Early in the summer, Salvador Fidalgo had arrived in Neah Bay, part of the extensive territory under the influence of Chief Tatoosh, with orders to locate and prepare a site for a possible Spanish establishment. In July 1792 the ship *Venus* arrived at Yuquot with a letter from Fidalgo informing Quadra that the pilot Serantes had been attacked and killed. In retaliation Fidalgo had sunk two canoes, killing eight men and saving only three children.[42] Angered by Fidalgo's brutal and arbitrary act of revenge, Tatoosh had gone to seek assistance from Wickaninish at Clayoquot and Captain Hanna, chief of the Ahousaht.[43]

Like all chiefs along the west coast, Wickaninish and Hanna were closely related to Tatoosh. Wickaninish's sister, possibly the same sister who was the widow of the Nootka Sound chief, Callicum,[44] was in 1792 married to a chief from the Strait of Juan de Fuca who was probably a relative of Tatoosh's.[45] In 1794 Captain Hanna's daughter was promised to Tatoosh, although the marriage was not scheduled until the following year.[46] Maquinna was also related by marriage to these chiefs and his daughter was to marry Wickaninish's son[47] (see diagram, below). This meant that Wickaninish and Hanna would be expected to view with sympathy a request from Tatoosh for combined action against the Spanish and that Maquinna would inevitably be drawn into the dispute.

A second violent incident took place later that summer between the Clayoquot Sound people and Captain Brown of the *Butterworth*, fuelling the tension. Soon after the incident, Joseph Ingraham of the *Hope* met the *Butterworth* and was told by Brown that the Natives had attacked him without provocation and that he had been forced to fire on them, killing one man and wounding two others.[48] Two days later, Captain Magee of the *Margaret* met Ingraham and told him a very different story. Magee reported that sailors had attempted to steal furs from the people at one of the villages but the villagers had fought back, prompting the sailors to fire on them, killing four people. Wickaninish's men then arrived

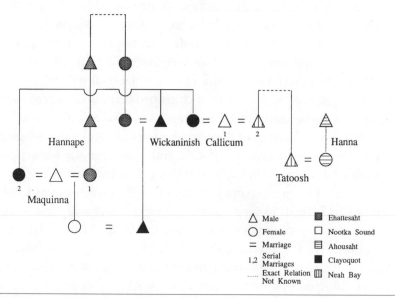

Marriages between key west coast chiefs, 1785-95

on the scene, pursued the sailors in their canoes, and would have caught them had not Magee fired a cannon shot between the two groups. Brown later took revenge. Upon meeting some canoes out fishing he took their occupants, whipped them, and threw them overboard. The *Jenny*, 'being astern, fired at them and ended the tragedy.'[49] This account was confirmed by the second mate of the *Jenny*.[50]

When Quadra received Fidalgo's letter concerning the violence in Neah Bay he wrote a reply, counselling humanity and greater restraint, and admonishing Fidalgo for his unnecessarily violent response.[51] Maquinna immediately offered to carry the letter to Neah Bay, but it did not get far.[52] Maquinna returned around 7 August and went to dine with Quadra. On seeing Captain Brown seated at the table Maquinna took Quadra aside, gave back the undelivered letter, and explained that Brown had killed the occupants of a Clayoquot canoe and that now Wickaninish, Hanna, and Tatoosh were 'arranging the manner of revenge.'[53] The three southern chiefs had sent Maquinna back to Yuquot, insisting the letter should not be delivered and advising him against trusting his Spanish allies.[54]

At this point the situation was potentially explosive. Spurred by their unsuccessful attempts to seize a trading vessel for their own operations and provided with a convenient campaign platform by the brutal actions of Fidalgo and Brown, Chiefs Wickaninish, Hanna, and Tatoosh now planned united action against the Europeans. Part of the rationale behind this plan may have been to exclude the Europeans from the west coast and thereby make room for Wickaninish to develop direct trade with China. Although factionalism made united action very difficult, once a critical level of support was reached no west coast group would be able to risk remaining outside the plan. To be politically isolated was to court aggression and potential annihilation. Because Maquinna held such a high rank and occupied a crucial strategic location his decision could tip that balance.

Although Maquinna never directly divulged that he was asked by Wickaninish, Hanna, and Tatoosh to abandon his alliance with the Spanish at Yuquot and unite with them against the Europeans, a speech he made six weeks later clearly indicated that an exchange of this kind must have taken place. In questioning Maquinna about the death of a cabin boy Quadra implied that Maquinna might have been implicated in the murder. Maquinna's indignant reply is unequivocal. 'Do you presume that a chief such as I would not commence hostilities by killing the other chiefs and placing the force of my subjects against that of their *meschimes*? You would be the first whose life would be in great danger if we were enemies. You well know that Wickaninish has many guns as well as powder and shot; that Captain Hanna has more than a few, and that they, as well as the Nuchimanes, [Nimpkish] are my relatives and allies, all of whom, united, make up a number incomparably greater than the Spanish, English, and Americans together, so that they would not be afraid to enter combat.'[55]

Maquinna's prominence as a leader and his wealth stemmed from trade with other west coast groups and with Europeans. It had been built using his skills as a diplomat, as had both the achievement and mainte-nance of his position and wealth. Maquinna saw that he was likely to lose both his position and his access to further trade if widespread conflict broke out. Furthermore, war, except as a last resort, was contrary to his normal operation. Yet, to go against the call for united action would be to gamble with possible annihilation. If Maquinna opposed the planned action but did not gain the support of other chiefs, Wickaninish would not only attack the Europeans but also treat Maquinna as their ally and pur-sue his destruction. At stake was not only who would decide how the Euro-peans and their trade were to be managed but also who could command the greatest influence and highest status – Maquinna or Wickaninish.

Maquinna decided in favour of negotiation and recruited Quadra to assist him. Several days after Maquinna had returned with the undeliv-ered letter, Captain Hanna came to Maquinna's village ostensibly 'on account of his children,'[56] although the real purpose of the visit was prob-ably to discuss the planned action. Maquinna took this opportunity to speak of the strength and advantages of his friendship with the Spanish, especially Quadra. He convinced Hanna to meet with Quadra, confident that the latter would do the rest. Quadra records that Hanna became 'so reconciled and satisfied that after having been two days in my house he took the letter [to Fidalgo] and brought the reply, [and] pacified the rest-lessness of the rest of the Chiefs.'[57] It could not have been an easy victory, for Hanna was one of Wickaninish's closest associates; for him to decide in favour of Maquinna must have cost him dearly with Wickaninish. It was a clear demonstration of Maquinna's high standing that he was able to sway Hanna from Wickaninish and thereby completely defuse the situation. Furthermore, as Maquinna's gamble was successful, his actions further enhanced his position.

Two weeks later on 28 August 1792, Captain George Vancouver arrived in Nootka Sound. Following the trying events of August, Vancouver, with his strong regard for the importance of stately ceremony and protocol and respect for the discrete direction offered by the experienced Quadra, confirmed Maquinna's heightened stature and peaceful policies. Relations however, started out rather badly. When Maquinna approached the *Discovery* on the morning of 29 August, he was prevented from boarding. Vancouver's officer on deck had failed to recognize him because, typically among Nootka Sound chiefs, 'there was not in his appearance the smallest indication of his superior rank.'[58] Over dinner that evening, Quadra was called upon to use his charm and diplomacy to smooth over this insult.

Quadra then proposed an official 'state' visit to Maquinna's residence at Tahsis.[59] Having the day before sent advance notice to Maquinna, Quadra and Vancouver, attended by officers and crew, set out in four boats on the morning of 4 September. They were received by Maquinna with pageantry, dancing, and gift-giving, the ceremonies concluding with a large feast. For this state dinner Quadra had brought with him food, cooks, and his silver service, and Vancouver supplied the drinks.[60] Maquinna constructed a table using a large house plank at which the Europeans, accompanied by the local chiefs, took their dinner. Meanwhile, the people of Tahsis enjoyed a traditional repast of tuna and dolphin stew.[61] That evening, as the guests departed Maquinna gave a speech of appreciation, in which he acknowledged the unusual honour accorded him by their visit, adding 'that neither *Wacananish*, nor any other chief, had ever received such a mark of respect and attention from any visitors.'[62] Maquinna, quite justifiably, interpreted the visit and Quadra's special efforts to provide the occasion with all the significant trappings of a full state ceremony as direct recognition by Quadra of his status and influence throughout the west coast of Vancouver Island and not just in Nootka Sound.

Unfortunately, this did not last. On 20 September 1792, Quadra called Maquinna aside to explain he was leaving the next day.[63] Not surprisingly, Maquinna was visibly upset. Having just gone out on a limb to support the Europeans, thereby risking his life and position, Maquinna

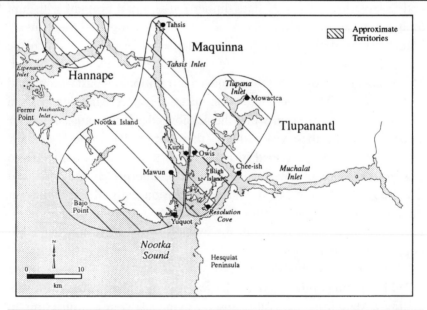

The territories and trading boundaries of Chiefs Hannape, Maquinna, and Tlupanantl

would now lose the only European ally he was ever able to rely upon. Indeed, little more than a week later, when Salvador Fidalgo arrived from Neah Bay to take command at Yuquot he refused to admit Maquinna, his brother, and Nanaquius into the commandant's house when they came to pay him the courtesy of a welcoming visit. Citing the murder of his pilot at Neah Bay as the reason, Fidalgo ordered the chiefs and all Native people to be kept at a distance and not to be allowed near the settlement without a strict watch.[64] Relations essentially stayed this way until the Spanish abandoned Yuquot in 1795.

In September 1794, Vancouver returned to Nootka Sound where he was immediately honoured by visits from Maquinna, Tlupananutl, and other chiefs.[65] Again a 'state' visit to Maquinna's village at Tahsis was undertaken. Because Maquinna's relations with the Spanish following Quadra's departure had not continued on the elevated plane of 1792, this second visit may have been even more significant than the earlier one. Maquinna appears to have interpreted Vancouver's second visit as renewed confirmation of both his social position and political policies. This is laid out in Maquinna's long welcoming speech to his guests. 'Maquinna informed the assembled crowd ... that our visit was to be considered as a great honour done to him, and that it had taken place in consequence of the civil and orderly behaviour of all inhabitants of the sound under his authority toward the English and the Spanish. This, he observed, was not the case with *Wicananish*, or any other chief whose people committed acts of violence and depredation on the vessels and their crews that visited their country; but that such behaviour was not practised at Nootka.'[66]

Maquinna's speech is explicit in its continuing commitment to peaceful intercourse with European visitors, a policy originally adopted by his father when Captain Cook arrived in Nootka Sound in 1778, and pursued ever since. However, maintaining this policy after Quadra's departure probably proved increasingly difficult, for Maquinna's speeches seemed to suggest that Vancouver's visits to his Tahsis residence had been instrumental in helping him maintain his superior standing and peaceful policies.

Wickaninish also continued to pursue his chosen policy, the acquisition of a European vessel. However, by 1793 he was pursuing this objective peacefully. During the winter of 1793-4, he agreed to purchase the schooner *Resolution* from Captain Roberts for fifty prime sea otter furs, but the *Resolution* disappeared while trading along the Columbia River before it could be delivered.[67] Wickaninish tried again in 1795. First, he offered to purchase Charles Bishop's ship *Ruby*, but Bishop declined. He then asked Bishop to bring him out a ship on his next visit, and gave him his preferred specifications.[68] Sadly, Wickaninish never received this ship either.

Although the events discussed here occurred over 200 years ago, they remain pertinent today because of the insight they offer into Nuu-chah-nulth political history. Of particular interest is the way they presage in three fundamental ways the later formation of the Nuu-chah-nulth Tribal Council. First, the confederative structure of polity in Nootka Sound, with its formal system of shared power and authority, provided a foundation on which Maquinna and Quadra were able to develop friendship, respect, and mutual trust. Similarly, it would underpin Maquinna's later relations with Vancouver. Because Maquinna was able to establish strong, cordial relationships with these European diplomats, his actions consolidated and enhanced his already elevated social position and promoted the value of power sharing and consensual political practice. Second, the extensive trade, marriages, and other social intercourse among the various west coast groups ensured that the connections necessary to plan and launch a united action against the European newcomers were both in place and workable, even though no war against the Europeans ever occurred. Third, Maquinna's powers of diplomacy and persuasion led the Nuu-chah-nulth to choose peaceful resolution of conflict over united, confrontational action.

These fundamental socio-political principles and practices were able to survive and grow over the ensuing 200 years even in the barren soils of colonization. By the 1950s, a united political body known as the Allied Tribes of the West Coast had begun to form among the Native inhabitants of Vancouver Island's west coast.[69] In 1978 it was reconstituted as the Nuu-chah-nulth Tribal Council. Each of the fourteen-member tribes was accorded equal status and authority. Unification under a common name occurred at the same time as the formal adoption of the name Nuu-chah-nulth. Characteristically, this name refers to a distinctive and common feature of the component tribes' places of origin and residence, the central mountain range which runs the length of Vancouver Island.[70]

The creation of tribal councils has been one of several strategies employed in recent decades by Canadian Native groups trying to overcome entrenched problems arising from ineffective government.[71] Among these councils the Nuu-chah-nulth Tribal Council stands out as 'one of the most established and authoritative' in Canada.[72] Yet, according to both Paul Tennant's historical account of Native politics in British Columbia and Philip Drucker's account of Native brotherhoods,[73] the Nuu-chah-nulth people were not, until very recently, major participants in the long struggle to form large umbrella political bodies to fight for Native rights, particularly land claims. It is suggested that this was because the primary factors fostering the emergence of the Nuu-chah-nulth Tribal Council were internal to the cultural and political history of the region. Its roots lie in long-established political structures and practices which valued the sharing of power, diplomacy, and consensus and not in the wider concerns of European-Native political relations in Canada.

The events of 1792 show that the Nuu-chah-nulth people were at this time unified in practice though not in name, and the principles of confederative political organization which would lay the basis for the Nuu-chah-nulth Tribal Council 200 years later were vigorously at work in west coast society in the late eighteenth century. That is not to say that, because Nuu-chah-nulth unity was prefigured in 1792, the tribal council was somehow inevitable. On the contrary, we might pay tribute to the Nuu-chah-nulth people, who, despite the oppression of 200 years of colonialism, remain strong in their ability to draw from the richness and vitality of their history in order to envision and to accomplish a positive, unified future.

Art and Exploration: The Responses of Northwest Coast Native Artists to Maritime Explorers and Fur Traders

Victoria Wyatt

Today's growing historical interest in the experiences and expressions of minorities entails more than a shift in focus: it demands a broadened methodology to embrace sources outside the written record. Often the voices of minorities are not well represented in written sources, either because their writings were not preserved in archival contexts or because – like the northwest coast Native peoples who first met Captain George Vancouver – they had developed highly effective, non-written means of expression. Such sources, including oral history, ceremony, and artwork, can provide voices that are absent from the written record.

The discussion that follows considers ways in which Native artworks may lend insight into creative responses of Native artists to contact with non-Native peoples in the late eighteenth and early nineteenth centuries. Long before they met George Vancouver and other Europeans, Native peoples on the northwest coast used artistic expression to keep lasting records of philosophies, histories, and genealogies. Along with song, dance, and oral tradition, the visual arts dramatically recorded spiritual and cultural information. Artists responded imaginatively to the arrival of non-Native maritime fur traders and explorers, embracing new opportunities to experiment artistically. Their choices as artists – what they chose to perpetuate and what they chose to change – reflect responses to these early encounters.

The period of maritime exploration prompted three types of responses – two which do not show fundamental change, and one which does. The first response is the one that was both most obvious and most pervasive – the artists' use of new materials. In the late eighteenth and early nineteenth centuries, artists gained access to foreign materials in previously unknown quantities. These trade goods included iron, which made wood carving more efficient; wool cloth, which stays warm when wet; and foreign copper, buttons, metal coins, and mirrors. Some of these materials may have been available in limited quantities through indirect trade prior to direct encounters with Europeans. Their impact has been documented in several works and does not need much attention, except to note the ways in which northwest coast Native artists experimented with these trade goods.[1]

Artists used materials creatively to add new twists to already existing artistic traditions, but they did not radically change those traditions. Artists incorporated new materials into tools and utensils without altering basic designs. Metal barbs replaced bone barbs in halibut hooks, but the construction of the hook – and the tradition of decorating it – remained the same. Similarly, in ceremonial art, the new materials embellished well-established artistic themes. Artists had long used abalone shells and sea mammal teeth to highlight some masks; now they added metals, coins, and mirror fragments for the same effect. A pair of elaborate Chinese coins mark the eyes in one Tlingit mask – and the effect in firelight would be dramatic – while the other features of the mask, and the masking tradition itself, remain the same.

Trade materials inspired artists to experiment with some new art forms that emulated the roles, if not the appearance, of Native ones. For example, button blankets emerged in the mid-nineteenth century. Made of wool trade cloth, these blankets are decorated with mother-of-pearl buttons in designs often signifying family crests. The new trade goods gave birth to a new type of blanket, but the innovation did not reflect a fundamentally new artistic concept. Rather, button blankets perpetuated a tradition seen in the woven Chilkat blankets shown in Figures 1 and 2 – the tradition of displaying a crest design in a blanket form to be worn on ceremonial occasions.[2]

This is not to say that button blankets brought no notable changes. They probably made crest blankets much more accessible to people in a wider range of social and economic status. The Chilkat blankets were primarily woven by skilled Tlingit artists, who traded them southward

Figure 1. Three Tlingit leaders in Angoon Alaska, c. 1900

for high prices. In contrast, button blankets required no knowledge of weaving and could more easily be made by the people who would wear them. Although this probably contributed to their popularity, the blankets undoubtedly owed part of their appeal to their fitting into an existing costume tradition.

In button blankets, trade goods form designs in Native styles to be worn in Native contexts. Despite their greater accessibility, the button blankets did not render Native artworks obsolete. Artists continued to make and wear Chilkat blankets, and people wore indigenous artworks along with new materials in ceremonial contexts. The photograph in Figure 1, taken around 1900, shows Tlingit men wearing Chilkat blankets and tunics along with a vest and a neck ornament made of trade wool and beads. These men combined new and old artistic materials to create a single costume.

Figure 1 also illustrates another phenomenon that reflects the integration of new materials into existing artistic traditions. Northwest coast artists were very interested in artworks from other regions brought by European and Euro-American trading ships. Occasionally they incorporated these artworks into existing ceremonial traditions. The feather cape shown at the right of Figure 1 was made by Natives of the Society

Figure 2. Tlingit man in Klukwan, Alaska, c. 1985

Islands. Presumably a non-Native maritime trader obtained it there and brought it to the northwest coast. A Tlingit clan in Angoon, the Deisheetaan, made it one of their valued artistic possession, displaying it with other clan artworks.[3]

The Society Islands cape reflects a one-of-a-kind exchange, but some non-Native artworks became fairly standard ceremonial items in some regions of the northwest coast. Tlingit traders snapped up Chinese camphorwood chests from maritime fur traders who bought them in China. These pigskin-covered chests were often brightly decorated with floral designs.[4] A camphorwood chest can be seen to the right in Figure 2 where it is partially covered by a Chilkat blanket.

Like other peoples on the central and northern coasts, Tlingit artists made their own ceremonial storage chests using a bentwood technique, decorating them with complex, painted designs in a distinctive style known today as Northern Formline. The Chinese camphorwood chests had a different artistic style, but they fit well into the tradition of elaborately decorated storage chests. Tlingit leaders used the camphorwood chests precisely as they used their own bentwood storage chests, that is, for storing clan items. In Figure 2, taken around 1895, a Tlingit man in Klukwan poses surrounded by clan possessions, including both a carved ceremonial chest and a camphorwood chest. He includes a United States flag in this display of clan art – another example of borrowing a non-Native artwork.

Northwest coast Native artists eagerly explored the use of trade materials in their visual arts. They also incorporated certain foreign artworks into their artistic and ceremonial traditions. Neither the trade goods nor the foreign artworks forced new artistic traditions or altered the cultural meanings of artistic expression. Native art from the maritime fur trade era reflects an openness toward experimentation; but the artists used new materials and new artworks to support, rather than to challenge, existing artistic traditions

Other catalysts *did* lead artists to experiment with new art forms. This was the second response. When Native peoples obtained new trade goods and habits from non-Native traders, they needed new accessories. Often they could make these goods less expensively and more efficiently than they could buy them. Artists did not copy the prototypes available from Europeans, but took this new opportunity to create functional works of art.

Traditionally, northwest coast artists made functional and utilitarian items into works of art. They decorated fish hooks, trap sticks, spoons, weaving and carving tools, baskets, cradleboards, clothing, and almost every other necessity of daily life. No boundaries separated 'art' from 'life.' The images on tools and utensils carried important philosophical and cultural meanings, daily reminding their users of these messages.

When artists developed new accessories in response to new needs, they decorated these new art forms – like their old ones – with images potent with spiritual and cultural meaning, blurring the boundaries

Figure 3. Tlingit powder measure of mountain goat horn

between 'tool' and 'art.' A fine example is the Tlingit powder measure of mountain goat horn illustrated in Figure 3. When northwest coast peoples obtained firearms from maritime fur traders, they began making powder measures and shot pouches, incorporating these new accessories into their existing artistic traditions. This Tlingit powder measure, now in the Princeton University Museum of Natural History, was collected in Yakutat around 1886 and probably post-dates the maritime fur trade, but it exemplifies an accessory transformed into an exquisite work of art. Artists were accustomed to steaming and bending mountain goat horn into spoons, and the same technique is used here. The image, an eagle, may represent a family crest and is integrated so gracefully that it is neither a powder measure decorated as an eagle nor an eagle decorated as a powder measure; the boundaries between its form – the tool – and its content – the image – are brilliantly merged.

For certain firearm accessories, artists simply used already existing art forms in new contexts. Some Tlingit shot pouches, woven of spruce root, were composed of a cylinder that slides inside a slightly larger cylinder. They could be woven in any size, creating a lightweight, durable, and watertight container for purposes such as holding bird down, which was distributed at ceremonies to welcome guests.

Pipes were another new art form developed to meet new needs. Although some northwest coast Natives chewed tobacco before they met Europeans, they learned to smoke from foreigners. For this new habit they needed pipes, and artists followed the time-honoured tradition of decorating functional objects. Designs on pipes came in many forms. Some closely resembled existing artworks, such as raven rattles.[5] Others show great experimentation, depicting narratives such as the Haida account of the discovery of the human race in a clamshell. In both cases, they perpetuate the tradition of making three-dimensional utensils into artworks with great spiritual and cultural significance.

New customs needed new accessories, and artists rose creatively to the challenge. They developed new art forms for those needs, but did so using imagery and ideas from existing traditions. The new artworks did not threaten the role of art in societies nor question the messages that artworks conveyed.

The employment of new materials for artwork and new contexts for artistic expression speaks of the artists' eagerness to explore materials and customs introduced by foreigners. It also suggests that these explorations reflected no intent to depart radically from artistic and cultural traditions, that experimentation was not a rejection of tradition, and that the artists' cultures were flexible enough to accommodate new influences without being threatened by them. Since Natives on the northwest coast had traded with other Natives for thousands of years, this comes as no surprise. The lack of cataclysmic change in the artwork suggests that this previous trade had prepared northwest coast Natives to deal with foreign influences effectively.

But what of artwork that *is* radically different? What historical conclusions can we draw from art styles that *are* new? These questions are answered by examining a third response: the development of artworks depicting non-Native peoples. Such a development could reflect these artists' attitudes toward foreigners. Stylistic anomalies may give us some glimpse of Native voices not on the written record, although conclusions can never be more than speculative.

Departures from the common stylistic choices are significant because they reflect philosophies. Artworks in northwest coast societies often served in place of writing to keep records and convey ideas. Artists developed art styles that expressed in visual form concepts being conveyed through the content.

On the northern parts of the northwest coast, individuals belonged to hereditary clans. These clans had animal crests that members displayed to identify their genealogy. Similar to European coats of arms, the crests also recorded information about ancestors. The right to claim the crest often stemmed from an ancestor's encounter with that animal spirit – an encounter that took place when the boundaries between humans, animals, and spirits were more fluid than they are today; when humans, animals, and spirits could transform into each other and sometimes even intermarry. The crest image speaks of the fluidity of boundaries and of relationships between past and present, ancestors and descendants.

In many regions of the coast, ceremonial artworks empowered dancers to change identities and travel back in time to re-experience encounters between animals and spirits. Some dramatic masks used by the Kwakwakawaq people in the *tseyka* winter ceremonies helped descendants relive an encounter between an ancestor and a spirit known as Bakhbakwalanooksiwey. Described much too simply, in these ceremonies the performers portrayed the experiences of an ancestor who left his village and, in his wanderings, met a wild spirit called Bakhbakwalanooksiwey attended by supernatural cannibal birds (represented in the tseyka by masks). Eventually the ancestor escaped from Bakhbakwalanooksiwey and his attendants and returned to his village in a wild, almost non-human state. He had to be tamed – to recross that boundary between humans, animals, and spirits. Once tamed, he taught his people the dances he had learned from the cannibal birds. When a descendant of that ancestor performed those dances, the presence of the masks helped them to relive the ancestor's experience and, in that moment of the dance, to collapse the boundaries between humans, animals, and spirits; between past and present; and between ancestor and descendant.

Some artworks facilitated communication with spirits. Some enabled shamans, or spiritual healers, to communicate with spirit helpers. Artworks such as the delicate, yet elaborate, Tsimshian shamans' charms helped spiritual healers bridge those boundaries between humans, animals, and spirits. Among the Coast Salish, each individual had spirit helpers as fellow travellers throughout life. Images on artwork would be very personal to that individual and would facilitate communication with the spirit helpers. There is much reference to collapsing boundaries. One rattle of mountain sheep horn, for example, shows a face; its eyes, mouth, and cheek are made up of other animals, all sharing the same boundaries. Such artworks simultaneously help their users to cross boundaries to relate to spirits and illustrate how boundaries are shared through the artistic style used.

Thus, artworks on the northwest coast have various spiritual roles. The artistic styles used in northwest coast art had to enable the artworks to convey a specific spiritual or philosophical message – but, as the art is a functional one, the style must also be compatible with the shape to be decorated. The artist must combine the necessary form with the philosophical content, and in a way that does not compromise statements about shared essences and shared boundaries. The various art styles that developed served these needs.

The spruce root hat (see Figure 4) shows the shape typically worn by

Figure 4. Haida spruce root hat, with frog design, painted by Charles Edenshaw

the Haida in the nineteenth century. An artist from a Western art tradition would depict a frog on a hat of this shape by probably painting an outline of a frog, and it would be easily recognizable as such – but there would be no harmony, no points of convergence, no shared boundaries between the form of the hat and its content. Instead, the Haida artists identified the few common characteristics between a frog and this hat – their three-dimensionality and their symmetry – and emphasized them. Wrapping the frog around the hat, they collapsed the boundaries between form and function.

To collapse these boundaries – to make a statement about the nature of boundaries – the artistic style must emphasize the boundaries themselves. An art that emphasizes *lines* is well suited to do so. In the northern northwest coast, a two-dimensional artistic system now known as Northern Formline developed at least 1,000 years ago.[6] In this system, lines of varying widths and curvatures define the outlines and body parts of crest animals. The lines converge and diverge to describe standard elements that play similar roles in all species. Thus, ovoids commonly represent eyes and joints, and U-forms commonly represent ears, noses, fins, and flukes. Combinations of elements serve important purposes: ovoids and U-forms together represent the pectoral fin of a killer whale or the wing of an eagle. All animals are made of the same elements, the same visual vocabulary.

A system that uses the same formations of lines – the same types of boundaries – to represent the body parts of all animals is very well adapted to making statements about shared boundaries. The Haida bowl in Figure 5 speaks eloquently about common identities. The whale, whose head is represented on one end, has its pectoral fin described by an ovoid and a U-form on the side of the bowl. The same ovoid and U-form signify the wing of the eagle, whose head is represented on the bowl's opposite end. The ovoid doubles as the joint in the fin of the whale and the joint in the wing of the eagle, and the U-form reflects both a fluke and feathers.

This bowl literally shares or collapses boundaries. It vividly demonstrates that two things really can coexist at the same time. The same collapsing of boundaries is addressed by art that records ancestral encounters with spirits, such as crest designs; art that collapses the boundaries between past and present, ancestor and descendant, such as the tseyka dance

Figure 5. Haida wood bowl, with whale and eagle design

mask; and art that helps people cross boundaries into the spiritual world to communicate with spirit helpers, such as art used by spiritual healers.

The art styles developed on the northwest coast are designed to speak well to this concept of shared and collapsible boundaries. Sometimes it is subtle and sometimes it is very literal. Perhaps the best-known examples are Kwakwakawaq transformation masks, which open and close to allow the dancer to change identities instantaneously.

If art styles convey philosophical messages, then departures from those art styles may make very deliberate philosophical statements. On the northwest coast there are some intriguing artworks depicting Europeans that do appear to depart from tradition. Not all artists who depicted Europeans used different art styles – in fact, a statistical study would probably show that most did not. However, such departures may still be deliberate even if artists who chose that route were in a minority. Artists are individuals, and individuals' choices can be significant even if they are the exception rather than the norm.

Haida argillite carvings made for sale to sailors in the mid-nineteenth century invite such speculation.[7] Haida artists began selling argillite carvings to foreigners as early as the 1820s, perhaps seeking a new trade commodity as the sea otter populations declined. Many, such as the pipe in Figure 6, showed images from Native cosmology. In these pipes, several presences intertwine, the boundaries between them fluid

Figure 6. Haida argillite panel pipe

Figure 7. Haida argillite ship panel pipe

and amorphous. It is difficult to tell where one entity begins and the other ends. Each presence takes its identity from its relationship to the whole. The three-dimensional art style employed in these pipes conveys concepts that complement the two-dimensional Northern Formline style.

Other argillite pipes, such as that in Figure 7, depict non-Native people. Some of these – not all, but some – adopt a style that contrasts dramatically with that commonly used for images from cosmology.[8] In these pipes, the Europeans are stiff and autonomous. Even when people touch, it is obvious where one entity begins and the other ends. There is no sense of shared boundaries, of commonality or community.

This stiffness and lack of fluidity appears in Haida argillite carvings other than pipes. Sculptures of sea captains, popular in the mid-nineteenth century, were often rigid, as were some freestanding sculptures showing Europeans in other poses.

Some Haida artists who depicted non-Natives in argillite abandoned the art style that emphasized shared boundaries and shared essences. If an art style seems to have developed to express a certain philosophy, and if some artists chose a different art style to portray images outside their cosmology, then perhaps these artists are suggesting that the philosophy conveyed through the art style is incompatible with the depiction of foreigners. Perhaps these artists did not see Europeans as part of a community, people able to bridge boundaries to communicate with the other presences in the tangible and spiritual world. Perhaps they felt Europeans could not be realistically portrayed in a style designed to emphasize communal relationships, shared essences, and the collapsing of boundaries.

This is clearly speculation and should never be presented as anything else. A number of questions suggest themselves before this argument can go much further. Are we looking at images of non-Natives made by just a few artists or many? These questions may not be crucial, as artistic choices can reflect an individual artist's attitudes even if only one artist made that choice. Questions of how many become critical only if we seek to determine an entire society's attitudes by looking at the expressions of a few – never a very safe exercise.

However, it *is* essential to ask whether the artists were simply unskilled at portraying unfamiliar subject matter. After all, even such accomplished European artists as John Webber were a bit awkward at representing Native art and subject matter. Possibly this explains the rigid Europeans, but it is neither a satisfactory nor a satisfying explanation. Haida artists were accustomed to representing a range of subject matter in their traditional art styles; the styles, which emphasized shared essences, gave artists versatility.

Furthermore, we know about some later experimentation on the northwest coast with images from non-Native cosmologies that was very successful. One such image is the late nineteenth-century sculpture of the Sphinx, carved in wood by a Haida artist, probably either Simeon Stilthda or Gwaytihl, now in the British Museum.[9] Some artists also experimented with *crossing boundaries* between Native and non-Native cosmology. The wooden sculpture in Figure 8, also by Gwaytihl, shows a Haida spiritual healer merging with a European angel.[10] The shaman/angel wears the apron of a spiritual healer painted in Northern Formline design, and has angel's wings, resembling those of Christian angels, which are decorated loosely with Northern formline elements. There is no way to confirm that this figure represents a merging of Native and Christian symbolism, but other artworks also appear to effect such a synthesis. A late nineteenth-century argillite figure based on the Mother Bear narrative – in which a woman marries a bear and gives birth to bear cubs – depicts a mother with human and bear characteristics suckling a

Figure 8. Haida wood sculpture of a spiritual healer

child while seated in a stylized Madonna-like pose.[11]

Clearly, some artists were very thoughtful about the way they portrayed non-Native concepts: it is reasonable to suggest that many were. Because artists were so accomplished in emphasizing the shared characteristics of very different living things – the fin that is also a fluke, the nose that is also a bird – they certainly could have shown the same sort of commonality, of shared essence, in non-Natives if they felt it was appropriate.

The images of Europeans that do not reflect traditional styles are probably not simply the fumblings of unpractised artists. They do not seem like failed attempts to integrate new images into an old style. Rather, they are departures from that style entirely. If there is a philosophical significance to the original style, there is also a significance when some artists choose not to use it.

This line of inquiry is, and always will be, clearly speculative. Many images of non-Natives – perhaps most – did follow more traditional art styles. Nevertheless, this case study has suggested that questions about the meaning behind stylistic choices are worth investigating; that it is worth asking whether nineteenth-century voices, so absent from the written record, can speak to us through artwork.

As we move toward a history that includes the thoughts and experiences of those peoples who are now minorities, we need to seek their voices in all their media of expression. Examinations of Native artwork can be very helpful to historians who study Native-white encounters. The absence of widespread major change in artistic styles and contexts during the maritime fur trade suggests that artists did not reject their heritage or their ethnic identity, even as they sought new trade goods and explored new customs. Against this backdrop of continuity, the change that does occur – the depiction of some non-Natives in an anomalous style – seems strikingly significant.

Artworks demand a different type of analysis for historians: the questions they address may differ from those addressed by written sources, and the information they suggest can never be termed 'answers.' However, they give some valuable angles for seeking Native voices; angles that, for historians studying Native history, are absolutely essential. Much more than written language, art was a vehicle of self-expression for nineteenth-century northwest Natives. We must listen for these peoples in their own modes of communication – not solely our own – if we seek to hear their voices.

Kidnapped: Tuki and Huri's Involuntary Visit to Norfolk Island in 1793

Anne Salmond

At the Hokianga discussions of the Treaty of Waitangi signed in 1840 between Maori chiefs and the British Crown, Mohi Tawhai (a local chief) spoke to the assembled gathering of Europeans and Maori and said: 'Let the tongue of everyone be free to speak: but what of it. What will be the end? Our sayings will sink to the bottom like a stone, but your sayings will float light, like the wood of the whau tree, and always remain to be seen. Am I telling lies?' The image was that of the net – a seine net that might be 1,000 metres long, with whau-wood floats along its top edge and sinker stones woven into a seam along its base. Like the net of memory, the seine was not cast at random; and the combined labour of many people was needed to haul it up.

In some ways Mohi Tawhai's metaphorical statement was prophetic. Maori commentaries and points of view have often been forgotten in New Zealand when popular tradition and historians have cast their narrative nets. The tapu-laden talk of tribal elders has been concealed or is inaccessible, while stories based on European documents have floated 'light, like the wood of the whau tree, and always remain to be seen.' This may have been inevitable, for parts of tribal knowledge have been closely guarded, and documents can have the advantage of a vivid proximity to the events being described. On the other hand, not everything in tribal history is hidden, and many early documents in Maori as well as those in English still survive. If history is to be faithful it cannot afford to be ignorant, and events that involved protagonists from different societies cannot be fairly interpreted from just one point of view.

The unpredictable, dramatic, action-packed first meetings between Maori and Europeans provide a case in point. From one contemporary perspective they were simply puzzling, extraordinary interludes in the lives of various tribal communities. The ships – floating islands, mythological 'birds,' or canoes full of *tupua* ('goblins') – came into this bay or that, shot local people or presented them with strange gifts, were welcomed or pelted with rocks, and after a short time went away again and were largely forgotten. Local comment might well have echoed a proverb quoted by Ngai-te-Rangi chiefs when they said farewell to an early governor of New Zealand in 1853: 'Haere and koe ko ngaa pipi o te aaria; ka noho maatou ko ngaa pipi o te whakatakere' ('You go, the shallow-rooting shellfish, while we, the shellfish of deep waters, stay behind'). From another contemporary vantage point, however, that of their seventeenth- and eighteenth-century European chroniclers, the same encounters were simply episodes in the story of Europe's 'discovery' of the world – more voyages to add to the great collections of 'Voyages' that had already been made. The genre of discovery tales was an ancient one in Europe, with a well-worn narrative line – explorers ventured into unknown seas; found new lands and named their coastal features; described exotic plants, animals, and inhabitants; and survived attacks by tattooed savages (or worse still, cannibals) with spears. These stories were very popular with ordinary people at the time, for they defined Europeans as 'civilized' in contrast with the 'savages' and 'barbarians' to be found elsewhere, and told exciting tales of giants and 'opposite-footers,' 'Indians' with outlandish customs, lost continents where people cooked in vessels of gold and silver, and humans with tails or the heads of dogs.

After 200 years or more of shared history in New Zealand, one would have thought that scholars might have considered each of these interpretative traditions, if only to set them to question each other. By and large this has not happened. Modern histories of these first meetings, although meticulous and well documented, clearly trace their lineage from the ancient European discovery tales. Europeans are depicted as being in charge of the drama, the explorers are the heroes, while Maori either sit as passive spectators or act anonymously behind cloaks and tattooed masks. Just as clearly, though, this is not the way it was. Both Maori and European protagonists were active in these meetings and fully human, despite their mythologies of each other, and followed their own practical and political agendas, quite unlike those of their modern-day descendants in many ways.

For the sake of accuracy as well as fairness, the story of the early meetings between Maori and Europeans in New Zealand – and that of European 'discovery' in general – has to be rethought. This requires an ethnographic approach to the past, reflecting upon manuscripts in ways drawn from tribal knowledge as well as European history, and grounding the sayings of both local people and Europeans about these meetings in the physical detail of their daily lives. The search is for an intellectual middle ground, a place at the interface between European explorers and local communities, a 'border zone' to quote the anthropologist Renato Rosaldo, where one might grasp something of the cross-cultural complexities of these early encounters and the creative or destructive implications of their dealings with one another.

In the case of the kidnapping of two young Maori men by Vancouver's supply ship, the *Daedalus*, off the Cavalli Islands (in the north of New Zealand) in 1793, the encounter was fraught with paradox and the long-term implications were profound.

George Vancouver, in his Introduction to *A Voyage of Discovery to the North Pacific Ocean and Round the World*, began with a paragraph in praise of European exploration:

> In contemplating the rapid progress of improvement in the sciences, and the general diffusion of knowledge since the commencement of the eighteenth century, we are unavoidably led to observe, with admiration, that active spirit of discovery by means of which the remotest regions of the earth have been explored; a friendly communication opened with their inhabitants; and various commodities, of a most valuable nature, contributing either to relieve their necessities, or augment their comforts, introduced among the less-enlightened part of our species. A mutual intercourse has also been established, in many instances, on the solid basis of a reciprocity of benefits; and the productive labour of the civilized world has found new markets for the disposal of its manufactures.[1]

According to Vancouver, 'the less-enlightened part of our species' characteristically contributed food and refreshments, or the skins of hunted animals and similar goods to these exchanges. In return they received from the 'civilized world' friendship, valuable commodities, and above all in the Georgian era, knowledge: 'It should seem, that the reign of George the Third had been reserved by the Great Disposer of all things, for the glorious task of establishing the grand key-stone to that expansive arch, over which the arts and sciences should pass to the furthermost corners of the earth, for the instruction and happiness of the most lowly children of nature.'[2]

Yet Tuki and Huru were kidnapped and taken to Norfolk Island to teach the convicts there how to work the local flax – for the instruction and happiness, if you like, of the most lowly children of England. Their extraordinary experiences in Norfolk Island in 1793, as tutors for 'civilized men,' captured yet living free and in friendship with the governor in an island prison, were to have profound and long-lasting effects on Maori-European relations in New Zealand.

The almost casual way in which the entire Pacific basin had become incorporated into the strategic thinking of Vancouver's Admiralty masters is evident from Vancouver's final set of instructions. Drafted in England on 20 August 1791, these were dispatched to Vancouver on the northwest coast of America via the *Daedalus*, supply ship to his expedition. In these instructions, Lieutenant Hergest, the commander of the *Daedalus*, was required to leave England with a shipload of provisions and supplies, and to deliver these with the additional instructions to Vancouver at Nootka Sound on the west coast of Canada. If Vancouver was not at Nootka Sound, Hergest was instructed to find him in the Sandwich (Hawai'ian) Islands or elsewhere, to accompany the expedition to Nootka Sound, if necessary, to assist in receiving back British land and buildings from the Spanish, and then to go south west across the Pacific to Port Jackson in Australia, with livestock and other supplies for the convict colony there. On his way to Port Jackson, Hergest was required 'to touch at New Zealand ... from whence he is to use his best endeavours to take with him one or two flax-dressers, in order that the new settlers at Port Jackson may, if possible, be properly instructed in the management of that valuable plant.'[3]

The Admiralty's interest in New Zealand flax had originally been sparked by Cook's first voyage to the Pacific, when the *Endeavour* with her contingent of scientists and artists circumnavigated those islands in

1769-70. In New Zealand, Joseph Banks and Dr Solander described the plant botanically for the first time, and Banks also described Maori weaving techniques and collected hanks of processed flax fibre (*muka*), cordage, and finely woven garments. Cook and Banks both drew attention to the potential uses of New Zealand flax for naval cordage and canvas,[4] and this, together with their reports of forests of large trees fit for masts and spars, ensured the Admiralty's strategic interest in the islands.

By 1791, however, the story had become more complicated. After circumnavigating New Zealand, the *Endeavour* had visited Botany Bay on the south coast of Australia in April 1770. Nine years later, when the British government was casting around for places to exile convicted criminals (because the newly independent Americans would no longer take them, and the British hulks and jails were packed and pestilential), Banks appeared before a House of Commons committee and suggested Botany Bay as a likely destination.[5] A convict colony was finally established in 1788 at Port Jackson just north of Botany Bay, with an eastern outpost at Norfolk Island, found by Cook during his second voyage in 1774.

The British Government hoped that these 'thief colonies' would soon become self-sufficient for food and clothing, and New Zealand flax or its Norfolk Island equivalent seemed the best local source for weaving fibre. Three years after their establishment, however, the colonies were still desperately short of both food and clothing, and many convicts were dressed in rags.[6] Maori warriors were a formidable obstacle to establishing any flax trade with New Zealand. In fact, Arthur Phillip, the first governor of New South Wales, had suggested handing over any convict who committed murder or sodomy to them 'and let them eat him. The dread of this will operate much stronger than the fear of death.'[7] Nor had any adequate way yet been found to process the flax on Norfolk Island.[8]

Philip Gidley King, the commandant of Norfolk Island, had been pleading since his island prison was established for European flax-dressers (presumably convicts) to be sent to New Zealand to study Maori weaving,[9] and then to Norfolk Island to teach the convicts to work the local flax. This was regarded as impractical and probably too dangerous, but King was a persistent man. In December 1790 he arrived in London on leave, and on January 1791 wrote a report (backed up by discussions with both Lord Grenville, the secretary of state, and Sir Joseph Banks, president of the Royal Society and the Admiralty's trusted advisor on

Pacific colonies and exploration), which put forward another suggestion: 'The Flax Plant of New Zealand, grows spontaneously, in many Parts of [Norfolk] Island, but mostly abounds on the Sea Coast, where there is a very great Quantity of it ... Every Method has been tried to work it, but, I much fear that, until a Native of New Zealand, can be carried to Norfolk Island, the Method of dressing that valuable Commodity will not be known. Could that be obtained, I have no doubt but Norfolk Island would soon clothe the Inhabitants of New South Wales.'[10]

In April 1791 at Tenerife, on his way back to Norfolk Island on the *Gorgon,* King repeated this plea in a letter to Under Secretary Evan Nepean and spelled out the precise, practical nature of the problem: 'Should the manufacturing of the flax-plant on Norfolk Island be thought an object, which it must be, were it only to cloath those who are now there, two or three New Zealanders would be necessary, to show how the operation of separating the flaxy from the vegetable part of the flax is performed ... Without that assistance I do not think we shall succeed, as every method we could devise has been tried already, but without success.'[11]

Later in the voyage, in July, King met Captain Vancouver at the Cape of Good Hope and asked him 'if it should be in his power during his Stay in these Seas, to procure Two or three New Zealanders of that Country, that it would be an Act of Publick Utility to send them hither.'[12] This time King's persistence finally paid off. Vancouver's additional instructions were drafted one month later in London.

The ship that carried Tuki and Huru from New Zealand to Port Jackson was the *Daedalus,* a Whitby-built ship of 310 tons chartered as transport for Vancouver's expedition.[13] Lieutenant Hergest, a close friend of Vancouver's, had been appointed as its agent (the title then given to a lieutenant in charge of a supply ship). Unfortunately, at this stage, detailed information on the *Daedalus* is lacking. Neither the ship's muster roll and manifest, nor the ship's log (which Vancouver evidently had when he drafted his *A Voyage to the North Pacific Ocean and Round the World),*[14] nor any other logs or journals from the voyage can be located. The *Daedalus'* voyage from England to the Marquesas, Hawai'i, Nootka Sound, the west coast of North America, back to the Marquesas, Tahiti, and then to New Zealand and Port Jackson has therefore to be reconstructed from secondary reports by Vancouver, Governor Phillip at Port Jackson, and others.

Vancouver's ships, the *Discovery* and *Chatham,* had left England in April 1791, headed for Nootka Sound via the Cape of Good Hope. En route they touched at King George III Sound on the south coast of Australia, and then Dusky Bay on the south coast of New Zealand. The *Chatham* then visited Rekohu, which the British named Chatham Island after the first lord of the Admiralty at that time.[15] The two ships met again at Tahiti and sailed for Hawai'i, where Vancouver hoped to meet the *Daedalus.* The supply ship had left England in late August and sailed via Cape Horn to the Marquesas, where some of the supplies on board were ruined in a fire caused by spontaneous combustion of improperly stowed stores. The *Daedalus* did not reach Hawai'i until May 1792, almost two months after the *Discovery* and *Chatham* had left the islands, and Lieutenant Hergest, the astronomer William Gooch, and a sailor were killed on their first landing at Oahu. After this disaster, the *Daedalus* left Hawai'i under the command of its master, Thomas New, and sailed for Nootka Sound, finally meeting Vancouver there on 28 August 1792. Here the supply ship's stores were restored, and Lieutenant James Hanson, second in command of the *Chatham,* was appointed to succeed Hergest as her commander.

Negotiations began at Nootka Sound between Vancouver and Bodega y Quadra, the Spanish commandant of San Blas and California, for the return of land and buildings at Nootka Sound claimed by the British. These discussions continued at Monterey, California, when the expedition arrived there on 26 November. Diplomatic courtesies included an exchange of charts,[16] perhaps including a version of Surville's 1769 chart of Tokerau (Doubtless Bay) in New Zealand. Quadra also offered cattle and sheep for transport to Port Jackson, and Spanish sailors to make up the complement of the *Daedalus,* which had been depleted by death and desertion. The *Daedalus* was partly unloaded at Monterey, some sick sailors were discharged into the ship for passage to Port Jackson, and twelve cows, six bulls, twelve ewes, and six rams[17] were housed in stalls built on board. On 29 December Hanson received his orders from Vancouver, with letters for Governor Phillip at Port Jackson[18] instructing the *Daedalus* to proceed to the Marquesas for food, water, and refreshment and, from there, to Tahiti to procure pigs and hens as well as to pick up twenty-one English sailors stranded when the transport *Matilda* was wrecked on a reef. After Tahiti he was to proceed to

a bay lately visited and surveyed by the French in the northern part of
New Zealand, called by Captain Cook, Doubtless Bay ... a sketch of
which is herewith inclosed for your information ... At [Doubtless] or
any port near the north extremity of New Zealand ... you are from
thence to use your best endeavours to take with you one or two of the
natives of that country versed in the operations necessary for the manufacture of the flax-plant of which their garments are mostly made, for
the purpose, if possible, of instructing the new settlers at Port Jackson
in the management of that very valuable plant, and this being a subject
of no small importance you are to pay particular attention to the
effecting it, in the execution whereof the native of the Sandwich Islands
you have on board may be essentially serviceable from his speaking
nearly the same language, you will therefore endeavour to attach him
as much as possible to your interest by attention and civil treatment.[19]

The 'native of the Sandwich Islands' on board the *Daedalus* was
almost certainly Kalehua (Tarehooa or 'Jack') from Kauai, a bilingual
sailor who had spent six months crewing on an American fur-trading
ship before joining the *Discovery* at Hawai'i in March 1792.[20] The
Daedalus sailed from Monterey on 29 December, and after visiting the
Marquesas and Tahiti (where seventy pigs were purchased and one of the
surviving sailors from the *Matilda* came on board),[21] Hanson set sail for
New Zealand. By the time *Daedalus* arrived off the Cavalli Islands, it was
a floating piggery. Of the other animals on board, only one cow, three
ewes, and a ram eventually survived the journey to Port Jackson.

It has often been assumed, in keeping with Vancouver's instructions,
that Lieutenant Hanson now proceeded to Doubtless Bay, in New
Zealand. Furthermore, Lieutenant-Governor King later identified the
place where 'two Natives of New Zealand' were captured as 'Knuckle
Point,' that is, Karikari Peninsula on the northern side of Tokerau
(Doubtless Bay).[22] As no journals or logs from the *Daedalus* have been
found, they cannot fix the precise time and place where Tuki and Huru
were taken.

The best surviving European account of the capture of Tuki and Huru
comes from Edward Bell in his *Chatham* journal, when he reported a conversation at dinner on the *Discovery* between Mr Puget and Lieutenant
Hanson in Nootka Sound on 25 October 1793. According to Bell,

At New Zealand they did not anchor, their business at this place was to endeavour to get two or three of the Natives to go with them to Botany Bay, for the purpose of cultivating the Flax plant, but as the Natives came off to the vessel in great numbers, and knowing them to have the character of a very troublesome, daring, insolent people, Lieut. Hanson did not think it prudent to stop to make a strict scrutiny into the abilities of any particular people, more especially as the crew of the *Daedalus*, at all times weak, but then were much more so, from a number of sick among them, he therefore by presents inveigled two young men out of a Canoe, and taking them below, under pretence of giving them something more, he instantly made all sail; Victuals were given to these poor fellows, and different methods used to keep their attention alive below for a couple of hours, when going on Deck, instead of finding themselves in the same place as when they Came on board, and their canoe alongside, into which they were ready to jump – to their inexpressible grief and astonishment they found themselves some Leagues from the Land, and no Canoe to get on shore in; In a little time they appeared contented.[23]

When he wrote this journal entry, Bell argued that what Hanson had done was justified, because 'a large ship, valuably laden, poorly manned, and with the best part of the crew sick, must act with prudence,' even though this might not meet with 'the feelings of these people, who ... Philosophise by the Fireside.' In 1815, though, he wrote a marginal note to this entry, 'I dont think so now 1815, I am 20 years older.'[24]

Bell's account, although revealing European attitudes, does not indicate precisely where these two young men were taken. The best evidence on this comes from Tuki and Huru's own description of their capture, as reported second hand (and no doubt with gaps and errors due to cross-linguistic confusion) by Lieutenant-Governor King on Norfolk Island in November 1793.[25]

According to this account, 'Tooke' (Tuki) was visiting 'Woodoo' (Huru) at his home near the Bay of Islands when a European vessel was sighted far out to sea. The ship was close to two inhabited islands, 'Komootu-kowa' and 'Opanake,' which can be identified as Motukawanui and Panaaki, two of the Cavalli Islands north of the Bay. Seized with curiosity, Huru's chief 'Povoreck' (Poho-reka?), Tuki, Huru, Huru's brother, one of Huru's wives, and a priest launched several canoes and all went out to the largest island, Motu-kawanui. There they were joined by the local chief 'Tee-ah-wor-rock,' Huru's father-in-law, and his son, who controlled Panaaki at that time. The canoes then went on to the *Daedalus* to see whether they could obtain iron, and according to King's account from Tuki and Huru:

> They were some time about the Ship, before the Canoe in which Tooke and Woodoo were, ventured alongside; when a number of Iron Tools and other Articles were given into the Canoe, the Agent Lieutenant Hanson (of whose kindness to them they speak in the highest terms) Invited and pressed them, to go on board, which Tooke and Woodoo were anxious to do immediately, but were prevented by the persuasion of their Countrymen; at length [they] went on Board, & according to their Expression, they were blinded by the Curious things they saw; Lieutenant Hanson prevailed on them to go below, where they Eat some meat; At this time the Ship made sail, One of them saw the Canoes astern, and perceiving the Ship was leaving them, they both became frantic with Grief, & broke the Cabbin Windows, with an intention of leaping Over Board, but were prevented; whilst the Canoes were in hearing, they advised Povoreek to make the best of his way home for fear of his being taken also.[26]

Lieutenant Hanson was probably wise not to land in the Bay of Islands. At the time the *Daedalus* arrived, the Bay was populated by perhaps 10,000 people living in fortified and open villages, supported by prodigal local fisheries and fertile inland gardens. Captain Cook and other members of the *Endeavour* expedition had almost been cut off there in November 1769 by a large war party. This was an affray in which a number of local people were shot. There had also been shootings off the Cavallis, when the local people had attacked the *Endeavour* with a barrage of sticks and stones. Three years later in June 1772, after a month spent anchored in the Bay in relative tranquillity, Marion du Fresne and a number of his men were killed for violating a death tapu, and for interfering (disastrously, if unwittingly) in local politics. The rest of his expedition retaliated with musket and cannon fire, and hundreds of local people (including old people and women) were shot.[27] By 1793 the inhabitants of the Bay of Islands may have learned to covet iron, but they also had long memories, and it was not surprising that they treated the *Daedalus* with extreme caution.

Nor was it surprising that members of Tuki and Huru's party had tried to dissuade them from boarding the *Daedalus*. In December 1769, after a two-week visit to Tokerau (Doubtless Bay), the French explorer Jean-François-Marie Surville had retaliated for the loss of his ship's yawl (washed up on Tokerau Beach by a storm and claimed according to local custom by the residents) by burning houses, canoes, and nets, and by kidnapping a local chief. This chief, Ranginui, had earlier offered food and shelter to a group of Surville's sick sailors, when they were marooned below his *paa* ('fortified village') during the same storm. A later tribal account showed the extent of local mystification and anger at Surville's behaviour:

> A gale came on and the sick people of these salts (maitai) from the other side of the sea were on shore, and the people of Patuu tribe attended to and fed these sick people, and they were kind to these white skins (Pakeha) till the gale subsided ... [Then] the chief who was called Ranginui was tied by orders of the chief of those salts, and the ship sailed away with Te Ranginui on board, and the vessel was lost to sight out far on the sea and sailed away no one knew where. There was not any cause given for which Ranginui was made prisoner by these salts, nor was there any reason for his being taken out to sea, but for such acts as this the Maori retaliated on the salts, who might come to these islands, that the Maori might have revenge for the evil bought on them by the salts, or those from over the sea.[28]

Tuki was from Oruru, a rich agricultural valley in Tokerau, and he must have known about that earlier kidnapping. The two young men, however, 'blinded by the curious things they saw' and perhaps reassured by Kalehua, the Hawai'ian sailor on board, were incautiously inquisitive. They boarded the *Daedalus*, and like Surville's ship more than twenty years earlier the *Daedalus* 'sailed away ... and was lost to sight out far on the sea.' Another tribal account, collected from an anonymous source by John White in about the year 1850,[29] recorded their kidnapping as follows: 'Two of our people were taken by the European on board of a ship to teach the European to make the tow from the flax leaf. These two men went out in a canoe to fish for kahawai, they were called Tuki and Hurukokoti, or Toha-mahue who were one a priest and his friend, who was a warrior. They were occupied in fishing when a ship made her appearance and they two went on board of her, and the canoe was lifted on board also, and the ship sailed way on the sea for many days and then she came to an Island, where there were many Europeans.'[30]

From their own and other reports, Tuki and Huru were well-treated on board the *Daedalus*, although their grief at being so unceremoniously snatched from their families, and their consternation at being on board a European vessel (with its cargo of peculiar animals and European goods) can only be imagined. On 20 April the *Daedalus* arrived in Port Jackson with its cargo of sick sailors, Tuki and Huru, Vancouver's supplies, seventy squealing pigs,[31] one calf, and four sheep. Almost as soon as the ship anchored, Lieutenant-Governor Grose ordered Tuki and Huru transferred to the *Shah Hormuzear,* an East Indiaman then in the port.

The *Shah Hormuzear,* a 400-ton Indiaman crewed by Lascars, had arrived at Port Jackson from Calcutta on 24 February 1793, with a cargo of sheep, horses, donkeys, goats, beef, flour, rice, wheat, sugar, wine, and a large quantity of spirits.[32] Its commander, Matthew Wright Bampton, and his wife had embarked on the voyage to bring supplies to Port Jackson as a private speculation. Several weeks after the arrival of *Shah Hormuzear,* Malaspina's exploring expedition appeared off The Heads at Port Jackson, and, about a month later on 20 April, the *Daedalus* anchored in the harbour. By now Governor Phillip had returned to England, and Lieutenant-Governor Grose was in charge at Port Jackson. When the *Daedalus* was sighted, the *Shah Hormuzear* had unloaded its cargo and was about to sail, but Grose persuaded Bampton to wait several days so that he could send a dispatch to England confirming the store ship's arrival. In a letter to Henry Dundas, Grose reported that 'Captain Vancouver has sent here two Natives of New Zealand, for the purpose of teaching us their manner of manufacturing the flax-plant.'[33] Remembering King's constant requests for New Zealanders to instruct the convicts at Norfolk Island in flax-working, Grose ordered Tuki and Huru to be transferred at once to the *Shah Hormuzear,* accompanied by Lieutenant Hanson who stayed with them until the ship sailed past The Heads.[34] On 24 April, after three days in port during which they had seen little or nothing of Port Jackson, Tuki and Huru sailed on the *Shah Hormuzear,* with its crew of shivering Lascars,[35] five freed convicts, and

220 tons of provisions (including 2200 gallons of wine and spirits),[36] six Bengal ewes, and two rams for Norfolk Island.

Norfolk Island in 1793 was a community at the remotest edges of the world. The island, 1670 kilometres north east of Port Jackson, was small (about five by nine kilometres), rugged, and extremely isolated. Its cliffs dropped straight into the sea, and its best landing place was guarded by a rocky reef, making getting ashore difficult and often dangerous for sea-borne travellers. Two high hills covered with dense sub-tropical rainfor-est dominated the skyline, their ridges and the coastal cliffs bristling with the island's characteristic pines. In places, the forest was almost impene-trable, its underwood tangled with barbed and twisting creepers. Poly-nesians had settled there at some time, because the first European settlers had found Polynesian rats, two canoes (which suggested to Governor Phillip a relatively recent visit from New Zealand), a carving, cultivated banana trees, stone adzes, and artifacts (including one greenstone amulet discovered later).[37] By 1788, however, when the first party of convicts came ashore, the Polynesians had gone again and the island was abandoned.

Norfolk Island's pines, the flax that grew on many coastal cliffs, and its strategic location in the Pacific sea lanes recommended it to the Admiralty planners. As an island prison it also had compelling advan-tages, being uninhabited and surrounded by a 1000-mile wide moat. The soil of the valleys and coastal flats also proved to be fertile, and so Norfolk Island was established as a convict farm and flax factory. The difficulty was that, try as they might (and they tried extremely hard), the Europeans could not work the local flax. Philip Gidley King had there-fore continued to plead for New Zealanders to be brought to the island to instruct the convicts in flax-working. The Admiralty had responded to his arguments in London, but King did not know this, and his letters to Grose and others often repeated the request. On 15 January 1792, for instance, soon after his return to the island King wrote to Lord Grenville: 'The Piece of Canvas that covers these Letters I have sent as a Specimen of the very imperfect State that the Flax is brought to, nor do I imagine that it can be meliorated without some of the New Zealanders to point out the Manner of their dressing that valuable Article. As every Method has been unsuccessfully tried to attain that desirable Perfection which the New Zealanders give it (many Specimens of which are in the Possession of Sir Joseph Banks, which he obtained from these Natives when there) and the very great Quantity they gave in Return for trifling things, may be a Reason to suppose that the Manufacturing of it is not tedious, but very simple.'[38]

In the same letter, King reported to Lord Grenville that he had asked the master of the *William and Ann*, a convict transport on a whaling expedition, 'who is going to fish on that coast, to get 2 of them, and to return here with them.' Because the master had raised difficulties about this proposal, King had offered him £100 if successful. In his journal a week later,[39] King reported that the master of the *William and Ann* had agreed, and had sailed from Norfolk Island on 19 January for the northeast coast of New Zealand.

On 29 March 1792, however, King told Dundas that the *William and Ann* had not returned to Norfolk Island, although a marginal note in his journal later added 'The Ship went to Doubtless Bay but (not surprisingly after Ranginui's kidnapping) could not prevail on any of the Inhabitants to go with him.'[40] Again he asked the government to bring New Zealanders to the island.[41] He repeated this request to Governor Phillip on September 1792 of that year, and finally in April 1793 received the answer he had been waiting for:

> Since writing the above, the Daedalus, Store Ship has arrived from the North-West Coast of America. The Agent, Lieut. Hanson (Lieut. Hergest having been killed by the Natives of one of the Sandwich Islands), according to Instructions he received from Captain Vancouver, has brought with him two men, Natives of New Zealand, and the Lieut. Governor [now Grose] has sent them to you by Captain Bampton for the purpose of giving such Information as they possess respecting the Manufacture of the Flax Plant. The Lieut. Governor thinking it perfectly unnecessary to recommend them to your care, desires me only to add that, he hopes much Benefit may be derived from their Introduction among us. You will of course victual and clothe them.[42]

At the time of Tuki and Huru's arrival at Norfolk Island in 1793, the community on the island was in many ways extraordinary. Its population of 1,026 numbered 495 convicts, 126 children, 318 free settlers, 76 military and 11 civil personnel,[43] and included only 237 women, of whom all but 11 were convicts, and 3 'Natives' (presumably Aborigines).[44]

Almost half of the population were convicts brought from England's hulks and jails. Many had been transported to Port Jackson on the second and third fleets, in conditions that horrified even contemporary observers – shackled in irons with a short bolt and penned below decks with the hatches shut, the water up to their chests. Rations and clothing were so pitifully inadequate that Captain Hill of the New South Wales Corps was moved to comment in 1790: 'The slave trade is merciful compared with what I have seen in this fleet.'[45] Not surprisingly, the health of the survivors had suffered, and this was made worse by recurrent food shortages and the lack of adequate clothing for most convicts once they arrived in the 'thief colonies.' In March 1792 Governor Phillip was forced to report to the Admiralty from Port Jackson: 'I am very sorry to say that most of the convicts who were received by the last ships still continue in the same debilitated state in which they were landed, and of whom, in less than seven months, two hundred and eighty-eight men have died ... The returns of sick this day is – civil and military, eighteen; male convicts, three hundred and ninety-four; and females, seventeen ... The cloathing that has been rec'd for the use of the convicts is so very slight that most of the people are naked a few weeks after they have been cloathed.'[46]

On Norfolk Island, too, rations were in short supply at this time, and clothing was poor. Many convicts were weak, emaciated, and unable to do much work. Their physical condition cannot have been much helped by the frequent punishments administered during 1790-1 by the acting commandant, Major Ross, and his quartermaster, Lieutenant Ralph Clark. Clark's journal during this period gives a chilling calendar of lengthy floggings of male and female convicts (including both the young and the very old), and of their being put in the stocks, chained to the grindstone, or confined in the island's jail.

By May 1793, however, the situation had improved somewhat. King had returned to the island in late 1791 as lieutenant-governor, and proved less harsh and arbitrary a master than Ross had been. He established a system whereby the chaplain, Reverend Bain, the surgeon, William Balmain, and Lieutenant Abbott of the 102nd Regiment took turns as 'justice of the week,' and adjudicated on cases with the help of *Burns Justice*.[47] Heavy penalties had to be discussed in detail with the lieutenant-governor, and orders which established strict rules for public behaviour were publicly promulgated. Punishments included shooting on sight any convict out after curfew; issuing no more clothing to any convict convicted of theft; and for women convicts who swore, cutting off their hair for a first offence, shaving their bodies for a second, and getting a whipping at the cart's tail for a third.

The floggings and other punishments decreased markedly under this system. Some severe sentences were still meted out, however, including sentences of 800 lashes for theft, commuted to 200-250 lashes on a promise of good behaviour, and 300 lashes for idleness, commuted to 100.[48] In addition, King had reduced the public labour required of the convicts to forty hours a week and allowed 'those who were industrious' to clear gardens on the government's lands to supplement their rations. Convict labourers were also allocated to help the free settlers (who included some convicts whose sentences had expired). As a result, the 1792-3 grain harvest increased five times; fruit trees, pineapples, strawberries, melons, sugar cane, bananas, grapes, figs, indigo, coffee, cotton, potatoes, and yams were planted; and livestock on the island had multiplied to about 1500 pigs, 80 goats, 30 sheep, and large numbers of ducks, geese, and chickens, supplemented by thousands of muttonbirds caught on Mount Pitt, eels from the creeks, and fish caught out at sea.[49]

The physical layout of the island at the time of Tuki and Huru's arrival is shown in several sketch surveys produced by Deputy-Surveyor Charles Grimes in 1793. These showed Sydney (where Tuki and Huru lived) as a cluster of stone and wooden buildings built along five short streets by the sea front. A number of convicts' houses, the surgeon's stone house, and the hospital were located to the east of the settlement; a stone storehouse and the Deputy Commissary's house (also built in stone) by the landing place; two granaries, a timber yard, the jail and the jailer's house around the barracks, with its guardhouse and Dark Hole; and overlooking them all, Government House, an eight-roomed, two-storied, Georgian stone building, sixty feet long by thirty feet wide, with a small stockade behind it.[50] A flagpole on Mount George flew the British flag. In its architecture and physical layout, Norfolk Island in 1793 echoed England's penal system, with settlers on the farms, and convicts and jailers crammed together in a prison settlement dominated by the barracks (the military), the jail (the law), and above them all, the flagpole and Government House (the Crown).

Much of the activity on the island at this time was focused on agriculture and building. There were no (or very few) cattle or ploughs and only very rudimentary machinery (the crane on Cascade Wharf, for instance). Although the Industrial Revolution may have been under way in England, Norfolk Island in 1793 was very much a craft- and subsistence-based community, propped up by infrequent shipments of supplies from India and the Cape of Good Hope, rather than from England.

From the time they first arrived at Norfolk Island, Tuki and Huru's position on the island was paradoxical. Although they were captives, and 'savages' to boot, they lived in Government House with Lieutenant-Governor King, ate at his table, and were excused from manual labour. Lieutenant-Governor Grose had instructed that they should be treated kindly, and so they were. They were issued clothing and provisions from the public store[51] – '7lb Flour, 2lb of Rice, 7lb of Beef, 4lb of Pork, 3lb of Dholl (Indian peas) and six ounces of oil for each free man each week'[52] – and lived in friendship with King's family at the pinnacle of Norfolk Island society.

Tuki and Huru were the first Maori to spend any time in a European community. The Europeans on Norfolk Island had known of the New Zealanders' reputation as ferocious cannibals, and they were surprised and disarmed by the geniality of their guests. In November 1793, Assistant-Surgeon Thomas Jamison wrote to a friend in England: 'The New Zealanders are pleasant and good-natured beyond anything one could expect to meet with amongst so barbarous a people as they have always been considered to be. One of them is called Odoo[Huru], the other Tugee [Tuki]. The former is son to one of the princes of that country; the other is son to one of their priests.'[53] Lieutenant-Governor King probably knew Tuki and Huru better than anybody else on the island, and his description of his two guests is worth quoting in detail:

> Hoo-doo Co-co-ty To-wai-ma-how-ey [Huru Kototi Toha Mahue?] is about twenty four years of age; five feet eight inches high; of an athletic make; his features like those of a European, and very interesting. He is of the district of Teer-a-Witte [Te Raawhiti] ... about the Bay of Islands. Both [Tuki and Huru] agree that the distance between their dwellings is only two days journey by land, and one day by water ...
>
> Hoo-doo is nearly related to Po-vo-reek, who is the principal chief of

Teer-a-Witte. [In a letter to Banks, King added that Huru was 'a warrior, and a Superior Rank to Tookee, he is always treated by great deference and respect by the latter. Five years ago his Father was killed in
battle and he says Eat by the Natives of T'Sou duckey (Hauraki)].'[54] He
has two wives and one child, about whose safety he seemed very apprehensive; and almost every evening at the close of the day, he, as well as
Too-gee, lamented their separation in a sort of half-crying and half-
singing, expressive of grief, and which was at times very affecting.

Too-gee Te-ter-re-nu-e Warri-pe-do [Tuki Te Terenui Whare pirau?] is
of the same age as Hoo-doo; but about three inches shorter, he is stout
and well made and like Hoo-doo of an olive complexion, with strong
black hair. Both are tattowed on the hips. Too-gee's features are rather
handsome and interesting; his nose is aquiline, and he has good teeth.
He is a native of the district of Ho-do-doe [Oruru] (which is in
Doubtless Bay), of which district Toogee's father is the Etang-a-roa [He
Tangaroa – god of the sea], or chief priest; and to that office the son
succeeds on his father's death. Beside his father, who is a very old man,
he has left a wife and child; about all of whom he is very anxious and
uneasy, as well as about the chief (Moo-de-wy [Muriwai]), whom he
represents as a very worthy character.

Too-gee has a decided preference to Hoo-doo both in disposition and
manners; although the latter is not wanting in a certain degree of good
nature, but he can at times be very much of the savage. Hoo-doo, like a
true patriot, thinks there is no country, people, nor customs equal to
his own; on which account he is much less curious as to what he sees
about him than his companion Too-gee, who has the happy art of
insinuating himself into every person's esteem. Except at times, when
he is lamenting the absence of his family and friends, he is cheerful,
often facetious, and very intelligent ... It is not, however, meant to be
said that if Too-gee were not present, an indifferent opinion would
have been formed of Hoo-doo; on the contrary, the manners and disposition of the latter are far more pleasing than could have been
expected to be found in a native of that country.[55]

In the beginning he was impressed by them, and Lieutenant-
Governor King's interest in Tuki and Huru was pragmatic. Almost as
soon as they came on shore he had tried to get them to show the convicts

how to work the local flax. He sent a hurried report to the secretary of state by the *Shah Hormuzear* which commented: 'The New Zealanders method of dressing the flax has a present appearance of being very tedious, perhaps when they have been longer with us, we shall mutually improve. A Flax dresser & Three Women attend them as often as we can prevail on them to instruct; As yet it requires entreaty, to persuade them to give us the least information.'[56]

Their reluctance to instruct the convicts was not surprising, however, for during their first few days on the island, Tuki and Huru were still grief-stricken and in shock. The experience of being snatched onto the *Daedalus*, with its cargo of pigs, sheep, and cattle (all unknown to the Maori), then being taken on board by the *Shah Hormuzear* with its lascar crew and transported to Norfolk Island must have seemed a nightmare; and King's urgent enquiries about flax-working can only have added to their confusion. Tuki, a priest's son, and Huru, the young chief, knew little enough about flax work, for in their communities weaving was a woman's art. Furthermore, as the one tribal account of their capture describes, Tuki as a priest was in a state of tapu at the time, which made the attempt to get him to work flax doubly inappropriate. All of King's planning and effort to bring them to Norfolk Island for this purpose proved largely futile, for as King later reported in frustration: 'Every information that could be got from them, respecting their mode of manufacturing the Flax plant, was obtained in One day ... and which turned out to be very little, as this operation is the peculiar Occupation of the Women, & as Woodoo is a Warrior, & Tookee a Priest, they gave us to understand, that Dressing of Flax, never made any part of their studies.' Such little information as he could immediately obtain King sent in a letter to Sir Joseph Banks on 24 May 1793, along with a jar containing processed flax:

> Their method of preparing the flax is this, the leaf is plucked green, the longer the better, the middle part of the leaf is stripped off with the finger & thumb & thrown away being too hard – the leaf is then split into narrow Stripes, and each Stripe cut across, in the middle, but great nicety is required here, so as not to separate the filaments, the Stripe is then held between the finger & Thumb of the left hand, whilst the right holds the Knife or a Sharp shell, on the under part just below the cut across; It is then drawn down, & the Vegetable part seperates from the Flaxy part.[57]

King added that Tuki and Huru seemed very familiar with the local vegetation and had already taught the Europeans on Norfolk Island to eat some plants previously thought poisonous; and that they had joyfully recognized some stone axes that had been dug up on the island as *Etoki* of *Eaheinomawe* (*He toki* ['adzes'] of *He ahi no Maui* ['Maui's fire'] or *Hiia no Maui* ['fished up by Maui'] – the north island of New Zealand).

At the time of the *Shah Hormuzear*'s departure in May, King hoped that he still might learn more about working flax from Tuki and Huru. Taking a 'coloured general chart' of the Pacific, he showed them the relative positions of Norfolk Island, Port Jackson, and New Zealand, and promised them that, if they would teach the women on Norfolk Island everything that they knew about flax-work, he would send them home in five or six months' time. Then he gave them a choice: either leave Norfolk Island and go to England on the *Shah Hormuzear* or stay pending their return home. Without hesitation, Tuki and Huru chose to remain, but when Captain Bampton and his wife 'took their leave, they were sensibly affected, and cryed bitterly, however kind treatment soon made [them] Chearful.'[58]

Philip Gidley King, their host on Norfolk Island, was a professional naval officer who, in 1793, was serving his second term as commandant of the convict colony. King had gone to sea when he was twelve years old, had served in the East Indies, and had fought in the War of Independence from 1775 to 1778, when his ship was sunk by the French. On his return to England, King had been posted to the Channel fleet on the *Ariadne* under Captain Arthur Phillip. Phillip later arranged King's commission as second lieutenant on the *Sirius*, which sailed with the First Fleet to Port Jackson; and, as governor of New South Wales, he appointed King as first commandant of Norfolk Island in 1788.

King was a conservative, dutiful officer, with a conventional faith in God, King, and Empire; yet he had liberal leanings. He also seems to have been compassionate, and Tuki and Huru's misery over their captivity moved him: 'The daily lamentations of Two sensible men, who were continually reminding me of my Promise, & repeating their anxious fears, respecting the safety of their Familys, from whom they were separated in a sudden manner made me feel for them as a Father & a Husband.'[59]

King's sympathy for Tuki and Huru was evidently shared by his wife. Anna Josepha was King's cousin whom he had married hastily in March 1791 during his leave in England, when he was ill with chronic gout and under orders to return to Norfolk Island. When they returned in late 1791, Anna was heavily pregnant and caring for Norfolk, one of King's two illegitimate sons by a convict woman born during King's first term of duty on the island. William Neate Chapman, King's secretary and protégé, said of Anna King, 'She is so good a woman that it is a pleasure for any person to be near her.'[60] Certainly she did everything she could to make Tuki and Huru at home in Government House.

By 1793 King's household included four-year-old Norfolk, two-year-old Phillip, baby Maria, and twenty-year-old William Chapman, King's secretary and the island's storekeeper, who often stayed with them. Family relations were warm and affectionate, and a close friendship grew up between Tuki and Huru and the Kings over the months. King wrote to Banks just before leaving Norfolk Island with Tuki and Huru, 'Our intelligent and worthy friends the two New Zealanders ... have now been here seven months during which time they have lived with me and we are so much attached to each other that much real concern will be shown by every description of people here when they leave us.'[61] According to Chapman, when King finally said goodbye to Tuki and Huru off the north coast of New Zealand in November, 'they cryed terribly and everybody on board was very much affected at the parting particularly the Governor who said he never parted with his mother with more regret than he did with those two men.'[62] In 1819, when Samuel Marsden met Huru in the Bay of Islands, he reported that 'the great kindness of Governor King towards [Tuki and Huru] made the most favourable impression on all the Natives who heard of it, and to the present day they always speak of it with gratitude and pleasure, and make enquiries after Governor King's oldest daughter, whose name is Maria, and who was only a few years [sic-months] old when Hooratooki [Huru and Tuki?] was at Norfolk Island. When [Huru] asked me about Maria, I told him she now lived at Parramatta. He said he would go and live with her till he died.'[63]

During their time on Norfolk Island, Tuki and Huru seem to have mixed mainly with King's family; with the civil and military officers who visited his house – the Reverend James Bain, the chaplain; Charles Grimes, the deputy surveyor-general; Thomas Jamison, William Balmain, and D'Arcy Wentworth, the assistant surgeons; Lieutenant Abbott and the other officers of the 102nd Regiment (the New South Wales Corps) – and with the settlers.

It is difficult to know what Tuki and Huru themselves thought of their situation on Norfolk Island. Although they were free and well treated, they must have been acutely aware of the misery of many convicts and the repressive penal regime of trials and harsh punishments on the island. Despite King's relative clemency, in July 1793 two men were imprisoned pending transfer to Port Jackson for stealing a bottle of rum, a dollar, and a silk handkerchief; another was sentenced to fifty lashes for harbouring them; a fourth was sentenced to 300 lashes for stealing files from the blacksmith's shop; and a fifth was sentenced to 100 lashes and six months in the penitentiary for disobeying an overseer. In August a man was sentenced to fifty lashes, an iron collar, and two months in the penitentiary for swearing at a soldier; another to 100 lashes for striking a convict who was with a soldier; and an inveterate thief was chained to the public grindstone for stealing a watch and twenty dollars, until he could be sent to Port Jackson for trial.[64]

Such punishments were quite unknown in Maori communities, where offenders were plundered, ostracized, and sometimes killed, but never confined. Later Maori visitors to European settlements, such as Te Pahi in Port Jackson 1806,[65] were horrified by the treatment meted out to prisoners for what seemed to them trivial offenses, but Tuki and Huru's reactions were not reported. On the one hand, given their aristocratic backgrounds, they may have taken their privileged position on the island for granted, and thought of themselves as chiefly guests, living with the most important family on the island, in a community composed mainly of *toa* ('warriors') and *taurekareka* ('slaves,' 'war captives'). On the other hand, it is obvious that their own captivity (and perhaps that of others) deeply grieved them. According to King, they 'often Threatened to Hang themselves on very slight occasions, & sometimes made very serious promises of putting it into execution, if they were not permitted to return to their own Country.'[66]

Events on the island during Tuki and Huru's visit included the celebration of King George's birthday on 4 June, when 5 large hogs were killed and 20 gallons of American spirits issued to the working convicts. The civil and military officers attended a dinner at Government House on this occasion (where Tuki and Huru no doubt were also present), which was followed by a bonfire and festivities on the beach. A school and an orphanage were established on the island during this period, with the help of Mrs. King, and, in August, several plays were performed by convicts and free men supervised by the surgeon William Balmain.[67]

While they were on Norfolk, Tuki and Huru must have visited some of the settlers in their houses up the valleys in Phillipsburgh and Queensborough, and they must have seen something of domestic life outside of Government House. As agricultural and construction work was going on all over the island, they must also have learned a great deal about European stock-rearing, cropping, boat-building, and stone masonry.

Like other people on the island, Tuki and Huru were subject to the curfew, signalled by a roll of drums at 8 P.M. and policed by the night watch, who patrolled the streets of Sydney and called the hour every half hour throughout the night.[68] After six months on the island, the rhythms of local life may have dulled their initial shock upon being landed in so strange a place. According to King, they learned to speak some English and he and some officers on Norfolk Island learned to speak some Maori: 'It may be expected that after a Six Month residence among us, that we should not be entirely ignorant of each others Language. Myself & some of the Officers (to whom I am obliged, for their communicating the information they gained from the two New Zealanders) have made such a progress that we could make ourselves well understood, & communicate our ideas to our visitors. They by intermixing what English words they knew ["which is not a little," King added in a letter to Banks[69]], with what we knew of their Language, could make themselves sufficiently understood by us.'[70]

King regretted that he had no copy of any of Cook's voyages on the island, 'to compare their language with that of the other 1.ds in these Seas,' but commented that 'to the New Holland language it has as little affinity as the New Hollanders have the accomplished manners, amiable disposition & ingenious turn of Tooke and Woodoo.'[71] This was an interesting prelude to the many unflattering comparisons made during the early colonial period between Maori and Australian Aborigines, to the Aborigines' disadvantage. King and the surgeon (Jamison?) eventually produced an extensive and quite accurate vocabulary of Maori,[72] and the development of a mutual linguistic capacity allowed King to record some quite complex information from Tuki and Huru about Maori social hierarchies, cosmology, and flax processing.

According to King, for instance, there were four 'classes' of persons in New Zealand:

E Tanga teda E tiketica [He rangatira tiketike – a high chief]. A principal Chief, or Man in very great authority, his Superior Consequence is
signified by a repetition of the word Etiketica [tiketike – 'high?']. This
Title appears hereditary. E tanga roak or E ta-honga [Tangaroa (the sea
god), or he tohunga – 'priest']. A priest whose Authority in many cases
is equal, and in some Superior to the E tikatika. A tange teda Epodi [He
rangatira?]. A subordinate chief or Gentleman. Te Ane E moki [taane
mookai]. A labouring man.[73]

These Categories involved a subtle re-shaping of the flexible, negotiated
hierarchies of *mana* ('ancestor power') into a European-style class system.
King added:

> The dead are burned in graves; and they believe that the Third day after
> the Interment; the heart separates itself from the Corpse. This separa-
> tion is announced by a Gentle air of wind, which warns an inferior Ea-
> Tooa [atua – spiritual being] (or Divinity) hovering over the Grave of
> its approach and carries it to the Clouds. In Tooke's Chart he has
> marked an imaginary road which goes the length ways of Ea-kei-no-
> maue [Te Ika-no-Maui, i.e., North Island], viz. from Cook's Streight to
> the North cape which Tooke calls Terry-inga [Te Reinga]; whilst the
> soul is received by the good Eatooa; an evil spirit is also in readiness to
> carry the impure part of the Corpse to the above road, along which it is
> carried to Terry-inga from whence it is precipitated into the Sea.[74]
> Every undertaking whether it is to fish or any other common occupa-
> tion is preceded by a prayer E kara kee a -[he karakia] addressed to the
> Supreme Ea Tooa.[75]

This is an illuminating account, well supported by later information
about the use of *karakia* ('god chants') and the passage of the *hau*
('wind,' 'breath of life') of a dead person along the spirits' pathway to Te
Reinga in the far north of the North Island. King also commented that
suicide was very common among the New Zealanders, and that if a
woman were beaten by her husband she would hang herself immediately.

According to Tuki and Huru, flax was sometimes cultivated in New
Zealand by separating the roots and planting them three in a hole about
a foot apart. King reported on how they had helped improve local flax
processing, saying that the flax workers now found it much easier to
strip the outer vegetable matter from the fibre. They stored bundles of

flax leaves in a closed room for seven days, stripped them with a knife, twisted the fibre into hanks and soaked it in a tub of water, washed and beat it, then dried, hackled, and spun it. By November twenty workers were processing flax on the island and between them produced twenty yards of No. 7 canvas in a week, although with a proper loom and weavers' tools, he thought that better results might be accomplished.[76] Tuki and Huru would not have agreed, however, for as the tribal account of their capture reported, 'Though the Europeans wished to learn to make *muka* ('flax fibre') as the Maori did, they could not succeed, as they cut the muka in short lengths, and also because the flax of the Island was not the *Tihore* (the best flax for making muka) and hence the muka broke in short lengths.'[77]

The most remarkable record of Maori thinking obtained in Norfolk Island, however, and a tribute to the eventual quality of communication between Tuki and King, was Tuki's map of New Zealand, sent by King in November 1793 to the secretary of state.[78] David Collins, the judge-advocate at New South Wales, gave the best account (presumably based on later conversations with King) of the production of this map:

When they began to understand each other, Too-gee was not only very inquisitive respecting England &c. (the situation of which, as well as that of New Zealand, Norfolk Island and Port Jackson, he well knew how to find by means of a coloured general chart); but was also very communicative respecting his own country. Perceiving he was not thoroughly understood, he delineated a sketch of New Zealand with chalk on the floor of a room set apart for that purpose. From a comparison which Governor King made with Captain Cook's plan of those islands [unavailable on Norfolk Island until after the arrival of the *Brittania*[79]], a sufficient similitude to the form of the northern island was discoverable to render this attempt an object of curiosity; and Toogee was persuaded to render his delineation on paper. This being done with a pencil, corrections and additions were occasionally made by him, in the course of different conversations; and the names of districts and other remarks were written from his information during the six months he remained there.[80]

Entire treatises have been written about Tuki's map of New Zealand.[81] Other maps were produced by Maori in the early contact

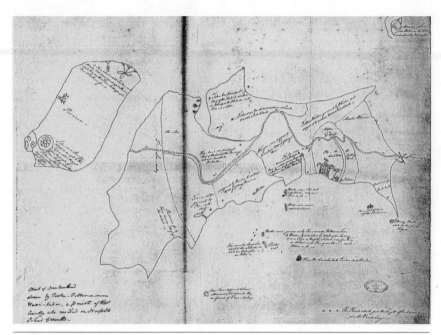

Tuki's map of New Zealand

period,[82] but Tuki's is unique in that it includes social, mythical, and political information written at his dictation. In effect, Tuki's chart is a socio-political description of upper North Island, with some brief comments (and inaccurate coastlines) for southern New Zealand. The key features of Tuki's map included 'Manoui-tavai' (Manawatawhi, the largest of the Three Kings Islands), said to have no water on it but inhabited by thirty people; 'Modey-Mootoo on which Te-kapa has an Hippah' (Murimotu, where the chief Te Kapa was said to have had a fortified village or paa), presumably the fort described by Cook on this small island off the North Cape; 'Terry-inga' (Te-Reinga), the spirits' place for leaping off into the underworld, which was shown at the termination of a spirits' pathway (Te Ara Whaanui) running from the bottom to the top of North Island, where it terminated at a symbol which represented the tapu tree there; 'Moodo Whenua' (Muriwhenua), whose boundaries on the map extended from around Ahipara on the west coast to north of Tokerau on the east;[83] and 'Ho-do-do' (Oruru), whose boundaries crossed the spirits' path and which was said on the map to have 2,000 fighting men (although King's journal says 1,000).[84] Within Oruru,

Tuki's habitation was fixed on the north coast of the valley, while the dwellings of two of his chiefs, 'Moodeewye' (Muriwai) on the south coast and 'Te Wy-te-wi' further south were marked with symbols that probably represented carved houses; the habitation of a secondary chief, 'Wytoa' (Waitoa), was marked far inland.

Further south on the east coast was the district named 'Wongar-ooa' (Whangaroa), supposed to contain 2,000 fighting men, whose chief, 'Tu-ko-rawa' (Tukarawa), was said to be 'inimical to Hododo [Oruru] and Teer-a-witte [Te Raawhiti], but in league with T'sou-duckey [Hauraki] & Moodoo Whenua [Muriwhenua] & Tettua Woodoo [Te Tai Hauauru?].' 'Tettua Woodoo,' to the south of Muriwhenua on the west coast, was said to be governed by 'Whadu' (Wharo) and to have 4,000 inhabitants. 'Choke-ang'-a' (Hokianga), further south on the west coast, was described as having 100,000 inhabitants, headed by the principal chief 'Toko-ha,' who was at peace with Oruru and Te Raawhiti. On the east coast, again, 'Woodoo's' (Huru's) habitation was marked in a district in the south of the Bay of Islands (presumably Te Raawhiti), which was supposed to contain 'Tea-worock,' father-in-law to Woodoo, with 100 people, very few trees, but much flax and water; and 'Pani-ke' (Panaaki) with 50 people (two of the Cavalli Islands), where Tuki and Huru were captured in the seas to the east.

South of these districts was 'T'sou ducky' (Hauraki), and then another large island 'Poenammoo' ('Te Wai Pounamu' – the South Island), with a 'tree about which Tookee and Woodoo tell some wonderful stories,' which apparently they had been told by the Hauraki people; and a lake where 'stone for Hatchets are got' – presumably the greenstone waters of that island.

In explanation, Tuki told King that the North Island of New Zealand was divided into eight districts, governed by their respective chiefs, the principal one being Hauraki, often at war with other tribes. According to Tuki, on occasion the Hauraki tribes were allied with Muriwhenua, 'Tettua – Whoodoo [Te Tai Hauauru],' and Whangaroa, but at other times those last tribes allied with Hokianga, Te Raawhiti, and Oruru against the Hauraki people. This seems to fit in well with the volatile tribal histories for that period, which tell of numerous raids between various Northern and Hauraki tribes.

Tuki added that there were long periods of peace, when flax and greenstone for axes and ornaments were exchanged and groups visited one another. He was prepared to concede that all the inhabitants of the South Island and Hauraki were cannibals, but vehemently denied that all New Zealanders ate people, expressing 'the greatest horror at the idea.'[85] Tuki also described a large fresh water river on the west coast, with a bar, which he called 'Choke-han-ga' (Hokianga). The chief here, Tokoha, lived half way up the river, where the country was covered with immense pines. When King obtained a copy of Cook's chart of New Zealand from the master of the *Brittania*, he pointed out to Tuki that Cook had not noticed a river in that region. Tuki asked whether Cook had seen an island covered with birds, and when King pointed to Gannet Island (off the Kaawhia harbour) he suggested that this must be the place. In fact Gannet Island was too far south, but Tuki's description of Hokianga, its bar, and its kauri forests was accurate. Tuki identified the chiefs of his own district, Oruru, as 'Te wy-te-wye' (Te Wai-te-wai), the principal chief whose house was ornamented with the heads of enemies killed in battle; 'Wy-too-ah' (Waitua), 'Moode-wye' (Muriwai), 'Wa-way' (Wawae), 'To-moco-moco' (Tomokimoki), 'Pock-a-roo' (Pokaru), and 'Tee-koo-ree' (Te Kurii), the principal chief's son. Milligan has attempted to identify all the chiefs mentioned by Tuki, either on the map or in King's account, but a more detailed study of Northern tribal histories is necessary to assess many of his claims.[86]

From my knowledge of place names and politics in the Northland region of North Island during this time, Tuki's account seems accurate and reliable. Together, he and King seem to have recorded a fascinating synopsis of Northern geo-politics in the 1790s.

On 2 November 1793, the store ship *Brittania* (301 tons, six guns, with a crew of twenty-four)[87] anchored off Norfolk Island.[88] Two other ships, the *Sugar Cane* and *Boddingtons*, had arrived in late October but, as they were leaving for India, King had not been able to fulfill his promise to Tuki and Huru that they could leave Norfolk Island on the next ship. When the *Brittania* arrived, therefore, they redoubled their pleas, begging King with 'hourly lamentations' to keep his promise and send them home. This time, King agreed. A sense of honour, and perhaps also a sense of adventure, persuaded him to assert his authority as lieutenant-governor. He drafted orders for the master of the *Brittania* to divert his course southwards to New Zealand, before resuming the trading voyage on behalf of the New South Wales Corps from Port Jackson to Bengal.

The *Brittania*, owned by Enderby's of London and commanded by Captain William Raven, had arrived in New South Wales with a certificate from the East India Company, which allowed it to go sealing in southern waters. Raven had already made one profitable trading voyage for the Corps to the Cape of Good Hope (combined with a sealing expedition south). Now he embarked on a voyage to India for a similar purpose.

Captain Nepean of the Corps was on board the *Brittania*, returning to England on leave. King decided to ask Nepean to make a thorough survey of Norfolk Island for a report on the colony to the Admiralty, and left him in charge while he returned his two friends. There was an exchange of documents, which included instructions for both Captain Nepean and Captain Raven, and a letter to Under Secretary Evan Nepean, to be delivered by the under secretary's brother, the captain. In this letter King suggested that enough flax could be got from New Zealand to clothe all the inhabitants of New South Wales. He added, 'If it should be thought necessary to settle New Zealand and I should happen to be the person fixed on, I hope my family, which is now growing numerous, will be considered.'[89]

On 8 November King embarked on the *Brittania* for New Zealand with Tuki and Huru and a number of other passengers, including Reverend Bain; Thomas Jamison, the assistant-surgeon; William Chapman, the storekeeper (who had gifts with him); two non-commissioned officers; seventeen privates; and one convict.[90] If the voyage took only three days, King intended to land at New Zealand 'and make such Cursory Observations (on the Soil and Quantity of Manufactured Flax which could be obtained) as I might be able to make *in One Day*.' For that reason he had included soldiers in his party.

The winds were favourable but light, and it was not until 12 November that North Cape was sighted. Houses and a fortified village (paa) were seen on Murimotu, and then a very large paa on a hill 'just within the Cape [Tokatoka Point].' At 4 P.M. six large canoes (according to Chapman, forty to sixty feet long), with about thirty men in each, came out from this paa to the *Brittania*. They recognized Tuki immediately, and as other canoes joined the fleet, most of their crews boarded the *Brittania*. The chiefs 'embrac[ed] and shed Tears of joy over Tooke, whose first, & earnest Enquiry was after his Family, & Chief, on those heads, he got the most satisfactory information from a Woman, who he informed us, is a near relation of his Mothers [according to Chapman, his sister-in-law]. His Father & Chief were still inconsolable for his loss; the latter ... was about a fortnight ago, on a visit to the Chief of the Hippah above mentioned, where he remained Four days, and Terry-te-wye [Tere-te-wai], the Principal Chief of Tooke's district, was dayly expected; this information pleased him very much.'[91]

The people of the far North and those at Oruru were evidently on very friendly terms, with frequent visits being exchanged between their senior chiefs. One chief from the first fleet of canoes told Tuki and Huru that the Muriwhenua people were currently allied with those of Oruru, Whangaroa, and Te Raawhiti, and that they had just returned from an attack on the Hauraki tribes.

There were about 100 people alongside, but Tuki greeted only his mother's kinswoman, and the chiefs 'who were distinguished from the rest by the Tattowing on their faces; & by the Respectful deference which was shewn them by the Emoki's [*mokai* – "slaves"] (i.e., the Working Men, who paddled the Canoes) who at times were beat most unmercifully.'[92] This last comment is interesting, as it indicates that slaves were, on occasion, harshly treated in Maori communities.

King gave gifts of iron tools to the 'Epodis' (or subaltern chiefs) at Tuki's direction, and then scraps of iron were exchanged for prepared flax, cloth, *patupatu* ('hand weapons'), spears, greenstone ornaments, fish hooks and lines, and paddles.[93] At 7 P.M., the canoes left the *Brittania,* and the ship sailed for the Bay of Islands. Later at 9 P.M. a canoe with a crew of four men came out to the *Brittania* and all willingly boarded. They traded their canoe to the master of the *Brittania* and stayed for supper. After the meal Tuki and Huru asked them for news of events since they had left New Zealand. In answer,

[They] began a Song, in which all the Four Men who came in the Canoe took a part, & used some fierce and Savage Gestures, & at other times sunk their voices, according to the different passages and events which they were relating, Woodoo, who was paying great attention to the Subject of their Song, suddenly burst into Tears, which were occasioned by an Account they were giving of the T'Sou duckey Tribe, having made an irruption into Teer-a-witte, (Woodoo's district) & killed the Son of Povoreek the Chief, and Thirty Warriors. Woodoo was too much affected to hear any more, he retired into a Corner of the cabbin, where he gave vent to his Grief, which was only interrupted by his vowing Revenge.[94]

The ship was virtually becalmed that night. At 6 A.M. the next morning, eight canoes came out from the main paa led by a canoe with thirty-six men and a chief on board, who stood up and signalled to the *Brittania*. As the canoe came alongside Tuki recognized 'Koto-ko-kee' (Tokoki?), the senior chief of the paa. King described Tokoki as an old man dressed in white, whose face was heavily tattooed. Tuki greeted him affectionately, and then introduced him to King. They pressed noses, the chief put his cloak around King's shoulders, and King in return presented him with a cloak of green baize, decorated with broad arrows. Seven more canoes, with twenty or more men and women in each, now approached the *Brittania*, and their crews boarded. William Chapman wrote, 'They are the finest set of men I ever beheld, the shortest we saw was at least 5ft 11in & very strong & muscular. The Women are small but have very pleasing countenances. I have heard it remarked that the women of most country's have the greatest flow of spirits, much greater than the male sex & I assure you it is so in New Zealand.'[95] At Tuki's request King declared the poop tapu, so that only Tokoki and two other chiefs had access to it.

King had become uneasy about the increasing length of his absence from Norfolk Island, and earlier that morning he had asked Tuki and Huru whether they wished to land at Muriwhenua, or to stay on board and return with him to Norfolk Island. Tuki was not enthusiastic about disembarking at Muriwhenua, saying that so far only subordinate chiefs had assured him that there was peace between his own people at Oruru and the Muriwhenua people, but neither did he want to return to Norfolk Island. When Tokoki came on board, however, all of Tuki's doubts vanished. Tokoki assured Tuki that their people were indeed at peace, and that he would personally return Tuki to Oruru the next evening. King was still uneasy, fearing that this might be a subterfuge to get hold of Tuki and Huru's gifts from Norfolk Island. Tuki answered 'with an honest Confidence that E tiketica no E teka [a pidgin phrase] ie. That an E tiketica [high chief] never deceives, and that he rather wish'd to go with Ko-to-ko-ke than to return to Norfolk Island before he had seen his family & Chief.'[96]

King took the old chief into the cabin, and with Tuki's help explained how concerned he was that Tuki and Huru should be immediately returned to Oruru. In three months' time, he added, he would go himself to Oruru, and if Tuki and Huru had been safely returned home, he would return to Muriwhenua and give the chief many additional gifts.

According to King: 'The only answer Ko-to-ko-ke made was by putting both his Hands to the sides of my Head, (making me perform the same Ceremony) & Joining our Noses, in which position we remained Three Minutes, & the Old Chief muttering in a very earnest manner, what I did not understand; After which he went through the same Ceremony with Tookee & Woodoo, which ended with a dance, when the Two latter joined Noses with me, & said that Kotokoke was now become their Father, & would in Person conduct them to Hododoe.'[97]

This ceremonious *hongi* ('nose-pressing') accompanied by *karakia* ('incantations') was probably intended to establish an honorary kinship among the chief, King, Tuki, and Huru, and was thus of deep significance for subsequent relations between King and the Maori. Tuki now gathered the people in a circle around Tokoki and 'recounted to them what he had seen during his absence; at many passages they gave shouts of admiration.' When they refused to believe that Norfolk Island was only three days' sail from Muriwhenua, he ran to the poop and fetched a cabbage, telling them to their astonishment that it had been cut five days earlier in King's garden.

Tuki and Huru now passed on a request from Tokoki for the soldiers to exercise and to fire their muskets and the great guns. King assured the gathering that as long as the New Zealanders and his own people remained good friends and neighbours, these weapons would never be used against them. The soldiers then paraded in front of the 150 Maori, went through their drill, and fired off three rounds. Next they fired a cannon loaded with grapeshot 'which surprized them greatly, particularly the Chief, who [King] made notice the distance the shot fell from the Ship.'[98]

A wind now blew up from the south, and a high surf began to run on shore. Tuki and Huru already had with them a bag containing six sets of linen, two green suits faced with orange, three swords, needles, thread, knives and looking glasses; before they left the ship King had also given Tuki and Huru thirty hand axes, forty-six chisels, carpenters' tools, six spades, hoes, knives, scissors, razors, two bushels of seed maize, one of wheat, two of pease, garden seeds, seven young sows, and three boars (three goats King had intended to give to them had died on board, and hats, jackets, and frock trousers for Tuki and Huru were not handed over in the haste of their departure).[99] He also presented the local people with 100 mirrors and 100 hundredweight of biscuit. All these gifts were loaded into the canoes, and Tuki and Huru affectionately farewelled everyone on board, reminding King of his promise to return in two or three months' time, when they and their families would go with him to Norfolk Island. To-ko-kee pronounced King's name carefully, and taught King to pronounce his name in turn (probably a ceremonial exchange of names, to ratify their new relationship). The local people now performed a *haka* ('war dance') to Chapman's utter astonishment: 'I never heard such a noise, nor saw such ugly faces as they made in my life in any country.'[100] As the canoes left the *Brittania* the Europeans gave them three cheers, and at Tuki's direction the local people replied with three cheers of their own.

Upon his return to Norfolk Island, King wrote a detailed report to the Right Honourable Henry Dundas, secretary of state for home affairs, telling him about the expedition to New Zealand, and enclosing a cloak and fishing lines made in New Zealand from New Zealand flax. He also wrote another letter to Under Secretary Nepean, suggesting that 'much publick good would result to the commerce of Great Britain and these colonies if a settlement was made [in New Zealand] at the Bay of Islands or the River Thames,' and offering to spend two months on an expedition to New Zealand to assess its suitability for settlement from Britain.[101] A box of New Zealand 'curiosities' was sent to the under secretary, which no doubt eventually arrived in England. Two basalt hand weapons (*patu onewa*), now in the Australian Museum, were said to have been presented to King by Tuki and Huru 'in gratitude for his action in returning them to New Zealand in November 1793 from Norfolk Island, where they had been taken by Lieutenant Hanson in the transport *Daedalus* earlier in the same year for the purpose of showing the methods of treating New Zealand flax.'[102] These are the last souvenirs of Tuki and Huru's stay in Norfolk Island.

When Lieutenant-Governor Grose heard that King had diverted the *Brittania* from its trading voyage to India, he was furious. Grose was at that time the commander of the New South Wales Corps, as well as lieutenant-governor. The Corps had underwritten the voyage as a profit-making venture, and King was a naval officer, technically subordinate to Grose. Shortly after King returned to Norfolk Island there had been a mutiny among the New South Wales Corps contingent there, and Grose may also have been looking for a scapegoat for that event. Grose wrote a very angry rebuke to King, and King countered with several lengthy ones to Grose and Dundas.

This episode did King's career no lasting harm, however. King was able to argue that in taking Tuki and Huru back to New Zealand, he was simply fulfilling his instructions to treat them well. The furore over this escapade and the mutiny eventually died down, and King continued to be promoted, eventually becoming governor of New South Wales.

There were at least three lasting consequences of Tuki and Huru's stay with Lieutenant-Governor King in Norfolk Island. First, local flax processing improved to the extent that some garments (including trousers and aprons), and a fore topgallant sail, ropes, and a logline (later tested on the *Daedalus)* were made. This kept alive the hope that a flax industry in Norfolk Island or New Zealand might eventually prove profitable.[103]

Second, the effective introduction of pigs, maize, and potatoes to Northland can be dated to 1793. The one tribal account of Tuki and Huru's adventures ends, 'the Europeans gave them some pigs, male and female, and some Indian corn and potatoes, these increased (*tupu*) and were distributed to the other tribes of Ngapuhi [in Northland].'[104] Both men came from extensive horticultural areas, and Oruru (Tuki's homeland) in particular was intensively cultivated with irrigated, drained hillside garden systems along a fertile river valley. The maize and potatoes may have been first planted there, or in gardens on the volcanic soils of the inland Bay of Islands. In any case, the potatoes flourished (for they could be grown very like *kuumara* ('sweet potatoes'), as did the pigs, and these new domesticates were distributed along the gift exchange networks of the region. Te Pahi, who later visited King in Port Jackson in 1806 when he was governor there, told King that he had been asked by his father to visit the governor, so that 'his country [might be] benefited by his Visit, as it had been by the great Blessing bestowed on it by the two New Zealanders return from Norfolk Island who introduced the Potatoe which is now in the greatest Abundance.'[105] Furthermore, Joseph Mathews, one of the first missionaries in the North, reported in 1837 that Tuki and Huru not only brought the plants and animals with them, but also a fair knowledge of how to care for them, and it may have been this which made the critical difference. In Northland at least, it seems likely that Tuki and Huru's kidnapping revolutionized local agriculture.

Third, Northland Maori established close ties with 'Kaawana Kiingi' (Governor King) and his family. When the *Fancy* visited Tokerau in 1795 and asked for Tuki, the people exclaimed, 'My-ty Governor King! My-ty Too-gee! My-ty Hoo-doo!'[106] *Maitai* was an archaic word for 'good,' and King's reputation in this part of the North was evidently widespread and excellent. Tokoki, the old chief in Muriwhenua, who had ceremonially established a kind of kinship with King (and had possibly assumed his name), would never have forgotten him, and both Tuki and Huru were high-born Maori with their own wide networks of kinship and alliance in the North. Other chiefs (including Te Pahi from the Bay of Islands and his sons) were later to stay with Governor King in Government House at Port Jackson. Much of the term *Kaawana* ('governor') in Northland Maori in the late eighteenth and early nineteenth centuries derived from what people knew about Philip Gidley King. He was the governor whom the Maori knew best, who had learned some of their language, had treated their kinsfolk with honour, and had shown his chiefly prestige with generous hospitality and gifts. King behaved like a man of *mana* ('prestige'), and it seems that Northland Maori came to expect other *Kaawana* to do the same. In 1840, when the Treaty of Waitangi was signed, the Northern chiefs ceded *Kaawanatanga* ('governorship') to the British Crown. Part of their willingness to treat with the Crown, surely, can be traced back to Norfolk Island, where young Maori aristocrats had lived with a governor, had become his friends, and had been treated as his equals in a society of convicts who, by contrast, were treated like white *taurekareka* ('slaves').

On reflection, Vancouver's description of European exploration was not entirely wrong. There was friendship on occasion (as well as considerable mutual violence), and exchanges of goods and information. Yet in the context of Tuki and Huru's visit to Norfolk Island, it is difficult to say with any conviction just who, in that particular story, were 'the bar-barous people,' 'the most lowly children of nature.' Lieutenant-Governor King himself, and Assistant-Surgeon Jamison, after six months' acquain-tance with Tuki and Huru, no longer wished to call them 'savages.' But George Vancouver, and most other Europeans of that period, would have no such compunction.

Vancouver's 'grand keystone to that expansive arch,' which linked Europeans to other peoples in the eighteenth century, requires closer examination. It may prove, on inspection, to have been not knowledge, but a resilient mythology about 'savages' which even contrary experience could not shift. It is also worth remembering that, in the shock of the first close encounters between Europeans and 'others,' imputations of savagery were not all one way.

Local people were not simply objects of curiosity in these early meet-ings. They, too, were historical actors who were curious about what they saw. A more faithful scholarship of 'European exploration' could try to take better account of these complexities, rather than simply replicating the explorers' rather unilateral viewpoints. We might cast the net of memory wider and haul it more cooperatively, and consider views from the shore as well as those from the decks of the European ships.

Banks and Menzies: Evolution of a Journal

W. Kaye Lamb

Because the story of the Archibald Menzies journal begins and ends with Sir Joseph Banks, attention must first be directed to him. Banks was born in 1743, a son of well-to-do parents with estates in Lincolnshire. Young Joseph was sent first to Harrow and then to Eton, but the usual school subjects interested him not at all. He never learned to spell, let alone punctuate. At the age of fourteen, however, he suddenly discovered botany, and plants and gardens became the primary interest in his life. In 1761 his father died and he and his mother moved to the London suburb of Chelsea, near the Chelsea Physic Garden. Banks found a friend in its director, and through him met William Aiton of the Royal Botanic Gardens at Kew. King George III took a keen personal interest in Kew, and he and Banks became friends to such a degree that Banks was advising the king on all matters relating to botany and gardening.

In 1764 Banks came of age, took possession of his estates, and was free to indulge his interests and hobbies. He had already conceived of searching the globe for new plants that might be propagated at Kew and other gardens, and in 1766 he was able to test the plan in person. A frigate was sent to Newfoundland on fisheries patrol, and Banks sailed in her as a passenger. This was arranged by his friend, Lord Sandwich, a former and future first lord of the Admiralty. As this indicates, Banks' circle of influential acquaintances was expanding rapidly. Sociable by nature and disinterested in politics, he found friends and influence everywhere.

Banks brought home specimens or records of at least 340 plants.[1] He returned to find that, in his absence, he had been elected to the Royal Society – a remarkable honour to receive at the age of twenty-three. Thanks to a warm endorsement by the Society, he was included in Captain James Cook's first great voyage of discovery to the Pacific to observe the transit of Venus due in 1769. The staff he took with him included D.C. Solander, already a botanist of note. When the expedition returned in the summer of 1771, Banks' fame became evident: he and Solander, not Cook, were greeted as the conquering heroes, and one newspaper actually identified Cook as a person who had 'sailed round the Globe' with Banks and Solander.[2]

Banks had kept a brief journal on the Newfoundland expedition, in which he had jotted down, in somewhat pell-mell fashion, notes about anything that had caught his interest. His famous, 250,000-word journal of his voyage aboard the *Endeavour* with Cook is a remarkable record of what he saw and experienced. It is not primarily a botanist's journal, but that of an ardent naturalist accompanying a voyage of discovery. Botany in a formal sense he left to Solander, who kept a systematic listing of plants observed and collected.

The adulation he had received seemed to have made Banks lose all sense of proportion. He was anxious to sail with Cook on his second voyage, and the way in which his excessive demands for accommodation for himself and a large staff made this impracticable is well known. But if he could not go foraging for plants himself, Kew Gardens might be able to sponsor collectors who could. In 1772 Francis Masson, the first of such emissaries, was sent to the Cape. Others followed, and seeds, dried specimens, and live plants came to Banks and Kew. Professional collectors were soon supplemented by interested amateurs, including consular staffs, private traders and travellers, and naval officers on distant stations.

This was how Archibald Menzies first came in contact with Banks. Menzies was born near Aberfeldy, Perthshire, in 1754, into a family in which most of the menfolk became gardeners and botanists. To better his education he went to Edinburgh, Scotland, where he studied under Dr John Hope, both professor of botany at the University and superintendent of what were to become the Edinburgh Royal Botanic Gardens. Botany and medicine were closely allied studies in those days, and in 1781 Menzies qualified as a surgeon. Eager to broaden his experience and participate in the search for new plants, he joined the Royal Navy and was appointed assistant surgeon of the *Nonsuch*. In her and subsequently in the *Formidable* and *Assistance* he spent five years on the West Indies and Halifax stations. Because of what Hope termed the 'indulgence of the Commander' he enjoyed many opportunities to botanize.[3]

Menzies' first personal contact with Banks came in May 1784, when, at Hope's request, he sent Banks a letter and a parcel of seeds from Halifax. Banks replied cordially, and other letters and parcels followed. In August 1786 the *Assistance* arrived at Chatham at the end of her commission, and Menzies immediately wrote to Banks, telling him that 'a ship, a private adventurer' was fitting out at Deptford 'to go round the world'; appointment to her as surgeon would not only gratify one of Menzies' 'greatest earthly ambitions' but also would 'afford one of the best opportunities of collecting Seeds and other objects of Natural History' for Banks and his other friends.[4]

As it happened, Banks was already fully informed about the expedition. In 1784 he had been approached by Richard Cadman Etches, a London merchant, head of a group organizing the expedition led by captains Portlock and Dixon – one of the first fur-trading ventures to the northwest coast. Etches was preparing a follow-up venture with the *Prince of Wales* (under Captain Colnett) and the *Princess Royal*. By now Banks was so widely known that he was consulted about many overseas projects, official and unofficial. In 1785 he had been in touch with David Scott, the chief promoter, and James Strange, the commander, of a fur-trading voyage being organized in Bombay. He had been interested in the proposal to found a convict colony in New South Wales, and the First Fleet had sailed in 1787. The same year he would approve the ship that became William Bligh's *Bounty*. And in 1789 Alejandro Malaspina would seek advice and approval of his plans for his great voyage to the Pacific in 1789-95.

Banks responded immediately to Menzies' appeal, and within a fortnight had him appointed surgeon of the *Prince of Wales*. The voyage lasted nearly three years, and when Menzies returned to the Thames in July 1789, he wrote at once to Banks. He had heard that the Admiralty was preparing an expedition to distant parts, and he was eager to join it as naturalist. The expedition's destination was somewhat vague. An African survey seems to have been the original intention, with the northwest coast probably added in view of the maritime fur trade developing there, and as a response to Spain's active interest in the region. The command was first intended for Lieutenant Henry Roberts, who had sailed with Cook. In time, with changes in commander and destination, this would become the Vancouver expedition.

Banks was well positioned to secure an appointment for Menzies. As Kew would be a beneficiary of Menzies' collecting, the king would be interested. Both the Admiralty and the secretary of state for home affairs were involved in organizing the expedition, and Banks had powerful friends in both places: Philip Stephens, the long-time secretary of the board at the Admiralty, among others; and William Grenville, the secretary of state, and Evan Nepean, the under secretary. Grenville was a cousin of both William Pitt, the prime minister, and the Earl of Chatham, first lord of the Admiralty. This list illustrates how far Banks had penetrated the sources of power and the way in which he was able to forward Menzies' career.

There was a short delay, which an impatient Menzies found trying, but on 3 October Nepean informed him that the king had approved his appointment as naturalist. From Nepean Menzies also learned that a ship under construction had already been purchased for the expedition; it would be named *Discovery* when launched in December. Roberts took command on 1 January 1790, and George Vancouver, who had been appointed second in command, came on board six days later. Within a fortnight the first garbled reports about the seizure of British ships at Nootka Sound by the Spanish reached London. In February more details became available, and it became clear that Spain was claiming exclusive jurisdiction over the northwest coast, a pretension to which the British had no intention of submitting. In March a tentative decision was made to meet the Spanish claim head on by establishing a permanent British settlement in the disputed area.

The idea was not new. Etches had discussed it with Banks in 1785, and the Portlock-Dixon expedition had been instructed to establish a post on the coast; to Etches' fury it had not done so. The Meares expedition to Nootka Sound in 1789 was owned in part by Etches, and its evident intention of founding a permanent settlement prompted Captain Estaban José Martínez to seize the British ships.

Events quickly caught up with this 1790 settlement project; and the dispatches concerning it were never sent. Relations between Britain and Spain worsened, and war soon threatened. When mobilization came, the

Discovery became a receiving ship; Roberts and Vancouver left to join the formidable fleet known as the Spanish Armament. Menzies was in limbo and remained so until late in 1790 when the Nootka Sound Convention ended the danger of war and gained for Britain the right to navigate the Pacific Ocean and to found establishments 'in places not already occupied for the purpose' by the Spanish. The immediate requirement became an adequate knowledge of the coast, and a detailed survey was given top priority – this, and a meeting with a Spanish commissioner at Nootka Sound to settle damage and territorial claims arising out of the 1789 seizures. The result was the Vancouver expedition of 1791-5.

Preparations began immediately. On 17 November 1790 the Admiralty recalled Vancouver to London, and the Deptford Yard was instructed to give the fitting out of the *Discovery* and its small companion, the *Chatham*, 'preference to all other works.'[5] Then came the change in command. The *Discovery* was paid off, and when it was recommissioned on 15 December Vancouver succeeded Roberts.

Menzies was in a difficult position. Roberts was still expected to lead an expedition to Africa, but nothing definite had been arranged, and the complement of the recommissioned *Discovery* had no provision for a naturalist. On 13 December, most opportunely, Menzies had received his warrant as a Royal Navy surgeon[6] (as distinct from his former rank as assistant surgeon). He himself tells what followed: 'As a state of tedious suspence was more intolerable to me, than the hardships of a long Voyage ... I requested leave of the Treasury to go out as Surgeon of the Discovery, promising at the same time that my vacant hours from my professional charge, should be chiefly employed ... in making such collections and observations as might elucidate the natural history of the Voyage.'[7] Banks and the secretary of state were at once involved, and Banks set about drafting the terms upon which Menzies should be appointed. Some of Banks' rough notes include the earliest reference to a Menzies journal: he was 'to deliver his journal to his employers on his return Provided that [if] it was thought proper for Publication, he should be allowed to publish it for his own benefit.' The term 'employers' is ambiguous, but to Banks it certainly meant the secretary of state. Banks gave his draft of the proposed terms of employment to Nepean on 15 December, and on 22 December Nepean told him that Grenville (now Lord Grenville) 'had agreed to the whole proposition & ordered a Letter wrote ... to request the appointment of Surgeon for Mr M[enzies].'[8] His salary was to be £80 a year.

Menzies continues the story: 'The Treasury gave a favourable hearing & readily agreed to my proposal, but the Commander of the Expedition made some Objections, what they were I never heard.' In the end the battle was tied: Vancouver was able to have Alexander Cranstoun appointed as surgeon in place of Menzies, but Banks and Grenville arranged to have Menzies appointed to a supernumerary position as botanist at a higher salary of £150 a year, but this was to include 'every charge of Salary mess servants wages &c &c.'[9] Banks was apt to assume that if he took an interest in a project this gave him the right to interfere, and evidence that friction had developed between Vancouver and himself is reflected in his oft-quoted warning to Menzies: 'How Capt Van will behave to you is more than I can guess unless I was to judge by his Conduct towards me which was not such as I am used to receive from Persons in his situation.'[10]

Banks signed Menzies' instructions (which he had drafted at Grenville's request) on 22 February 1791 from his own residence in Soho Square. The preliminary paragraph outlined the vast field of inquiry in which Menzies was expected to be active. It was to include 'an investigation of the whole of the Natural History of the Countries you are to visit as well as an enquiry into the present State & comparative degree of civilization of the inhabitants you will meet with.' The concluding paragraph dealt with his journal: 'You are to keep a regular Journal of all occurrences that happen in the execution of the several Duties you are to perform, & enter in it all the observations you shall make on every subject you are employed to investigate, which Journal, together with a compleat collection of specimens of the animals, vegetables & minerals you shall have obtained as well as such curious articles of the cloths [sic], arms, implements and manufactures of the Indians as you shall deem worthy of particular notice, you are on your return to deliver to His Majesty's Secretary of State for the Home department, or to such person as he shall appoint to receive them from you.'[11]

The Vancouver expedition somewhat resembled Banks' voyage with Cook, and Banks' own *Endeavour* journal probably suggested that a record by Menzies would be valuable. So far as is known, Menzies kept no journal of his voyage in the *Prince of Wales*, but his letters to Banks had shown

The Discovery on the Rocks in Queen Charlotte's Sound, sketch by Zachary Mudge, engraved by B.T. Pouncy

that he was quite capable of keeping one. The overriding consideration, however, on the Vancouver expedition was Banks' conviction that Menzies should keep a journal for his own protection. In the same letter in which he expressed doubts about Vancouver's treatment of Menzies, he stressed this point. As it could be 'highly imprudent' of Vancouver 'to throw any obstacles in the way of your duty I trust he will have too much good sense to destruct it if he does the instances whatever they are will of course appear as they happened in your Journal which as it will be a justification of you will afford ground for impeaching the propriety of his conduct which for your sake I shall not Fail to make use of.'[12]

Vancouver and Menzies had minor differences regarding messing arrangements and other details even before the expedition sailed, but all went relatively well during the early stages of the voyage. Vancouver's health had caused some concern and, significantly, he chose Menzies, rather than Cranstoun, to act as his personal physician. Indeed, Banks stated later that 'Menzies Savd Vancouvers Life by putting him upon a nutritive diet when he thought himself within a few days of his dissolution by having adhered to a shore one this was soon after the Ship left Teneriff.'[13] At the Cape of Good Hope, dysentery on board a ship that arrived from Batavia spread to the *Discovery*, and took the life of a marine. Cranstoun was seriously ill, and (in Menzies' words) 'Captain Vancouver in this situation requested me to take charge of the sick for him, which I readily complied with.'[14]

As it happened, Cranstoun's health continued to be a problem, and by the time the expedition reached Nootka Sound, Vancouver decided that he must be discharged and invalided home to England. Menzies describes the sequel: 'As Capt. Vancouver did not conceive himself warrantable to make a new Surgeon ... while I was on the spot, he solicited me to take charge of the Surgeon's duty ... & this he urged with a degree of earnestness that I could not well refuse, especially as he requested at the same time that in case of my not accepting of it, to state my having refused it in writing, & as I did not know how far this might operate against my interest in the Navy Office, I with considerable hesitation accepted of the appointment.'[15]

His new duties as surgeon placed Menzies much more directly under Vancouver's authority, but some time seems to have passed before he realized that this might have some bearing on the future of his journal. Meanwhile a plant frame (or miniature greenhouse) built on the quarter deck to bring live plants back to England caused difficulties. It had been built 'from a particular plan of Sir Joseph Banks, Bart.' and perhaps for that very reason irritated Vancouver. On 18 November 1793, Menzies sent a note to Vancouver that reveals how strained relations had become: 'It is really so unpleasant to me to represent to you verbally any thing relative to the Plant-frame on the Quarter-deck that I have now adopted this method to mention to you all the alterations or rather additions which I wish to be made to its original plan, for the security of the plants within it.' He had two immediate needs in mind. First, 'the Fowls have been in it again last night, and have done irreparable damage'; the frame must be covered with a strong netting, to protect the plants when it is open. Second, Vancouver should 'appoint a Man, who will be suffered from his other duty, to look after it, and execute my orders concerning it, while I am out of the Ship or pursuing my duty on Shore.'[16] After some delay Vancouver dealt with the first request, but, as subsequent events were to show, he was unwilling to let Menzies have any authority over crew members of the *Discovery*.

It is not known when Menzies became aware that the Admiralty had instructed Vancouver to impound all journals, logs, etc. executed by 'the officers, petty officers and gentlemen on board the *Discovery*,' but he was worried about the prospect by the time the expedition reached Valparaiso on the home run. On 28 April 1795, he wrote to Banks: 'When the Journals of the Voyage &c. are demanded by Captain Vancouver, I mean to seal up mine, & address them to you, so that I hope you will receive them.'[17]

On 2 July, as the ships were nearing St Helena, Vancouver decided that the time had come to carry out the Admiralty's directive. The journals and logs kept on the *Discovery* were gathered in, but Menzies requested permission to retain his until the end of the voyage, and Vancouver consented. This suggests that relations between the captain and himself had improved, but the plant frame was soon to cause a resounding clash. On 28 July, without any prior warning, Vancouver reassigned to other duties the crew member who was to follow Menzies' directions regarding the hutch. It was left open, a torrential rain fell, and great damage resulted. Vancouver and Menzies fell out. On 13 September, when the *Discovery* dropped anchor in the Shannon, Vancouver wrote at once to the Admiralty, accusing Menzies of having treated him with 'great contempt and disrespect'[18] and asking that he be tried by court martial. The following day Menzies gave his version of the dispute in a letter to Banks: though suffering 'all the pangs of disappointed expectations' he had 'coolly & without either *Insolence* or *contempt* complained to Captain Vancouver of being unjustly used in this proceeding. He immediately flew in a rage, and his passionate behaviour, and abusive language on the occasion, prevented any further explanation – and I was put under Arrest, because I would not retract my expression, while my grievance still remained unredressed.'[19]

Truth to tell, the plant frame had been a repeated disappointment to Menzies, particularly in the later stages of the voyage. Writing to Banks from Nootka Sound in September 1794 he had lamented that the 'severe & quick transition of Climate [from Hawai'i to Alaska] killed the greatest part of the live plants, I had in the Frame.'[20] In March 1795, off the coast of South America, he informed Banks that the voyage southward 'had proved fatal to many of my little favourites, the live-plants from the North west coast & California, notwithstanding my utmost endeavours to save them.' He was still hopeful that he would 'be able to fill up the vacancies, before we leave this coast,'[21] but if he did so, many new specimens must have perished in the rain on 28 July. To have this last mishap occur when the long voyage was within a few weeks of ending must indeed have been a bitter and exasperating disappointment.

As the voyage ended, Vancouver renewed his demand for the surrender of Menzies' journals; Menzies again refused to comply. Vancouver recalled that at St Helena, Menzies had 'requested that the same (for their more perfect completion) might be suffered to remain in your possession during the passage to Europe, which request I have thus complied with; and the coast of Ireland being now in sight, I desire that the same may, in the course of this day, be delivered to me ... For which this shall be your Order.'[22] To which Menzies replied, pointing out the dual nature of his employment: 'I have received your Order of this day's date, Addressed to me as Surgeon of His Majesty's Sloop *Discovery*: Demanding my Journals, Charts, drawings etc of the voyage, but I can assure you that, in that capacity, I kept no other Journals than the Sick-book, which is ready to be delivered if you think this necessary.' Menzies then recalled a conversation with Vancouver in which he had discussed 'the mode of conveying the Journals, Papers, Drawings, etc.' he had 'kept on the Voyage in compliance with my Original Instructions to the Secretary of States' Office.' He concluded: 'I therefore beg leave to acquaint you that I do not conceive myself authorized to deliver these Journals etc. to anyone till they are demanded of me, by the Secretary of State for the home department, agreeable to the tenor of my Instructions.'[23]

Vancouver's remark that Menzies had wished to retain his journals after St Helena 'for their more perfect completion' refers no doubt to Menzies' efforts to complete a fair copy. In the letter to Banks in which he reported his arrest, Menzies wrote: 'I am at present hard at work in bringing up the clean copy of my Journal of the Voyage, & I am afraid I shall require the indulgence of a few months after I get home to have it completed; as I am but a very slow hand at the pen and our constant and frequent movements during the voyage took up much of my time on shore, in examining the different countries we visited.'[24] But, as shall be seen, years, not months, were to pass before Menzies completed the version of his journal available today.

Vancouver left the *Discovery* at the Shannon and hurried to London; Menzies stayed on board, arriving in the Thames on 20 October. Being under arrest, he could neither go ashore nor land his papers and his surviving live plants. Meanwhile Banks had been active. On 1 October he had informed Menzies that it had given him 'infinite pain' to hear of his quarrel with Vancouver; he understood fully how exasperating the loss of his live plants had been, and he was writing 'instantly' to Evan Nepean (who had recently succeeded Philip Stephens as secretary of the board of Admiralty). After a circumspect reference to the dispute with Vancouver ('no doubt the Capt had good reasons for his Conduct but I incline to believe that Flesh & blood ... could not see its whole hopes destroyed without uttering some Complaint'), he was forthright about Menzies' status and his journals: 'As Menzies was wholly under my orders he has declined to deliver up his Journals to the Capt they being under the instructions given to him by me their Lordships will please to decide whether these Journals shall be sent up to the board or be delivered immediately to me and Menzies will instantly obey their will on this subject.'[25]

Vancouver rejoined the *Discovery* when it reached Deptford, and events moved rapidly. Banks was urging Nepean to allow Menzies to land his collections; two days later, in a brief note that probably reflected pressure by Nepean on both parties, Vancouver informed him that Menzies had 'made an ample apology for his conduct to me on the 28th July last' and requested permission to withdraw his application for a court martial.[26] His request was granted; Menzies was released from custody and was permitted to land his plants. No mention was made of the journals, but there is no doubt that Menzies and Banks retained possession of them.

The *Discovery* was paid off on 3 November 1795, and Menzies found himself without employment and with the fair copy of his journal still far from complete. Late in the month he was sent to Sheerness to supervise fumigating the hospital ship *Union* and units of a visiting Russian squadron in which typhus had broken out. Visits to Sheerness continued until February 1796. On 3 February Banks sent an appeal on Menzies' behalf to the Duke of Portland, who had succeeded Grenville as secretary of state. His letter explained the dual nature of Menzies' employment in the *Discovery* and continued: 'In consequence of this double duty he found it impossible properly to arrange and digest the Journal he was ordered to keep ... My petition in his favour was therefore that his salary being £150 a year, might for the present be continued to him in order to enable him to complete his journals which when finished are to be delivered to your Grace.'[27]

For once, Banks' appeal was unsuccessful. Not long after this rebuff – probably in March 1796 – the Admiralty informed Vancouver that they wished him to prepare his journal for publication. Within a month Vancouver heard that a scheme was afoot to include Menzies' journal in the project. On 8 April he protested directly to the Earl of Chatham, the first lord of the Admiralty: 'As I find it is the intention of the Admiralty, that the observations made by Mr Menzies, on the various subjects of the Natural History of the different Country [sic] we visited, should in some way be connected with my account of the Voyage; and that under such considerations Mr Menzies is to be benefited by a proportion of the profits that may result from the sale of the work; and on that subject in a letter to the Board [of Admiralty] I have pointed out the disadvantages I labour under ... the pay of Mr Menzies during the Voyage was much more than double mine which together with his expenses, has been paid him since his return; and hence it is natural to conclude; since he has been so amply paid by government that the results of his employment are the intire property of government and totally at their own disposal.'[28] At this time Vancouver had not yet been paid for his services as commander of the expedition, and the account would not be settled for another eighteen months.

This proposal certainly originated with Banks, and the precedent he had in mind would be his own journal of the *Endeavour* voyage with Cook. When Hawkesworth was commissioned to prepare Cook's journal for publication, Banks' own journal was one of several turned over to him to 'enhance' Cook's narrative. He used it freely; Beaglehole's comment is interesting: 'There is therefore a great deal of Banks in Hawkesworth, including a great deal that can hardly be said to be even paraphrased – unless the providing of punctuation and the correction of spelling can be deemed paraphrase.'[29] Banks evidently proposed that the Vancouver and Menzies journals should be melded in somewhat the same fashion.

Vancouver's protest was successful. Rebuffed a second time, Banks proposed nothing less than to forestall Vancouver and to have Menzies' journal completed, and even in print, before Vancouver's official account appeared. The difficulty was that Menzies had to have an income, and he had to resume service in the navy. On 30 November 1796, he joined the Admiralty yacht *Princess Augusta*, and, except for a brief transfer to the frigate *Tamer*, remained there until 1799. His duties cannot have been onerous, but any duties at all would interfere with journal revision. At times, however, he was evidently able to concentrate on the task, and on 3 January 1798, he sent Banks a revealing progress report:

> I received your kind letter this morning and return my sincerest thanks for your friendly admonitions & solicitations respecting the finishing of my Journal before Captain Vancouver's is published. – It is what I most ardently wish, for more reasons than one, and therefore have lately applied to it very close. – I generally get up at five in the morning and continue at it, with as little interruption as possible till six or seven in the evening daily. The volume I am now at work upon (and which is nearly finished) I once thought would include the whole of the remainder of the Narrative, but I find it will not, though it is much larger than either of those you have got. A desire of making it a full and continued narrative of the Voyage and my being but a slow hand at the pen, are the princi-pal reason for its taking so much of my time in finishing, but the most fagging part of it is nearly over, and can assure you that I will continue with unremitting application until the whole is accomplished.[30]

Banks' urgings were in vain. Vancouver died on 12 May 1798, but most of his half-million-word narrative had already been set in type. Only a hundred pages remained to be revised, carried out promptly by his brother John, who had been assisting him for a year or more. *A Voyage of Discovery* was published later in 1798, probably in August or early September.

In his essay on Menzies, J.J. Keevil remarks that 'in spite of Banks' and Menzies' mutual interests and long associations a certain coolness now appears to have crept into their relations, a circumstance to which the court-martial incident may have contributed.'[31] Much more likely, Menzies' failure to complete his fair copy in time to enable Banks to embarrass Vancouver was the cause.

Banks retained Menzies' journal, or at least the three volumes to which Menzies had referred in his letter of 3 January 1798. They carried the narrative as far as 16 February 1794, when the ships were preparing to leave the Hawai'ian Islands, bound for Alaska and the third and last sur-veying season. The unfortunate way in which Banks' papers were dis-persed after his death in 1820 is well known. He had no children, and the first custodian of the papers was Lady Banks' nephew, Sir Edward Knatchbull. He was succeeded by his son, who later became the first Baron Brabourne. As late as 1886 Menzies' journal was still part of what was left of the papers. F.R.S. Balfour, who inherited some of the Menzies papers in 1942, concludes the story: 'The history of this voluminous work ... is that it came up for sale at Sothebys on 13 March 1886. It must have belonged to representatives of Banks, as at the same sale there appeared other Banksian Mss. The sale lot is number 977 ... it was mis-described in the catalogue as the Journal of Banks in the "Discovery." It then consisted of 420 folios.'[32] Purchased by the British Museum, the Menzies journal is now Add. MS 32641 in the Manuscript Department of the British Library.

Menzies intended to complete the narrative of the voyage in a fourth volume, describing the last survey season. This final part of the extant journal carries the account forward to 18 March 1795, ten days before the homeward bound ships entered Valparaiso harbour. Vancouver states that on the 14th, 'to my utter astonishment and surprise, I was given to understand from Mr. Menzies that sea scurvy had made its appearance amongst the crew.' Oddly enough, Menzies makes no mention of this outbreak in his own journal, though he mentioned it in a letter to Banks sent home in the whaler *Lightning*. For a clue as to why Menzies carried the fair copy of his journal no further we may look in the preface that John Vancouver contributed to Vancouver's published narrative. Only the account of the voyage from Valparaiso, around Cape Horn and, thence, to St Helena and England remained to be revised when the captain died, and John Vancouver felt that this could be dealt with in somewhat summary fashion: 'As no new incidents occurred in this part of the voyage, and as the insertion of log-book minutes, over a space which is now so frequently traversed, cannot either be useful or entertaining, I have endeavoured to compress this portion of the journal into as few pages as possible.' Menzies may well have felt the same way. There is the further point that changed circumstances probably made further work on the journal impracticable. Within a few months of the publication of Vancouver's *Voyage*, Menzies became surgeon of the *Sans Pareil*, flagship of Lord Hugh Seymour, and he served in it on the West Indies station until September 1802. Broken in health, he then retired from active service and set about establishing a medical practice in London. It is an interesting coincidence that the part of Vancouver's *Voyage* that John Vancouver revised personally and Menzies' journal both end within a few days of one another.

Banks lost interest in Menzies' journal when Vancouver's narrative was published, and it is unlikely that the last year was ever part of his papers. The format of the manuscript, 259 pages (or 130 folios) in length, is similar to that in the British Library. For its later history we must go to Australia. Edward Augustus Petherick (1847-1917) was first employed by George Robertson, the Melbourne publisher and bookseller, who sent him to London in 1875 as a buyer. Petherick began to compile a bibliography of Australia and the Pacific, and during his more than thirty years in England he not only expanded the bibliography but also acquired thousands of the items listed in it. In 1909 this great collection found a permanent home in the National Library of Australia, which numbers Petherick amongst its 'great benefactors.' His manuscripts included the last year of the Menzies journal (when and how he acquired it does not appear). It is now MS 155 in the Library's Manuscript Collection.[33]

One question remains: to what extent did Banks determine the character of the journal as it appears today? During the expedition Menzies wrote to Banks whenever possible. His letters were dated from Tenerife, the Cape of Good Hope, Hawai'i, Nootka Sound, Monterey, San Diego, Valparaiso, and, finally, Shannon. Zacariah Mudge and William Broughton both carried letters to Banks when they returned to England with dispatches in 1792; others were sent from California through Mexico to Europe; the rest were entrusted to trading ships encountered here and there by the *Discovery*. Some were a year or more on the way, but only one seems to have been lost in transit. In all, Menzies wrote fourteen, mostly lengthy, letters to Banks, giving him an excellent, if concise, first-hand account of most of the highlights of the voyage.

It is clear that from the first Menzies intended his journal to be the 'full and continued narrative of the Voyage' to which he referred when writing to Banks. In three seasons on the northwest coast the ship's boats carried out about fifty surveying expeditions. Menzies only accompanied about a third of them, but knew the officers in charge of the others – notably Peter Puget, James Johnstone, and Joseph Whidbey – and he borrowed their journals, which enabled him to keep his account of the expedition reasonably complete.

Occasionally the letters to Banks supplement the journal. At Tenerife a shore party and Spanish guards unfortunately clashed. Vancouver (who was not in uniform) was roughly handled and thrown into the harbour. He did not report the incident to the Admiralty or mention it in the *Voyage*, but Menzies described it in some detail, first in a letter to Banks and later in his journal.[34]

The letters also fill a curious gap in the journal's record of the ships' visit to the Cape. As they were arriving, Menzies gazed upon 'a country so celebrated for the uncommon variety of its vegetable productions' and promised himself 'no small degree of pleasure in the pursuit of these favourite objects during our stay.' But the journal leaps forward five weeks until sailing day, when Menzies made a brief shore excursion with his friend Captain William Paterson, a soldier-naturalist well known to Banks, who had shared in the hunt for new plants for Kew. Paterson was travelling with the Third Fleet to New South Wales, where he would later serve as lieutenant-governor. The gap is explained by dysentery, which had broken out on the *Discovery*. Cranstoun, the surgeon, was soon gravely ill, and much of Menzies' time was absorbed by emergency medical duties. Here again the letters give missing details. Menzies wrote that he met Francis Masson back in South Africa to secure plants for Kew, and that Masson 'was good enough to accompany me in some of my excursions up Table Mountain and in the neighbourhood of False Bay.' Menzies did little collecting; he assumed that Masson, whose study it had been 'for many years' had 'already collected everything new and rare.'[35]

The accounts of his visits to King George Sound, in southwestern Australia, and to Dusky Bay, New Zealand, essentially summarize his activities as a botanist. In King George Sound he describes his shore excursions in detail, followed by a concluding section of general observations. The account of Dusky Bay follows much the same pattern. As for the Pacific northwest, botanical references are frequent in the 1791-2 journal which covers the first (1792) survey. Occasionally, an individual bird, fish, or plant is singled out and described in full scientific detail.

The account of the 1793 survey season, however, is another matter; it has no more than about thirty specific botanical references, and the record of the 1794 survey season is almost as bare. Is it fanciful to see in this a response to pressure from Banks to press on with a revision that would deliberately forestall Vancouver's general account?

The deficiencies of the journal as a botanical record have long been a subject of comment. In 1929 Willis Linn Jepson contributed an article on Menzies to a series on early California botanists published in *Madrono*. His comments are interesting:

> It was at once obvious that one possessed a valuable historical document, but it was also apparent that it contained comparatively scanty records regarding the Native vegetation. In the journal Menzies from time to time makes a few notes, in more or less general terms, of his botanical excursions ashore, but on account of the utter strangeness of the vegetation his comments are not, on the whole, of much significance. At that time the importance of a strictly scientific journal with a numbering of specimens in sequence by stations and dates as collected were not appreciated ... On the other hand the journal is amply filled with other matters. Save for the references to himself as a botanist just noted one might suppose from reading the manuscript that Menzies was the navigator or geographer of the expedition. The progress of the *Discovery* or its consort the *Chatham*, every storm that impeded, every wind that aided their movement, is faithfully set down.[36]

This view is extreme, but Balfour echoed it in his centennial lecture to the Linnean Society in 1942: 'It is to be regretted that Menzies' Journal records so few of the localities of his botanical discoveries ... We would have preferred this information to the prolix daily accounts of the weather experienced and the nautical observations taken.'[37]

These, of course, were the views of readers who would have welcomed a journal devoted exclusively to botany and botanizing. Instead, this is a journal in which Menzies' special interests are evident but not predominant, especially in the later years. The change in the journal does not necessarily mean that Menzies abandoned botany. It seems certain that, in addition to the journal, he kept notes on his botanizing expeditions, recording the new and interesting plants found along the way. But these were evidently kept separately, perhaps with the precedent of Banks and Solander in mind – Banks writing the *Endeavour* journal, while Solander maintained a systematic record of botanical discoveries. Unfortunately, Menzies' notes have disappeared, and all that remain are his letters and the notes on the mounts of his dried specimens (now scattered through many herbaria), which Eric Groves of the British Museum (Natural History) has hunted down with incredible patience and persistence.

Finally, watermarks in the paper used by Menzies in preparing his fair copy give some indication when the manuscript was written. From the initial entry in December 1790 to the entry for 29 May 1792 (folio 134), the paper is watermarked 1794, meaning that the text could have been written any time after Menzies' return to England in 1795. With folio 135, however, there is a significant change. After a blank page, Menzies made a fresh start with a different pen, and from folio 135 to folio 420, the end of the British Library's manuscript, the paper is watermarked 1796. Thus, it was written when Banks was pressing Menzies to complete the manuscript for possible publication. The text in folio 420 stops with Menzies' last visit to Hawai'i in February 1794. MS 155, the Australian manuscript, picks up the story a few days later and breaks off abruptly in March 1795, when the ships were off the coast of Chile.[38] Its paper is watermarked 1798.

Was the copying abandoned because the manuscript could not possibly be ready in time to forestall Vancouver? The jury may still be out, but the verdict appears to be that Menzies' journal, as it appears today, was written after the *Discovery* returned to England and was drafted in great part to specifications laid down by Sir Joseph Banks.

The Intellectual Discovery and Exploration of Polynesia

K.R. Howe

The terms *exploration* and *discovery* are usually employed in a geographic sense, but they also have intellectual dimensions. After European explorers had located a cultural region to become known as Polynesia,[1] more exploration and discovery were required to know, understand, and explain the apparent characteristics of the Polynesians. As they strove to catalogue their new knowledge, European investigators seldom tried to interpret Polynesians in terms of themselves. Instead, Polynesians were frequently likened to something familiar and explicable in European terms. Ultimately Polynesia was a European-created, cultural artifact.

Modern scholarship has surveyed the ways in which European commentators since the late eighteenth century have variously stereotyped Pacific peoples as Noble Savages, ignoble savages, dying savages, and Romantic savages.[2] There is good coverage, too, of how European scholars have, for 200 years, attempted to locate the original homeland of Pacific peoples in general and Polynesians in particular. Answers have ranged from the Mediterranean, to Asia, to India, to the Americas, to sunken continents, and even to outer space.[3] Modern scholars have accepted for some time now that such commentators, to quote M.P.K. Sorrenson, read into the search for 'origins and culture what they wanted and expected to find, on the basis of theories derived from their own cultural and philosophical traditions.'[4]

Although such a quest has been described, the imperatives behind it have been far less understood. Polynesian origins and cultures were not persistently and extensively studied for 200 years merely out of idle or antiquarian curiosity. On the contrary, among key commentators was a need to interpret and define Polynesians, the 'other,' in order to help to locate and define the 'self.' Such commentators were in effect looking for their own reflections in their mirror on the world. Eventually they saw Polynesians as having Aryan/Caucasian ancestry like themselves, which was, of course, a major act of intellectual appropriation and colonization.

The propensity of European visitors to the Pacific to liken the 'other' to familiar images was first demonstrated by the later eighteenth-century explorers. Wherever they located Pacific Islanders between the extremes of Noble or brutish savages, their observations, their simple ethnographies, were often underpinned with explicit comparisons. Louis-Antoine de Bougainville and Joseph Banks gave Tahitians Greek names as befitted their appearance and characters – Hercules, Mars, Lycurgus, Ajax, Epicurus. Explorers constantly sought parallels with European sociopolitical systems. Thus Tahiti and Hawai'i had kings and queens. Tahitian social structure was graded from king to baron, to yeoman, to gentleman, to vassal, to slave or villein.[5] Even in less hierarchical societies, such as New Zealand, where primitivism was deemed a little harder than in 'soft' Tahiti, explorers like Dumont D'Urville, as late as the 1820s, saw in 'spontaneous comparison' Greek landscapes, towns, and characters everywhere – including a seaborne war party which, apart from lacking a Homer, resembled 'perfectly the victors of Troy.'[6]

Bernard Smith has rightly pointed out that 'we must not be misled by the colourful parallels developed by Bougainville, Banks and others, into thinking that all Polynesians evoked classical visions of the Golden Age ... Yet it was the classical vision which first permeated the European imagination.'[7] Philosophers, painters, poets, and writers in Europe created sensational, exotic South Seas fantasies that bore little or no relation to Native life. In particular they constructed a whole mythology of Tahiti as Arcadia. Even the living specimens taken back to Europe by explorers, notably Mai (or Omai) and Aotourou, were not studied as representatives of Oceanic cultures, but as adaptations and thus reflections of the supposedly more refined European mores.[8] Their pictures were predetermined too: Mai was invariably depicted dressed like some eastern prince. The exotic image of the South Seas was never really destroyed (and still exists in many forms today) despite another view based on the essentially evangelical concept of the ignoble savage, together with a historico-literary tradition that European contact was responsible for destroying the paradise in the Pacific.[9]

This early propensity to compare the cultures of the Polynesians to earlier societies in Europe, especially the Greeks, was *not* motivated by a random convenience or simply an instinctive reflection of the prevailing artistic and literary concern with neo-classicism. Rather, Greek and similar iconography provided a powerful reference point for those explorers groping toward a Polynesian ethnography. The unfamiliar, the wildly exotic could be made meaningful through cultural comparison to elements of both remote, but familiar, past civilizations. There was more to it than this, however. The growing scholarly interest in early European history provided a window on the past self, particularly as longstanding antiquarian views about primitivism became more sociologically informed.[10]

The opening of the Americas greatly stimulated the study of early or 'natural man,' particularly in the 1750s,[11] and the 'discovery' of Oceanic cultures shortly thereafter added examples. If at least some New World and Oceanic societies could be shown to be similar to early Mediterranean civilizations, then a study of such cultures might be a way of catching live, as it were, aspects of Europe's own prehistory. For example, Lord Monboddo, an eighteenth-century advocate of human progression through an evolutionary process, thought that discoveries in the South Seas would 'improve and enlarge the knowledge of our own species as much as the natural history of other animals, and of plants and minerals.'[12] Indeed, Monboddo believed that the inhabitants of the South Seas, 'living in the natural state,' would provide much better examples than those of America because North American Indians and Peruvian Incas had been changed so much since the time of Columbus.[13]

There are many examples of how explorers' categorizing of Pacific peoples contributed to the growing knowledge about the human race in general. One of the most influential of the early recorders of Pacific life was J.R. Forster, the scientist who sailed on Cook's second voyage. He graded the Polynesians according to their own internal hierarchy (Tahitians first, followed by Marquesans, Tongans, Easter Islanders, Maori), and distinguished this general group from the darker-skinned peoples later categorized as Melanesians. Forster, himself opposed to the more simplistic notions of the Noble Savage, nevertheless found much to admire, particularly in Tahitian lifestyles, aspects of which he likened to 'the true antient Greek style' and 'the same manner as at Rome.'[14] Forster wanted to explain the differences and varieties in Pacific cultures, which he put down to such factors as climate and resources. Like many others, his aim was not so much to study Oceanic peoples per se, but to begin to construct an anthropology of the human race, investigating the progress from primitive states toward higher levels of civilization. For Forster, societies followed the 'progress of man as an individual.' Infancy he likened to animal life, childhood to savagery, the 'violent passions' of adolescence to barbarism, and maturity to civilization.[15] Pacific cultures were in various stages of savagery and so provided clues to the 'infant state of humanity.'[16]

Forster's commentaries had an application that reached far beyond Pacific studies. For example, they influenced Johann Friedrich Blumenbach, who graded the world's population into descending categories – Caucasians, Malays (including Pacific Islanders)/Americans, and Mongolians/Ethiopians.[17] Such classifications had less to do with explaining, say, Polynesians, than with an apparently rational explanation for, and legitimizing of, the European world view, based on assumptions of its own cultural superiority. Placing the cultures of 'others' on a Eurocentric yardstick was more a commentary on the yardstick and those who used it than those it purported to measure. Polynesians or others were examined only in relation to self and in that process self or past self was explained – 'The Moral Philosopher ... who loves to trace the advances of his species through its various gradations from savage to civilised life, draws from voyages and travels, the facts from which he is to deduce his conclusions respecting the social, intellectual and moral progress of Man.'[18]

Long before Darwin it was appreciated that there was not just a cultural distance between modern European civilization and primitive ones – some of which, like those of Polynesia, were now coming to European attention – but also a distance in time. Just as the barbaric Gauls and Britons had eventually reached the high point of human civilization, could not Pacific (and other cultures) do the same? Several commentators indeed contemplated the rise of modern civilizations among the Natives of the Antipodes and Oceania. One foresaw a time 'when New Zealand may produce her Lockes, her Newtons, and her Montesquieus;

and when great nations in the immense region of New Holland, may send their navigators, philosophers, and antiquaries, to contemplate the ruins of *ancient* London and Paris, and to trace the languid remains of the arts and sciences in this quarter of the globe.'[19] Dumont D'Urville expressed similar sentiments,[20] all of which foreshadowed T.B. Macaulay's 1840 vision of a Maori standing on the remains of London Bridge sketching the ruins of St Paul's. Such apparently fanciful musings reflected serious and complex formulations about human socio-economic progress deemed to involve four basic stages – hunting, pastoral, agricultural, commercial. To a considerable extent, such theories were based on observations of the contemporary 'savage.'[21]

Explorers were far less systematic and overtly ideological in their ethnographic endeavours than many who came after them, in particular missionaries. If explorers' comparative reference points were commonly derived from neo-classicism, those of missionaries were primarily biblical. Missionaries nevertheless retained some important elements of eighteenth-century Enlightenment thought on the nature and development of the human race. For example, they similarly believed in the unity of the race, though they specifically identified as progenitors first Adam and Eve and then the descendants of Noah after the Flood. This fitted nicely with Blumenbach's categories of humans, of which some evangelical missionaries were well aware.[22] In their view, the more 'advanced' savages, including Polynesians, were the descendants of Shem, and the allegedly more 'primitive,' such as the Papuans and Australian Aborigines, were the sons and daughters of Ham.[23]

Scriptural interpretation also allowed for considerable fluidity in human historical development, though the missionaries injected a righteous dimension and emphasized progression and regression according to the respective moral worth of a people. European societies, in their view, had advanced and gained commercially and technologically because of their spiritual and moral excellence, whereas Pacific and other heathen societies had clearly degenerated on the scale of human existence. The evangelical vocation, then, was to rescue Pacific societies from the brutish levels to which they had sunk.

In point of fact, in their general explanations of Polynesian peoples, missionaries reflected their own world views. In trying to understand Polynesian cultures, the evangelical mind resorted to familiar images, that in turn reinforced the missionaries' perceptions of their own past and present status in the development of the human race. The notion that the peoples of Polynesia had semitic origins seems to have been first advanced about the Maori by Samuel Marsden, who considered that, on the basis of various customs, including their 'natural turn for traffic,' the Maori had 'sprung from some dispersed Jews ... and have by some means got into the island from Asia.'[24] Until the 1870s numerous missionary and non-missionary writers established and entrenched a now well-annotated tradition of the Maori as one of the Lost Tribes of Israel.[25]

Semitic influences in Polynesian cultures were diligently recorded elsewhere. For example, William Ellis, who wrote one of the better early accounts of Polynesia, concluded that, if Polynesians were not actually Jewish, then at least their language and customs 'shew that the nation, whence they emigrated, was acquainted with some of the leading facts recorded in the Mosaic history of the primitive ages of mankind.'[26] Island legends similar to biblical tales of the Creation and the Flood were widely illustrated. For example, George Turner found in Samoan traditions a story 'like the Mosaic account of the deluge,' a tale reminiscent of 'Jacob's ladder,' and a Samoan 'Paethon' whose efforts to slow the sun seemed to echo the 'sublime description in the book of Joshua ... when that man of God stood in the sight of Israel and said: "Sun, stand thou still upon Gibeon."'[27] Similar legends were recorded in Fiji and Tonga,[28] and can be found scattered throughout mission literature on Polynesian culture.

The quest for Polynesian origins also involved considerable debate about their alleged migration routes into Oceania. This debate need not be reiterated here, other than to say that, in crude terms, it boiled down to whether the Polynesians came from the west, directly out of Asia, or from the east, out of Asia via the Americas. The debate, rekindled by Thor Heyerdahl's 1947 *Kon Tiki* expedition, has a very long ancestry.[29] Missionary and non-missionary scholars also made substantial inquiry into the settlement routes within Oceania itself.[30] However, the question as to ultimate origins was not much in dispute (apart from those like J.A. Moerenhout, who argued for a sunken continent theory)[31] with most writers, and certainly most evangelicals in agreement with Russell: 'The traces of primeval belief which prevail among the people of the South Sea, will be found to lend great probability to the conclusion, that the nations whence they originally emigrated must have been well acquainted with some of the leading facts contained in the Mosaical history.' Russell also drew attention to the close similarities between island religions and those of ancient Greece and Rome: 'The classical scholar, while he may regret the absence of the pleasing mythology ... will acknowledge that the gross rites of Otaheite may be traced to the same source with the more elegant adoration which was offered to the deities of Delphi and Eleusis.'[32] Other missionaries likewise noted similarities with the Hindu religion.[33] The traces of either classical or Indian elements were readily explained as being picked up during the Polynesians' wanderings from their biblical homeland.

The missionaries' substitution of the image of the ignoble for that of the Noble Savage can be deceptive. Without question, the evangelicals regarded all 'heathen' societies that had no contact with Christianity and 'civilization' as utterly degraded. Yet there were levels of degradation. Polynesians, for all their alleged abominations, were usually considered relatively superior heathens because of their light skin and the apparent openness and responsiveness of many of their societies. Certainly the potential for their improvement was there. As John Williams claimed, in terms of 'mental capacity' the 'South Sea Islander does not rank below the European.'[34]

Furthermore, some more astute missionaries displayed a complex and contradictory attitude to aspects of island cultures. On the one hand they came to destroy totally abhorrent customs and superstitions; on the other, they were intrigued by certain aspects, especially since Native tradition might contain hidden references to the times of Noah. Recording such tales, however 'ludicrous and puerile' they might be, might nevertheless provide some recognizable 'fragment, or corroboration, of Scripture.'[35] Thus might savage life confirm biblical truths. For William Ellis, the similarities between Polynesian oral traditions and key biblical events, such as the Flood, 'furnish strong additional evidence that the scripture record is irrefragable.'[36] Thomas Williams agreed, claiming that Fijian religion, in spite of its 'wild and contradictory absurdities,' was capable of 'shadowing forth ... some of the great facts in the history of mankind.'[37] It was all good material to lead scholars, in the words of John Dunmore Lang, back to the very 'infancy of society, when the earth was still wet, as it were, with the waters of the deluge.'[38]

The evangelical missionaries' ability to relate to Polynesian societies by finding in their abominations something that was familiar, even though distant, could provide intellectual support. For some it became something of an anthropological challenge; for the unfortunate few, the challenge became all too dangerous. Thomas Kendall, an early missionary in New Zealand, was one who became both physically and intellectually seduced by the Maori. Kendall believed that the Maori had come out of Egypt and he made their religion all too familiar by finding in its beliefs and carvings remnants of Old Testament ideas and pythagorean concepts.[39] Elsewhere in Polynesia missionaries such as Benjamin Broomhall, Samuel Wilson, and George Vason were tempted into island lifestyles at least in part through an empathy with certain Native values. Others too 'fell,' though usually out of lust.

More commonly, many missionaries simply had a lively curiosity and were keen observers of Native culture, motivated by varying degrees of abhorrence and fascination, with attitudes ranging from the arrogant to the empathetic. Missionaries collectively have left an extensive ethnography, well picked over by modern historians and anthropologists but as yet little studied for its own sake. In general terms it was a literature that attempted to make Polynesian culture meaningful by interpreting it in terms of missionary understandings of human societies and history. In particular the theory of degeneration performed the vital dual role of confirming the utter depravity and general childlikeness of the Polynesians, while allowing for their fundamental humanity by virtue of their ancient Mediterranean heritage. Such views offered to missionaries a people who had lost their way, but who could yet be recovered and transformed. It confirmed missionaries' view of themselves as superior beings and the pivotal role that they and their culture were playing in human development.

In the second half of the nineteenth century the semitic Polynesian was largely replaced by the Aryan/Caucasian Polynesian because of the growing sophistication of techniques that had already been used gropingly – comparative linguistics and comparative mythology. These twin sciences emerged in the later eighteenth century and flowered from the mid-nineteenth on, particularly in Indian studies. In 1786 William Jones, the founder of the Asiatic Society, announced links between Sanskrit and European languages. This began a longstanding oriental tradition in European scholarship whereby Indian language and literature were regarded as perhaps the finest in the world. In the first half of the nine-teenth century a succession of linguists, many German, unravelled the complex derivative relationships that existed among languages known as the Indo-European language family.[40] One leading scholar was Max Müller, the German-born professor of comparative linguistics at Oxford. Müller was something of an academic cult figure in England with his astonishingly popular lectures and books on the 'science' of language, religion, and mythology. Among his most influential works were *Lectures on the Science of Language* (2 volumes, 1861-4) and *Chips from a German Workshop* (4 volumes, 1868-75). Müller not only extolled ancient Indian culture and language, which he thought was seminal in the Western cul-tural tradition, but also believed in a single Aryan ancestry for most Europeans and Indians. In addition to his comparative linguistic research, which included translations of some of the sacred Indian Vedas, Müller revolutionized comparative mythology that had been mainly antiquarian and literary. His solar mythology entailed an inter-pretive methodology that, he claimed, could explain the origins of all Aryan tradition and mythology. Early humans in a 'mythopoeic age,' he argued, personified nature and created nature myths based primarily on the sun. These later became the Aryan or Indo-European peoples who fancifully elaborated the ancient myths. Müller's breakthrough in com-parative mythology had been to demonstrate how the names and attrib-utes of the ancient Vedic deities had evolved into the gods of the Greeks.[41]

Edward Tylor, a founding father of anthropology, extended Müller's comparative mythology by using ethnographic rather than philological material and by applying it to non-Aryan races. He also introduced his doctrine of 'survivals,' which maintained that in both European peasant and 'savage' societies certain beliefs and customs were preserved rem-nants of human cultures at an ancient formative stage. The study of sur-vivals thus offered a window not only on the early condition of the human race but also on the present.

This was by no means a new idea and was in essence simply a restate-ment of views common enough by the later eighteenth century. What was different were the highly refined techniques of the new comparative sciences, especially in the context of Indo-European or Aryan studies. For those involved in Polynesian studies, such scholarship provided ready-made techniques for interpreting Polynesian culture. It offered a much more comprehensive framework to investigate what previously had been discrete and impressionistic evidence that Polynesians had some vestiges of Mediterranean and/or Hindu heritage.

Just as linguists had defined the Indo-European language family, so were languages elsewhere eventually classified into families. Pacific island languages were, by the early nineteenth century, lumped into a single language group known as Malayo-Polynesian, and comparative linguists were soon checking for links between the Malayo-Polynesian and the Indo-European language families.[42]

Wilhelm von Humboldt was the first to suggest that Polynesian languages contained traces of an early form of Sanskrit. In 1841 Franz Bopp claimed that Malayo-Polynesian had emerged from a decayed form of Sanskrit. Other scholars, like J.R. Logan, noted linguistic and other cultural affinities between Polynesians and Indians. The first island-based researcher to follow up these alleged links was John Rae, who lived in the Hawai'ian Islands. He concluded that rather than Polynesian languages deriving directly from Sanskrit, it was the other way round: 'The original seat of the Polynesian race was in Central or Western Asia ... [and] all those tongues which we designate as the Indo-European languages have their true root and origin in the Polynesian language.'[43] Müller was quick to defend this remarkable idea: 'Strange as it may sound to hear the language of Homer and Ennius spoken as an offshoot of the Sandwich [Hawai'ian] Islands, mere ridicule would be a very inappropriate and very inefficient answer to such a theory. It is not very long ago that all Greek and Latin scholars of Europe shook their heads at the idea of tracing the roots of the classical languages back to Sanscrit.'[44] Such a process was by no means unique to the Pacific. W.H.I. Bleek argued that 'the origin of grammatical forms, of gender and number, the etymology of pronouns, and many other questions of the highest interest to the philologist, find their true solution in Southern Africa.'[45] As far as Polynesia was concerned, Rae's proposition was generally accepted, and in the 1870s numerous journal articles appeared, especially in the *Transactions and Proceedings of the New Zealand Institute*, suggesting Indian/ Aryan origins on the basis of philological comparisons. Non-linguistic similarities were also noted. J.B. Thurston argued that parallels between Fijian land tenure customs and those of India pointed 'to a bygone existence of the communal family.'[46]

The comparative mythologists followed similar paths. Müller introduced missionary William Gill's *Myths and Songs from the South Pacific*
(1876), noting the apparent similarities between Mangaian (Cook
Islands) sun, moon, and storm gods and those of ancient Greece and
Germany.[47] Adolf Bastian, professor of ethnology in Berlin, firmly linked
Polynesian legends with those of Aryan nations,[48] and Tylor noted in
1882 that 'the possibility of ... [a] connection in mythology between the
South Sea Islands and Northern Europe is proved almost beyond dispute.'[49] Just as Rae had reversed the earlier assumed derivation of the
Polynesian language from Sanskrit, Edward Shortland did the same for
comparative mythology, believing that it was possible to 'observe a similarity between the more antient form of religious belief and mythological
tradition of the Aryans and that still existing among Polynesians.'[50]

The major scholarly statement about the Polynesians' Aryan ancestry came independently from Abraham Fornander of Hawai'i in *An
Account of the Polynesian Race* (1878-85)[51] and from Edward Tregear of
New Zealand in *The Aryan Maori* (1885).[52] Both Fornander and Tregear
acknowledged recent linguistic and mythological scholars, particularly
Müller, from whom they had gained their understanding of Aryan origins and history, as well as of comparative philology and mythology.
Summarizing Müller's views, they described how the ancient Aryan peoples who lived on the high plains east of the Caspian moved off in two
great migrations. One went west into Europe, the other swept over Persia
and India. Sanskrit-speaking Aryans eventually became the ruling peoples of India. Fornander and Tregear went on to argue, on the basis of
their own research, that some of these people had moved through the
Southeast Asian archipelago and out to the Pacific islands.[53] Thus they
both found in Hawai'ian and Maori language, mythology, and customs
extensive 'survivals' of this Aryan/Indian heritage. These clues unlocked
the secrets of Polynesian culture. Using comparative science it was now
possible to interpret every aspect of life in Polynesia, from the technological to the spiritual. Moreover, such science offered glimpses of the very
formation of Aryan culture itself. As Tregear commented, 'these
uncivilised brothers of ours [the Polynesians] have kept embalmed in
their simple speech a knowledge of the habits and history of our ancestors, that, in the Sanscrit, Greek, Latin, and Teutonic tongues, have been
hidden under the dense aftergrowth of literary opulence.'[54]

Polynesians were attributed with Aryan origins, apparently, for the same reasons as, earlier, they were attributed with semitic origins. These explanations offered a demonstrable interpretation of cultures that otherwise would have remained alien and unfathomable. More specifically, and perhaps not coincidentally, the major statements of the Polynesians' 'Aryan' heritage came from Hawai'i and New Zealand – the two Oceanic locations of extensive European colonization. Indeed the Aryan/Caucasian theory was possibly at times a conscious effort at intellectually colonizing new lands and their Native peoples. This certainly applies to Edward Tregear, the foremost advocate of Aryan origins for Polynesians.[55] A brief summary of his thinking in this connection may illustrate what is probably a much more widely shared intellectual phenomenon.

Tregear was born into an old Cornish family in Southampton in 1846. He was a sensitive lad who wrote poetry, could read and write Greek at age seven, and steeped himself in medieval legend and Celtic and Nordic mythology. His father, a captain with P & O Shipping, lost money gambling and, when he died of typhoid in India, left the family penniless. In 1863 seventeen-year-old Tregear brought his mother and two younger sisters to New Zealand. He spent the next fifteen years as a soldier and surveyor on the remote frontier of the North Island. It was a time of great physical hardship and emotional turmoil, for he saw himself as a poet torn from his homeland and cast adrift in a dreadful landscape. He spent a great deal of time in Maori communities, learnt their language, and puzzled over how to interpret it. Initially, he attempted to cope with his alienation by writing escapist poetry peopled with figures and deeds from classical and Arthurian legend. Then he began a more serious study of the Maori language, and, in particular, devoured the works of Müller. His first major result was *The Aryan Maori*. Tregear's study was only at one level a study of Maori. More fundamentally it was a search for self and an attempt to come to terms with his strange new world. With his alleged 'discovery' that the Maori were Aryan, Tregear's New Zealand was no longer a hostile, barren land without history and full of savages. Now he could see that New Zealand had an imaginative and historical landscape similar to England's and as ancient; its Maori inhabitants were no longer primitive aliens, but shared with Europeans a common, if remote, ancestry. Maori myth, custom, language, and culture generally were no longer strange and unknowable. He had cracked the code and found them permeated with 'survivals' from a shared Aryan past. In a stroke Tregear had filled a desolate land with people, history, mythology, and culture that he could understand, relate to, and willingly embrace. It was a feat of intellectual occupation, possession, and control.[56]

Tregear's general thinking and emotions were not uncommon among sensitive intellectuals transported to strange parts of the world who tried to interpret alien cultures. Tregear's deconstruction of Polynesia was remarkably similar to that of Abraham Fornander's in Hawai'i. Indeed Fornander's career has some very close parallels with Tregear's.[57] Both Fornander and Tregear faced considerable scorn from some quarters over their 'Aryan heresy' but, wrote linguist F.W. Christian, were soon 'triumphantly vindicated.'[58] Indeed several scholars, apart from Fornander and Tregear, vied for the honour of having been the first to discover the Polynesians' Aryan heritage.[59] From the mid-1880s it was commonly accepted that Polynesian cultures had at least some Aryan ancestry and/or influence. Many adapted and modified the extensive volumes of Fornander for their own particular location, as for example did Basil Thomson for Fiji,[60] and F.D. Fenton for New Zealand. Fenton's study, which is a highly detailed and now largely unreadable study of Chaldean, Babylonian, Cushite, and Akkadian history, and which claims that the Polynesians 'walked with Abraham,' must rank as among the most bizarre accounts of Polynesian origins.[61] Of all those writing on the subject, apart from Tregear who spent more than twenty years after publishing *The Aryan Maori* extending and refining his views, Percy Smith was probably most prominent in gathering evidence placing Polynesians firmly in the 'Caucasian family of the human race.'[62]

Such opinions persisted well into the twentieth century. John Macmillan Brown, a longtime supporter of Aryan origins for Polynesians, argued in 1927 that Polynesian language 'represents the primeval form of Indo-European.'[63] The tradition was as strong elsewhere. In lectures delivered to Hawai'i's Kamehameha schools by leading anthropologists in 1933, Hawai'ian origins were placed in 'central Asia' and shared 'the common ancestor from which the north Europeans and the early Polynesian types derived.'[64] As late as 1938, the New Zealander Peter Buck of the Bishop Museum wrote in his *Vikings of the Sunrise* that Polynesians may have originated in the Middle East and 'probably did live in some part of India.'[65] German scholars also supported the tradition into the 1930s and saw particular links between Polynesian and Scandinavian culture. Félix Speiser summarized and attempted to debunk such views, though he was impressed enough with 'constant similarities' between Polynesian and European myths to attribute them to a common 'Asiatic diffusion centre.'[66]

To return to the nineteenth century, Darwinism seems not to have had too dramatic an impact on Polynesian scholarship. The earlier seminal works by Müller and Tylor that had so influenced Polynesian studies knew nothing of Darwinism. Yet these works allowed for ascending as well as descending human types and thus were quite compatible with the Lamarckian-based 'social Darwinism' of Herbert Spencer. Now extra care was needed to ensure that studies of modern savages, as living examples of the past, had not had ancestors living in a higher state. In general terms Darwinism in the Pacific context reinforced rather than modified the pervasive Christian notions of degeneration. Nor was Darwinism responsible for heralding the idea of Polynesian depopulation. That had been a longstanding belief originating in the eighteenth century and was well entrenched by the 1830s. Darwinism provided a rather more persuasive explanation for such a phenomenon,[67] and certainly added urgency to ethnography. Percy Smith made a hasty trip to the islands in 1897: 'Time was pressing – the old men of the Polynesian race from whom their history could be obtained were fast passing away – civilization was fast extinguishing what little remained of ancient lore – the people themselves were dying out before the incoming white man – and, to all appearances, there would soon be nothing left but regrets over lost opportunities.'[68]

The predominance of New Zealand-based scholarship, particularly in the 1880s and 1890s, needs emphasizing for, in addition to the particular psychologies of individual investigators combined with theoretical constructs from the European sciences, a collective national psychology was also at work. In both Australia and New Zealand at that time, there was a concern to express national, not British, identity. An Australian identity emerged in the image of the Outback and the romanticized lifestyles and democratic values of the stockman.[69] Such images were not appropriate in New Zealand because its frontier experience differed from Australia's and, more important, because people in New Zealand wished to distinguish themselves from Australians. One solution attempted by intellectuals was to plunder Maori culture for national emblems.[70] New Zealand was even commonly referred to as Maoriland. The Polynesian history of New Zealand, given a heroic interpretation with Percy Smith's compilation of Maori fleet traditions into a grand synthesis of a Great Fleet,[71] was another aspect of this process.

The Maori increasingly came under particularly intense study, since it was assumed that the race would soon disappear. The purposeful capturing of the last moments of a culture is exemplified by an old Maori woman sitting for the portrait painter C.F. Goldie. Alongside him stood composer Alfred Hill, scoring her songs and chants, and Tregear, recording her legends. This was far more than simply salvage ethnography, as important as that was. Certainly Polynesian scholars were acutely conscious of the potential significance of their Polynesian scholarship for a national identity. Tregear believed that such scholarship would 'be looked upon in New Zealand as sacredly as the modern American Treasures, relics of those who "came over in the Mayflower" – as Tennyson says "For we are the Ancients of the Earth, And in the morning of the Times."'[72] As for the attempt at a Maoriland identity, it was not particularly successful, for New Zealand's national identity became based instead on alleged prowess in rugby and war in the early twentieth century.[73] However, many remnants of a symbolic/ceremonial celebration of New Zealand's Polynesian heritage still remain.[74]

The Aryan/Caucasian history of Polynesia was interpolated and exploited elsewhere. For example, the Fijians had no traditions of origins. But, in the 1890s at the Navuloa mission school, pupils were finally enlightened about their distant past by the principal, anthropologist Lorimer Fison, among others. He explained how the Fijians' ancestors had come from the ancient city of Thebes via Lake Tanganyika and eventually reached Fiji in the Kaunitoni migration. This won a Fijian-language newspaper's competition held in 1892 to select a 'definitive version of the legendary history of the people.' Fijians soon embraced such a story, particularly to advance their ancestral land claims before the Native Lands Commission. Soon deeply entrenched in oral tradition, the Kaunitoni migration eventually provided a socially cohesive history to help underpin Fiji's recent transition to political nationhood.[75]

Hawai'i's Polynesian history was also put to particular purposes. The

entrepreneurial publicist Rollin Daggett, United States minister to
Hawai'i, mangled Fornander's *An Account of the Polynesian Race* and
produced *The Legends and Myths of Hawai'i* (1888), ostensibly authored
by King Kalakaua of Hawai'i. Daggett's introduction attempts to give
Hawai'ian Polynesians a glorious, unified past from their origins in
Arabia, and traces the ancestry of the modern monarchy unerringly back
to AD 1095. It amounts to tidying up a history of a people whose voices
finally 'will be heard no more for ever,' and to preparing their islands for
their destiny: 'The Hawai'ian Islands with the echoes of their songs and
the sweets of their green fields will pass into the political, as they are now
firmly with the commercial, system of the great American Republic.'[76]

Such local uses of Polynesian studies must be set firmly against what
was regarded as their more universal significance – evidence of the
ancestral lifestyles of those people who were now among the civilized
nations. George Grey claimed that there was a 'strong probability that
the social state of our British ancestors in many respects closely resembled that of the New Zealanders.'[77] Tylor thought that Grey's collection of
Polynesian mythology 'will set before us the description of the great
events of nature ... the higher mythologies of India, Greece, and
Scandinavia is admirably represented from the contemplation of nature
in the early stage of its growth among the Polynesians.'[78] Tregear was certainly one who became increasingly convinced that the unwritten literature of the South Seas had major clues about human antiquity: 'What we
shall ever know of our most ancient progenitors lies embalmed in these
apparently foolish but priceless and almost indestructible traditions
passed on from 'mouth to ear' through innumerable centuries.'[79] Thus
Pacific-based scholars were always concerned to feed their Polynesian
findings back to the 'greats' of European science – Müller, Tylor, Andrew
Lang, J.G. Fraser – as further evidence in the quest to unravel the distant
human past. In fact, a huge correspondence network not only linked
scholars within Polynesia but also gave them ready access to the scientists
throughout England and Europe. And, judging by the international
character of journal publications, Polynesian studies probably had a
wider and more diverse readership than it does today. The Polynesian
Society in New Zealand and the Hawaiian Historical Society, both established in the early 1890s, greatly enhanced the longstanding exchange of
information.

Interpretations of Polynesian culture and history, even well into this century, are largely a European creation. What is striking is the extent to which the proponents of the three main traditions discussed here – neo-classical, biblical, comparative scientific – shared some fundamental beliefs and concerns, even if their respective interpretations differed. They all adhered to monogenesis and the notion of a cradle of humanity, thus assuming that the homeland of Polynesia had to lie outside the Pacific. They all accepted the notion that human cultures could ascend or descend; they all believed Polynesians to be relatively superior among the savages; and they all were commonly preoccupied with viewing progress, or the lack of it, in the context of the broadest possible scale of human history. The idea of the past was a much more finite and unified concept than is now fashionable. Overall, students of Polynesia of the late eighteenth-/early nineteenth-century would probably have felt quite comfortable had they been able to read the *Journal of the Polynesian Society* 100 years later. Furthermore, these three traditions offered to their proponents a means of likening the unfamiliar to the familiar and hence provided convincing explanations or interpretations of what otherwise was unfathomable. As the particle physicists have argued for most of this century, knowledge has no reality beyond that attributed to it by those who claim it as true, and we know how a body of belief/knowledge/truth is accepted by groups for as long as it serves the needs of those groups.

Edward Said has demonstrated how the image and ideology of the Far East was but a figment of European scholarly imaginations and that, as a consequence, oriental studies were essentially an act of academic occupation and control, one that excluded the ostensible subjects themselves.[80] The European discovery and exploration of Polynesia shows a similar process. Polynesian history and culture came to exist for outsiders quite without reference to its own meanings or understandings. Its peoples, their history, mythology, and tradition were examined, plotted, located, categorized, stereotyped, fixed, given origins, chronologies, and interpretations according to European concepts and frameworks. Moreover, as with orientalism, it was institutionalized by these outsiders in journals and books, scholarly institutions, and museums. It appeared in school readers and encyclopaedias, in opera, art, and literature.

Since its discovery by eighteenth-century explorers, Polynesia and its inhabitants have consistently been interpreted in constructs that Europeans have found familiar and thus meaningful. The ultimate act in this process was to reconstruct Polynesians on the basis of claimed Aryan/Caucasian origins. This discovery and definition of the unknown 'other' was not just an act of intellectual occupation and control, but also, and ultimately, a means of locating, defining, and understanding 'self' both within the span of human progress and amidst strange new worlds. There is indeed double meaning in Tylor's claim in 1867 that the 'study of the lower races is capable of furnishing most important knowledge about ourselves, about our own habits, customs, laws, principles, prejudices.'[81]

The Burden of *Terra Australis*:
Experiences of Real and Imagined Lands

David Mackay

On his first visit to Tahiti in the Southern winter of 1773 on board the *Resolution*, the learned Dr Johann Reinhold Forster revealed how even scientists could be ensnared by the lure of the Pacific. His account of the island was paradisal and, in a classic environmentalist interpretation, attributed the fortunate situation of the islanders to the lush beauty of their habitat. They were a hospitable, gentle, fertile, and happy people in tune with their surroundings. As the *Resolution* prepared to sail, he summarized his views: 'The fine shady plantations, the agreable Walks, the fine rivulets, the powerfull Sun, the quick Vegetation, the delicious & salubrious food, the sweet breezes blowing constantly to cool the Air, the beautiful tropical sky at Sunrising & Sunsetting, & every other circumstance contribute towards the happiness of its Inhabitants.'[1] At this point emotion overwhelmed him, and he lapsed into Latin, citing Virgil on the glories of the Elysian Fields.

It is scarcely surprising that such a scholarly man as Forster should fall captive to the lure of Tahiti. The spell of exotic new lands had been exerted for centuries and, in European colonial terms, can be traced to perceptions of North America in the sixteenth century and to schemes for its settlement. Early descriptions sent back across the Atlantic offered tantalizing glimpses of rich and accessible lands. Superficial appearances formed the basis of substantive accounts of new lands as promoters sought to attract investment. Reporting to his master, Sir Walter Raleigh, on 13 July 1584, Commander Arthur Barlowe described Hatteras Island thus:

Wee viewed the lande aboute us, being whereas we first landed, very sandie, and lowe toward the water side, but so full of grapes, as the very beating, and surge of the Sea overflowed them, of which we found such plentie, as well there, as in all places else, both on the sande, and on the greene shrubbe, as also climing towardes the toppes of the high Cedars, that I thinke in all the world the like aboundance is not to be founde. Wee found the people most gentle, loving and faithfull, void of all guile, and treason, and such as lived after the manner of the golden age. The earth bringeth foorth all things in aboundance, as in the first creation, without toile or labour.[2]

In temperate terms, grapes, more than any other crop, conveyed a sense of lushness and plenty to the European. The Bacchanalian overtones suggested a cornucopia of abundance and fructification and invoked classical and picturesque images of leisure and plenty. Grapes also provided something of a benchmark of the fertility and richness of an environment, their early success in New South Wales, for example, being used by Governor Phillip to convince the English of the agricultural potential of his colony.[3]

Such tales of bounty were rife in the histories of the new worlds of the Americas and the Pacific, and they can be viewed as part of the preliminaries to European involvement, exploitation, and settlement. In some cases, they can be regarded as cynical, hyperbolic promotion designed to attract investment, patronage, or government support. In other cases they were more ingenuous descriptions of landscapes and peoples beyond European experience, but with places in European tradition and imagination. Sometimes they were both, elaborated with limited experience, geographical analogy, and a smattering of elementary science. Typical of such plans were those of James Mario Matra, who had sailed with Captain James Cook on the *Endeavour* and had combined experience and imagination in his 1783 scheme for settling New South Wales.

Accounts such as those of Forster, Barlowe, and Matra involved self-deception, but of course this element was intrinsic to depictions of Arcadian societies. Forster's quotation from Virgil suggests that the poetic and reflective elements were informed by a prior set of beliefs. These became part of the imaginative baggage explorers carried with them to the Pacific. Although many voyagers were immune to this influence, for some its distorting power could be considerable, particularly, at dramatic moments, or when a Native society was used as a counter-model to European society. This could lead to a temporary or sustained suspension of the critical faculties in favour of a received version of what Arcadia should be like and often produce, peculiar perspectives. Once again Forster provided a fine example. One month after the *Resolution* left Tahiti it was back in Ship Cove, New Zealand. Shortly after dining with the officers, Forster witnessed a blatant act of cannibalism by some Maori on board the vessel. He contrasted the rather callous, light-hearted way some of the crew dealt with the incident with the mortified reaction of Mahine, a young man from Bora Bora, travelling with them. He had fled to his cabin in tears. For Forster, this was 'a proof that all our artificial Education, our boasted civilization, our parade of humanity & Social virtues, was in this case outdone by the tender tears & feelings of the innocent, goodnatured boy, who was born under the benign influ-ence of the Sun within the Tropics, had the Education suitable to a Man of Quality in his country, where it seems cruelty & ferociousness have not so much gained ground, as to destroy the principles of humanity.'[4] This could well have been written by Diderot and illustrates how indige-nous communities were used as contemplative devices in analyzing Euro-pean society. It also has its echoes in Fanny Burney's contrast between the *'pedantic Booby'* – Mr Stanhope – and the *'thoroughly well bred'* Omai.[5] The paradox in Forster's case lies in the rather eccentric context in which he has chosen to document Polynesian sensibility and British inhuman-ity. However, also contained within this incident, and within this para-dox, were the elements which could enable a sudden switch in stance, producing a sharp reaction against the Pacific and its peoples.

Such assessments of real places and peoples were influenced by con-ceptions of imaginary ones. Forster, like many other observers of the Pacific before and since, was investing the ocean, its lands, and inhabi-tants with the qualities and virtues of ideal societies in an Arcadian mould. One obvious general source were the utopian tracts which prolif-erated in Europe between the sixteenth and eighteenth centuries. The biblical allusion in Barlowe's report is also illuminating in that it points to the more ancient heritage of the Arcadian ideal, with its paradisal labour and sustenance. Many eighteenth-century perceptions of the Pacific invoked similar images. Writing of Tahitians Joseph Banks proclaimed, 'Scarcely can it be said that they earn their bread with the sweat of their brow when their chiefest substance, Breadfruit, is procur'd with no more trouble than that of climbing a tree and pulling it down.'[6] This was akin to the Garden of Eden before the Fall. Philibert Commerson, on Bougainville's voyage, saw the leisure implications of this, remarking that 'the good Utopian enjoys endlessly either the sensation of his own pleasures or the spectacle of those of others.'[7]

The intellectual climate of eighteenth-century England in particular predisposed some toward an Arcadian view of the Pacific. The Platonic vision of traditional England as a vast garden was exemplified in the fascination for landscape gardens and their embellishments. A traditional, nostalgic conception sought to recapture the simplicities and virtues of a past age and blot out corruption, luxury, and urban vices. Pocock has identified this political dimension as being in the Harringtonian strain of thought which informed the beliefs and actions of the country party, the Tory gentry, and some political opposition in the Walpole and Pelham years.[8] It reached its most forceful literary form with William Blake. Such a vision affected the perception of the Pacific and anticipation of new lands, and the concept of the noble savage in particular owed much to this nostalgic vision: hence the way in which Ahutoru and Omai were credited with virtues which were in many senses classical.

The self-delusion applied to a real world obviously operated more forcefully and creatively when applied to imaginary ones, but many of the same processes were clearly at work. Geographers, promoters, and writers scripted what they wanted to find into the unknown lands which they described, and the reflective power of works such as *Gulliver's Travels* is sufficiently well known and allusive for historians to avoid it. Such avowedly fictional works were merely part of the backdrop to voyages of discovery and plans for commercial or strategic development in the Pacific in the eighteenth century, and demonstrate the manner in which the voids on the globe were filled in inventively to support the perceived needs or deficiencies of Europe. This took the form of continents, strategic islands, or seaways expediting passage to the riches of other lands.

At its simplest, one could say that armchair geographers and the more optimistic discoverers read what they wanted to see into new lands, informed by the prevailing Arcadian tropes. They employed prophetic geography which saw only opportunities. No dark, tortured mind hypothesized a frigid southern continent in high, unreachable latitudes. No commentators on Australia before Flinders postulated a dry, barren interior. No one in the eighteenth century accurately predicted the very different, but equally formidable, northern coast of British Columbia and Alaska. No one suggested that all those coastal indentations were simply that – dead ends which provided no channels to the East. No one suggested that the inhabitants of undiscovered lands would be poor, lacking in goods, precious metals, and a diverse diet.

In the context of the eighteenth-century Pacific, discussion of ideal societies was most significant with respect to the anticipation of *Terra Australis Incognita*. The conceptions of the continent put forward by writers such as Callander, De Brosses, and Dalrymple were generally Arcadian in the way they presented its fertility, productions, and people. This is not the place to give a historical account of what Joseph Banks mournfully described as 'our aerial fabric called continent,' but possibly men such as Forster and Philibert Commerson were, in part, projecting onto the real worlds they visited expectations of the imaginary one. When the notion of a habitable southern continent was finally destroyed by Cook, some of its projected benefits were transferred to other places, such as Tahiti and New South Wales. This is one of the senses in which the phrase 'burden of *Terra Australis*' is appropriate, for its shadow lingered on to influence notions of the benefits from the Pacific. When some of these were not forthcoming, those who had speculated about the Pacific or had idealized its lands often suffered a backlash.

The expectations of *Terra Australis* were to a degree reflected in the narrowing range of oceans in which it was supposed to exist. Although the southern continent was in many accounts described as circum-polar in shape – appearing therefore in the Atlantic, Indian, and Pacific oceans – by the mid-eighteenth century it was generally confined to the Pacific. Expectations for the South Atlantic focused more on islands to serve as suitable strategic and commercial bases for the Pacific or Indian oceans, as the boundaries of any continent were pushed progressively south.[9] Both Anson's and Byron's expeditions were interested in the Falkland and Pepys islands for these very reasons. In the late eighteenth century, the Isla Grande became the main object of interest. Although Pepys Island and Isla Grande were mythical, the Falkland Islands dispute of 1770-1

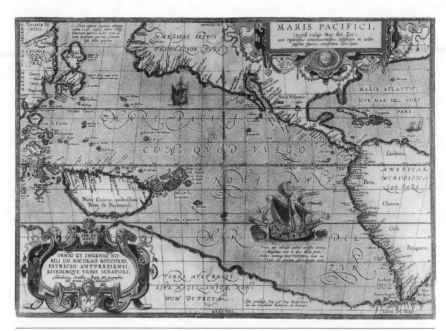

Map of the Pacific by the cartographer Abraham Ortellius, printed in 1589

indicated the intensity of European interest in such bases at the time, although the imperatives shifted elsewhere by the end of the century.

The South Indian Ocean had been crossed to quite high latitudes by ships in the East India trade, exploiting the driving winds of the 'roaring forties.' Even by the early eighteenth century it was generally assumed that any land masses there would be frigid and uninviting. Dutch contacts with the west and south coasts of Australia from 1616 on did not suggest that it was any more promising, a view confirmed by Dampier at the end of the seventeenth century.

The 10,000-mile breadth of the Pacific appeared much more promising, partly because so much of the unexplored area lay in tropical or temperate zones. The tentative forays of Spanish, Dutch, and some English expeditions before 1700 provided tantalizing glimpses of what the ocean had to offer; even the most chaotic voyages and fragmented rumours were invested with great speculative significance. Whereas Asia by the eighteenth century was too familiar as despotic, indolent, or corrupt, the Pacific was utopian because so much of it was unknown. The Arcadian society had to be a place virtually free of trade in the European sense of luxury, material wants, factional politics, divisive religious issues, and/or social pretensions. Many early voyagers and writers on the Pacific saw the islands as simple, fertile, and healthy, with great regenerative powers. By definition then, the first European settlement in the Pacific corrupted the ideal. It could only be discovered to be destroyed.

One surprising aspect in the optimistic depictions of real and imagined lands was how their essential elements endured over time. Campbell, De Brosses, Dobbs, Dalrymple, and Matra endowed their real and imagined lands with the same qualities as writers and voyagers of 200 years before. According to these propagandists *Terra Australis* was, in all senses, a counterweight to lands of the northern and western hemispheres. Dalrymple projected its population to be fifty million, opening prospects of lively trade and exchange. It embraced many degrees of latitude, and in its various climates would thrive products ranging from tropical spices to the flaxes, grasses, and forests of temperate lands. Beneath its soils, mineral wealth, equivalent to that of Spanish America, must inevitably be found. In strategic terms it would confer inestimable benefits on the nation that controlled it. Arthur Dobbs' anticipation of the land of Yedso in the North Pacific was not on quite such a grandiose scale, but, like the other fabulous countries of the North Pacific, it, too, was inhabited by civilized people who crafted their household implements from silver and gold.[10]

When Francis I of France sent Jacques Cartier across the Atlantic, his purpose was 'to discover certain islands and lands where it is said a great quantity of gold and other precious things are to be found.'[11] The bullionist conception and expectations of undiscovered lands were therefore another remarkably resilient element. Of course, the precious metal discoveries of the Spanish and Portuguese in South America proved the riches existed, in the same way that the Portuguese and Dutch exploitation of Southeast Asian spices did in the other hemisphere. Travellers' tales, mythical or just highly exaggerated, heightened the expectation of discovery and fuelled the enthusiasm needed to provide investment, royal patronage, and shipping.

For Britons, Sir Francis Drake's voyage had conflated gold, silver, and the lure of the Pacific. Bullion was awaiting those with the enterprise and courage to pierce the South Seas. William Hawkins had bluntly stated the agenda in the 1580s: 'Ther is no hope for money ... but by passynge the Straytes.'[12] This spirit infected the Cavendish and Fenton expeditions. Although the lure of the South Seas was powerful, the attractions and profit to be derived were generally conceived in rather vague and non-specific terms. One particular focus of attention was the Manila galleon, plying between Acapulco and the Philippines, which became a prime target for privateers from Francis Drake to George Anson. In Anson's view the riches of New Spain were the vital elements of state power. The Iberian monarch, 'by his settlements in that part of the globe, became possessed of many of the manufactures and natural productions with which it abounded, and which, for some ages, had been the wonder and delight of the more polished and luxurious part of mankind.' It was this wealth which Anson sought, but the vicissitudes of the Pacific made it elusive, and he lamented, 'a fatality attends me.' However, the capture of the bullion-laden galleon *Cavadonga* was seen as offsetting the earlier disasters of the expedition.[13]

There seemed to be an assumption that the known mineral wealth of South America naturally extended, in the west, to the Pacific. Joseph Banks thought that New Zealand would be mineral rich, because it was in the same latitudes as Chile. Off the coast of Stewart Island, New Zealand, in March 1770 he condemned the commander for refusing to anchor when large, shiny veins of some mineral were seen in the cliffs: 'What it was I could not guess at but it certainly was some mineral and seemd to argue by its immense abundance a countrey abounding in minerals, where if one may judge from the corresponding latitudes of South America in all human probability something very valuable might be found.'[14] When Jacob Roggeveen discovered Easter Island, he took it to be *Terra Australis,* and from a distance the crew believed they saw silver and mother-of-pearl earrings on the islanders. Closer investigation proved this to be wrong, and the bullionist intentions of the voyage were made transparent: 'It was unanimously judged as indisputable that the above mentioned Paasch Island does not in the least fulfil the description of high land, being only of average height, where also fine metals could not possibly exist, as experience by ocular inspection has taught us that the inhabitants are devoid of them, and merely use for covering and ornament a certain field plant.'[15] Having established this point the mercenary commander moved on. Later in the voyage he reiterated his earlier observation about the objectives of the voyage: 'Moreover, it must be noted that low and medium lands cannot produce fine metals, because these are not found anywhere but in high mountainous land; these two types are not the object of our expedition and enterprise.'[16]

Further west, for 200 years the voyage of Alvaro de Mendaña to the Solomon Islands had exerted a bullionist influence magnificently out of proportion to its achievement. Supposedly first visited by the Inca Tupac Yapanqui, the Solomons were the object of Quiros, Le Maire, Schouten, and Tasman, and in the eighteenth century, of Roggeveen and Byron. A dismissive report by an official of New Spain defined negatively all that the islands were reputed to contain: 'In the course of those discoveries they found no specimens of spices, nor of gold and silver, nor of merchandise, nor of any other source of profit, and all the people were naked savages.' Far from acting as a deterrent to interest, this disclaimer only served to convince the British that the Spanish were determined to keep the riches to themselves.[17] This is an exaggerated example of the principle that *Terra Australis* needed only the most fragile foundations for its support.

It was the myth of the Solomon Islands which also tempted John Byron off his prescribed course. Ignoring his instructions to search the South Atlantic for an island base and then find the northwest passage from the Pacific end, he headed across the Pacific for the lands of Mendaña and Quiros. Like Anson, he presumably believed that a haul of gold and silver would compensate for failing to achieve the prescribed objectives. His inability to find the islands caused great disappointment.[18]

Not only in the South Pacific were lands of gold and silver supposed to exist. The Spanish explored the Pacific coast of America in the sixteenth century in response to Native accounts of mineral-rich lands to the north, and these stimulated inland journeys through to the nineteenth century.[19] The objects behind the search for the northwest passage were not only the advantages of a rapid passage to the wealth of East Asia, but also the discovery of lands in the North Pacific supposedly rich in minerals. James Knight, appointed governor in Hudson Bay in 1713, absorbed Indian accounts of lands laced with copper and gold to the north and west through the Straits of Anian. He proved 'pathetically eager to glean any scrap of information about their [Indian] country,' and his fateful expedition set out from Gravesend in June 1719, supposedly with large, iron-bound chests in which to bring back the gold.[20] In his unpublished memorial in support of a search for the northwest passage in 1731, the propagandist Arthur Dobbs recalled the rumours about a Spanish vessel driven by storms to the bullion-rich land called Yedso.[21] Other islands in the North Pacific would be similarly endowed.

With bullion, as with other commodities, the virtues of *Terra Australis* and even known lands were partly determined by location, as geographers and propagandists argued largely by analogy. Thus Emmanuel Bowen on a map of 1744 concluded that by a 'parity of reason' *Terra Australis* must be a wealthy land: 'It is impossible to conceive a Country that promises fairer from its scituation [sic], than this of Terra Australis ... if Peru overflows with Silver, if all the Mountains of Chili are filled with Gold, and this precious Metal & Stones much more precious are ye products of Brazil.'[22] John Campbell, editor of the volume in which this map appeared, shared these assumptions, projecting onto *Terra Australis* all the commodities found in similar latitudes elsewhere.[23] Alexander Dalrymple employed the same logic thirty years later.

This comparative process was not limited to imaginary lands, for such projections covered known lands as well, and in the late eighteenth century there was respectable scientific support for it. The Matra proposal for settling New South Wales pointed out that 'the climate and soil are so happily adapted to produce every various and valuable production of Europe, and of both the Indies ... Part of it lies in a climate parallel to the Spice Islands, and is fitted for the production of that valuable commodity, as well as the sugar-cane, tea, coffee, silk, cotton, indigo, tobacco, and the other articles of commerce that have been so advantageous to the maritime powers of Europe.'[24] Sir George Young's plan made this connection more explicit, observing that 'the variety of climates included between the forty-fourth and tenth degrees of latitude gives us opportunity of uniting in one territory almost all the productions of the known world.' He went on to list a splendid array of well-endowed countries which fell between these latitudes and also considered it axiomatic that, because of its vast size, Australia would also be home to a variety of precious minerals.[25]

Scientific support for such a belief came from none other than the respected president of the Royal Society, Sir Joseph Banks. In the 1780s and 1790s he promoted plans for transplanting commercial species in British tropical colonies, such species including breadfruit, cotton, tea, spices, indigo, and opuntia, the host plant for the cochineal insect. The assumption behind his elaborate program of plant interchange was also that similar latitudes and climates produced, or could produce, similar products. This was particularly true of the tropics, and Banks declared in 1787 that there were 'few if any instances being known of Plants brought from one intertropical climate refusing to thrive in another.'[26] This elaborate network of plant exchange could also be seen in some ways as an attempt to rectify the deficiencies of nature. To the extent that these drew on the Pacific, as in the case of Bligh's breadfruit expedition, they too were part of the burden of *Terra Australis* because they sought to capture the bounty of the Pacific and transfer it to less favoured parts of the world.[27]

One reason for the resilience of myths of imaginary lands and the inflated virtues of real ones was the slight evidence which was required for their support or, conversely, the substantial evidence needed to destroy them. Indeed, even highly negative reports from another country could be taken as evidence of *Terra Australis*. One of the last proponents of *Terra Australis,* the Frenchman Baron de Gonneville, believed that the British and Dutch had perfidiously concealed its existence.[28]

More specifically, the slightest sign was sufficient to point to a continent. The seventeenth-century voyages of Davis, Schouten, and le Maire provided hints of the great land to the south. In Davis' case, from a low sandy island 500 leagues off the Spanish American coast, a range of high mountains were seen in latitude 27° west, with flocks of birds flying from it.[29] Schouten and Le Maire, when about 4,000 miles from Peru in the region of the Tuamotus, found calm water to the south, breaking the great Pacific swell. The natural conclusion was that a large land mass was responsible.[30] Elsewhere sea birds, suspicious cloud banks, floating bits of wood and foliage, and some normal indicators of nearby land were taken as evidence. Islands were also frequently seen as outliers of a greater land mass. Bouvet's Cape of the Circumcision, dimly perceived in the fog of the South Atlantic in 1739, offered hope of a continent there. In John Callander's *Terra Australis Cognita,* the numerous islands seen by Drake, Narborough, Dampier, and others were positive proof of a Pacific continent.[31] Roggeveen saw the island of Juan Fernandez as the gateway to *Terra Australis,* believing that whoever claimed it would 'become in a few years master of a country as rich as Mexico and Peru, or Brazil.'[32] To the navigators sailing across the Pacific it is not surprising that every little atoll could be viewed as a harbinger of greater things to come.

In the case of the northwest passage the encouraging signs were somewhat different, but generally just as slight. Slender openings, flood tides from unusual directions, the sight of whales on the move, or accounts of Indian hunters were all grist for the mill. Chesterfield Inlet, Roe's Welcome, and Wager Bay within Hudson Bay were all seen as possible routes to the Pacific coast in the first half of the eighteenth century, and for those like Arthur Dobbs it took much convincing that any of these ended in unnavigable streams. Returning from his voyage of 1742 the unfortunate Christopher Middleton had to face an Admiralty Committee of Inquiry after Dobbs accused him of deliberately concealing a passage in Wager Bay.[33] On the other side of the American continent the evidence of possible openings to the east was even greater, but just as illusive. The accounts of de Fuca and de Fonte, the sketchy information about Spanish and Russian voyages, the deceptive maps of Müller and Stählin, and the tantalizing inlets of a heavily indented and fragmented coast are all sufficiently well known. But the spell of these shadowy pieces of evidence was sufficiently strong to lure even Cook.[34]

Another link between these real and imaginary lands was the propagandists' opinions of the advantages likely to flow from their discovery and occupation, and the qualities required for their successful exploitation. John Campbell outlined the general theme well in his 1744 edition of John Harris' *Complete Collection of Voyages and Travels*, a mercantile and strategic call to arms. Britain had to throw off the lassitude which seemed to beset it: 'Does not that Change in Point of Cultivation, Magnificence in Building, and great increase in Shipping, which within these last two Ages, has happened in the old World, arise from the Discovery of the new? Why then do we not pursue this Track? Why not prosecute new Discoveries, at least, why not enlarge our Commerce by the invention of new Branches? ... We have Commodities, we gave Manufactures, we have Shipping, we have Sailors, we have Merchants, what can we possibly want if we have the Will to employ those as we ought?'[35] This same spirit infused the author of *Anson's Voyage*, who echoed Campbell's refrain: 'Since as our fleets are at present superior to those of the whole world united, it must be a matchless degree of supineness or mean-spiritedness, if we permitted any of the advantages which new discoveries, or a more extended navigation may produce to mankind, to be ravished from us.'[36] In his memorial urging a sustained search for a northwest passage Dobbs, too, stressed the mercantile and national advantages that vigorously pursued discovery would bring.

The principal benefits were obviously strategic and commercial. Strategic concerns were common, particularly in relation to South America. The author of *Anson's Voyage* lamented the Spanish monopoly of the wealth of that continent and saw the voyage as an attempt to wrench it from them. Critical to the success of such a venture was occupying certain key strategic points in the South Seas such as Pepys Island and the Falklands in the South Atlantic.[37] Grand claims were made for such places. After Byron's voyage the Earl of Egmont described the Falklands as '*the Key to the whole Pacifick Ocean.* This Island must command the Ports & trade of Chili, Peru, Panama, Acapulco, & in one word all the Spanish Territory upon that Sea.'[38] This claim was subsequently made for Juan Fernandez, Tristan de Cunha, the mythical Isla Grande, the Galápagos, and even Botany Bay.[39] Underlying this strategic interest was the continuing bullionist fascination with the wealth of New Spain. Of course, discovering the northwest passage would pose the same threat to the wealth of New Spain and to the Manila galleon, a point made in Dobbs' memorial. A base on the Pacific coast, such as at Nootka Sound, would do likewise.

Shortly after leaving Tahiti in 1773 Johann Forster expressed doubts about the existence of a habitable *Terra Australis*, but still felt that the search had proved useful: 'It will however appear that there is no Land, where our Philosophers suspected to find great tracts of Country & even that is a very great Discovery: & the Exploration of the Antarctic Ocean is another great point in Navigation & Geography gained.' The bitter cold of the Antarctic in that summer subverted this relaxed view as the prospects of finding land diminished. He began to link the failure to find *Terra Australis* to the state of his own career, bewailing the fact that Joseph Banks and Daniel Solander would probably preempt him in publishing natural histories of the Pacific, and that in being deprived of a new continent he had also been deprived of a huge quantity of new species and, consequently, of fame and fortune. These things 'cast a damp on my prospects in these gloomy Circumstances & regions.' Shortly after Christmas 1773, with the thermometer barely above freezing, the contrasts with the Tahitian environment of August became acute: 'The Islands of Ice surrounding the Ship look like the wrecks of a destroyed world, everyone of them threatens us with impending ruin, if you add our solitary Situation & being surrounded by a parcel of drunken Sailors hollowing & hurraing about us, and peeling our Ears continually with Oaths & Execrations, curses & Dam's it has no distant relation to the Image of hell, drawn by the poets.'[40]

Although the poets may actually have depicted a hotter realm, one could hardly imagine a sharper contrast with the bountiful land that *Terra Australis* was supposed to be. In those nights without darkness in Antarctica, Forster even suggested that there was a vanity in searching for lands where none existed, and that nature took its revenge for such effrontery: 'The Ocean & the winds raged all night. The former had no *pacific* aspect, and seemed to be displeased with the presumption of a few intruding, curious, roving, puny mortals.' Nature could be perverse and capricious, as well as bountiful. In a sense, experience had uncovered in the Pacific the obverse of the ideal world. Forster was carrying the burden of *Terra Australis*.

In this fashion, discovery was propelled by myths which drove governments, propagandists, speculators, navigators, and settlers. These myths set up expectations of new lands which generally could not be fulfilled. When discovery, scientific investigation, familiarity, and settlement determined that these optimistic projections of real and imaginary lands faded or collapsed, people were required to make a sometimes painful adjustment to the actual environment in which they found themselves. As Williams noted about Anson's expedition, there was a 'demoralizing contrast between carefree expectation and sombre reality which occurred as the expedition struggled to round Cape Horn.'[41] This contrast could often lead to a bitter and recriminatory reaction against those who had promulgated or popularized the earlier perspective or to morbid and introspective speculations such as those of Forster.

The collapsing expectations of *Terra Australis* had important consequences as voyagers, traders, and settlers attuned themselves to the actual conditions in the Pacific, for, as Spate has suggested, 'The great circumnavigations made the Pacific a real place, less adapted to Utopian purposes, and so narrowed the range of choice.'[42]

One of the earliest casualties of the more rigorous examination of the Pacific exemplified by Cook's voyages was the last possible actual model of an ideal society in the Arcadian mould. Although the first accounts of Tahiti by Wallis and Bougainville suggested that the model was plausible, the difficulty with such Arcadian utopias was that geographical discoveries had made them testable in a way in which urban or futuristic utopias were not. In the latter the ideal conditions are never met, the laws never framed, the technology never put in place. By contrast, in the Arcadian models, be they Tahitian or North American Indian, once the blemishes became known, or alternatively once the model became contaminated, it no longer served its utopian purpose.

The role of science and technology in this process was rather ambiguous. In one sense the ideal societies of the Pacific had represented a kind of rejection of the values of technological change and were looking back to a previous and simpler age in European society. Correspondingly, reassessing the natural world of the Pacific was paralleled in Europe by a new appreciation of technology. From this point, philosophers looked to a scientific methodology or to the rational operation of enlightened self-interest as the basis of their ideal societies. The devotees of Adam Smith and Jeremy Bentham had no respect for Rousseau's notion of natural man. This ambiguity also applies to science in the reevaluation of the Pacific. In one sense it was the precision which scientific methods brought to exploration which was critical in the discovery and evaluation of the societies of the South Seas. Shipboard philosophers such as Commerson, Banks, and Forster perversely played their part in reinforcing the validity of the utopian model, and the notion that the charm and success of those societies lay in their ignorance of science, since nature in its bounteousness provided for their material wants. Banks and Forster held similar views on the economy of the Tahitians, believing that the habitat was fertile and adequate to the needs of the people, without a high demand for sustained labour. This perspective appeals to modern environmentalism, as the islanders, like the Australian Aborigines, had temperate demands attuned to the capacity of nature to support them.

Paradoxically, from Cook's voyages onwards, the islands of the Pacific were subjected to a closer and more empirical analysis by navigators, natural historians, artists, and missionaries. The world they depicted often fell far short of the Arcadian ideal, even if, for a moment, those such as Forster could be entranced by swaying palms. In bringing back

Ahutoru and Omai to Europe, voyagers were providing specimens of natural man for scrutiny and analysis: the noble savage could, as it were, be placed in the laboratory to see whether he measured up. In Leonie Kramer's view, utopias were always rational, schematic places that left no place for human response to experience.[43] In Tahiti and the other islands of the Pacific, this taste of experience undermined the mythology.

Attacks on philosophers, armchair geographers, and persuasive navigators who had generated or fostered the myths about real and imagined lands were, not surprisingly a consequence of the burden of *Terra Australis*. As he searched the southern oceans in the wake of Davis, Schouten, and Le Maire, Jacob Roggeveen became increasingly bitter about the misleading accounts on which his search was based. He concluded that the calm water they had detected resulted from the protective screen of the Tuamotus breaking the swell, rather than a *Terra Australis*. Then he vented his spleen: 'I must in a few words observe that one must be greatly astonished at finding people who contrive to become famous through the general publication of their writings in which they seek to establish embellished lies as clear truth, as applies to a so-called Captain David, William Dampier and Lionel Wafer ... these three (for they were English) were as much robbers of the truth as of the goods of the Spanish.'[44] Eventually his compatriot Schouten fell victim to similar attacks.

James Cook showed a similar impatience with armchair geographers during his second voyage, as the notion of a habitable *Terra Australis* was systematically and stubbornly destroyed. However, his strongest feelings were revealed on the final voyage, for whereas he had taken the writings of men such as Callander, Dalrymple, and De Brosses with a grain of salt, in his search for the northwest passage he had allowed himself to be drawn in by the Stählin map and, as Glyndwr Williams argued, suspending his disbelief. The anger was thus with himself, as well as the cartographer and it mounted to a final outburst in October 1778, similar to that of Roggeveen almost 60 years earlier: 'If Mr *Stæhlin* was not greatly imposed upon what could induce him to publish so erroneous a Map? in which many of these islands are jumbled in a regular confusion, without the least regard to truth and yet he is very pleased to call it a very accurate little Map? A Map that the most illiterate of his illiterate Sea-faring men would have been ashamed to put his name to.'[45]

This disillusionment also affected the peoples of the Pacific. The noble savage stereotype had always been restricted in its hold on the European imagination, but in the post-Cook era its well-documented erosion occurred. James Burney was perhaps a little naive in his expectations of the people of Tahiti: 'I must confess that I was a little disappointed on my first coming here as I expected to find People nearly as white as Europeans.'[46] Generally however, more frequent contact, attacks on ships and crews, and the occasional evidence of cannibalism in New Zealand and infanticide in Tahiti forced a reassessment of Pacific peoples as in any sense noble savages. Once again the philosophers came in for their share of abuse. Crozet damned their view of the 'affable, humane and hospitable' Polynesian after the killing of Marion du Fresne. La Pérouse was just as vehement: 'I am however a thousand times more angry with the philosophers who so exalt the savages than with the savages themselves ... A navigator, on leaving Europe, ought to consider the savages as enemies.'[47] In his case, the observation was laced with the contempt of a man who had never been victim to the lure of the Pacific in the first place.

Another aspect of the burden was the way in which the hopes that Europeans vested in *Terra Australis* were located elsewhere once the continent was found to be illusory, often giving rise to yet more inflated and unrealistic expectations. Before Cook's voyage the focus of attention had been on the unknown centre of the Pacific. Once that centre had been revealed, largely, as a commercial vacuum, interest was renewed in what is now referred to as the Pacific Rim. In particular, East Asia became the focus of attention as manifested in the Macartney embassy, the voyage of James Colnett, and the energetic trading at Canton. In the words of the great French historian of that interest, 'To the myth of the Austral continent ... succeeded the reality of China, a vast market whose prospects demanded the exploitation of the Pacific.'[48] New South Wales was a national example of this transference of expectations and the trader Charles Bishop an individual case.

In the case of New South Wales even the scrupulous Cook was to a degree saddled with the burden of *Terra Australis*, becoming a scapegoat by virtue of his alleged claims. The planners of the Botany Bay penal colony and the first European settlers in New South Wales looked to the voyages of James Cook, interpreted through Hawkesworth, for their reli-

able, first-hand accounts of the country. Once at Botany Bay the first settlers repeatedly referred to the record of Cook's voyage and to the
accounts of the Botany Bay area in particular, contrasting his observations with the land they found themselves. The comments were usually
suffused with confusion and even bitterness. How could a great navigator, renowned for the accurate and matter-of-fact nature of his observations, have erred so fundamentally in his evaluation of New South Wales?

Had Cook, Banks, and the other scientists on board given inaccurate
accounts of the Botany Bay region? Had the burden of *Terra Australis* infected their judgments with unfortunate consequences for the settlement
at Port Jackson? Or was the problem with the way the accounts of the first
voyage had been retailed to the reading public and official mind? Had
the vision of *Terra Australis* warped the accounts of the 'retailers' of Cook?

Cook sighted the Australian coast on 19 April 1770 near Point Hicks,
and left it over four months later on 23 August in Endeavour Strait. The
Endeavour anchored in Botany Bay on Sunday 29 April and sailed again
on 7 May. The only other significant contact with the eastern mainland
was after the ship ran on a reef and had to be repaired at Endeavour
River near present-day Cooktown. This task kept the expedition on
shore from 15 June until 16 August. Cook's immediate experience of the
area later settled was therefore limited to little more than a week in
Botany Bay in the early winter of 1770. During this short stay the crews
experienced very mild weather with light winds. In the middle of the
week winds dropped, and there was a spell of that beautiful, crisp,
opalescent weather which the Sydney region often experiences in winter.
Cook described it as 'serene.'

The original accounts of Cook and Banks concur about Botany Bay.
Although a rich, black soil was found near the mouth of the Georges
River, the land was described as generally of light, sandy soil covered
with dispersed trees or long grass which in Banks' words, 'resembles
something our Moors in England.'[49] Although the trees were often
impressive in size they were regarded as useless for shipbuilding or general building, and their hardness suggested difficulties in clearing the
land. Excursions further afield revealed land of less promise: travelling
inland on the north side of the Bay, Cook offered this unflattering view:
'We met with nothing remarkable, great part of the Country for some
distance in land from the sea Coast is mostly a barren heath diversified

with marshes and Morasses.'[50] There was nothing in these descriptions to match Cook's recommendations of the River Thames, or Bay of Islands in New Zealand, both of which he regarded as suitable for European settlement. Rather deceptively Cook described Botany Bay itself as a 'capacious safe and commodious' harbour, and marked six watering places around its edge. In fact the entrance to the Bay is rather narrow and much of it is exposed to winds. Governor Phillip's early judgment in January 1788 was that there was insufficient water for his 1500 men, women, and children.

There was one respect in which the area was undeniably rich, and the Bay's name suggests it. Banks and Solander were literally overwhelmed with the flora and fauna. They encountered more new plant varieties here than at any other single point on the three-year voyage, and some genera were starkly different from anything found before. The bird and animal life likewise presented great colour and variety, and although it was early winter, the fishermen had little difficulty in getting a good daily catch. This lushness of natural history was reflected in the rethinking of the name which Cook eventually chose for the Bay. 'Sting Ray Bay,' originally chosen because of the enormous size of those fish caught within it, gave way first to 'Botanists Bay' and then to 'Botany Bay.' Cook himself explained the reasoning: 'The great quantity of New Plants &c Mr Banks and Dr Solander collected in this place occasioned my giving it the name of Botany Bay.'[51]

For the natural historian then, this was a kind of New-World paradise, yielding one new variety after another in a profusion and splendour fitting for a *Terra Australis*. Collecting, classifying, naming, and storing this wealth overtook the more prosaic task of assessing the land thoroughly in terms of its potential for European settlement. In the years after the voyage, when the collections in the herbarium survived better than human memory, Botany Bay was reinterpreted, and the enormous variety of plant and animal life bespoke of a climate, soil, and vegetation ideal for a European colony. A correspondent in the *Gentleman's Magazine* in December 1786 wrote supporting the Botany Bay scheme, urging readers to 'revolve immediately in your mind the mild climate of 34°, the very name of the spot the convicts are going to,' as providing evidence of how well they would be provided for.[52] Not for the last time did the Australian environment cast its deceptive spell over the observer, hinting at a fertility which in reality it could not match.[53] The burden of *Terra Australis* ensured the spell would work.

Cook should bear no more than his share of the blame for this predicament. His journals, and those of Banks, were not particularly fulsome about the Botany Bay area, as has been seen, and his final remarks on the eastern coast of what became New South Wales are fairly dismissive. It was a land of indifferent fertility and water supply, including many rocky, barren, or savannah-like parts. Although there were many discoveries of new plants, few of these were of any utility – 'The Land naturly produces hardly any thing fit for man to eat.' Banks' summary judgments were more harsh:

> For the whole lengh [sic] of coast which we sail'd along there was a sameness to be observd in the face of the countrey very uncommon; Barren it may justly be calld and in a very high degree, that at least we saw. The Soil is generally sandy and very light: on it grows grass tall enough but thin sett, and trees of a tolerable size, never however together, in general 40, 50, or 60 feet asunder. This and spots sometimes very large of loose sand constitutes the general face of the countrey as you said along it, and indeed of the greatest part even after you have penetrated inland as far as our situation would allow us to do ... A Soil so barren and at the same time intirely void of the helps derivd from cultivation could not be supposed to yield much towards the support of man.

Even the Reverend John Hawkesworth, so prone to distorting the record of the voyages, captured accurately the tone of the voyagers themselves: 'The soil in some parts seemed to be capable of improvement, but the far greater part is such as can admit of no cultivation.'[54]

From Cook's myth-dispelling second voyage onwards, New Holland (Australia) began to rise in the estimation of Europeans, almost by default. As the only considerable land mass left unoccupied by Europeans it became almost the surrogate *Terra Australis,* and as time went by it came to be invested in the minds of many with its attributes and virtues. In this process the qualifications of Cook, Banks, and other observers were played down. The actual descriptions of soil, vegetation, and animal life gave way to speculation about what lay in the interior or as yet undiscovered parts of the continent. It was symbolic of the changes that on his third voyage Cook called at Adventure Bay, in Van Dieman's Land, in January 1777, to collect water and greens. The great commander himself was part of the process of reassessment. Time also softened Banks' views to some degree, to witness his evidence before House of Commons committees in 1779 and 1785.

Since the concern here is with attitudes to the land, I will not rehearse the reasons for the British choice of New South Wales as a convict colony. The manner in which the proposal to ship convicts to Botany Bay was packaged is, however, of immediate concern, because this shaped perceptions of the new land and vitally affected the attitudes to their environment, to the settlement itself, and, indirectly, toward the homeland. The attempt by speculators such as Matra, Call, and Young to make New Holland serve many purposes reawakened the dream of *Terra Australis*, locking in the burden of *Terra Australis*. Great Britain, recently defeated and humiliated in a colonial war, was susceptible to the lure of a new utopia.

James Mario Matra's plan for settling New South Wales established the scale of this burden. The discoveries of British explorers might 'in time atone for the loss of our American colonies.' The natural resources and trading potential of Australia were sketched in a way which would to a large extent cover the range of commodities and markets available in North America. In opposition to Cook and Banks in 1770, Matra claimed the coast had a great variety of soil, 'and great parts of it were extremely fertile.' Following the reasoning of Dalrymple, Matra also pointed out that New South Wales would put Britain in a strong position to trade with China, Japan, Korea, and the northwest coast of America, all highly accessible. Britain would also be well placed to exploit trading potential in the Spice Islands (Moluccas). A side benefit would arise from the strategic situation of New South Wales, enabling it to be exploited as a base against Dutch and Spanish colonies in the East Indies and South America. With *Terra Australis* gone the Pacific could be compressed.[55]

More visionary plans involving New South Wales surfaced in 1784 and 1785, and as with the Matra proposal the chief concern of the individuals behind them was self-interest. The Young and Call plans nevertheless reveal the same faith that New South Wales would serve as a complete substitute for the riches of *Terra Australis*.[56]

The combined effect of these schemes was first to recast the observations of Cook and Banks. Their reservations about the soil of New South Wales were swept away – it became a land more fertile than the United States. Similarly, the explorers' comments about the uniformity of the vegetation and appropriateness of the land for agriculture were conveniently ignored. A form of geographical determinism had sidelined the judicious assessments of the explorers. That determinism had replaced the riches of *Terra Australis* with the bounty of New Holland. Although the official documents ordering the dispatch of convicts to New South Wales were a little more prosaic, referring to its 'fertility and the salubrity of the climate,' the more optimistic expectations were fed into the consciousness of its first settlers.

The fleet arriving in Botany Bay in January 1788 at first saw a land much as Cook had described it. The 'park-like' character was apparent from the ships and the climate was mild under the influence of sea breezes; although once the eleven vessels of the fleet were all within the Bay, it looked less commodious than they had been led to believe.

Very quickly, however, the limitations of Botany Bay became apparent. The search for an adequate supply of fresh water proved fruitless: most of the sites Cook had marked were little more than bogs, inadequate to support almost 1500 people. That alone was enough to rule out Botany Bay as a suitable site for the settlement. Other disadvantages were soon apparent. Arthur Bowes, surgeon on the first fleet, summed up the general view: 'Upon first sight, one wd be induced to think this a most fertile spot, as there are great Nos. of very large & lofty trees reachg. almost to the water's edge & every vacant spot between the trees appears to be cover'd wt. verdure: but upon nearer inspection, the grass is found long & coarse, the trees very large & in general hollow, & the wood itself fit for no purpose of buildg. or anything but the fire ... the Soil to a great depth is nothing but a black sand ... add to this, that every part of the ground is in a manner covered with black and red ants of a most enormous size.'[57] Surgeon John White was one of the first to quarrel with Cook's appraisal of the Bay, which, he said, 'does not, in my opinion, by any means merit the commendations bestowed on it by the much-lamented Captain Cook and others. The fine meadows talked of in Captain Cook's voyage I have never seen, though I took some pains to find them out; nor have I heard of a person that has seen any parts resembling them.'[58]

In justifying to the secretary of state the removal of the colony to Port Jackson, Phillip's views were more tempered, as was generally to be the case in future. The harbour of Botany Bay was too exposed to easterly winds to accommodate ships safely. Although there was fresh water at a number of sites around the Bay, it was either inconveniently placed in terms of settlement or it was not in sufficient volume to provide for the needs of the whole contingent. The land in most places appeared swampy and potentially unhealthy. Initial impressions of Port Jackson were much more favourable. The capaciousness of the harbour, the shelter it offered, the capacity to moor close to the shores of the Cove, and its sheer beauty impressed itself on many in the fleet. Phillip pronounced it the 'finest harbour in the world,' which could accommodate 1,000 ships of the line. John White, unhappy with Botany Bay, was initially won over by Port Jackson: 'Port Jackson I believe to be, without exception, the finest and most extensive harbour in the universe and at the same time the most secure, being safe from all the winds that blow.'[59]

Over the next five years divergent views emerged. The original assessment of the harbour itself was sustained, although some argued that an asset so distant from every other British settlement was of doubtful utility, no matter how impressive and capacious it was. Various other factors moulded attitudes toward the environment. Convict and officer alike were overwhelmed by nostalgia and homesickness which exalted their memories of the old country and sharpened the contrasts with New South Wales. The Reverend Johnson wrote in this vein to his friend Henry Fricker: 'And all almost, at least but with few exceptions, are heartily sick of the expedition, and wish themselves back safe in old England.'[60] The green, orderly, and humanized landscape of rural England was compared to the dry, dull, uniform, and even inverted wilderness of their new home. During an expedition to Broken Bay in 1789 Watkin Tench recorded: 'Here again they again wandered over piles of misshapen desolation, contemplating scenes of wild solitude, whose unvarying appearance renders them incapable of affording either novelty or gratification.'[61] It was an environment which not only refused to provide bodily sustenance but also refused to provide a lift to the soul. Away from the harbour the landscape appeared dull or monotonous and the picturesque imagination drew little nourishment from it. This unrelenting character affected more than just the officer journalists. In the view of one woman convict, it was a 'solitary waste of creation.'[62] A far cry from *Terra Australis.*

The sense that the colonists had been misled by early visitors persisted as knowledge of the Cumberland Plain area grew. Watkin Tench was speaking for all when, after a survey of Botany Bay and the area immediately to the south in 1789, he observed: 'We were unanimously of opinion, that had not the nautical part of Mr Cook's description, in which we include the latitude and longitude of the bay, been so accurately laid down, there would exist the utmost reason to believe, that those who have described the contiguous country, had never seen it. On the sides of the harbour, a line of sea coast more than thirty miles long, we did not find 200 acres which could be cultivated.'[63] Cook's famous 'meadows' were nowhere to be found, and the implication was that the great navigator had somehow suspended his judgement on visiting Botany Bay or had been hoodwinked by a malign environment. Phillip thought he had the probable explanation. Commenting to the secretary of state on the difficulty of clearing the land for agriculture, and the lack of open grassland, he wrote: 'I presume the meadows mentioned in "Captain Cook's Voyage" were seen from the high grounds about Botany Bay, and from whence they appear well to the eye, but when examined are found to be marshes, the draining of which would be a work of time, and not to be attempted by the first settlers.'[64]

This deceptiveness of the landscape was one of its most intolerable vices. To Cook and Banks its park-like nature had offered the hope of a decent pastureland at least. The first fleet found the vegetative cover to be a sham, offering the appearance of greenness and therefore fertility but actually disguising the real poverty of the soil. The great range of flowering plants, the rich, chattering and cawing bird life survived in a near desert environment where water resources were inadequate. The hopes of growing tropical spices and other products, or of finding mineral wealth, were derisory. Many early crops withered in the ground or were attacked by insect pests or caterpillars. More than any other environment outside frozen wastes, it seemed a land condemned for Cain. The burden of *Terra Australis* afflicted it.

The case of Captain Charles Bishop may be dealt with more briefly, but his peripatetic voyaging symbolized the hopes, fantasies, and disillusionment which often characterized perceptions of the Pacific. He also represented a strain of attitudes to the Pacific which retains currency today. His ostensible mission, as defined by Sydenam Teast, the owner of his ship, was simple: to sail via Cape Horn for the Pacific, head for the northwest coast of America, and make two trading voyages to Canton with sea otter furs. His instructions foresaw no great difficulties in the voyage, unless he was forced to put into the Sandwich (Hawai'ian) Islands, where the lure of the Pacific might infect the crew and he could get caught up in local political feuds.[65]

As it happened, around Cape Horn a series of Pacific events intruded to cast his plans in rather different directions. He visited the Falklands, Easter Island, the northwest coast of America, the Sandwich Islands, Canton, Amboina, Taiwan, Kamchatka, Tahiti, New South Wales, Bass Strait, Norfolk Island, Kiribati, and New Zealand. His economic interests, or rather hopes, deviated from sea otter furs to embrace spices, seal furs, the Tahitian pork trade, transporting ejected missionaries, and general merchandise. He sold his first ship in Canton and purchased another at Amboina. But his fortunes were, to say the least, mixed. The Pacific, which had promised him so much and seemed so readily accessible, never lived up to his commercial expectations. The quick profits were elusive. The ocean and its peoples proved unpredictable and often violent, recurrently diverting the voyage in new directions. In Hawai'i there was a sense of Arcadia already tainted by dangers. The beckoning women on the beach provided many temptations; 'the sight of so much beauty for it was a fine moon light night, did not fail to awaken in the minds of our Weather beaten crew, Sentiments kindred to love.' But only kindred, for the Islands carried forbidden fruit and perils for the Utopist. Bishop and his ship were not equipped to deal with the chaotic political environment severely exacerbated by the intrusion of the West.[66]

Charles Bishop serves to exemplify another dimension of the burden of *Terra Australis*. One of the enduring features of the economic development of the Pacific through to 1840 was the extractive nature of its early industries. This stretched back to the Spanish mining of Latin America, which was the envy of other nations. The vision of the Pacific as a region of bounteous production cannot be unconnected with the facts of its exploitation in the eighteenth and nineteenth centuries.

Like many setting out for the sea otter trade, Bishop did not initially see any limits to the harvest, but by 1797 he was becoming aware that conditions were unpredictable and the trade might have passed its best. Equally illuminating was his interest in the sealing potential of Más Afuera, one of the Juan Fernandez group, for he was influenced by the accounts of Carteret, written up by Hawkesworth, which had claimed: 'The seals were so numerous, that I verily think if many thousands were killed in a night, they would not be missed in the morning.'[67] From such reports Bishop believed that 20,000 seal skins could be procured there in ten weeks, and he returned to this possibility repeatedly in his correspondence with backers in Canton. It seemed that he was looking to the bounty of this island to make up for the losses which he had suffered in the sea otter trade.[68]

Bishop never actually got to Más Afuera because of weather, ship, and crew problems. However, sealing began there in 1797 and within eight violent but profitable years its fur seal population had been exterminated. This was a story endlessly and depressingly repeated throughout the Pacific. European exploitation in the eighteenth century affected ethnographic material (the artificial curiosities traded on a vessel's return) seals, sea otters, whales, bêche de mer, pearling, sandalwood, timber, and the Pacific pork trade. All these industries were dealing with a limited and easily depleted resource.

The burden of *Terra Australis* was to suggest that these resources were unlimited; that the vastness of the Pacific gave it abundance, resilience, and regenerative powers uncharacteristic of Europe. Forster's *Journal* commented on the natural fertility of the Tahitians. Plants grew and were cropped with great rapidity. Scientists revelled in the profusion of species and the abundance of plant, fish, and bird life. This abundance hid an ecological fragility and made it possible to harvest these resources voraciously, to pollute, infect, people, and overfish in the belief that the huge Pacific swells would cleanse and renew endlessly.

Yet the warning signs were there from the earliest days. Cook soon became aware of the limits of the pork supply in the Pacific and the effects of European intrusion on the food supply, health, and welfare of Pacific peoples. In the South Island of New Zealand, in Australia, and in Alaska, he realized the harshness and fragility of some indigenous lifestyles and the industry and balance required to preserve them. The sea otter trade had barely been going a decade before the traders realized the population decline. In the islands of Bass Strait, off New Zealand,

and in the sub-Antarctic, it soon became apparent that seal colonies could not sustain the slaughter they were being subjected to. The sperm whale had been chased out of the North Atlantic: in the 1780s its pursuit began in the Pacific. But the persistent perception of Pacific meant that once one industry expired, extractors moved on to another and, as the technology improved, the intensity of the harvest increased. The burden of *Terra Australis* leads to the obscenity of the drift net, stretching for up to fifty kilometres, sweeping the Pacific of its marine life.

Appendices:
Vancouver's Instruments, Charts, and Drawings

Prepared by Andrew David

Appendix 1: Instruments Supplied to Captain George Vancouver[1]

(a) A list sent from the Admiralty to the Navy Board, 19 January 1790

1 Sextant by Dollond
1 Sextant, 5 inch radius
1 Astronomical Quadrant
1 Achromatic Telescope of 42 inch radius on a polar axis
1 Military Telescope of 2 feet
1 Dipping Needle by Nairne and Blunt
2 straight bars ⎤
1 Horseshoe ⎦ Magnets
1 Plane Table complete
1 Theodolite
1 Protractor with a Nonius
1 Surveying or Pocket Compass
2 Azimuth Compasses, one large by Gregory, one by Knight
2 Boat Compasses
1 Copying Glass
1 Parallel Ruler
1 Chain and Lines
1 Three-foot Rule, brass-edged
1 Marine Barometer
2 Thermometers with a Case for sinking
1 Pocket Thermometer
2 Station Pointers
1 case of Quicksilver for an Artificial Horizon
1 Portable Observatory

[In addition Vancouver signed for:

1 Case of Instruments
1 Beam Compass]

(b) Items requested by Lieutenant Henry Roberts

[On 14 January Roberts requested the following extra articles, which, presumably, were also supplied to Vancouver.]

1 Boats Cutter of 16 feet
2 Tents with poles &c complete
1 Marquee, Camp Tables and Utensils
1 Boat's awnings
2 Drawing Boards
Various seine nets and trawls with lines and hooks in proportion

Appendix 2: Schedule of Mathematical, Optical and Astronomical Instruments Put into the Hands of Mr. William Gooch, going as Astronomer to the North-West Coast of America[2]

An Astronomical Clock, by Earnshaw ⎤
A Journey-man Clock ⎦ With their common stand[3]
Two time-keepers by Arnold
An Alarum Clock
A good Pocket-Watch, with a second hand, by Earnshaw[4]
An Achromatic Telescope of 46-inch focus, with a divided Object-glass, Micrometer, and stand; by Dollond
A reflecting Telescope, by Burton
Three Setts of coloured Wedges to darken the sun, by Nairne
A Universal Theodolite, or Altitude and Azimuth Instrument, by Ramsden
A Transit Instrument, by Troughton
A Theodolite, by Burton
A Steel Gunter's Chain, for Surveying
Four Thermometers
A new Hadley's Sextant, with a Stand for use at Land, by Troughton
A Hadley's Sextant, by Dollond, new divided, by Troughton
A Night Telescope, by Dollond
A Four feet Hand Perspective, by Dollond
A Knight's Azimuth Compass, by Adams
A Marine Dipping Needle ⎤
A Small Pocket Compass ⎥ by Nairne
A Sett of Magnetic Steel bars ⎦
A Bason to hold quicksilver, with glass roofs, by Dollond
A Quantity of quicksilver, in a Bottle
A reflecting level of Black Glass, truly flat, adjusted by a glass level ground flat beneath, by Troughton
A stand for the Dipping Needle
A[5] ten feet rod of Deal made of the true standard length
A five feet brass standard; these two[6] to examine and correct the Gunter's Chain
A beam Compass scale of equal parts, by Troughton
A circular Protractor, by Troughton
A circular Protractor, by Troughton
A board to draw on
An Instrument[7] to lay a place down in a Chart from the two   observed angles between 3 given places, by Troughton[8]

Books and Charts
The Nautical Almanacs of 1769 & 1774.
The Nautical Almanacs of 1791, 2, 3, 4, 5, 6; two setts.
Tables requisite to be used with the Nautical Almanac; 3 setts.
General Tables of refraction and parallax.
Taylor's Sexagesimal Tables.
Mayer's Tables & Charts, Mason's Lunar tables in one.
Hutton's Mathematical Tables.
Folio Distances of the Moon from the Sun and Stars.
Robertson's Navigation.
Wild's Surveying.
Dalrymple's Surveying.
Mackenzie's Marine Surveying.
Astronomical Observations to Cook's Voyage, by W. Wales 1777.
Original Astronomical Observations in a Voyage &c by W. Bayly 1782.
Astronomical Observations made in Voyages, by Byron, Wallis &c by W. Wales, 1788.
A Variation Chart of 1756 by Mountain and Dodson.
Celestial Atlas by Mr Bode of Berlin.

Appendix 3: The Graphic Records of Vancouver's Voyage

British Charts

A   British Library, London
    A Chart shewing part of the sw Coast of New Holland; with *inset* A Sketch of King George
    III^d Sound on the sw Coast of New Holland, with View of the Entrance of King George the
    third Sound. *Map Room, Kings Topographical Collection, Vol.* CXVI *52-71*

B   Cambridge University Library
    William Gooch's journal: A Plan of the Harbour of Port Praya in the Island of St. Jago.
    Mm. 6.48, p. 133

C   Hydrographic Office, Taunton
    1   Port Quadra, Gulf of Georgia ... Mr Whidbey. H. Humphrys delin. *224 on Ac2*
    2   Grays Harbour ... Mr Whidbey. Jos^h Baker delin. *224 on Re*
    3   A Chart shewing part of the Western Coast of N. America ... from the Latde. of 43° 00'
        N. and Longde. 234° 00' E. to the Latde. of 36° 36' N. and Longde 238° 36'E ... in the
        Summer of 1792 ... Prepared by J. Baker. *226 on Ac1*
    4   A Chart shewing part of the Western Coast of N. America ... from the Ltde. of 42° 30'
        N. and Longde. 230° 30'E. to the latde. of 52° 15' N. and Longde 238° 03'E ... in the
        Summer of 1792. The parts of the Coast red, are copied from Spanish Charts ...
        Prepared by J. Baker. *228 on 82*
    5   A Sketch of Columbia River by W. Broughton. *229 on Rv*
    6   James Johnstone's 'roughs':
        (a) [sw Coast of Western Australia]. *231/1 on Ac1*
        (b) [Second boat expedition from Restoration Bay, 9 to 18 June 1793]. *231/2 on Ac1*
        (c) [Strawberry Bay to Birch Bay and islands north and west of Haro and Rosario
            straits]. *231/3 on Ac1*
        (d) [Johnstone Strait]. *231/4 on Ac1*
        (e) [Straits between Banks Island, Pitt Island, and adjacent mainland]. *231/5 on Ac1*
        (f) [First boat expedition from Restoration Bay, 30 May to 3 June 1793]. *231/5 on Ac1*

(g) [Galapagos Islands, 8 February 1795]. *231/7 on Ac1*

(h) [Third boat expedition from Restoration Bay, 22 June 1793]. *231/8 on Ac1*

(i) [Fourth boat expedition from Salmon Cove, 22 to 31 July 1793]. *231/9 on Ac1*

(j) [Coast in vicinity of Cabo St Lucas; track through the Tres Marias; Magdalina Islands on the coast of California]. *231/11 on Ac1*

(k) [Isle of Cerros, 9 December 1794]. *231/12 on Ac1*

7 A chart shewing parts of the sw Coast of New Holland; with *inset* A Sketch of King George III^rds Sound on the sw Coast of New Holland *with* View of the Entrance of King George the third Sound. H. Humphrys delin. *436/1 on Xf*

8 A chart shewing part of the sw Coast of New Holland; with inset A Sketch of King George IIIrd Sound on the sw Coast of New Holland with View of the Entrance of King George of third's Sound. *436/2 on Xf*

9 A rough survey in pencil of the Marquesas Islands [by W. Gooch]. *446 on Pu.*

10 Marquesas Islands by W. Gooch.

11 A Chart shewing part of the Western Coast of N. America from Latde. 29° N to Latde. 37° in the Summer of 1792. Josh Baker delin [a continuation of 226 on Ac1 above, with the overlap at Monterey showing considerable differences]. *523 on He*

12 Chatham Island by W. Broughton. *523 Pac fol. 3*

13 sw Coast of Australia and King George III Sound by W. Broughton. *523a on Xf*

14 Dusky Bay in New Zealand by Lieut. Broughton; Facile Harbour; Pickersgill Harbour from Cook; Anchor Harbour from Vancouver. Copied by J. Walker, December 1797 [appears to be a compilation drawing for the engraved chart]. *523b on Xv*

15 The Snares by W. Broughton. *523c in New Zealand fol. 1*

16 Port Stewart by P. Puget. *558 on Rc*

17 Port St Salvadore, Brazil, by P. Puget. *559 on Af2*

18 Chart of Tres Marias, Port Blas, by P. Puget. *560 on Ac2*

19 Port Protection by P. Puget. *561 on Rc*

20 Anchor Island Harbour, Dusky Bay, by P. Puget. *562 on Xu*

21 A Sketch plan of the Snares, with two views. *Sykes' Sketch Book, fol. 7v*

D Public Record Office, Kew

1 Columbia's River [almost certainly a copy of Gray's chart, which Vancouver obtained at Nootka Sound; removed from CO 5/187]. *MPG 557(1)*

2 Outline sketch plan of Burke's Channel [removed from CO 5/187]. *MPG 557(2)*

3 Chart of the Coast of NW America and Islands adjacent North Westward of the Gulf of Georgia as explored ... in the Months of July & August 1792 [from 50° 00' N to 51° 48' N; removed from CO 5/187]. *MPG 557(3)*

4 A Chart of the NW Coast of America from 40° 00' N to 50° 30' N [removed from CO 5/187]. *MPG 557(4)*

5 A Chart showing part of the Coast of NW America. [Although a manuscript chart, it carries the legend 'London Published May 1st 1798 by J. Edwards Pall Mall & G. Robinson Paternoster Row' and thus, although lacking the three inset plans, is almost certainly the compilation drawing for Plate 5 of the Vancouver's *Atlas*.]

6 Henry Humphrys' journal (*Adm 55/26*):

(a) Chart of King George the Third's Sound ... Surveyed by Mr Whidbey Master. *fol. 47*

(b) Anchor Island Harbour in Dusky Bay, New Zealand ... by Mr Whidbey. *fol. 56*

(c) Chart of Port Discovery or Port Quadra in the Streights of Juan de Fuca, surveyed by Mr Whidbey. *fol. 98*

7 John Stewart's journal (*Adm 55/28*):

(a) A Sketch of King George ye IIIds Sound. *fol. 27*

(b) A Scetch of Wytete Bay on the S° side of Woahoo. *fol. 83*

(c) Port Stewart NW Coast of America. *fol. 207*

8 Joseph Baker's journal (*Adm 55/32*):

(a) A Sketch of King George III Sound. *fol. 59v*

(b) Anchor Island Harbour in Dusky Bay New Zealand. *fol. 73v*

9 John Sherriff's log (*Adm 53/334*):

(a) King George the Third's Sound West Coast of New Holland. *fol. 53*

(b) [A pencil outline of two stretches of unidentified coastline opposite entries for 9 to 22 May 1792; possibly of Port Discovery]. *fol. 58*

(c) [An incomplete and unidentified survey of an intricate area, containing a number of islands or tips of peninsulas opposite entries for 23 May to 2 June 1792; probably of the San Juan Islands]. *fol. 59*

(d) [A pencil outline of an unidentified stretch of coastline opposite entries for 28 June to 16 July 1792]. *fol. 62*

(e) Marias Islands. *fol. 63*

(f) Commencement Bay. *fol. 100*

(g) Port Stewart. *fol. 107*

(h) [Port Protection]. *fol. 110*

10 James Johnstone's log (*Adm 53/335*):

(a) [King George III Sound]. *fol. 73*

(b) [SW Coast of Western Australia]. *fol. 74*

(c) [Anchor Island harbour]. *fol. 91*

(d) [The Snares]. *fol. 92*

(e) Chatham Island. *fol. 96*

11 Lists of charts and drawings brought back from Monterey by Broughton: see under Drawings below

E Thomas Heddington's surveys: In 1808 Heddington applied to the Admiralty for the return of his surveys and drawings. This was granted and their present whereabouts, if they have survived, is not known. Heddington's request was accompanied by a list of his charts, but not his drawings. *PRO, Adm 1/1936, letter Cap H 178, dated 24 October 1808*

Spanish Charts

Vancouver possessed a number of Spanish manuscript charts, some of which have survived. One was sent out in the *Daedalus*, the others were presented to him in Nootka by Quadra and Galiano.

A Public Record Office, Kew

Carta reducida que comprehende parte de la Costa Septentrional de California, corrigida y enmendada hasta la Boca del Estrecho de Fuca ... [por] Dn Manuel Quimpert en el año de 1790. Construida por su primer Piloto Dn Gonzalo López de Haro. [This chart fits the description of the chart forwarded to the Admiralty by Henry Dundas (later Viscount Melville), a copy of which was sent to Vancouver aboard the *Daedalus*.[9]]. *MPK 203(2)*

B Hydrographic Office, Taunton

1 Plano de los Canales Imediatos a Nutka y de la Navegatión (sic) hecha para su reconocimiento por las Lanchos de las corvetas *Descubierta* y *Atrevide* en el Año 1791. Para el uso de Mendendez. *355/1 on Ac11*

2 [A tracing by an English draughtsman of a Spanish survey of Vancouver Island from Nootka to Cape Classet and the Strait of Georgia; with plans of] Pᵗᵒ Clayocaut, Pᵗᵒ de Nuestro Sd de los Angles, Pᵗᵒ de la Sta Cruz and Pᵗᵒ San Rafael. *355/2 on Ac1 fol. 1*

3   Chart of the West Coast of North America, with the Isles adjacent from the Latde 50°
    45' N & Longde 30°: copied from one constructed ... by Dⁿ Caamaño ... in ... 1792
    [traced by an English draughtsman]. *355/3 on Ac1*

These charts correspond to three of the nine charts presented to Vancouver and brought
back to England by Broughton.[10]

Drawings

A   British Library, London
    1   Four views of King George III Sound on one sheet (copies of original drawings by
        Sykes).
    2   *View of the Entrance of King George the third Sound* (inset on chart referred to above).
        Map Room, Kings Topographical Collection, Vol. CXVI: 52-71

B   Bishop Museum, Honolulu
    1   *Karakakoa Bay, Owhyee*. Drawn on the spot by Thomas Heddington. Engraved by M.
        Dubourg. Published by Captain Thomas Heddington, RN, March 1814.
    2   *Village of Macacoupah, Owhyee*. Drawn on the spot by Thomas Heddington. Engraved
        by M. Dubourg. Published by Captain Thomas Heddington, RN, March 1814.
        Tinted aquatints based on two of Heddington's missing drawings.

C   Cambridge University Library
    William Gooch's journal: Three ethnographc drawings, one natural history drawing, and a
    pencil sketch of the *Daedalus. Mm.6.48*

D   Dixson Library, State Library of New South Wales, Sydney
    The Discovery on the Rocks in Queen Charlotte Sound. A detailed water-colour drawing
    attributed to Zachary Mudge because of the close similarity to Plate VI in
    Vancouver's *Voyage*, with an identical title. *Pd 695*

E   Hydrographic Office
    1   *View of the Entrance of King George III^rds Sound*. H. Humphrys delin. *Inset on
        436/1 on Xf*
    2   *View of the Entrance of King George the third's Sound*. *Inset on 436/2 on Xf*
    3   An album containing 100 sheets of drawings by John Sykes and Henry Humphrys,
        together with a list of 25 drawings brought back from Monterey by Broughton (see also
        list below) and 90 drawings in Sykes' Sketch Book, delivered to Vancouver prior to the
        Discovery's arrival at St Helena. *Sykes' Sketch Book*

F   National Library of Australia, Canberra
    1   *Karakakoa Bay, Owhyee*. Drawn on the spot by Thomas Heddington. Engraved by M.
        Dubourg. Published by Captain Thomas Heddington, RN, March 1814. *NK 262*
    2   *Village of Macacoupah, Owhyee*. Drawn on the spot by Thomas Heddington. Engraved
        by M. Dubourg. Published by Captain Thomas Heddington, RN, March 1814. *NK 4866
        Tinted aquatints based on two of Heddington's missing drawings. The library also holds
        two lithographs versions of the latter view at NK 4865.*

G   Public Record Office
    1   Henry Humphrys' journal: Thirteen coastal views on ten sheets. *Adm 55/26*
    2   Peter Puget's journal: Three coastal views on two sheets. *Adm 55/27*
    3   Robert Pigot's journal: Four coastal views on three sheets. *Adm 55/30*
    4   Joseph Baker's journal: Six coastal views on four sheets and a view of the *Discovery*
        aground on 7 August 1792. *Adm 55/32*
    5   Zachary Mudge's log: Two coastal views. *Adm 51/4533*

6   John Sherriff's log: Seven coastal views on two sheets. *Adm 53/334*

7   James Johnstone's log: One coastal view. *Adm 53/335*

8   Thomas Manby's log: Six coastal views on four sheets. *Adm 51/2251*

9   *A View of Friendly Cove* (showing the parcel of land that Quadra was prepared to cede to Vancouver), by H. Humphrys. MFQ *127*

10 Lists of charts and drawings brought back from Monterey by Broughton. *Adm 1/2629, letter dated 13 January 1793.*[11]
Broughton brought back from Monterey a collection of Vancouver's original surveys, together with copies of various Spanish surveys presented to Vancouver by Quadra and Galiano, as well as drawings by John Sykes and Henry Humphrys. The accompanying letter contains a list of twenty charts, including nine received from Quadra and Galiano, a list of twenty-seven drawings signed by Sykes (see also list above), and a list of twelve drawings signed by Humphrys. The surviving charts and drawings are probably among those now held in the Hydrographic Office.[12]

H   Royal Botanic Gardens, Kew
A number of original botanical drawings done by Archibald Menzies on the northwest coast have recently been identified by Eric Groves in the herbarium of the Royal Botanic Gardens, Kew. Some may relate to Vancouver's voyage, while others have been identified as belonging to Menzies' voyage in the *Prince of Wales*, under Captain James Colnett.

I   Newberry Library, Chicago
Drawings by William Alexander: On his return to England, Vancouver set about preparing his journal for publication and also selecting suitable sketches by Sykes, Humphrys, and Heddington to illustrate it. William Alexander, who had been one of the official artists with Macartney's embassy to China, was employed to redraw the sketches for the engravers. Alexander was instructed to amend some of the drawings Vancouver had selected to illustrate his journal, apparently to add human interest. A collection of seventeen of these drawings is held in the Newberry Library, of which fourteen were eventually engraved and included in Vancouver's *Voyage*. The original drawings of two of the remaining three are by Sykes and are held in the Hydrographic Office, the original drawing of the third, by Humphrys, has not survived.

Notes

The following abbreviations appear in this section:

AGI   Archivo General de las Indias
AGN   Archivo General de la Nación, México
AHN   Archivo Histórico Nacional, Madrid
ANL   Australian National Library
ATL   Alexander Turnbull Library, Wellington
CUL   Cambridge University Library
HOMDT Hydrographic Office, Ministry of Defence, Taunton
HRNSW *Historical Records of New South Wales*
Kew   Royal Botanic Gardens, Kew
ML   State Library New South Wales: Mitchell Library
MN   Museo Naval, Madrid
NMM   National Maritime Museum, Greenwich

Introduction

1   W. Kaye Lamb (ed.), *George Vancouver, A Voyage of Discovery to the North Pacific Ocean and Round the World, 1791-1795* (London: Hakluyt Society 1984), II:583.

2   George Vancouver, *A Voyage of Discovery to the North Pacific Ocean and Round the World; in which the Coast of North-West America has been Carefully Examined and Accurately Surveyed ...* (London: G.G. and J. Robinson 1798); Lamb, *Vancouver's Voyage*, I:290.

3   Vancouver to Philip Stephens, Secretary of Admiralty, 8 September 1794, in Vancouver, *Voyage*, 182.

4   Vancouver to Evan Nepean, Under Secretary of State, 7 January 1793, Lamb, *Vancouver's Voyage*, I:1580.

5   Lamb, *Vancouver's Voyage*, I:242.

6   Lamb, *Vancouver's Voyage*, I:243-4.

7   George Godwin, *Vancouver: A Life* (London: Philip Allan 1930); F.W. Howay, *Captain George Vancouver* (Toronto: Ryerson 1932).

8   Bern Anderson, *Surveyor of the Sea: The Life and Voyages of Captain George Vancouver* (Toronto: University of Toronto Press 1960).

9   Ronald Wright, *Stolen Continents: The 'New World' Through Indian Eyes Since 1492* (Toronto: Viking 1992); a similar line is taken in Thomas R. Berger, *A Long and Terrible Shadow: White Values, Native Rights and the Americas, 1492-1992* (Vancouver/Toronto: Douglas & McIntyre 1991).

10 Wright, 5.

11 Lamb, *Vancouver's Voyage*, IV:1391. The emphasis is Vancouver's.

Chapter 1: Discovery of Polynesia

1   John C. Beaglehole (ed.), *The Endeavour Journal of Joseph Banks, 1768-1771* (Sydney: Angus and Robertson 1962), I:399.

2   John C. Beaglehole (ed.), *The Journals of Captain James Cook on his Voyage of Discovery, Vol. I: The Voyage of the Endeavour, 1768-1771* (Cambridge, England: Hakluyt Society 1955), 169.

3   Beaglehole, *Cook Journals*, I:286 and 288; Beaglehole, *Endeavour Journal*, II:37.

4   John C. Beaglehole (ed.), *The Journals of Captain James Cook on his Voyages of Discovery, Vol. II: The Voyage of the Resolution and Adventure, 1772-1775* (Cambridge, England: Hakluyt Society

1961), 320-4. Though not before a young midshipman, George Vancouver, ran out to the bowsprit to stake his claim to being furthest south by yelling 'Ne Plus Ultra!' – or so Vancouver claimed. Sparrman, who had stayed in an aft cabin during the tacking operations, made a similar claim to glory. As the ship made a little stern way before the sails filled on the new tack, Sparrman thought that he had gone 'a trifle farther south than any of the others in the ship.' See Beaglehole, *The Life of Captain James Cook* (London: Hakluyt Society 1974), 365n; and Lamb, *Vancouver's Voyage*, 1:5.

5   Beaglehole, *Cook Journals*, 11:327.

6   Ibid., 325.

7   George Forster, *A Voyage Round the World in his Britannic Majesty's Sloop Resolution, Commanded by Capt. James Cook, during the years 1771, 3, 4, and 5* (London: B. White 1777), 1:557.

8   Beaglehole, *Cook Journals*, 11:339n.

9   Ibid., 354.

10   John C. Beaglehole (ed.), *The Journals of Captain James Cook on his Voyages of Discovery, Vol. III: The Voyage of the Resolution and Discovery, 1776-1780* (Cambridge, England: Hakluyt Society 1967), 263-4.

11   Ibid., 262n.

12   William H. Goetzmann, *New Men, New Lands* (New York: Viking 1986), 1-15.

13   Beaglehole, *Banks Journal*, 1:370-3; 11:252-8. Banks was not the first to make this discovery. Sixty years earlier a Dutch scholar, Adriaan Reeland, had published a dissertation comparing word lists from Malaya and Java with those from islands in Melanesia and the western edge of Polynesia and had established that they belonged to the same language family. See Hadriani Relandi, *Dissertationum Misscelanaearum, Pars Tertia et Ultima* (Guliemi Broedelet: n.p. 1706).

14   This habit of cultural-linguistic inquiry apparently made a strong impression on George Vancouver during his service as a midshipman on Cook's second and third voyages. Although his journals from those two voyages were unfortunately lost, Lieutenant King's testimony reveals that Vancouver quickly developed an extraordinary facility in the Hawai'ian language, which served not only to recover Cook's body (King in Beaglehole, *Cook Journals*, 1:554), but also to help reestablish good relations between the British and the Hawai'ians when Vancouver returned to Hawai'i fifteen years later commanding his own expedition. On that voyage, his linguistic facility and interest led Vancouver to discover the Tahitian practice of *pi*, or word replacement, and to correctly forecast that it would be a problem in comparative Polynesian linguistics. Upon returning to Tahiti, Vancouver found that in the years since he was last there a radical change in vocabulary had taken place because of the Tahitian practice whereby a high-ranking chief's name becomes taboo upon his ascension to power, causing even common words that contained syllables of the chief's name to be banished from use and replaced by neologisms. 'The new-fashioned words,' Vancouver wrote, 'produce a very material difference in those tables of comparative affinity which have been constructed with so much attention and labour,' – a situation which has since proved problematic for linguists. George Vancouver, *A Voyage of Discovery to the North Pacific Ocean and Round the World ...* (London: G.G. and J. Robinson 1798), 1:135-6; Ralph White, 'Onomastically Induced Word Replacement in Tahitian,' Genevieve A. Highland, Roland W. Force, Alan Howard, Marion Kelly, and Yoshihiko H. Sinoto (eds.), *Polynesian Culture History* (Honolulu: Bishop Museum Press 1967), 323-38.

15   Thor Heyerdahl, *American Indians in the Pacific* (Chicago: Rand McNally 1953); *Early Man and the Ocean* (Chicago: Rand McNally 1978), 332.

16   Beaglehole, *Cook Journals*, 1:154n.

17   Peter Bellwood, *The Polynesians: Prehistory of an Island People*, rev. ed. (London: Thames and Hudson 1987); Roger Green, 'Lapita,' Jesse D. Jennings (ed.), *The Prehistory of Polynesia* (Cambridge, MA: Harvard University Press 1979), 27-60; Ben Finney, *Voyage of Rediscovery*

(Berkeley: University of California Press, in press).

18 Beaglehole, *Cook Journals*, I:154.

19 Celsus Kelly, *La Australia del Espiritu Santo* (Cambridge, England: Hakluyt Society 1966), II:309.

20 Clements Markham (trans. and ed.), *The Voyages of Pedro Fernandez de Quiros, 1595-1606* (London: Hakluyt Society 1904), II:152; Kelly, *La Australia*, II:309.

21 Andrew Sharp (ed.), *The Journal of Jakob Roggeveen* (Oxford: Clarendon Press 1970), 153-4.

22 H. Ling Roth (trans.), *Crozet's Voyage to Tasmania, New Zealand ... in the Years 1771-1772* (London: Truslow and Shirley 1891), 71.

23 Beaglehole, *Cook Journals*, III:279.

24 Andrew Sharp, *Ancient Voyagers in the Pacific*, Polynesian Society Memoir, No. 32 (Wellington: Polynesian Society 1957); *Ancient Voyagers in Polynesia* (Berkeley: University of California Press 1963).

25 Beaglehole, *Cook Journals*, III:87.

26 Ibid., 87n.

27 Anderson in Beaglehole, *Cook Journals*, III:960.

28 Charles De Brosses, *Histoire des Navigations aux Terres Australes* (Paris: Durand 1756), I:80.

29 J. Dumont-d'Urville, *Voyage de la Corvette L'Astrolabe ... Pendant les années 1826, 1827, 1828, 1829 ...* (Paris: J. Tastu 1830), II:614-16.

30 Beaglehole, *Cook Journals*, III:503-4, 529-30, 537, 541.

31 Ibid., 279.

32 Although Cook notes a few resemblances to Polynesian tongues among the other languages spoken on Vanuatu and New Caledonia, evidently neither Cook nor Johann Forster picked up the underlying linguistic relationship of eastern Melanesian and Polynesian tongues as members of the Austronesian language family. For example, Forster declares that although the languages spoken on the islands of Polynesia 'are hardly sufficient to constitute dialects, the languages spoken at the New-Hebrides, New-Caledonia, and New-Holland, are absolutely distinct from the above general language, and likewise differ among themselves.' Johann Reinhold Forster, *Observations Made during a Voyage Round the World* (London: Robinson 1778), 461.

33 Ka Leo Staff, 'Indigenous Speakers Address Genocide in Hawaii,' *Ka Leo O Hawai'i (The Voice of Hawai'i)*, LXXXVI (52): 1, 7 November 1991.

34 Gananach Obeyesekere, 'The Apotheosis of James Cook: European Myth-making in the Pacific,' seminar paper presented 24 January 1991 at the Department of Anthropology, University of Hawaii, Honolulu.

35 John F.G. Stokes, 'Origin of the Condemnation of Captain Cook in Hawaii,' *Thirty-Ninth Annual Report of the Hawaiian Historical Society for the Year 1930*, 68-104.

36 Boswell in Beaglehole, *Cook Journals*, III:234n.

37 Forster, *A Voyage Round the World*, I:368.

Chapter 2: Myth and Reality

1 J.C. Beaglehole, *Cook Journals*, III:1531-2.

2 The best discussion of the de Fuca voyage printed in Purchas' *Pilgrimes* of 1625, and of the de Fonte account published in 1708, remains H.R. Wagner, 'Apocryphal Voyages to the Northwest Coast of America,' *Proceedings of the American Antiquarian Society*, New Series, XLI (1931):179-234.

3 Beaglehole, *Cook Journals*, III:293-4.

4 Ibid., 335.

5 *The Gazetteer*, 17 Oct. 1780.

6 See Daines Barrington (ed.), 'Journal of a Voyage in 1775. To explore the coast of America,

Northward of California,' *Miscellanies* (London: J. Nichols 1781); William Coxe, *An Account of the Russian Discoveries between Asia and America* (London: 1780).

7   J.R. Forster, *History of the Voyages and Discoveries made in the North* (Dublin: Luke White and Pat. Byrne 1786), 454.

8   For a recent study, see James R. Gibson, *Otter Skins, Boston Ships, and China Goods: The Maritime Fur Trade of the Northwest Coast, 1785-1841* (Seattle: University of Washington Press 1992), especially Chapter 1.

9   James Cook and James King, *A Voyage to the Pacific Ocean* ... (London: 1784), III:440.

10 James Strange, 'A Narrative of a Voyage,' India Office Library, Home Series, Misc. 800/1, 98.

11 See Catherine Gaziello, *L'expédition de Lapérouse 1785-1788* (Paris: C.T.H.S. 1984), 83.

12 John Dunmore and Maurice de Brossard (eds.), *Le Voyage de Lapérouse 1785-1788* (Paris: Imprimerie Nationale 1985), II:183.

13 [William Beresford], *A Voyage round the World 1785-1788 by Captain George Dixon* (London: Geo. Goulding 1789), 216.

14 Ibid., introduction by Dixon, xiv.

15 W. Kaye Lamb, 'The Mystery of Mrs. Barkley's Diary,' *British Columbia Historical Quarterly*, VI (1942):43.

16 Charles Duncan, *Sketch of the Entrance of the Strait of Juan de Fuca, 15 August 1788* [Sketch] (London: 1790).

17 F.W. Howay (ed.), *Voyages of the Columbia to the Northwest Coast 1787-1790 and 1790-1793* (Boston: Massachusetts Historical Society 1941), 73.

18 Ibid., 99.

19 Public Record Office (PRO), London, Adm. 55/146, fol. 232.

20 Howay, *Voyages of the Columbia*, 99-100.

21 Alexander Dalrymple, *The Spanish Pretensions Fairly Dismissed* (London: George Bigg 1790), 15-16; see also his *A Plan for Promoting the Fur-Trade* (London: George Bigg 1789) and *Memoir of a Map of the Lands around the North-Pole* (London: George Bigg 1789).

22 PRO, CO 42/72, 501, Dalrymple Memoir, 2 Feb 1790.

23 John Meares, *Voyages made in the Years 1788 and 1789, from China to the Northwest Coast of America* (London: 1790), 179.

24 For the differing versions of the voyage of the *Washington* given by Meares, see F.W. Howay (ed.), *The Dixon-Meares Controversy* (Toronto: Ryerson Press 1929), 14; Meares, *Voyages in 1788 and 1789*, lvii.

25 Beaglehole, *Cook Journals*, III:367.

26 See PRO, CO 42/72, 495-8; *The Gentleman's Magazine*, LX (Mar. 1790):197-9.

27 See R.H. Dillon (ed.), 'Peter Pond and the Overland Route to Cook's Inlet,' *Pacific North West Quarterly*, XLII (1951): 324-9.

28 See *Historical Records of Australia*, Series I, Governors' Despatches, I (Sydney 1914), 161-4.

29 For Duncan's expedition, see Glyndwr Williams, *The British Search for the Northwest Passage in the 18th Century* (London: Longmans 1962), 242-8.

30 Vancouver's instructions are printed in Lamb, *Vancouver's Voyage*, I:283-8.

31 See British Library, Eg. Ms. 2186, fol. 18.

32 For a convenient summary of these, see Warren L. Cook, *Flood Tide of Empire: Spain and the Pacific Northwest, 1543-1819* (New Haven, CT: Yale University Press 1973), especially Chapter 8.

33 Ibid., 163.

34 Herbert K. Beals (trans. and ed.), *Juan Pérez on the Northwest Coast* (Portland: Oregon Historical Press 1989), 149.

35 Cook, *Flood Tide of Empire*, 164.

36 H.R. Wagner (ed.), *Spanish Explorations in the Strait of Juan de Fuca* (Santa Ana: Fine Arts Press 1933), 12.

37 Ibid., 152.
38 This is a brief summary of confused and murky events stretching from the Spanish archives to Malaspina's ships in the Pacific. See Dario Manfredi's interpretation in Robin Inglis (ed.), *Spain and the North Pacific Coast: Essays in Recognition of the Bicentennial of the Malaspina Expedition, 1791-1792* (Vancouver: Vancouver Maritime Museum Society 1992), 119-24. For the Maldonado voyage generally, see Wagner, 'Apocryphal Voyages,' 218-34.
39 Cited by Catherine P. Hart in Inglis, *Spain and the North Pacific*, 78.
40 See Donald C. Cutter, *Malaspina and Galiano: Spanish Voyages to the Northwest Coast 1791 & 1792* (Vancouver: Douglas & McIntyre 1991), 24.
41 John Kendrick and Robin Inglis, *Enlightened Voyages: Malaspina and Galiano on the Northwest Coast, 1791-1792* (Vancouver: Vancouver Maritime Museum Society 1991), 13.
42 Pedro de Novo y Colson (ed.), *Viaje científico político alrededor del mundo por las cobetas Descubierta y Atrevida* (Madrid: 1885), typescript translation by Carl Robinson, Vancouver Public Library and UBC Library (Special Collections), 270.
43 Wagner, *Spanish Explorations*, 205-6.
44 See John Kendrick (trans. and ed.), *The Voyage of Sutil and Mexicana 1792: The Last Spanish Exploration of the Northwest Coast of America* (Spokane, WA: Arthur H. Clark 1991) 204.
45 H.R. Wagner and W.A. Newcombe (eds.), 'The Journal of Jacinto Caamaño,' *British Columbia Historical Quarterly*, II (1938):299.
46 PRO, Adm 55/27, fol. 93v.
47 Lamb, *Vancouver's Voyage*, II:504, 504n-505n.
48 Ibid., III:1023n.
49 Ibid., III:1024, 1062-3.
50 Ibid., IV:1243.
51 Ibid., IV:1382.
52 Ibid., I:275.

Chapter 3: Vancouver's Survey Methods and Surveys

1   Christine Holmes (ed.), *Captain Cook's Second Voyage: The Journals of Lieutenants John Elliott and Richard Pickersgill* (London: Caliban Books 1984), 30.
2   Beaglehole, *Cook Journals*, II:726.
3   Lamb, *Vancouver's Voyage*, I:1030.
4   British Library, Add. MS 31360, fols. 42 and 43.
5   'Chart of the NW Coast of America and part of the NE [Coast] of Asia with the track of his Majestys Sloops Resolution and Discovery from May to October 1778 by George Vancouver,' American Geographical Society Collection, University of Wisconsin-Milwaukee.
6   Hydrographic Office, Ministry of Defence, Taunton (HOMDT) r4 on Ag1. See also Mary Blewitt, *Surveys of the Seas* (London: MacGibbon & Kee 1957), 104-5.
7   Ibid. The survey was 'Published December 1st 1792 by John Leard & sold by Mount & Davison Tower Hill for Mess.rs Vancouver & Whidbey.'
8   Murdoch Mackenzie, *Orcades: or a Geogtraphic and Hydrographic Survey of the Orkney and Lewis Islands ...* (London: printed for the author, 1750), 3.
9   Beaglehole, *Cook Journals*, II:29, note 1, 13 August 1772.
10 William Wales and William Bayly, *The Original Astronomical Observations made in the course of a Voyage towards the South Pole, and round the World* (London: Board of Longitude 1777), 49.
11 PRO, HO 42/18, fols. 166-7. A draft of this letter with numerous crossings out and amendments, dated 19 February, is held in the Mitchell Library, Brabourne papers, IX, A 79/2 which also contains Bligh's discarded draft. This letter is reproduced, as amended, in the *Historical Records of New South Wales*, I (2): 456-7.
12 Sutro Library, University of San Francisco, SL Banks Ms. PN 1:2.

13 PRO, Adm 1/2395, Roberts to Philip Stephens, 4 and 14 January 1790.
14 National Maritime Museum (NMM), Adm/A/2827, Admiralty to Navy Board, enclosing a list of instruments to be supplied.
15 PRO, Adm 1/3522, Alexander Dalrymple to Philip Stephens, 7 August 1801, inquiring about his astronomical quadrant, which had been returned damaged.
16 Lamb, *Vancouver's Voyage*, I:313.
17 Cambridge University Library (CUL), RGO 14/9, fol. 59.
18 Lamb, *Vancouver's Voyage*, I:309.
19 CUL, RGO, 14/9, fol. 61v.
20 CUL, RGO, 14/13, fol. 155-5v, contains a list of the instruments supplied to Gooch, which he signed as a receipt on 2 July 1791. There is a preliminary list in this volume at fols. 153-3v, which does not include the station pointer and the quadrant with two moveable clamps, with another list in RGO 14/9, fols. 64-4v, attached to the Board of Longitude's instructions for Gooch.
21 CUL, Mm. 6.48, fol. 56v, Gooch to his parents, 31 July 1791.
22 CUL, RGO 14/17, fol. 231, Earnshaw's account to the Board of Longitude, dated 1 July 1791, includes 'To a silver Chronometer Name Thos Earnshaw No 1514, Jewell'd in the Escapement and Small Wheelholes – £47.5.0' and also 'Repairing a silver Chronometer for Mr Gooch – £5.5.0.' Since no other account by Earnshaw, dated 1791, was received by the Board of Longitude, it seems probable that this particular account was made out by Earnshaw with the date he originally supplied his clocks and the pocket watch to Gooch. According to George Gilpin, the retiring secretary to the Board of Longitude (in RGO 14/13, fol. 34), Earnshaw 1514 was one of the chronometers returned to the Board of Longitude by Captain Vancouver.
23 Among useful articles in the 1769 *Almanac* are remarks on Hadley's quadrant by Nevil Maskelyne, the Astronomer Royal, and in the 1774 *Almanac* two examples of calculating lunar distances.
24 Lamb, *Vancouver's Voyage*, I:284.
25 Ibid., 285.
26 The station pointer was a newly invented instrument, which enabled the ship's or boat's position to be fixed and plotted easily by measuring the two angles subtended by three objects ashore; see also Susanna Fisher, 'The Origins of the Station Pointer,' *International Hydrographic Review*, LXVIII:119-26.
27 John Robertson, *The Elements of Navigation* (London: J. Nourse 1764), II:460.
28 Alexander Dalrymple, *Essays on Nautical Surveying* (London: George Bigg 1786), 1, 2, 9.
29 PRO, MPG 557(3), depicting Vancouver's survey of July and August 1792, is on a plane projection. It was probably one of the surveys brought to England by Mudge.
30 James Lawson, 'Autobiography,' Bancroft Library, MS 32, quoted in William King, 'George Davidson and the Marine Survey in the Pacific North'est,' *Western Historical Quarterly*, X (3):295.
31 A meteorological journal kept during the voyage by the naturalist Archibald Menzies is held in the Royal Meteorological Society Archives in the Henry Ransom Humanities Research Center, the University of Texas, Austin. These archives are reportedly being returned to the Royal Meteorological Society in London.
32 Donald C. Cutter, *Malaspina & Galiano: Spanish Voyages to the Northwest Coast, 1791 & 1792* (Seattle: University of Washington Press 1991), 84. Cutter quotes Apuntes, 'Noticias y correspondencias pertenecientes a la Expedicion de Malaspina,' MS 427, Museo Naval, Madrid.
33 Lamb, *Vancouver's Voyage*, II:584 and note 1.
34 Ibid., 589 and note 1.
35 John Kendrick (trans. and ed.), *The Voyage of the Sutil and Mexicana, 1792* (Spokane, WA: Arthur Clark 1991), 113 and 250; Mercedes Palau (ed.), *Diario de viaje de Alejandro Malaspina*

(Madrid: 1984), 65 (identifies No. 61 as being by Arnold) and 332 (details the instruments transferred to Galiano).

36 Lamb, *Vancouver's Voyage*, II:531.
37 Ibid., 1:52-4.
38 Ibid., 531, 595, 685, and related footnotes, from which the accepted present-day longitudes have been taken here and elsewhere.
39 Ibid., II:617, 619-20.
40 Ibid., 685.
41 Ibid., III:939, 1028.
42 Ibid., IV:1263, 1298, 1363, 1391.
43 D.H. Sadler, *Man Is Not Lost: A Record of Two Hundred Years of Astronomical Navigation with the Nautical Almanac, 1767-1967* (London: National Maritime Museum and Royal Greenwich Observatory 1968) 8.
44 Matthew Flinders, *A Voyage to Terra Australis* (London: G. and W. Nichol 1814), Appendix I and II.
45 Ibid., 1:259.
46 Kendrick, *Voyage of Sutil and Mexicana*, 215.
47 When first calculated, this placed Nootka Sound 120°26' west of Cadiz. However, when the official account of Galiano's voyage was being printed, his longitude was recalculated to take into account errors in the tables he had used, revealed by observations obtained in Paris in 1792 by Mr Messier, giving an amended longitude for Nootka of 120°19' west of Cadiz. [Jose Cardero], *Relacion del viaje hecho por las goletas 'Sutil' y 'Mexicana' en el ano de 1792* (Madrid: 1802), 44. I am grateful to Mr John Roberts of Victoria for drawing my attention to this. The only instance that eclipses of Jupiter's satellites were observed during Vancouver's expedition appears to have been by Whidbey on 25 February 1793, when the *Discovery* was in Kealakekua Bay, Hawai'i.
48 Kendrick, *Voyage of Sutil and Mexicana*, 204.
49 Lamb, *Vancouver's Voyage*, IV:1664-5.
50 Ibid., II:901.
51 Ibid., III:791; see also Thomas Earnshaw, *Longitude* (London: 1808), 71-3, for further praise of this watch by Whidbey.
52 Earnshaw, *Longitude*, 232.
53 Lamb, *Vancouver's Voyage*, I:281.
54 HOMDT, 231/4 on Ac 1; see also Lamb, *Vancouver's Voyage*, II:610.
55 Henry Wagner, *Cartography of the Northwest Coast of America to the Year 1800*, facsimile ed. (Amsterdam: N. Isreal 1968), II:471.
56 HOMDT, 228 Press 82.
57 PRO, MPK 203(2) (extracted from FO 95/7, fol. 595).
58 Lamb, *Vancouver's Voyage*, I:287.
59 PRO, Adm 1/2630, Cap v4, Vancouver to Evan Nepean, 15 February 1798.
60 HOMDT, B504 on Pt.

Chapter 4: Vancouver's Chronometers

1 The term 'dead reckoning' was first used and characterized by William Barlow in 1597: 'The dead reckoning is an vncertaine ghess.' See Charles H. Cotter, 'Early Dead Reckoning Navigation,' *Journal of Navigation*, XXXI (1978): 20-7, who explains that 'estimating a ship's speed required accurate knowledge of the effect of wind force on the sails and ship's super-structure ... [which] ... varied with the type of vessel, area of sail carried, wind direction ... It was therefore necessary for a navigator to have wide experience of the behaviour of his ship in a variety of circumstances' (p. 25).

2   Eric G. Forbes, 'The Foundation and Early Development of the Nautical Almanac,' *Journal of the Institute of Navigation*, XVIII (4) (October 1965):391-401; D.H. Sadler, *A Record of Two Hundred years of Astronomical Navigation with the Nautical Almanac, 1767-1967* (London: HMSO for the National Maritime Museum and the Royal Greenwich Observatory 1968).

3   Derek Howse, 'Navigation and Astronomy in the Voyages,' Derek Howse (ed.), *Background to Discovery: Pacific Exploration from Dampier to Cook* (Berkeley: University of California Press 1990), 160-84, and 'The Principal Scientific Instruments taken on Captain Cook's Voyages of Exploration, 1768-1780,' *The Mariner's Mirror*, LXV (1979):119-35.

4   Eva G.R. Taylor, *Navigation in the Days of Captain Cook*, Maritime Monographs and Reports, No. 18 (Greenwich, CT: Trustees of the National Maritime Museum 1975).

5   There are numerous descriptions of Vancouver's use of lunar observations to ascertain longitude. For the first year of the expedition see, for example, Lamb, *Vancouver's Voyage*, I:311, 317-18, 326, and II:531.

6   Derek Howse, 'Captain Cook's Marine Timekeepers. Part 1: The Kendall Watches,' *Antiquarian Horology* (September 1969): 190-205; Humphrey Quill, 'Two Historic Chronometers by John Arnold: Very Early Instruments Belonging to the Royal Society,' *Horological Journal* (July 1960):418-23. The two Arnolds, now known as numbers 36 and 37, did not perform as well as K1, described by Cook as 'our never failing guide the watch.'

7   Vaudrey Mercer, *John Arnold and Son, Chronometer Makers, 1762-1843* (London: 1972); R. John Griffiths, 'Introduction,' Thomas Earnshaw, *Longitude: An Appeal to the Public* (London 1808; reprint ed., St Helens, Merseyside: British Horological Institute 1986).

8   A.C. Davies, 'The Life and Death of a Scientific Instrument: The Marine Chronometer, 1770-1920,' *Annals of Science*, XXXV (1978):509-25.

9   Edward J. Dent, *An Abstract from Two Lectures on the Construction and Management of Chronometers* (London: 1842), 5.

10 Janet Brown and Michael Neve (eds.), [Charles Darwin] *Voyage of the Beagle* (London: Penguin 1989). Appendix 1: 'Admiralty Instructions for the Beagle Voyage,' 379, containing extracts from Vol. 2 of FitzRoy's *Narrative of the Surveying Voyages of HMS Adventure and Beagle* (1839).

11 Howse, 'Cook's Marine Timekeepers: the Kendall Watches,' 199-203; Rupert Gould, *The Marine Chronometer: Its History and Development* (London: Holland Press 1978), 73-4. For Kendall, see Gerard L'E. Turner, 'The Auction Sale of Larcum Kendall's Workshop, 1790,' *Antiquarian Horology* (September 1967):269-75. Kendall's accounts with the Board of Longitude for 1776-87 are in RGO 14/17, 393-7. Kendall cleaned the Board's Harrison chronometers and between 1782 and 1787 was paid £34 10s for this work.

12 K1 went on the *Resolution*; K2, of course, was the *Bounty* watch.

13 *Gentleman's Magazine*, LX (part 2) (1790):1213.

14 CUL, RGO 14/17, 10 April 1776.

15 Howse, 'Cook's Marine Timekeepers: The Kendall Watches,' 199.

16 Lamb, *Vancouver's Voyage*, II:309.

17 CUL, RGO 14/13, 'Schedule of the Instruments of the Board,' 9. In 1785 its warehouse had eight timekeepers (H4, K3, a pocket Earnshaw [probably the one later replaced by 1514] and five box chronometers by Arnold). Gilpen, the storekeeper, noted that 'two were very old, no number, and I believe went with Cook.' These are now known as 'Royal Society Numbers 36 and 37.' On 20 February 1797 Gilpen wrote again to the Board to report the return of 'five timekeepers from Captain Vancouver: the one with three dials [K3], Earnshaw['s] pocket 1514, and Arnold's 14, 176, and 82.'

18 CUL, RGO MS 14/1, Account of the Board of Longitude with Arnold.

19 Joseph Banks, *Observations on Mr Mudge's Applications to Parliament for a Reward for his Timekeepers* (London 1793). For Banks' connection with Vancouver's voyage, see David

Mackay, 'A Presiding Genius of Exploration: Banks, Cook, and Empire, 1767-1805,' *In the Wake of Cook: Exploration, Science and Empire, 1780-1801* (London: Croom Helm 1985). Arnold's own assertion 'that there had scarce ever been less than a hundred of [his] watches employed in the preservation of Shipping' during the 1780s is nearer the mark. John Arnold, *Certificates and Circumstances relative to the Going of Mr Arnold's Chronometers* (London 1791).

20 CUL, RGO MS 14/1, accounts of Arnold's business with the Board of Longitude in the 1780s.

21 Andrew S. Cook, 'Alexander Dalrymple and John Arnold: Chronometers and the Representation of Longitude on the East India Company Charts,' *Vistas in Astronomy*, XXVIII (1985):189-95.

22 Howard T. Fry, *Alexander Dalrymple (1737-1808) and the Expansion of British Trade* (London: Cass 1970), 238-9, quoting Dalrymple's views that 'our Successors ... by the comon use of Chronometers, will acquire, without labour, a precision to which all our Investigations cannot reach'; and 'the more recent Improvements in Navigation which leaves the Lunar Observations as far behind, as they did the Variations, is by Chronometers.'

23 Derek Howse, *Nevil Maskelyne: The Seaman's Astronomer* (Cambridge, England: Cambridge University Press 1989), esp. Chapter 9, 'The Nautical Almanac,' 85-96.

24 I am grateful to Andrew Cook (of the India Office division of the British Library) for showing me his copies of these, including Dalrymple's *Instructions concerning the Chronometers, or Timekeepers, sent to Bombay, 1786*; see footnote 49 in Cook's 'Dalrymple and Arnold.'

25 CUL, RGO 14/9, 54, 55b-56a, 17 December 1789 and 11 March 1790.

26 CUL, RGO MS 14/1, Account of the Board of Longitude with Arnold.

27 Gould, *The Marine Chronometer*, 171, 206.

28 The details of the purchase of A176 are well documented in David Harries, 'A Late 18th Century "Expedition" Marine Chronometer: the John Arnold No. 176,' *Timecraft*, II (i) (January 1982):5-10. For the details of the sale, see *Guardian* (London), 22 September 1981; and also *Christie's Catalogue*, Wednesday, 25 November 1981, 74-9, for details of its provenance.

29 *Christie's Catalogue*, 75-6.

30 J. Eric Haswell, *Horology: The Science of Time Measurement and the Construction of Clocks, Watches, and Chronometers* (London: Chapman and Hall 1928; reprinted Boston: Charles River Books 1976), 253, explains that 'it is possible with these balances (Z type) to reduce considerably the centrifugal error: statistics show that, with an ordinary marine balance making about 1 1/4 turns, the centrifugal error causes a loss of as much as 12 seconds a day, whilst in a balance cut midway between the arms the loss only approximates 2 seconds a day.'

31 Haswell, *Horology*; CUL, RGO MS 14/1, entries for 6 February and 15 May 1801, 32-3. A14 and A176 were also given new gimballed boxes costing £2 12s 6d. each. The present box on A176 is not its original.

32 CUL, RGO 6/577, fol. 52^2, 20 September 1850.

33 CUL, RGO 14/9, letters 54, 55b-56a, 17 December 1789 and 11 March 1790.

34 A.G. Randall, 'Thomas Earnshaw's Numbering Sequence,' *Antiquarian Horology*, XVII (1988):367-71, notes that No. 58/1514, in its silver pair cases, had a spiral balance spring, and the 'Earnshaw type bimetallic compensation balance with brass wedge or segmental shaped weights.' Haswell, *Horology*, 245, stresses the importance of the technical contribution which Earnshaw made in this area: 'Earnshaw not only devised the spring-detent escapement which has survived practically unchanged to the present day, but also solved the difficulty of unifying [brass and steel] used in the compensation balance by fusing them together instead of riveting them or soldering them as Arnold had done.'

35 Lamb, *Vancouver's Voyage*, II:902. Vancouver's diagnosis was entirely plausible because water had got in the watch case. Earnshaw would never have admitted that he overoiled the watch.

36 A.G. Randall, 'Thomas Earnshaw's Numbering Sequence,' *Antiquarian Horology*, XVII (1988):367-71.

37 David S. Landes, *Revolution in Time: Clocks and the Making of the Modern World* (Cambridge, MA: Harvard University Press 1983), 135-8.

38 Howse notes that before sending a clock on an expedition, 'it was the practice to send it to Greenwich to be rated and for the pendulum rod to be marked so that the pendulum length could be kept constant: theoretically, the difference in the clock's rate of going in different latitudes (assuming a compensated pendulum of constant length) gives a measure of the difference in the force of gravity between the two places.' Derek Howse, 'Captain Cook's Pendulum Clocks,' *Antiquarian Horology* (March 1969):62-76, quotation 68.

39 Derek Howse and Beresford Hutchinson, 'The Saga of the Shelton Clocks,' *Antiquarian Horology* (December 1969):281-98.

40 Earnshaw's regulator at the Armagh Observatory was for a long time the world's most accurate clock. Made in 1790, and after brief spells in Greenwich and Dunsink observatories, it was sent to Armagh. There it was sealed in a case and not opened or oiled for twenty-five years. It was accurate to about a tenth of a second a day. See James A. Bennett, *Church, State, and Astronomy in Ireland: 200 years of Armagh Observatory* (Belfast: Armagh Observatory and the Institute for Irish Studies, Queens University of Belfast 1990), 24-7, and 51-2.

41 CUL, RGO 14/1, Accounts of Board of Longitude with Earnshaw. The accounts also noted 'repairing a Larum [an alarm clock] named Arnold, 18s.' The alarm clock was needed to wake up those in the tent observatory who might doze off, before a sighting needing to be timed.

42 Ibid., Accounts of Makers with the Board of Longitude. The account was settled on 11 May 1792.

43 Howse and Hutchinson, 'Shelton's Clocks,' 286-7.

44 Derek Howse, 'Captain Cook's Minor Clocks and Watches,' *Antiquarian Horology* (June 1969):138-45. Quotation on p. 141.

45 Howse, 'Cook's Minor Watches,' 142, quoting William Wales and W. Bayly, *Astronomical Observations made in the course of a Voyage towards the South Pole.*

46 PRO, Adm/2628: Captain's Letters, 1771-1792 (Vancouver 1790-2):625.

47 CUL, RGO 14/1, Accounts of the Board of Longitude with Earnshaw.

48 Lamb, *Vancouver's Voyage*, II:622, footnote 1.

49 CUL, RGO 14/16/387.

50 The painting *The Resolution and Discovery in Nootka Sound* by John Webber (the official artist of Cook's third voyage) is reproduced in David Cordingly (ed.), *Captain James Cook, Navigator* (London: National Maritime Museum 1988), on 40-1, and Plate 22 in Lamb, *Vancouver's Voyage*, II:101.

51 The best known contemporary account of chronometer making was that written by Dr Pearson for Abraham Rees' *Cyclopaedia; or Universal Dictionary of Arts, Sciencs, and Literature.* [See Rees' *Clocks, Watches, and Chronometers, 1819-20* (reprint ed., Newton Abbott, England: David & Charles 1970), 13-50, which contains descriptions of Arnold and Earnshaw's instruments.] The entries describe the layout and construction practised by the production houses of Arnold and Earnshaw at around the turn of the century, and were written before 1809. See Negley B. Harte, 'Rees's Clocks, Watches, Chronometers and Naval Architecture: A Note,' *Maritime History*, III (i)(1973): 92-5.

52 Lamb, *Vancouver's Voyage*, II:323. Vancouver took the established longitude of Cape Town as definitive: 'I did not think any observations were at all necessary for ascertaining the longitude, as that must have been accurately determined long ago by persons of greater information and superior abilities.' Again, Vancouver was anxious on his way home to check his chronometer rates 'at some place where longitude had been settled by professed astronomers.' Therefore he headed for Cape St Lucas, eight or ten days' sail from Monterey, where the transit of Venus had been observed (Lamb, III:1427).

53 Lamb, *Vancouver's Voyage*, II:790-1.

54 Ibid., II:918. Vancouver recorded that he would 'continue to allow the [Friendly Cove] rate and error, until I shall have authority sufficient to alter my opinion of its correctness.'

55 The number of lunar observations taken was prodigious. For example, in July 1793, 346 'sets' were made. Each set consisted of six observations 'to establish by the Observatory instruments the true longitude' of Observatory Inlet (Lamb, *Vancouver's Voyage*, III:1026). Several other exercises exceeded a hundred observations, and one scored 510 (ibid., I:323).

56 Ibid., 320.

57 William Wales, *The Method of Finding the Longitude at Sea, by Timekeepers: to which are added Tables of Equations, Altitudes, more extensive than any hitherto published* (London 1794; 2nd edition 1810). The Guildhall Library copies have handwritten errata.

58 Alexander Dalrymple, *Some Notes Useful to those who have Chronometers at Sea* (London 1779 or 1780). There is a copy in the Grenville Collection in the British Library.

59 Alexander Dalrymple, *Instructions concerning Arnold's Chronometers or Time-keepers* (London 1788). There is a copy in the Guildhall Library, London.

60 Arnold may have timed the publication of his own pamphlet to coincide with the publicity accompanying Vancouver's departure. John Arnold, *Certificates and Circumstances relative to the Going of Mr Arnold's Chronometers* (London 1791).

61 CUL, RGO 14/9/61b-64b contains detailed directions of how observations were to be made on ship and on shore. Howse, 'Captain Cook's Scientific Instruments,' reprints the 'Instructions to Observers,' 124-5. 'Wherever you land ... you are to set up the astronomical clock and to fix it very firmly on the stand ... you are to compare the Watch Machine [K1] with the astronomical clock at noon, and also about the times of the equal altitudes.'

62 'Whidbey, with the assistance of some of our young gentlemen, relieved me of considerable labour, by attending to nautical astronomy.' Lamb, *Vancouver's Voyage*, III:653.

63 Lamb, *Vancouver's Voyage*, IV:1639, cites a letter from Whidbey to an unidentified correspondent, 2 Jan. 1793: 'In consequence of his [Gooch's] death, the principal part of the Astronomical part of the Voyage [h]as fallen on me, which I find myself inadequate to ... I have got the Boards instruct[ion]s, and shall follow them as far as my abilities lays.' Joseph Whidbey, 'Remarks, On Timekeepers, The Compass, &c.,' *The Naval Chronicle*, II (1799):505-12.

64 CUL, RGO 14/12/(59)/482-3. Whidbey calculated that he had been absent from the ship for 140 days and nights, on a six-oared cutter, and often for eighteen days at a time, during which he averaged thirty miles a day. He complained that he had been 'drawn into very considerable expense owing to being obliged to be constantly on shore when the observatory was erected.'

65 Lamb, *Vancouver's Voyage*, I:221-2, citing PRO, Adm 12/74 (1797).

66 Ibid., 52.

67 Ibid., 481. 'I was led to believe,' wrote Vancouver, 'that our change in the climate (the thermometer having fallen from about 80 to about 60 since leaving the Sandwich Islands) had caused some acceleration in its (K3's) rate of going.' He believed that Earnshaw's watch had kept better time (until its breakdown) because it was newer than the Arnold models, and therefore 'least sensible of the change in the climate' (ibid., II:791).

68 Charles-Édouard Guillaume developed a group of nickel-iron alloys (*invar* and *elinvar*) 'whose modulus of elasticity varied only slightly within the ordinary range of temperature.' See David S. Torrens, 'Notes on Elinvar,' *Horological Journal*, LXXXI (January 1939): 26-8; [Nobel Foundation], *Nobel Lectures, including Presentation Speeches and Laureates' Biographies: Physics*, 3 Vols. (Amsterdam: Elsevier 1967), I (1901-21):439-75, especially 468-73. Their development came at a time when chronometers were being superseded by the new technology based upon radio time-signals. This permitted timepieces of ordinary quality to be regularly tuned to Greenwich time.

69 Thomas Earnshaw, *Longitude: An Appeal to the Public* (London 1808: reprinted St Helens 1986, with an introduction by R. John Griffiths), 23, 25, 26, 35, 59, 71-4, 226, 231-2, is replete with ref-

erences to No. 1514 and its alleged superiority over Arnold's instruments. The National Maritime Museum at Greenwich has a MS critique of Earnshaw's *Appeal.*

70 Silvio Bedini, *Thinkers and Tinkers: Early American Men of Science* (New York: Schribners 1975), 330-1. Lewis and Clark were to determine, inter alia, latitudes and longitudes. Lewis received special training in the proper procedures. Determination of longitude was to be made by the lunar method. Bedini notes that Jefferson had originally intended using an equatorial telescope; instead, Lewis was to be provided with a chronometer, specifically one by John Arnold. See also Silvio A. Bedini, 'The Scientific Instruments of the Lewis and Clark Expedition,' *Great Plains Quarterly,* IV (1984):54-69, especially 60-1. The Arnold cost $250 (plus 75 cents for the key) and had a balance wheel and escapement of 'the most improved construction.'

71 A good example was the 24-page pamphlet published in 1832 by the chronometer maker Parkinson and Frodsham, namely, *A Brief Account of the Chronometer, with remarks on those furnished by Parkinson and Frodsham to the Expeditions of Captains Ross, Parry, Sabine, King, Lyon, Foster, and other distinguished navigators, with the Rate of Others tried at the Royal Observatory, Greenwich, in the Years 1828-29-30-31* (London, n.d., but probably 1832). Christopher Wood, 'Extracts from a Parkinson and Frodsham Pamphlet,' *Antiquarian Horology,* IX (1) (December 1974):46-50, notes that its purpose was 'unashamedly commercial.'

72 CUL, RGO 14/24/472. After editing the history of his brother's voyage, John Vancouver had a few months free. The problem he chose to address was the means whereby a chronometer could be kept at a stable temperature 'at sea, on shore, either within the tropics, or under the polar circles, ... [not] ... to be interrupted by the successive alternatives of heat and cold.'

73 Earnshaw's 1514, originally bought for Gooch, was eventually returned to its maker, 'very much damaged by rust it having been in water.' It was repaired (at a cost of five guineas) and delivered to Joseph Whidbey, by 1798 master of the *Sans Pareil.* It was one of several chronometers tested in a sea trial, including Thomas Mudge's famous Green and Blue models, and two of Arnold's box chronometers. See CUL, RGO 14/1/ 5 June 1798: Account of Makers with the Board of Longitude: Earnshaw.

74 Randall C. Brooks, 'Magnetic Influence on Chronometers, 1798-1834: A Case Study,' *Annals of Science,* XLIV (1987):245-64. Disagreement over the solution to these technical problems continued over the years and blurred into the commercial rivalry between Arnold and Earnshaw's firms and their successors, Dent and Frodsham. British and American journals in the 1830s (*Nautical Magazine* and *American Journal of Science*) followed the rivalry. See, for example, the articles 'Magnetic experiments on Chronometers' by Arnold and Dent, and 'On the Sea and Land Rates of Chronometers,' by Parkinson and Frodsham, in *American Journal of Science,* XXVI (1834):121-7.

75 They were most likely supplied through J.H. de Magellan (1722-90) who settled in London in 1764 and supplied scientific instruments to the courts of Spain and Portugal. G. L'E. Turner, 'The Portugese Agent: J.H. de Magellan,' *Antiquarian Horology* (December 1974), 74-5.

76 Mercer, *Arnold and Son,* 7-101.

77 Lamb, *Vancouver's Voyage,* II:600.

78 Nathan Rosenberg, 'The Historiography of Technical Progress,' in *Inside the Black Box: Technology and Economics* (Cambridge, England: Cambridge University Press 1982), 3-33, especially 5-8.

79 A new technology, Rosenberg has noted, 'usually asserted its advantages over the old only slowly. Partly this is because the new technique has many "bugs" at first which need to be eliminated; partly because the capital goods sector takes time to learn to produce the new machine efficiently, and the diffusion of the new technology is closely linked to the gradual decline in price which is associated with this learning process; ... partly because improvements continue to be made in the old technique.' See Nathan Rosenberg, *Technology and American*

Economic Growth (New York: Harper & Row 1972), 85-6.

80 Beaglehole, *Cook Voyages*, II:78-9.
81 N.W. Emmott, 'Captain Vancouver and the Lunar Distance,' *Journal of Navigation*, XXVII (1974):490-5. Beaglehole, *Cook Journals*, II:78-9.
82 Sixty years later: Brown and Neve, *Voyage of the Beagle*, Appendix 1, 395.

Chapter 5: A Notable Absence

1 See James R. Gibson, *Otter Skins, Boston Ships, and China Goods* (Montreal: McGill-Queen's University Press 1992).
2 See James R. Gibson, 'The Tempo of Russian Eastward Expansion: Full Speed Across Siberia to the Pacific from the End of the 16th to the Middle of the 17th Century,' *The North Pacific in the Seventeenth Century*, Proceedings of the Great Ocean Conferences, II (Portland: Oregon Historical Society Press 1992), 100-29.
3 See N.N. Stepanov, 'Pervaya russkaya ekspeditsiya na Okhotskom poberezhye' [The First Russian Expedition on the Okhotsk Seaboard], *Izvestie Vsesoyuznovo geograficheskovo obshch-estva*, XC (1958):438-52.
4 See Michael E. Thurman, *The Naval Department of San Blas: New Spain's Bastion for Alta California and Nootka 1767 to 1798* (Glendale, CA: Arthur H. Clark 1967).
5 See William Lytle Schurz, *The Manila Galleon* (New York: E.P. Dutton 1939).
6 L.N. Naikov, *Razskazy Nartova o Petre velikom* [Nartov's Accounts of Peter the Great] (St Petersburg: Tipografiya Imperatorskoy academii nauk 1891), 99.
7 See N.A. Ivashintsev, *Russian Round-the-World Voyages, 1803-1849: With a Summary of Later Voyages to 1867*, Glynn R. Barratt (trans.) (Kingston, ON: Limestone Press 1980); N. Nozikov, *Russian Voyages Round the World*, Ernst and Mira Lesser (trans.) (London: Hutchinson n.d.); V.A. Yesakov, A.F. Plakhotnik, and A.I. Alekseyev, *Russkie okeanicheskie i morskie issledovaniya v XIX-nachale XX v.* [Russian Explorations of the Oceans and Seas in the Nineteenth and Early Twentieth Centuries] (Moscow: Izdatelstvo 'Nauka' 1964).
   The first Russian systematic, large-scale exploration of the interior of Russian America did not even take place until the first half of the 1840s. See Henry N. Michael (ed.), *Lieutenant Zagoskin's Travels in Russian America, 1842-1844: The First Ethnographic and Geographic Investigations in the Yukon and Kuskokwim Valleys of Alaska* (Toronto: Arctic Institute of North America 1967).
8 See V.A. Aleksandrov, *Rossiya na Dalnevostochnykh rubezhakh (vtoraya polovina XVII v.)* [Russia on the Far Eastern Frontier (Second Half of the Seventeenth Century)] (Moscow: Izdatelstvo 'Nauka' 1969); A.I. Krushanov (ed.), *Istoriya Dalnevo Vostoka SSSR v epokhu feodal-izma i kapitalizma (XVII v.-fevral 1917 g.)* [History of the Far East of the USSR in the Era of Feudalism and Capitalism (Seventeenth Century-February 1917)] (Moscow: 'Nauka' 1991), 191-201; George V. Lantzeff and Richard A. Pierce, *Eastward to Empire: Exploration and Conquest on the Russian Open Frontier, to 1750* (Montreal: McGill-Queen's University Press 1973), 141-182. Also see Mark Bassin, 'The Russian Geographical Society, the "Amur Epoch," and the Great Siberian Expedition 1855-1863,' *Annals of the Association of American Geographers*, LXXII (1983):240-56 and James R. Gibson, 'Russia on the Pacific: The Role of the Amur,' *Canadian Geographer*, XII (1968):15-27.
9 A.P. Okladnikov and V.I. Shunkov (eds.), *Istoriya Sibiri* [History of Siberia] (Leningrad: Izdatelstvo 'Nauka' 1968), II:78.
10 See Raymond H. Fisher, *The Voyage of Semen Dezhnev in 1648: Bering's Precursor* (London: Hakluyt Society 1981).
11 See James R. Gibson, *Feeding the Russian Fur Trade: Provisionment of the Okhotsk Seaboard and the Kamchatka Peninsula 1639-1856* (Madison: University of Wisconsin Press 1969), 9-13, and Lantzeff and Pierce, *Eastward to Empire*, 195-219. For a first-hand, comprehensive account of

Kamchatka dating from the last half of the 1730s, see S.P. Krasheninnikov, *Opisanie zemli Kamchatka* [Description of the Land of Kamchatka], 4th ed. (Moscow-Leningrad: Izdatelstvo Glavsevmorputi 1949); the best English translation of this classic is Stepan Krasheninnikov, *Explorations of Kamchatka 1735-1741*, E.A.P. Crownhart-Vaughan (trans.) (Portland: Oregon Historical Society 1972).

12 See Raymond H. Fisher, *Bering's Voyages: Whither and Why* (Seattle: University of Washington Press 1977) and B.P. Polevoi, 'The Discovery of Russian America,' in S. Frederick Starr (ed.), *Russia's American Colony* (Durham, NC: Duke University Press 1987), 13-31. Peter particularly needed to replenish his treasury to fund his costly military campaigns.

13 F.A. Golder, *Bering's Voyages* (New York: Octagon Books 1968), II:37; Georg Wilhelm Steller, *Journal of a Voyage with Bering 1741-1742*, Margritt A. Engel and O.W. Frost (trans.) (Stanford: Stanford University Press 1988), 75.

14 See A.P. Sokolov, '*Ekspeditsiya k Aleutskim ostrovam kapitanov Krentsyna i Levashova 1764-1769 gg*' [The Expedition of Captains Krenitsyn and Levashov to the Aleutian Islands, 1764-1769], *Zapiski Gidrograficheskovo departamenta Morskovo ministerstva*, Part 10 (1852), 70-103.

15 Avrahm Yarmolinsky (ed.), *An Anthology of Russian Verse 1812-1960* (Garden City, NJ: Anchor Books 1962), 2.

16 Avrahm Yarmolinsky (trans.), *The Unknown Chekhov: Stories and Other Writings Hitherto Untranslated* (New York: Noonday Press 1958), 295.

17 Yuri Semyonov, *The Conquest of Siberia*, E.W. Dickes (trans.) (London: George Routledge & Sons 1944), 147.

18 See Gibson, *Feeding the Russian Fur Trade*, especially Chapter 7.

19 Sir George Simpson, *Narrative of a Journey Round the World, During the Years 1841 and 1842* (London: Henry Colburn 1847), II:264-5.

20 Prokopy Gromov, '*Put ot Irkutsa v Kamchatku*' [The Route from Irkutsk to Kamchatka], *Pribavleniya k Irkutskim yeparkhialnym vedomostyam*, VII, 17-18 (1869):217.

21 [Peter Kropótkin] James Allen Rogers (ed.), *Memoirs of a Revolutionist* (Garden City, NJ: Anchor Books 1962), 123.

22 Golder, *Bering's Voyages*, I:33.

23 Evgenii G. Kushnarev, *Bering's Search for the Strait: The First Kamchatka Expedition 1725-1730*, E.A.P. Crownhart-Vaughan, trans. and ed. (Portland: Oregon Historical Society 1990), 30.

24 R.V. Makarova, *Russkie na Tikhom okeane vo vtoroy polovine XVIII v.* [Russians in the Eastern Ocean in the Second Half of the 18th Century] (Moscow: Izdatelstvo 'Nauka' 1968), 42, note 18; A.A. Pokrovsky (ed.), *Ekspeditsiya Beringa: sbornik dokumentov* [The Expedition of Bering: A Collection of Documents] (Moscow: Glavnoye arkhivnoye upravlenie NKVD SSSR 1941), 370.

25 Polevoi, 'Discovery of Russian America,' 23.

26 R.V. Makarova, *Vneshnyaya politika Rossii na Dalnem Vostoke: vtoraya polovina XVIII v. - 60ye gody XIX v.* [The Foreign Policy of Russia in the Far East: Second Half of the 18th Century - Sixties of the Nineteenth Century] (Moscow: Moskovsky gosudarstvenny istoriko-arkhivny institut 1974), 29.

27 D.M. Lebedev, *Ocherki po istorii geografii v Rossii XVIII v. (1725-1800 gg.)* [Essays on the History of Geography in Russia in the Eighteenth Century (1725-1800)] (Moscow: Izdatelstvo Akademii nauk SSSR 1957), 114-15. For this expedition, see G.A. Sarychev, *Puteshestvie po severo-vostochnoy chasti Sibiri, Ledovitomu moryu i Vostochnomu okeanu* [Journey to the Northeastern Part of Siberia, the Icy Sea, and the Eastern Ocean], 2nd ed. (Moscow: Geografgiz 1952) and Martin Sauer, *An Account of a Geographical and Astronomical Expedition to the Northern Parts of Russia ...* (London: T. Cadell Jr and W. Davies 1802); the former has been published in an abridged English translation as Gawrila Sarytschew, *Account of a Voyage of Discovery to the North-East of Siberia, the Frozen Ocean, and the North-East Sea* (London: Richard Phillips 1806).

28 It does not follow, however, that Russian expansion can be wholly or even partly explained by an 'urge to the sea,' that is, by a striving for warm-water or ice-free ports. This fallacy has been convincingly debunked by John A. Morrison, 'Russia and Warm Water: A Fallacious Generalization and Its Consequences,' *U.S. Naval Institute Proceedings*, LXVIII (1952):1, 169-79 [revised and reprinted as 'Russia and Warm Water,' in Sidney Harcave (ed.), *Readings in Russian History*, 1st ed. (New York: Thomas Y. Crowell 1962), 1:46-64].

29 See V.F. Gnucheva (comp.), *Materialy dlya istorii ekspeditsii Akademii nauk v XVIII i XIX vekakh* [Materials for a History of the Expeditions of the Academy of Sciences in the Eighteenth and Nineteenth Centuries] (Moscow-Leningrad: Izdatelstvo Akademii nauk SSSR 1940), 304-10.

30 See I.K. Kirilov, *Tsvetushcheye sostoyanie Vserossiiskovo gosudarstva* [The Flourishing Condition of the All-Russian State], 2nd ed. (Moscow: Izdatelstvo 'Nauka' 1977).

31 A.V. Yefimov, *Iz istorii velikikh russkikh geograficheskikh otkryty* [From the History of the Great Russian Geographical Discoveries], rev. ed. (Moscow: Geografgiz 1950), 291, citing TsGADA, fol. Müller portfolios, No. 512, d. 1.

32 For Golovin, see V.A. Divin, *Veliky russky moreplavatel A.I. Chirikov* [The Great Russian Navigator A.I. Chirikov] (Moscow: Geografgiz 1953), 66-71, citing TsGADA, fol. Gosarkhiv, raz. XXIV, d. 8 and fol. Senate, d. 1,089; for Saunders, see ibid., 71-4, citing TsGADA, fol. Gosarkhiv, raz. XXI, d. 9.

33 See L. Golenishchev-Kutuzov, *Predpriyatie imperatritsy Yekateriny II dlya puteshestviya vokrug sveta v 1786 g.* [Empress Catherine II's Venture of a Voyage Around the World in 1786] (St Petersburg 1840) and A.P. Sokolov, *'Priogotovlenie krugosvetnoy ekspeditsii 1787 goda pod machalstvom Muloskovo'* [The Preparation of the Round-the-World Expedition of 1787 under the Command of Mulovsky], *Zapiski Gidrograficheskovo departamenta Morskovo ministerstva*, part 6 (1848), 142-91.

34 For these points I am primarily indebted to Alexander Vucinich, *Science in Russian Culture: A History to 1860* (Stanford: Stanford University Press 1963).

35 Michael T. Florinsky, *Russia: A History and an Interpretation* (New York: Macmillan 1953), 1:357, citing Veselago.

36 A.I. Alekseyev, *'Russkaya gidrograf icheskaya nauka v XVIII v.'* [Russian Hydrographic Science in the Eighteenth Century], *Trudy Instituta istorii yestesvoznaniya i tekhniki*, XXVII (1961):82-3.

37 Beaglehole, *Cook Journals*, III (2):1, 247; cf. W. Ellis, *An Authentic Narrative of a Voyage Performed by Captain Cook and Captain Clerke ...* (London: G. Robinson, J. Sewell, and J. Debrett 1782), II:225-6. Cook's third expedition lost only seven men to sickness and three to accidents, and five were killed in Hawai'i.

38 See Gibson, *Feeding the Russian Fur Trade*, 29-31, 131.

39 Captain A.J. Von Krusenstern, *Voyage Round the World, in the Years 1803, 1804, 1805, & 1806 ...*, Richard Belgrave Hoppner (trans.) (London: John Murray 1813), 1:xx, xxiii-iv.

40 A.I. Andreyev (ed.), *Russkie otkrytiya v Tikhom okeane i Severnoy Amerike v XVIII veke* [Russian Discoveries in the Pacific Ocean and North America in the Eighteenth Century] (Moscow: Ogiz 1948), 281-2.

41 C.F. Newcombe (ed.), *Menzies Journal of Vancouver's Voyage April to October, 1792* (Victoria: Government of the Province of British Columbia 1923), 128.

42 William Coxe, *Account of the Russian Discoveries between Asia and America* (London: T. Cadell 1780), Part III.

43 Gibson, *Feeding the Russian Fur Trade*, 17.

44 Ibid., 28.

45 Gibson, *Otter Skins, Boston Ships, and China Goods*, 16, 54.

Chapter 6: Nootka Sound

The author thanks Dr R.J.B. Knight for his kind help in obtaining some of the details of this chapter. The title derives from Ronald Robinson and John Gallagher's famous essay, 'The Imperialism of Free Trade,' *Economic History Review*, 2nd series, VI(1953):1-15.

1   D.L. Mackay, 'Direction and Purpose in British Imperial Policy, 1783-1801,' *The Historical Journal*, XVII (1974):492. See also the Board of Trade's comment regarding whaling: 'It is of great importance in the present moment ... that a proper effort should now be made to secure to this Country, the advantages of a Fishery which was once so lucrative to the Americans' – PRO, BT 5/3, 457, Report, 3 May 1786.

3   For a detailed account, see V.T. Harlow, *The Founding of the Second British Empire, 1763-1793* (London: Longmans, Green 1952, 1964), II:293-328, 419-24.

4   PRO, PRO 30/8/183, fols. 254-7, 258-9, Wolfe Tone to [Pitt], 10 and 23 August 1788.

5   Kew, Banks papers, I, No. 319, Enderby to Banks, 26 August 1788; State Library, New South Wales: Mitchell Library (ML), Sydney, MS 322, 511-5, Account of the *Emilia*'s voyage, 6 March 1790.

6   Meares, *Voyages made in 1788 and 1789* (London: J. Walter 1790), 108-26 passim, 216-7, 146-50; and *Memorial presented to the House of Commons, May 13, 1790*, ibid., Appendix, note.

7   [Daniel Beale], Instructions to Colnett, 3 April 1789, in F.W. Howay (ed.), *The Journal of Captain James Colnett aboard the Argonaught from April 26, 1789* (Toronto: Champlain Society 1940), 19-23.

8   Cook, *Flood Tide of Empire*, 118.

9   See ibid., 119-30; and also PRO, FO 185/6, No. 2, enclosure, 'Extract of a Letter from Mexico dated 28th August 1789.'

10 PRO, FO 185/6, No. 1, Merry to Leeds, 4 January 1790.

11 Ibid., No. 2, Merry to Leeds, 7 January 1790, with enclosure.

12 Ibid., No. 6, Merry to Leeds, 15 January 1790.

13 PRO, PRO 30/8/341, fosl. 64-5, Del Campo to Leeds, 10 February 1790.

14 PRO, FO 185/6, No. 9, Merry to Leeds, 28 January 1790.

15 Ibid., No. 6, Merry to Leeds, 15 January 1790.

16 PRO, FO 72/16, fol. 87, Leeds to Merry, 2 February 1790.

17 PRO, PRO 30/8/341, fols. 64-5, Del Campo to Leeds, 10 February 1790.

18 Ibid. 30/8/151, fol. 43, Leeds to Pitt, 23 February 1790.

19 PRO, FO 72/16, fols. 126-37 (two drafts each in English and French), Leeds to del Campo, 26 February 1790.

20 See W.R. Manning, 'The Nootka Sound Controversy,' *The American Historical Association: Annual Report for 1904*, 369-73.

21 PRO, FO 72/16, fols. 87-8, Leeds to Merry, 2 February 1790.

22 For details, see Cook, *Flood Tide of Empire*, 54-84, 93-7, 146-99 passim.

23 See Alan Frost, 'New South Wales as *Terra Nullius*: The British denial of Aboriginal Land Rights,' [Australian] *Historical Studies*, XIX (1981), 513-23.

24 Mourelle, 'Journal of a Voyage in 1775,' in Daines Barrington, *Miscellanies* (London 1781), 469-534.

25 PRO, HO 42/16, No. 8, Banks to Nepean, 15 February 1790. Banks was wrong in this supposition, for Pérez had anchored at the entrance to Nootka Sound in 1774.

26 Sutro Library, Banks papers, PN 1/No. 6, 7, 9, Etches to Banks, 17 and 23 July 1788 and 19 May 1792.

27 PRO, CO 42/21, fols. 56-62, Alexander Dalrymple to [?], undated but around September 1789.

28 PRO, HO 28/7, fol. 49, [Evan Nepean], 'Sketch of a Letter to the Admiralty,' undated but early February 1790.

29 See Sutro Library, Banks papers PN 1/No. 11, 8, 18A & B, Alexander Henry to Banks, 25 March 1781, Etches to Banks, 30 July 1788, J.M. Nooth to [Banks], 4 November 1789, and Isaac Ogden

to David Odgen, 7 November 1789; and see also Williams, *Search for the Northwest Passage,* 212-40.

30 PRO, HO 28/7, fol. 50, [Nepean], 'Sketch of a Letter to the Admiralty,' undated but early February 1790.

31 Ibid., fols. 48-56 (in quoting these sentences, I have ignored subsequent emendations).

32 PRO, HO 42/16, No. 10, [Mulgrave], 'Heads of Instructions for an Expedition to NW.t Coast of America,' February 1790.

33 PRO, Adm 1/4155, No. 9, Grenville to Lords Commissioners, 9 February 1790.

34 PRO, HO 28/61, fol. 251, [Nepean], Draft to the Lords Commissioners, March 1790.

35 PRO, HO 28/61, fol. 249, [Nepean], Instructions to Roberts, March 1790.

36 PRO, CO 201/5, fols. 49-54, [Nepean], Instructions to Phillip, March 1790. The second set is at CO 201/1, fols. 19-24.

37 PRO, HO 28/61, fols. 253-5, [Nepean], Instructions to Cornwallis, 31 March 1790. Interestingly, as an indication of continuing intent, this set bears Grenville's signature.

38 PRO, HO 28/61, fols. 273-9, [Nepean], Draft instructions 'To the Captain of the Frigate to be dispatched from the East Indies to Owhyhee,' March 1790.

39 Many of these details are from David Mackay, *In the Wake of Cook* (Wellington: Victoria University Press 1985), 91-3.

40 Sutro Library, Banks papers PN 1/No. 17, Menzies to Banks, 4 April 1790, and Banks' List.

41 See Williams, *Search for the Northwest Passage,* 239-40.

42 Meares, *Voyages made in 1788 and 1789,* 216-7; and ibid., *Memorial,* n.p.

43 PRO, FO 72/17, fols. 17-19, Leeds to Merry, 4 May 1790.

44 Ibid., fol. 19.

45 *Historical Manuscript Commission (HMC): Dropmore Papers* (London: H.M.S.O. 1892), I, 579: Grenville, Cabinet Minute, 30 April 1790. As with so many documents relating to the Nootka Sound crisis, this was drafted by Nepean, with the version in FO 95/7/3, fol. 295 being in his hand.

46 PRO, Adm 1/4155, No. 26, Grenville to Lords Commissioners of the Admiralty, 1 May 1790.

47 Paul Webb, 'The Naval Aspects of the Nootka Sound Crisis,' *The Mariner's Mirror,* LXI (1975):135.

48 *HMC: Dropmore Papers,* I, 579-80, George III to Grenville, 1 May, Grenville to George III, 2 May 1790.

49 PRO, Adm 2/1343, Lords Commissioners, Secret Instructions to Commodores of the Mediterranean, Leeward Islands, Jamaica and North American stations, 2 May 1790; *HMC: Dropmore Papers,* I, 580: Grenville to Westmoreland, 3 May 1790; PRO, CO 123/9, 87-9, Grenville to Hunter, 15 May 1790.

50 PRO, FO 52/8, fols. 203-5, 207-8, Nepean to Matra, 1 and 4 May 1790.

51 India Office Records L/P & S/5/539, Secret Court, Circular, 7 May 1790 and Secret Board, Circular, 8 May 1790; PRO, CO 77/26, fols. 184, 243, 244, 246-7, 271-3, Chairmen of Court of Directors to Grenville, 10 May 1790, India Board, Minutes, 11 and 12 May 1790, Chairman to Captains of the China ships, 12 May 1790, Grenville to Commodore Cornwallis, 5 June 1790, Court of Directors to Nepean, 22 July 1790.

52 PRO, Adm 1/4155, Nos. 28, 29, 30, 31, 53, Grenville to Lords Commissioners, 6, 8, 15, 17 May and 29 July 1790; and Webb, 'Naval Aspects,' 146.

53 For intelligence reports, see, for example, PRO, FO 95/7/3, fols. 297, 305, 309, 377-8, 379-80, 385-8, 391-4, and 307 (Nepean to Simmons, 27 May 1790); Adm 2/1343 Lords Commissioners, Secret Orders to Forbes and Berkeley.

54 PRO, Adm 2/1343, Grenville to Lords Commissioners, 25 June 1790, and Lords Commissioners, Secret Order to Barrington, 26 June 1790; Adm 2/120, 214-98, Lords Commissioners, Orders to Howe, 8-30 July 1790.

55 See Manning, 'The Nootka Sound Controversy,' 404-6; and J.M. Norris, 'The Policy of the British Cabinet in the Nootka Crisis,' *English Historical Review*, LXX (1955):577-9.

56 PRO Adm 1/4155, No. 54, Grenville to Lords Commissioners, 30 July 1790; Adm 2/1343, Lords Commissioners, Order to Howe, 3 August 1790.

57 PRO, Adm 1/4155, No. 53, Grenville to Lords Commissioners, 29 July 1790; Adm 2/1343, Lords Commissioners, Order to Blankett, 30 July 1790, to Commodore Cornwallis, 30 July 1790.

58 For the reports on the state of the Swedish fleet, see PRO, Adm 1/5118/1; and Adm 2/1343, Lords Commissioners, Orders to Lawford and Roberts, 15 August 1790. See also Adm 2/120, 362, 368, Lords Commissioners, Order to Flood, 1 September, to Elliot, 8 September 1790.

59 PRO, Adm 2/1343, Lords Commissioners, Order to Pole, 30 August 1790; and FO 95/7/4,454-5 Blankett to Nepean, 26 August 1790.

60 PRO, FO 95/7/4, 479, Fitzherbert to Leeds, 6 October 1790; Adm 1/4155, No. 60, Grenville to Lords Commissioners, 10 and 25 October 1790; Adm 2/1344, Lords Commissioners, Order to Laforey, 25 October 1790. A. Aspinall (ed.), *The Later Correspondence of George III* (Cambridge, England: Cambridge University Press 1966), 1:479-80, Grenville to George III and reply, 25 October 1790.

61 PRO, FO 72/19, fols. 93-7, 123-4, Leeds to Fitzherbert, 2 October 1790.

62 See PRO, Chatham, 30/8/367, fols. 203-23 for the letters between Howe and Chatham, 22 October-4 November 1790.

63 PRO Adm 2/120, 498, Lords Commissioners, Order to Howe, 4 November 1790.

64 Miranda to Pitt, 8 September 1791, as printed in 'English Policy towards America in 1790-1791,' *American Historical Review*, VII (1902):711-12.

65 PRO, PRO 30/8/360, fols. 81-6, [Mulgrave] Memorandum, undated but around 1-12 May 1790.

66 See Miranda in 'English Policy towards America,' 712.

67 PRO, PRO 30/8/128, fols. 71-3, Dalrymple to Pitt, 10, 12 and 16 May 1790.

68 L.B. Kinnaird, 'Creassy's Plan for Seizing Panama,' *Hispanic American Historical Review*, XIII (1933): 46-78.

69 PRO, CO 77/26, fols. 185-9, [Memorandum] to Lord Cornwallis, 12 May 1790; India Office Records L/P & S/5/563,29-31, India Board (Dundas, Mulgrave, Campbell), Instructions to Lord Cornwallis, 21 May 1790; CO 77/26, fols. 246-7, 249-52, 275, Grenville to Lord Cornwallis and Commodore Cornwallis, 5 and 16 June 1790.

70 PRO, FO 95/7/4, fols. 509-12, Plan for employing the Baymen, undated; and Adm 1/4155, Nos. 28, 29, 30, Grenville to Lords Commissioners, 6, 8 and 15 May 1790.

71 PRO, FO 95/7/4, fols. 501-6, Campbell, 'Ideas regarding a War with Spain,' July 1790.

72 PRO, PRO 30/8/345, fols. 48-51 [Miranda], Declaration, 3 August 1790.

73 PRO, FO 95/7/4, fols. 481-5, Campbell to Pitt, 18 October 1790; PRO 30/8/120, fols. 56-60, White to Campbell, 25 October 1790, and Campbell to Pitt, 26 and 28 October 1790.

74 PRO, PRO 30/8/168, fols. 30-2, Popham to Pitt, 29 October 1790.

75 PRO, Adm 1/4155, Nos. 60, 69, Grenville to Lords Commissioners, 10 and 25 October 1790; FO 95/7/4, fol. 491, 'List of Officers who were on the Surveying Service with Mr Gauld,' 2 November 1790.

76 Webb gives these figures, 'Naval Aspects,' 136.

77 Roger Knight, 'The First Fleet: Its State and Preparation, 1786-1787,' John Hardy and Alan Frost (eds.), *Studies from Terra Australis to Australia* (Canberra: Australian Academy of the Humanities 1989), 121-36.

78 *Parliamentary History*, XXVIII (1790), col. 770, Report, 6 May 1790.

79 Ibid., col. 979, Report, 14 December 1790.

80 See E.H. Pritchard, 'The Crucial Years of the Early Anglo-Chinese Relations, 1750-1800,' *Research Studies of the State College of Washington*, IV (1936):236-64, 272-311.

81 Adam Smith, *An Enquiry into the Nature and Causes of the Wealth of Nations* (London: W.

Strachan and T. Cadell 1776), II, 235, 216, 224, 236-7, 242-56.
82 Ibid., 236-7.
83 William L. Clements Library, Melville papers, Dundas to Sydney, 30 November 1786.
84 See Pritchard, 'The Crucial Years,' 242.
85 Bowood House, Shelburne papers, S 161/11 Phillip to Lansdowne, 3 July 1788.
86 (In private hands), Phillip to Middleton, 6 July 1788.
87 See Harlow, *Founding of the Second British Empire*, II, 460-71.
88 British Library, Add. MS 40102, fol. 66, Dundas to Pitt, 22 July 1800.

Chapter 7: Seduction before Sovereignty

1   María Dolores Higueras Rodríguez and María Luisa Martín-Merás (eds.), *Relación del viaje hecho por las goletas Sútil y Mexicana en el año 1792 para reconocer el estrecho de Juan de Fuca* (Madrid: Museo Naval 1991), 111.
2   Nathaniel Portlock, *A Voyage Round the World; But more Particularly to the North-West Coast of America: in the King George and Queen Charlotte, Captains Portlock and Dixon* (London: J. Stockdale and G. Goulding 1789), 271.
3   Archivo General de la Nación, México (AGN), Sección de Historia, Vol. 61, Viceroy Antonio María de Bucareli to General de Flota Luis de Córdoba, 25 August 1773; Córdoba to Bucareli, Veracruz, 1 September 1773; and Bucareli to Juan Pérez, 24 December 1773.
4   AGN, Documentos para la Historia de México, Segunda Serie, Vol. 15, Nuevo método o gobierno de las misiones, Colegio Apostólico de San Fernando, October 1773.
5   Archivo General de las Indias (AGI), Estado, leg. 20, ramo 5, article 1, Antonio Bucareli y Ursúa, 'Instrucción que debe observar el Alférez de Fragata Graduado, Don Juan Pérez, Primer Piloto de los del número del Departamento de San Blas, a cuyo cuidado he puesto la Expedición de los descubrimientos siguiendo la Costa de Monterrey al Norte, 24 December 1773.' Another copy is in AGN, Historia, Vol. 61. For an English translation, see Manuel P. Servin (trans.), 'The Instructions of Viceroy Bucareli to Ensign Pérez,' *California Historical Quarterly*, XL (September 1961):237-48.
6   Ibid., Article 3. See AGI, Estado, leg. 43, ramo 10, 'Diario que yo Fr Juan Crespi, misionero del Apostólico Colegio de Propaganda Fide de San Fernando de México formó del viage de la Fragata *Santiago*, alias la *Nueva Galicia*, mandada por su Capitán y Alférez de Fragata, Don Juan Pérez,' 1774; and AGI, Estado, leg. 43, ramo 9, 'Diario del viage que por orden del R. P. Fr Junipero Serra ... hago desde el puerto de San Carlos de Monterey ... en la fragata de S.M. *Santiago*, mandado por Juan Pérez, por Thomas de la Peña.'
7   AGI, Estado, leg. 20, ramo 11, 'Continuación del Diario que formó el Alférez graduado de Fragata Dn. Juan Pérez, primer Piloto del Departamento de Sn. Blas con la titulada *Santiago* alias la *Nueva Galicia* de su mando, que comprehende su salida de Monterey a explorar la costa septentrional, y su regreso a este proprio puerto en 26 de Agosto de este año de 1774'; and AGI, Guadalajara, leg. 516, 'Copia del Diario de viage executado en la fragata *Santiago* alias la *Nueva Galicia* por el Piloto Esteban José Martínez, desde el Puerto de San Carlos de Monterey ... a descubrimiento de la Costa hasta los 55 grados 48 minutos segun la última demarcación hecha 55 grados 30 minutos: todo de orden del Exmo. Sr. Virrey Don Frey Antonio María Bucareli y Ursúa.' For an English translation of the Pérez journal and extract of Martínez' journal, see Herbert K. Beals (trans.), *Juan Pérez on the Northwest Coast: Six Documents of His Expedition in 1774* (Portland: Oregon Historical Society Press), 1989.
8   Ibid., Articles 15, 16, and 17.
9   Ibid., Articles 20 and 21.
10 Ibid., Articles 22 and 30.
11 See, for example, AGN, Historia, Vol. 68, 'Instrucciones secretas para el Teniente de Navío Don Francisco Eliza, Comandante de la Fragata *Concepción*, San Blas, 28 January 1790'; and Museo

Naval, Madrid (MN), Vol. 619, 'Instrucción que deben observar los capitanes de fragata Don Dionisio Alcalá Galiano y Don Cayetano Valdés en la exploración a que estan destinados del Estrecho de Juan de Fuca, situado entre los 48 y 49 de latitude N. en la Costa N.O. del Mar del Sur, 31 January, 1792.' For an English translation of this latter document, see John Kendrick (trans.), *The Voyage of Sútil and Mexicana, 1792: The Last Spanish Exploration of the Northwest Coast of America* (Spokane, WA: Arthur H. Clark 1991), 49-54.

12 AGI, Estado, leg. 20, ramo 11, Juan Pérez to Bucareli, San Blas, 3 November 1774.

13 AGI, Indiferente General, leg. 1630, Julián de Arriaga to Bucareli, El Pardo, 24 February 1775; MN, Vol. 330, unsigned and undated note, 1775; AGI, Estado, leg. 20, ramo 14, Inventario de las prendas cambalachados con los Indios descubiertos a la altura de 55 grados y 49 minutos, 27 December 1774; and AGI, Estado, leg. 20, ramo 28, Lista de los ropares, armas, e instrumentos, que en un caxoncito se remiten a España, 27 December 1779. Also see Christon I. Archer 'Spain and the Defence of the Pacific Ocean Empire, 1750-1810,' *Canadian Journal of Latin American and Caribbean Studies*, XIX (21) (1986):26-7.

14 'Navegación hecha por don Juan Francisco de la Bodega y Quadra, teniente de fragata de la Real Armada y comandante de la goleta *Sonora*, a los descubrimientos de los mares y costa septentrional de la California, 1775,' in Salvador Bernabeu Albert (ed.), *Juan Francisco de la Bodega y Quadra: El descubrimiento del fin del mundo, 1775-1792* (Madrid: Alianza Editorial 1990), 84-5. For a modern account, see Cook, *Flood Tide of Empire*, 75-7. Also see Christon I. Archer, 'The Making of Spanish Indian Policy on the Northwest Coast,' *New Mexico Historical Review*, LII (1) (January 1977):47-8.

Although Bodega y Quadra's paternal name was Bodega, and that is the name one might expect him to be known by, he signed himself either in full as 'Juan Francisco de la Bodega y Quadra,' or in short as 'Quadra.'

15 AGI, Estado, leg. 38-A, ramo 4, Navegación hecha por el Piloto segundo de la Armada, Dn. Francisco Antonio Mourelle en la Goleta de S.M. nombrada la *Sonora* del mando del Teniente de Fragata Dn. Juan Francisco de la Bodega y Quadra, a los descubrimientos de las Costas, y Mares Septentrionales de la California, que de orden del Exmo. Señor Don Antonio María de Bucareli y Ursúa, executaron el Año de 1775; AGI, Guadalajara, leg. 515, Informe a S.M. en que el Colegio de San Fernando de México da cuenta de los nuevos descubrimientos hechos en California desde 1769 hasta el presente de 1776, 26 February 1776; and Bernabeu Albert, *Bodega y Quadra*, 'Navegación,' 85.

16 Two sailors with the landing party had been seen attempting to escape by swimming out to the ship. Both were forced to turn back by the cold water and their eventual fate is unknown.

17 AGI, Estado, leg. 38-A, ramo 11, 'Diario de la navegación que debe hacer con el auxilio el Teniente de Navío Dn. Bruno de Hezeta en la fragata de su mando *Santiago*, alias *Nueva Galicia*, y en conserva de la Goleta *Sonora* que esta a su orden, y se dirijen a los descubrimientos de la California desde el Departamento de San Blas.' For an English translation, see Herbert K. Beals (trans.), *For Honor and Country: The Diary of Bruno de Hezeta* (Portland: Oregon Historical Society 1985), 78-9.

18 AGI, Estado, leg. 38-A, ramo 4, Navegacíon hecha por el Piloto segundo de la Armada, Dn. Francisco Antonio Mourelle.

19 Ibid. and Bernabeu Albert, *Bodega y Quadra*, 'Navegación,' 95-6.

20 AGI, Estado, leg. 38-A, ramo 11, 'Diario de la navegación que debe hacer ... el Teniente de Navío Dn. Bruno de Hezeta,' 1779.

21 AGI, Estado, leg. 38-B, ramo 17, 'Navegación que hace el Alférez de Fragata graduado y primer piloto Dn. José de Cañizares desde el Puerto de San Blas ... a los descubrimientos de la costa septentrional de California en la Fragata de S.M. *Nuestra Señora de los Remedios*, alias la *Favourita* ... de la que es comandante el Teniente de Navío de la Real Armada y caballero del orden de Santiago, Don Juan Francisco de la Bodega y Quadra,' 1779.

22   AGI , Estado, leg 38-B, ramo 19, 'Diario de navegación que con el favour de Díos y de su santíssima Madre principia a hacer Juan Pantoja y Arriaga, Segundo Piloto de la Fragata de Su Magestad *Nuestra Señora del Rosario* alias *Princesa*,' 1779.

23   MN, Vol. 332, 'Navegación hecha por el Alférez de Navío Don Francisco Antonio Mourelle destinado de segundo Capitán de la fragata *Favourita* ... desde el Puerto de San Blas ... a los descubrimientos de la Costa Septentrional de Californias,' 1779.

24   For published editions of the captains' journals, see Bodega y Quadra, 'Diario de 1779,' in Bernabeu Albert, *Bodega y Quadra*, 111-58; and 'Diario de la Navegación que con el favour de Díos y de la Virgen de la Regla, espera hacer el Teniente de Navío Don Ignacio de Arteaga, mandando la fragata de S.M. *Nuestra Señora del Rosario* (alias) la *Princesa* ..., 1779, in Consejo Superior de Investigaciones Científicas, Instituto Histórico de Marina, *Colección de diarios y relaciones para la historia de los viajes descubrimientos*, VII, 'Comprende los viajes de Arteaga en 1779 y de Caamaño en 1792, por la costa NO de América' (Madrid 1975), 17-162.

25   AGI, Estado, leg. 38-B, ramo 16, 'Diario de Navegación que con el favour de Díos y de su Ssma. Madre pretende hacer el Primer Piloto del número de la Real Armada Dn. José Camacho embarcado en la Fragata de S.M. *Nuestra Señora del Rosario* (alias) la *Princesa*,' 1779.

26   AGI, Estado, legl 38-B, ramo 19, 'Diario de navegación de Juan Pantoja y Arriaga,' 1779; MN, Vol. 332, 'Navegación hecha por el Alférez de Fragata Francisco Antonio Mourelle'; and AGI, Estado, leg. 38-B, ramo 16, 'Diario de Navegación de Dn. José Camacho,' 1779. The two hostages who had gone voluntarily with the Natives spent a frightening night in captivity and then returned to be awarded 100 lashes each and imprisonment for their desertion.

27   MN, Vol. 332, Mourelle, 1779.

28   MN, Vol. 575-bis, Tercera exploración hecha el año de 1779 con las fragatas del Rey la *Princesa* mandada por el Teniente de Navío Don Ignacio Arteaga y la *Favourita* por el de la misma clase, Don Juan Francisco de la Bodega y Quadra; and Juan Francisco de la Bodega y Quadra, 'Diario de 1779,' Bernabeu Albert, *Bodega y Quadra*, 150.

29   'Diario de Navegación que ... espera hacer el Teniente de Navío Don Ignacio Arteaga,' 1779, in Consejo Superior de Investigaciones Científicas, *Colección de diarios y relaciones*, VII:66.

30   Bodega y Quadra, 'Diario de 1779,' 127.

31   MN, Vol. 332, 'Navegación de Don Francisco Antonio Mourelle,' 1779. Padre Juan Riobó stated incorrectly that the children sold to the Spanish were abandoned by the Natives who did not want them. See 'An Account of the Voyage Made by the Frigates "Princesa" and "Favourita" in the Year 1779 from San Blas to Northern Alaska,' *Catholic Historical Review,* IV (2) (July 1918):227.

32   Bodega y Quadra, 'Diario de 1779,' 128.

33   MN, Madrid, Vol. 332, 'Navegación de Don Francisco Antonio Mourelle,' 1779; and AGI, Estado, leg. 38-B, ramo 17, 'navegación que hace el Alférez de Fragata graduado y primer piloto Dn. José de Cañizares.'

34   AGN, Californias, Vol. 42, Juan Francisco de la Bodega y Quadra to Viceroy Matías de Gálvez, Mexico, 1 October 1783.

35   Ibid., José de Gálvez to Viceroy Matías de Gálvez, El Pardo, 3 April 1783.

36   Biblioteca Nacional, Mexico, Caja Fuerte, Viceroy Manuel Antonio Florez to Governor José Camacho at San Blas, 3 November 1787.

37   AGI, Mexico, leg. 1529, 'Diario de la navegación que de Orden del Rey Nuestro Señor que Díos Gue. y por disposición del Exmo. Señor Dn. Manuel Antonio Florez, Virrey de N.E., executó el Alférez de Navío Dn. Esteban José Martínez, Comandante de la Fragata *Princesa* y Paquebot *San Carlos*, desde el Departamento de San Blas, a Descubrimientos sobre la Costa Septentrional de California en el presente Año de 1788.' As yet, Martínez did not know about the fur-trading expeditions of John Meares and others.

38   Biblioteca Nacional, Mexico, Caja Fuerte, 'Diario de navegación que con el favour de Díos y de su Madre Santíssima va a executar el Piloto de la Real Armada Don Antonio Serantes sobre la Fragata de S.M.C. la *Princesa* del porte de 16 cañones al mando del Alférez de Navío Don Esteban José Martínez,' 1788.

39   AGI, Mexico, leg. 1529, 'Diario de Esteban José Martínez,' 1788.

40   AGI, Estado 20, ramo 34, Florez to Minister of the Indies, Antonio Valdés, No. 686, 26 November 1788; and AGN, Historia, Vol. 68, Viceroy Conde de Revilla Gigedo to Bodega y Quadra, 8 December 1789. For details on the poor relations between Martínez, López de Haro, and other officers during the 1788 expedition, see Biblioteca Nacional, Mexico, Caja Fuerte, López de Haro to Florez, San Blas, 28 October 1788.

41   Biblioteca Nacional, Mexico, Caja Fuerte, Ms 1683, Florez to Antonio Valdés, No. 702, 23 December 1788.

42   'Charles Clerke's journal,' 1778, in Beaglehole, *Cook Journals*, III:1329, and Beaglehole, *Life of Cook*, 587.

43   AGI, Guadalajara, leg. 516, 'Diario de viage executado en la fragata *Santiago* alias la *Nueva Galicia* por el Piloto Esteban José Martínez, desde el Puerto de San Carlos de Monterey ... a descubrimiento de la Costa hasta los 55 grados 48 minutos ...' Martínez stated that the Natives did not board the ship. The journal of Padre Thomas de la Peña describes the arrival of fifteen canoes with some 100 men and women who traded sea otter skins, mats, and painted hats for old clothing, Monterey abalone shells, and knives. Again there is no mention of the Natives actually boarding the Spanish ship. See AGI, Estado, leg. 43, ramo 9 'Diario del Viage que por orden del R.P. Fr Junipero Serra ... hago desde el puerto de San Carlos de Monterey ... en la fragata de S.M. *Santiago* ... mandada por Don Juan Pérez, por Thomas de la Peña,' 1774.

44   AGN, Historia, Vol. 65, Escritura de posesión, Nootka Sound, 13 July 1789.

45   'Diario de la navegación que Yo el Alférez de Navío de la Real Armada Dn. Esteban Josef Martínez, voy a executar al Pto. de San Lorenzo de Nuca, mandando la Fragata *Princesa* y Paquebot *San Carlos*, 1789,' in Consejo Superior de Investigaciones Científicas, *Colección de diarios y relaciones para la historia de los viajes descubrimientos*, VI (Madrid: Instituto Histórico de Marina 1964), 60; and MN, Vol. 2128, Francisco Miguel Sánchez, Historia compuesta de todo lo acaecido en la expedición hecha al Puerto de Nuca, Año 1789. The *San Carlos* commanded by López de Haro arrived at Nootka Sound on 10 May.

46   Ibid., 63.

47   Joseph Ingraham to Martínez, 'Description of Nootka and Inhabitants,' Nootka Sound, n.d., 1789, and AGN, Historia, Vol. 65, Martínez to Florez, 13 July 1789. The interpreter used by Martínez was Corporal of Dragoons Gabriel del Castillo.

48   Ibid. Also see AGI, Mexico, leg. 1529, Martínez to Florez, Aboard *Princesa* at Nootka Sound, 13 July 1789.

49   MN, Vol. 331, Testimony of Francisco Antonio Mourelle, n.d.

50   For a good summary of the events surrounding the detention of the British ships, see Cook, *Flood Tide of Empire*, 151-79. Also see Howay, *The Journal of Captain Colnett*.

51   AGN, Historia, Vol. 65, Martínez to Florez, 13 July 1789. Martínez dispatched a schooner under Pilot José María Narváez to investigate the entrance to the strait.

52   AGI, Mexico, leg. 1530, Martínez to Florez, Nootka Sound, 24 July 1789; Viceroy Revilla Gigedo to Valdés, No. 244, 12 January 1790, and Revilla Gigedo to Valdés, No. 199, 27 December 1789. Also see AGI, Estado, leg. 20, ramo 96, Revilla Gigedo to the Conde de Floridablanca, No. 68, 30 December 1791. Revilla Gigedo opposed the conquest of the Hawai'ian Islands which he considered too dangerous and expensive.

53   AGN, Historia, Vol. 68, Revilla Gigedo to Bodega y Quadra, 8 December 1789. The viceroy noted that British and French expeditions had not been able to find a northwest passage. He compared Martínez's dreams with the apocryphal discoveries of Admiral Bartolome de Fonte.

54 Beinecke Library, Yale University, New Haven, CT, MS 621, Report of Fray Severo Patero, Nootka Sound, 13 July 1789.

55 Luis Sales, *Noticias de la provincia de Californias en tres cartas de un sacerdote religioso hijo del real convento de predicadores de Valencia a un amigo suyo* (Valencia 1794), 85. Although the friar is not identified, Padre José Espi was from Valencia. This volume also includes the report of Pilot José Tobar y Tamáriz.

56 AGN, Historia, Vol. 65, Fray Severo Patero to Florez, aboard *Princesa*, Nootka Sound, 13 July 1789.

57 Archivo Histórico Nacional, Madrid (AHN), Estado, leg. 4819, Fray Manuel de Trujillo, 'Relación de la Entrada de San Lorenzo de Nutka,' n.d.

58 MN, Vol. 2128, Francisco Miguel Sánchez, 'Historia compuesta de todo acaecido en la expedición hecha al Puerto de Nuca, año de 1789.'

59 Ibid.

60 AHN, Estado, leg. 4819, Fray Manuel de Triujillo, 'Relación.'

61 AGN, Historia, Vol. 65, Joseph Ingraham, 'Description of Nootka and Inhabitants,' 1789. For a discussion of cannibalism, see Christon I. Archer, 'Cannibalism in the Early History of the Northwest Coast: Enduring Myths and Neglected Realities,' *Canadian Historical Review*, LVI (4)(Dec. 1980):453-79.

62 AGN, Historia, Vol. 65, Informe que yo Don José Tobar y Tamariz, primer piloto de la Real Armada doy al Exmo. Sr. Virrey de N.E. en obedicimiento de su superior orden, comunicado con fecha de 29 de agosto de 1789.

63 MN, Vol. 2128, Francisco Miguel Sánchez, 'Historia compuesta de todo lo acaecido en la expedición hecha al Puerto de Nuca, año de 1789.'

64 AGN, Historia, Vol. 31, Padre Lorenzo Socies, 'Noticias de Nutka.'

65 AHN, Estado, leg. 4819, Fray Manuel de Trujillo, 'Relación.'

66 AGN, Historia, Vol. 65, Martínez to Florez, Nootka Sound, 13 July 1789.

67 MN, Vol. 2128, Francisco Miguel Sánchez, 'Historia'; and 'Diario de Esteban Josef Martínez,' 1789, 124.

68 AGN, Historia, Vol. 65, Martínez to Florez, Nootka Sound, 13 July, 1789; and 'Diario de Esteban José Martínez,' 1789, 111-12.

69 'Diario de Esteban José Martínez,' 1789, 94. Sánchez stated that the denigrating words were '*Jacobs pysec coelz capzal*,' meaning that Martínez was a bad man and a great thief who robbed everyone. See Francisco Miguel Sánchez, 'Historia,' MN, Vol. 2128. Martínez's spelling of the word for 'bad' was *pizac*. See C.M. Tate, *Chinook as Spoken by the Indians of Washington Territory, British Columbia, and Alaska* (Victoria, M.W. Wyatt 1889).

70 Pilot José Tobar y Tamariz stated that Martínez shot Callicum while Fray Francisco Miguel Sánchez said that the commander ordered the shot fired. See AGN Historia, Vol. 65; José Tobar y Tamariz, 'Informe,' 1789; and Sánchez, 'Historia,' MN, Vol. 2128.

71 Colnett wrote, 'The man [Martínez] had Cruelty enough to do anything, for he killed Caleacan the Greatest Chief at Nootka for only having told him it was wrong to stop his friend the English.' See Howay, *The Journal of Captain Colnett*, 62. Also see John Meares, *Voyages Made in the Years 1788 and 1789 from China to the North-West Coast of America* (New York: Bibliotheca Australiana 1967), 117-18. Meares depicted Callicum as a wonderful person who 'possessed a delicacy of mind and conduct which would have done honor to the most improved state of our civilization.' Having created this image, Meares expressed 'horror and detestation of that inhuman and wanton spirit of murder which deprived his country of its brightest instrument.' Many Spanish read the British sources and were highly critical of Martínez. See AHN, Estado, leg 4291, Marqués del Campo, Spanish Minister to London, to Conde de Floridablanca, 26 November 1790. Campo feared that if Meares' stories about the death of Callicum were correct, Spain would be hated by the northwest coast Natives for centuries. For other negative Spanish views of Martínez, see Iris Higbie Wilson (ed.), *Noticias de*

Nutka: An Account of Nootka Sound in 1792 by José Mariano Moziño (Seattle and London: University of Washington Press 1970), 75-6; and Francisco Xavier de Viana, *Diario de viaje* (Montevideo: Ministerio de Instrucción Pública 1958), II, 20.

72 AHN, Estado, leg. 4288, Revilla Gigedo to Conde de Floridablanca, 1 April 1792.

73 AGI, Mexico, leg. 1530, Revilla Gigedo to Antonio Valdés, No. 195, 27 December 1789.

74 AGN, Historia, Vol. 68, Revilla Gigedo to Francisco de Eliza, 17 November 1790.

75 MN, Vol. 575-bis, 'Instrucciones secretas dadas por el comandante de San Blas D. Juan Francisco de la Bodega y Quadra al teniente de navío D. Francisco de Eliza, comandante de la fragata *Concepción*, y de los buques *Filipino* [*San Carlos*], y *Princesa Real* [the captured British *Princess Royal*], 28 January 1790.' Another copy of this document is in AGN, Historia , Vol. 68.

76 AGN, Historia, Vol. 69, Francisco de Eliza, 'Costumbres de los Naturales del Puerto de San Lorenzo de Nuca, proporciones para su conquista, y utilidades que comprendo puede este producir,' Nootka Sound, aboard the frigate *Concepción*, 20 April 1791.

77 AGN, Historia, Vol. 68, Salvador Fidalgo to Bodega y Quadra, 1 December 1790.

78 Ibid., Diario de navegación que con el favour de Díos va a executar el Alférez de Navío de la Real Armada, D. Manuel Quimper en la balandra de su mando *Princesa Real* ... del Puerto de la Santa Cruz de Nuca ... al descubrimiento del Estrecho de Juan de Fuca,' 1790.

79 Ibid.

80 Ibid.

81 Joseph P. Sánchez, *Spanish Bluecoats: The Catalonian Volunteers in Northwestern New Spain, 1767-1810* (Albuquerque, NM: University of New Mexico Press 1990), 93-4; and Wilson, *Noticias de Nutka*, 78.

82 AGN, Historia, Vol. 69, Eliza to Revilla Gigedo, aboard *Concepción*, Monterey, 7 July 1792.

83 Ibid.

84 Ibid., Francisco de Eliza, 'Costumbres de los Naturales del Puerto de San Lorenzo de Nuca,' 20 April 1791.

85 AGN, Historia, Vol. 68, Manuel Quimper to Revilla Gigedo, Tepic, 13 November 1790; and Martínez to Quadra, Tepic, 2 December 1790.

86 AGN, Historia, Vol. 69, Jacinto Caamaño to Bodega y Quadra, Tepic, 8 June 1791.

87 Ibid., Jacinto Caamaño, 'Diario de las cosas particulares que he notado durante el tiempo que he estado en Noka,' July 1790 to February 1791; and 'Caracter, vida, y costumbres de los Indios de Noka, y sus inmediaciones.' For an account of the loss of Hudson's boat, see Cook, *Flood Tide of Empire*, 292-3.

88 AGN, Historia, Vol. 68, Salvador Fidalgo to Revilla Gigedo, 13 November 1790.

89 AGN, Historia, Vol. 69, Francisco Eliza, 'Costumbres de los Naturales del Puerto de San Lorenzo de Nuca,' 20 April 1791.

90 Ibid., Jacinto Caamaño, 'Caracter, vida, y costumbres de los Indios de Noka, y sus inmediaciones,' 1791.

91 Ibid., Revilla Gigedo to Bodega y Quadra, 25 May 1791.

92 Ibid., Francisco de Eliza to Bodega y Quadra, Nootka Sound, 9 March 1791.

93 AGN, Historia, Vol. 60, Bodega y Quadra to Revilla Gigedo, Tepic, 11 June 1791, and Eliza to Revilla Gigedo, No. 5, Nootka Sound, 20 April 1791; and Bancroft Library, University of California, Berkeley, Ms., fol. 46, Ensign Félix Cepeda, 'Memoria de los viages europeos a la Costa Nor-oeste de la América Septentrional,' carta segunda.

94 Pedro de Novo y Colson (ed.), *La vuelta al mundo por las corbetas Descubierta y Atrevida al mando del Capitán de Navío D. Alejandro Malaspina desde 1789 a 1794* (Madrid 1885), 191. For the original version, see Mercedes Palau (ed.), *Viaje científico y político a la América Meridional, a las Costas del Mar Pacífico y a las Islas Marianas y Filipinas verificado en los años de 1789, 90, 91, 92, 93 y 94 a bordo de las corbetas Descubierta y Atrevida de la Marina Real, mandadas por los capitanes de navío D. Alejandro Malaspina y D. José F. Bustamante* (Madrid: Ed. El

Museo Universal 1984), 309. Also see Francisco Xavier de Viana, *Diario de Viaje* (Montevideo: Ministerio de Instrucción Pública 1958), II, 88; and Lorenzo Sanfeliu Ortiz (ed.), *62 meses a bordo: la expedición Malaspina según el diario del Teniente de Navío Don Antonio de Tova Arredondo, 2 comandante de la 'Atrevida,' 1789-1794* (Madrid 1943), 165. For a summary in English of Malaspina's visit to Nootka Sound, see Iris H. Wilson Engstrand, *Spanish Scientists in the New World: The Eighteenth-Century Expeditions* (Seattle: University of Washington Press 1981), 67-75.

95 Tomás de Suria, *Quaderno que contiene el Ramo de Historia Natural y diario de la Expedición del círculo del Globo, 1791* (New Haven, CT: Yale University, Beinecke Library); and Henry R. Wagner (ed.), *Journal of Tomás de Suría of his Voyage with Malaspina to the Northwest Coast in 1791* (Glendale: Arthur Clark Company, 1936), 275.

96 Novo y Colson, *La vuelta al mundo*, 193; and Sanfeliu Ortiz (ed.), *62 meses a bordo*, 166.

97 Beinecke Library, Tomás de Suría, 'Quaderno,' 1791.

98 MN, Vol. 330, 'Descripción física de las Costas del NO de la América visitadas, 1791; and Novo y Colson, *La vuelta al mundo*, 355.

99 AHN, Estado, leg. 4289, Ramón Saavedra to Bodega y Quadra, aboard *Concepción*, Nootka Sound, 27 August 1791. The existence of cannibalism was examined again in 1792 by the officers with Dionisio Alcalá Galiano and Cayetano Valdés. They reviewed the old stories and speculated that the Spanish presence at Yuquot since 1789 had curbed this atrocious custom. See María Dolores Higueras Rodríguez and María Luisa Martín-Merás (eds.), *Relación del viaje hecho por las goletas Sútil y Mexicana en el año 1792 para reconocer el estrecho de Juan de Fuca* (Madrid: Museo Naval 1991), 131-2.

100 Novo y Colson, *La vuelta al mundo*, 361.

101 See, for example, AHN, Estado, leg. 4290, Ramón Saavedra to Viceroy Marqués de Branciforte, Nootka Sound, 21 August 1794. Saavedra reported a raid by Wickaninish, involving Nootkan participation against the Hesquiats, in which seventy died and many children were taken captive. Two children were brought for sale to the Spanish.

102 AGN, Historia, vol. 70, Alonso de Torres y Guerra to Bodega y Quadra, San Blas, 16 November 1792.

103 AHN, Estado, leg 4290, Marqués de Branciforte to the Duque de Alcudía [Manuel Godoy]. When the Spanish withdrew from Nootka Sound in 1795, there were twenty-eight Native children aboard the ships. Three children died previously after having received baptism.

104 AGN, Historia, vol. 69, Ramón Saavedra to Revilla Gigedo, No. 2 Nootka Sound, 26 May 1791; and Saavedra to Bodega y Quadra, 27 August 1791.

105 Ibid.

106 Madrid, Archivo y Biblioteca, Ministerio de Asuntos Exteriores Viaje a la Costa N.O. de la América Septentrional por Dn. Juan Francisco de la Bodega y Quadra, del orden de Santiago, Capitán de Navío de la Real Armada, y Comandante del Departamento de San Blas en las Fragatas de su mando *Santa Gertrudis, Aranzazu, Princesa,* y Goleta *Activo,* 1792. This document is printed in Bernabeu Albert, *Bodega y Quadra*, 129-237.

107 The body was thought by some observers to have had flesh cut off the 'calves of the legs and fleshy parts of the arms.' This renewed fears of cannibalism. Peter Puget of the *Chatham* felt that the boy had been involved in a sexual affair with a Native woman, and he was not convinced that the Nootkans were responsible. See C.F. Newcombe, *Menzies' Journal of Vancouver's Voyage, April to October, 1792* (Victoria: Archives of British Columbia, Memoir VI 923), 22; British Museum, Add. MS 17548, Peter Puget, Rough Journal of HMS *Chatham*, January 1794-September 1795; Rodríguez and Martín-Merás, *Relación del Viaje hecho por las Goletas Sútil y Mexicana*, 148-9; Wilson, *Noticias de Nutka*, 54-6; and Mark D. Kaplanoff (ed.), *Joseph Ingraham's Journal of the Brigantine Hope on a Voyage to the Northwest Coast of North America, 1790-2* (Barre, MA: Imprint Society 1971), 237.

108 AGN, Historia, Vol. 67, Salvador Fidalgo to Bodega y Quadra, aboard *Princesa,* Puerto de Nuñez Gaona, 4 July 1792.

109 MN, Vol. 575-bis, De Acapulco a Nutka, Goleta *Mexicana,* 1792.

110 MN, Vol. 280, Revilla Gigedo to Alejandro Malaspina, 22 November 1791.

111 See, for example, John Boit's Log of the Second Voyage of *Columbia,* in Frederic W. Howay (ed.), *Voyages of the 'Columbia' to the Northwest Coast 1787-1790 and 1790-1793* (Portland: Oregon Historical Society 1990), 411.

112 Edmund S. Meany (ed.), *A New Vancouver Journal on the Discovery of Puget Sound by a Member of Chatham's Crew* (Seattle, 1915), 21; and Lamb, *Vancouver's Voyage,* II:670-2.

113 Madrid, Archivo y Biblioteca, Ministerio de Asuntos Exteriores, 'Viaje a la Costa N.O. de la América Septentrional por Juan Francisco de la Bodega y Quadra,' 1792; and AHN, Estado, leg. 4290, Bodega y Quadra to Revilla Gigedo, Monterey, 24 October 1792.

114 MN, Vol. 330, Secundino Salamanca, 'Apuntes, incoordinados acerca de las costumbres, usos, y leves de los salvajes havitantes del Estrecho de Fuca, 1792.'

115 Meany, *A New Vancouver Journal,* 25.

116 MN, Vol. 2193, 'Extracto del diario de las navegaciones, hechos en la América Septentrional por D. Jacinto Caamaño, Teniente de Navío de la Real Armada y Comandante de la fragata *Nuestra Señora de Aranzazú,* 1792.'

117 AGN, Historia, Vol. 70, Salvador Fidalgo to Revilla Gigedo, Nootka Sound, 26 November 1792.

118 AGN, Historia, Vol. 71, Salvador Fidalgo to Ramón Saavedra, Nootka Sound, 31 May 1793.

119 AGN, Provincias Internas, Vol. 3, Ramón Saavedra to Revilla Gigedo, No. 11, Nootka Sound, 15 June 1794.

120 AHN, Estado, leg. 4290, Ramón Saavedra, 'Desde la salida de la fragata *Princesa* del mando del Teniente de Navío D. Salvador Fidalgo que verificó el 7 de junio del año pasado de '93 han ocurrido hasta el día las siguientes novedades en esta establecimiento,' 15 June 1794.

121 Ibid.

122 AHN, Estado, leg. 4290, Branciforte to the Duque de Alcudía, No. 9, 29 August 1794.

123 Ramón Saavedra, 'Desde la salida de la fragata *Princesa.*'

124 Ibid.

125 AGN, Historia, Vol. 71, Saavedra to Revilla Gigedo, Nootka Sound, 31 August 1794.

126 Ibid., Cayetano Valdés to Revilla Gigedo, Mexico, 6 March 1793.

127 Ibid., Secundino Salamanca to Revilla Gigedo, 6 March 1793.

Chapter 8: Dangerous Liaisons

The research from which this chapter is drawn has been made possible by financial assistance from the British Columbia Heritage Trust, the Mowachaht/Muchalaht Band, and the Department of Archaeology, Simon Fraser University. The author would like to thank Andrew Barton, John Dewhirst, Freeman Tovell, and Doug Sutton for their comments on an earlier draft.

1 John Meares, *Voyages Made in 1788 and 1789* (New York 1967), 228-31.

2 Ibid., 153.

3 Cecil Jane (trans.), *A Spanish Voyage to Vancouver and the Northwest Coast of America being the Narrative of the Voyage Made in the Year 1792 by the Schooners 'Sútil' and 'Mexicana' to Explore the Strait of Fuca* (London: Argonaut Press 1930), 32.

4 Meares, *Voyages Made 1788 and 1789,* 144. See Valerie Sherer Mathes, 'Wickaninnish, a Clayoquot Chief, as Recorded by Early Travelers,' *Pacific Northwest Quarterly* (July 1979), for a general account of Chief Wickaninish.

5 Meares, *Voyages Made 1788 and 1789,* 125.

6 Ibid., 146.

7 Howay, *The Journal of Captain Colnett,* 201-2. John Hoskins' Narrative, Feb. 1792, Robert

Haswell's Log, Feb. 1792, and John Boit's Log, Jan. 1792, in Howay, *Voyages of the Columbia* (Boston 1941), 271-4, 310-11, 387-9.

8   A general summary of Nuu-chah-nulth warfare can be found in Morris Swadesh 'Motivations in Nootka Warfare,' *Southwestern Journal of Anthropology*, IV (1948):76-93. Detailed accounts of individual Nuu-chah-nulth wars are recorded in Edward Sapir and Morris Swadesh, *Native Accounts of Nootka Ethnography* (Bloomington: Indiana University, Research Center in Anthropology 1955), 339-457, and in Philip Drucker, *The Northern and Central Nootkan Tribes* (Washington: Bureau of American Ethnology, Bulletin 144 1951), 332-65.

9   Meares, *Voyages Made in 1788 and 1789*, 113. Robin Fisher and J.M. Bumsted (eds.), *An Account of a Voyage to the North West Coast of America in 1785 and 1786 by Alexander Walker* (Vancouver: Douglas & McIntyre 1982), 62.

10 Meares, *Voyages Made in the Years 1788 and 1789*, 113. Fisher and Bumsted, *An Account of a Voyage*, 61.

11 Meares, *Voyages Made in 1788 and 1789*, 109. Alessandro Malaspina, 'Politico-Scientific Voyages Around the World ... from 1789-1794,' Books 1 and 2, Carl Robinson (trans.) (typescript, Vancouver: UBC Library), 284.

12 Wilson, *Noticias de Nutka*, 91.

13 William L. Schurz (trans.), [Don Estevan Josef Martinez] 'Diary of the Voyage which I, Ensign of the Royal Navy, Don Estevan Josef Martinez, am going to Make to the Port of San Lorenzo de Nuca ... in the present Year 1789' (transcript, Vancouver: UBC Library), 144.

14 Meares, *Voyages Made in 1788 and 1789*, 230.

15 Although Spanish, Mexican, and American historians prefer Bodega y Quadra, the British and Canadian convention of simply using Quadra will be followed here.

16 V.D. Webb (trans.), [Don Juan Francisco de la Bodega y Quadra] 'Voyage to the N.W. Coast of North America by Don Juan Francisco de la Bodega y Quadra ... in the Year 1792' (typescript, Vancouver: UBC Library), 15.

17 Freeman M. Tovell, 'The Career of Bodega y Quadra: A Summation of the Spanish Contribution to the Heritage of the Northwest Coast,' Robin Inglis (ed.), *Spain and the North Pacific Coast* (Vancouver: Vancouver Maritime Museum Society 1991), 172-80.

18 Webb, 'Voyage ... by Bodega y Quadra,' 47.

19 Ibid., 44.

20 Freeman M. Tovell, 'The Other Side of the Coin: The Viceroy, Bodega y Quadra, Vancouver and the Nootka Crisis,' *BC Studies*, XCIII (Spring 1992):3-29.

21 Jane, *A Spanish Voyage to Vancouver* 16 Wilson, *Noticias de Nutka*, 84.

22 Ibid.

23 Susan Golla, 'A Tale of Two Chiefs: Nootkan Narrative and the Ideology of Chiefship,' *Société des Américanistes* (1991):107-23. Sapir and Swadish, *Native Accounts of Nootka Ethnography*.

24 Wilson, *Noticias de Nutka*; Webb, 'Voyage ... by Bodega y Quadra.'

25 John R. Jewitt, *A Journal Kept at Nootka Sound by John R. Jewitt One of the Surviving Crew of the Ship Boston of Boston, John Salter, Commander, Who was Massacred on 22nd of March, 1803, Interspsed with some account of the Natives, Their Manners and Customs* (reprint of the 1807 ed., New York: Garland 1976); Hilary Stewart, *The Adventures and Sufferings of John R. Jewitt Captive of Maquinna* (Vancouver: Douglas & McIntyre 1987).

26 Jane, *A Spanish Voyage to Vancouver*, 16-7.

27 Wilson, *Noticias de Nutka*, 34-7. Bodega y Quadra, 'Voyage to the N.W. Coast of North America,' 45-6.

28 Jane, *A Spanish Voyage to Vancouver*, 18.

29 Ibid.

30 Malaspina, 'Politico-Scientific Voyages Around the World,' Books 1 and 2, 284-5, and Book 3, 215; Wilson, *Noticias de Nutka*, 84-5; Meares, *Voyages Made in 1788 and 1789*, 209-10; Newcombe,

Menzies' Journal of Vancouver's Voyage, 114.

31 Ibid., 127.

32 Wilson, *Noticias de Nutka*, 34.

33 Webb, 'Voyage ... by Bodega y Quadra,' 47.

34 Jane, *A Spanish Voyage to Vancouver*, 17.

35 Ibid.

36 Wilson, *Noticias de Nutka*, 63.

37 Henry R. Wagner (trans.), 'Journal of Tomas de Suria of his voyage with Malaspina to the Northwest Coast of America in 1791,' *Pacific Historical Review*, v (1936):274.

38 Jane, *A Spanish Voyage to Vancouver*, 18.

39 Webb, 'Voyage ... by Bodega y Quadra,' 47.

40 Jane, *A Spanish Voyage to Vancouver*, 18.

41 Lamb, *Vancouver's Voyage*, II:672.

42 Kaplanoff, *Joseph Ingraham's Journal, 1790-92*, 240; Webb, 'Voyage ... by Bodega y Quadra,' 29-30.

43 Ibid., 30.

44 Howay, *The Journal of Captain Colnett*, 193.

45 John Boit's Log in Howay, *Voyages of the Columbia*, 386.

46 UBC Library, Vancouver, Bernard Magee, 'Log of the *Jefferson*,' photocopy.

47 John Mills, 'The Ethnohistory of Nootka Sound, Vancouver Island' (unpublished Ph.D. dissertation, University of Washington 1955), 120.

48 Kaplanoff, *Joseph Ingraham's Journal, 1790-92*, 224.

49 Ibid., 225-6.

50 Ibid.

51 AGN, Historia, Vol. 67, Expediente 15, Letter to Fidalgo from Quadra, 5 August 5 1792.

52 Webb, 'Voyage ... by Bodega y Quadra,' 30.

53 Ibid., 36.

54 Ibid.

55 Wilson, *Noticias de Nutka*, 56.

56 Webb, 'Voyage ... by Bodega y Quadra,' 37.

57 Ibid., 38.

58 Lamb, *Vancouver's Voyage*, II:661-2.

59 Webb, 'Voyage ... by Bodega y Quadra,' 76.

60 Newcombe, *Menzies' Journal of Vancouver's Voyage*, 120; Lamb, *Vancouver's Voyage*, II:671; E.S. Meany (ed.), 'A New Vancouver Journal,' *Washington Historical Quarterly*, v (1914):304.

61 Ibid.; Newcombe, *Menzies' Journal of Vancouver's Voyage*, 120.

62 Lamb, *Vancouver's Voyage*, II:672.

63 Webb, 'Voyage ... by Bodega y Quadra,' 115.

64 Newcombe, *Menzies' Journal of Vancouver's Voyage*, 127.

65 Lamb, *Vancouver's Voyage*, III:1399.

66 Ibid., 1402.

67 UBC Library, Bernard Magee, 'Log of the *Jefferson*.'

68 Michael Roe (ed.), *The Journal and Letters of Captain Charles Bishop on the North-West Coast of America, in the Pacific and in New South Wales 1794-1799* (Cambridge, England: Hakluyt Society 1967), 107.

69 Paul Tennant, *Aboriginal People and Politics: The Indian Land Question in British Columbia, 1849-1989* (Vancouver: UBC Press 1990), 124.

70 John Dewhirst, 'Mowachaht Ownership and Use of Salmon Resources of the Leiner River and Upper Tahsis Inlet, Nootka Sound, B.C.' (unpublished report, Victoria, Archeo Tech

Associates 1990), 16.

71 Frank Cassidy and Robert L. Bish, *Indian Government: Its Meaning in Practice* (Lantzville, BC: Oolichan Books 1989). Tennant, *Aboriginal People and Politics.*

72 Cassidy and Bish, *Indian Government*, 90.

73 Tennant, *Aboriginal People and Politics.* Philip Drucker, *The Native Brotherhoods: Modern Intertribal Organizations on the Northwest Coast* (Washington: Bureau of American Ethnology, Bulletin 168, 1958).

Chapter 9: Art and Exploration

1 Works that discuss the impact of new materials include Wilson Duff, *The Indian History of British Columbia, Volume I: The Impact of the White Man*, Anthropology in British Columbia, Memoir 5 (Victoria: British Columbia Provincial Museum 1964); Bill Holm and Thomas Vaughan, *Soft Gold: The Fur Trade and Cultural Exchange on the Northwest Coast* (Portland: Oregon Historical Society 1982); and Victoria Wyatt, *Shapes of Their Thoughts: Reflections of Culture Contact in Northwest Coast Indian Art* (New Haven, CT: Yale Peabody Museum of Natural History and University of Oklahoma Press 1984).

2 For more on Chilkat blankets, see Cheryl Samuel, *The Chilkat Dancing Blanket* (Seattle: Pacific Search Press 1982). Button blankets are discussed in Doreen Jensen and Polly Sargent, *Robes of Power: Totem Poles on Cloth*, UBC Museum of Anthropology Museum Note No. 17 (Vancou-ver: UBC Press and the UBC Museum of Anthropology 1986).

3 See Adria H. Katz, 'The Raven Cape, a Tahitian Breastplate Collected by Louis Shotridge,' in Susan A. Kaplan and Kristin J. Barsness (eds.), *Raven's Journey: The World of Alaska's Native People* (Philadelphia: University Museum 1986), 78-90.

4 Camphorwood chests are illustrated in Vaughan and Holm, *Soft Gold*, 20.

5 An elegant example of a pipe inspired by a raven rattle is illustrated and discussed in Bill Holm and William Reid, *Form and Freedom: A Dialogue on Northwest Coast Indian Art* (Houston: Rice University Institute for the Arts 1975), 30-3. Compare it with the raven rattles discussed in the same volume on pp. 190-9.

6 The Northern Formline style is described by Bill Holm in *Northwest Coast Indian Art: An Analysis of Form* (Seattle: University of Washington Press 1965).

7 Sources that discuss and illustrate many examples of nineteenth-century argillite carving include Peter L. Macnair and Alan L. Hoover, *The Magic Leaves: A History of Haida Argillite Carving* (Victoria: British Columbia Provincial Museum 1984); Carol Sheehan, *Pipes That Won't Smoke; Coal That Won't Burn* (Calgary: Glenbow Museum 1981); and Leslie Drew and Douglas Wilson, *Argillite: Art of the Haida* (North Vancouver, BC: Hancock House 1980).

8 Anthropologist Marjorie Halpin deserves credit for making this observation.

9 This sculpture, British Museum No. 96.1202, is illustrated in Bill Holm, 'Will the Real Charles Edensaw Please Stand Up? The Problem of Attribution in Northwest Coast Indian Art,' (177) in Donald N. Abbott (ed.), *The World Is As Sharp As a Knife: An Anthology in Honour of Wilson Duff* (Victoria: British Columbia Provincial Museum 1981), 175-200. Bill Holm notes that while the work stylistically resembles those attributed to Gwaytihl, the British Museum catalogue cites Simeon Stilthda as the carver. He adds that if this information is accurate, some of the other pieces attributed to Gwaytihl may actually be by an associated carver.

10 This sculpture is also illustrated in Holm, 'Real Charles Edensaw,' 176.

11 This argillite sculpture is also illustrated in Aldona Jonaitis, *From the Land of the Totem Poles: The Northwest Coast Indian Art Collection of the American Museum of Natural History* (New York and Seattle: American Museum of Natural History and University of Washington Press 1988), 79.

Chapter 10: Kidnapped

1   Lamb, *Vancouver's Voyage*, I:272.
2   Ibid., 273, 436-7.
3   Ibid., 287.
4   *Historical Records of New South Wales* (HRNSW) (Sydney: Charles Potter, Government Printer 1891), I:2, 11-12, 19, 89 for Matra, 1783, Young, 1785, and for official documents making this point.
5   Jonathon King and John King, *Philip Gidley King: A Biography of the Third Governor of New South Wales* (North Ryde, NSW: Methuen 1981), 13.
6   HRNSW, I:596.
7   Ibid., 53, Phillip, 1787.
8   Ibid., 186, 211, 18-219, 271, 434, 437-8, 441, 442-3, 486, 529, 563.
9   Mitchell Library (ML) Sydney, CY C115, Journal of Philip Gidney King, 1786-90, xerox copy, 369.
10 ML, C187, Norfolk Letterbook of Philip Gidney King, 1788-99, 59.
11 Robert McNab (ed.), *Historical Records of New Zealand* (Wellington: John Mackay, Government Printer 1908), I:126.
12 ML, C187, King Letterbook, 225.
13 Lamb, *Vancouver's Voyage*, I:38.
14 Judging from his numerous references to information derived from such a source.
15 Lamb, *Vancouver's Voyage*, I:63.
16 Ibid., II:663, 678, 729.
17 Ibid., 734.
18 McNab, *Historical Records of New Zealand*, I:154-7.
19 Ibid., 159-60.
20 Lamb, *Vancouver's Voyage*, II:450-5.
21 Ibid., III:1082. See also Grose in McNab, *Historical Records of New Zealand*, I:165. According to Collins, however, about 100 pigs were loaded on board at Tahiti, and eighty pigs and four sheep survived the voyage. David Collins, *An Account of the English Colony of New South Wales, with Remarks on the Disposition, Customs Manners &c. of the Native Inhabitants* ... (London: T. Cadwell Jr and W. Davies in the Strand 1798), 282-3.
22 Australian National Library (ANL), MS 9/94a, King to Banks, 24 May 1793, 3.
23 Lamb, *Vancouver's Voyage*, II:540-1. See also Vancouver's much less detailed account in ibid., III:1081.
24 Ibid., II:541.
25 ML, A1687, King Journal, 179-81.
26 Ibid., 179-80.
27 Anne Salmond, *Two Worlds: First Meetings between Maori and Europeans, 1642-1772* (Auckland: Viking Press 1991), 359-429.
28 Ibid., 340.
29 Alexander Turnbull Library (ATL), Wellington, MS 75, Folder B19, White, 90.
30 ATL, MS 75, Folder B19, White, 90.
31 Lamb, *Vancouver's Voyage*, III:1082.
32 Collins, *New South Wales*, I:270, 273.
33 McNab, *Historical Records of New Zealand*, I:165.
34 Collins, *New South Wales*, I:283.
35 Ibid., 273.
36 Ibid., 281; ANL, MS 70, Philip Gidley King Journal, 71.
37 Specht gives tentative dates of AD 1000-1400, possibly with a second Polynesian settlement in AD 1400-1750: Merval Hoare in Raymond Nobbs (ed.), *Norfolk Island and Its First Settlement, 1788-1814* (Sydney: Library of Australian History 1988), 18-22; King in HRNSW, I(2), 187, 296;

ANL, MS 9/94a, King to Banks, 24 May 1793, 3; personal communication, Merval Hoare, 1991.

38 ML, C187, King Letterbook, 15 January 1792, 90.

39 ML, A1687, King Journal, 25-6; ANL, MS 70, King Journal, 13.

40 ANL, MS 70, King Journal, 13.

41 ML C187, King Letterbook, 29 March 1792, 98; David Collins, Secretary to the Governor, to Lieutenant-Governor King.

42 Ibid., April 1793, 146.

43 Nobbs, Norfolk Island, 5; ANL, MS 70, King Journal, 63-4.

44 HRNSW, I:228.

45 Ibid., 367.

46 Ibid., 596.

47 ANL, MS 70, King Journal, 12 November 1791, 5.

48 Ibid., 7-10, 33, 35, 39.

49 Nobbs, Norfolk Island, 118, 119.

50 Ibid, 130.

51 ML, A1958, Victualling Book, Norfolk Island, 18a.

52 ANL, MS 70, King Journal, 10 March 1793, 62.

53 McNab, Historical Records of New Zealand, I:183.

54 ANL, MS 9/95, King to Banks, 10 November 1793, 1.

55 Collins, New South Wales, I:519-20.

56 ML, A1687, King Journal 1793, 129-30.

57 Ibid., 135, 182.

58 Ibid., 136.

59 ML, C187, King letterbook, 225.

60 ML, A1974, Chapman letters, 3 November 1793.

61 ANL, MS 9/95, King to Banks, 10 November 1793.

62 ML, A1974, Chapman letters, 19 November 1793.

63 John Rawson Elder (ed.), The Letters and Journals of Samuel Marsden, 1765-1838 (Dunedin, NZ: A.H. Reed 1932), 155.

64 ML, King's journal, 1793, 82, 86, 87.

65 McNab, Historical Records of New Zealand, I:262-8.

66 ML, A1687, King letterbook, 187.

67 Ibid., 88.

68 Ibid., 61.

69 ANL, MS 9/95, King to Banks, 10 November 1793.

70 ML, A1687, King Journal, 192.

71 ANL, MS 9/95, King to Banks, 10 November 1793.

72 ML, CY Safe 1/10, King Journal, 173-88.

73 McNab, Historical Records of New Zealand, II:543.

74 Ibid., 543-4.

75 Paul Fidlon and R.J. Ryan (eds.), The Journal of Philip Gidley King: Lieutenant, RN, 1787-90 (Sydney: Australian Documents Library 1980), 364.

76 Ibid., 545.

77 ATL, MS 75, Folder B19, John White, 90.

78 ANL, MS 9/95, King to Banks, 10 November 1793, 2,3.

79 McNab, Historical Records of New Zealand, II:542.

80 Collins, New South Wales, 521-2.

81 See in particular R.R.D. Milligan (John Dunmore, ed.), The Map Drawn by the Chief Tuki-Tahua in 1793 (Mangonui, NZ: Estate of R.R.D. Milligan and J. Dunmore 1964).

82 Including one which tribal accounts say was drawn for Cook on the deck of the *Endeavour* at Whitianga, NZ (Salmond, *Two Worlds*, 207), another for Nicholas by Korokoro in 1814, and others for Shortland in the 1840s.
83 The most serious error in Milligan's interpretation of Tuki's map occurs here, when he assumes that the promontory marked at the western boundary of Muriwhenua is Cape Maria Van Diemen. I am certain that on the contrary, this is Tauroa Point at the end of Te Oneroa-a-Tohe (Ninety Mile Beach). Many of Milligan's subsequent disagreements with tribal authorities follow from this mistaken identification.
84 ML, A1687, King journal, 185.
85 Ibid., 183.
86 Milligan, *The Map Drawn by Tuki-Tahua.*
87 Ibid., 29.
88 ML, A1687, King Journal, 171.
89 McNab, *Historical Records of New Zealand*, I:168.
90 Ibid., 183-4.
91 ML, A1687, King Journal, 193-4.
92 Ibid.
93 Murray, 13 November 1793.
94 Ibid., 195-6.
95 ML, A1974, Chapman letters, 1792-1838, 19 November 1793.
96 Ibid., 199.
97 Ibid., 200.
98 Ibid., 201.
99 Fidlon and Ryan, *King Journal*, 367.
100 ML, A1974, Chapman letter, 37.
101 McNab, *Historical Records of New Zealand*, I:181.
102 ML, AK1/4, Letter about weapons presented to Governor King by Tooke and Woodoo, 29 November 1819.
103 ML, A1687, King Journal, 318-22.
104 ATL, MS 70, Folder 19, White, 81, 90.
105 ML, C186, King 1806, 135.
106 Milligan, *The Map Drawn by Tuki-tahua*, 135.

Chapter 11: Banks and Menzies
1 Patrick O'Brien, *Joseph Banks: A Life* (London 1987), 58.
2 *Gazetteer and New Daily Advertiser*, 26 August 1771; O'Brien, *Banks*, 149.
3 Royal Botanic Gardens, Kew (Kew), Hope to Banks, 22 August 1786.
4 Kew, Menzies to Banks, 22 August 22 1786.
5 PRO, Adm 106/2625.
6 J.J Keevil, 'Archibald Menzies, 1754-1842,' *Bulletin of the History of Medicine*, XXII (1948):799.
7 British Library, Menzies journal, December 1790.
8 ML, Brabourne papers, IX:50.
9 ML, Brabourne papers, IX:53.
10 ML, Brabourne papers, IX:95, Banks to Menzies, 10 August 1791.
11 Quoted from the original instructions, now in the Provincial Archives of British Columbia. Oddly enough, they were addressed incorrectly to Alexander, not Archibald Menzies.
12 ML, Brabourne, IX:95, Banks to Menzies, 10 August 1791.
13 Kew, undated memorandum by Banks.
14 British Library, Menzies Journal, 10 September 1791.
15 Ibid., 8 September 1792.

16   ML, Brabourne, IX:147, enclosure in Menzies to Banks, 6 December 1793.
17   Kew, Menzies to Banks, 28 April 1795.
18   PRO, Adm 1/2629, 62-3, Vancouver to Nepean, 13 September 1795.
19   Kew, Menzies to Banks, 14 September 1795.
20   ML, Brabourne, IX, 153, Menzies to Banks, 8 September 1794.
21   Ibid., 171, Menzies to Banks, 26 March 1795.
22   PRO, Adm 1/2629, 97, Vancouver to Menzies, 12 September 1795.
23   Ibid., 99-100, Menzies to Vancouver, 12 September 1795.
24   Kew, Menzies to Banks, 14 September 1795.
25   Brabourne, IX, 164, Banks to Nepean, 1 October 1795.
26   PRO, Adm 1/2629, 104, Vancouver to Nepean, 26 October 1795.
27   British Museum (Natural History), Botany Library, Banks to the Duke of Portland, 3 February 1796.
28   PRO, PRO 30/8/185, Vancouver to the Earl of Chatham, 8 April 1796.
29   Beaglehole, *Banks Journal*, I:ccxlix.
30   ML, Brabourne, IX:185-6, Menzies to Banks, 3 January 1798.
31   Keevil, 'Archibald Menzies,' 805.
32   F.R.S. Balfour, 'Archibald Menzies, 1764-1842, Botanist, Zoologist, Medico and Explorer,' *Proceedings*, Linnean Society of London, CLVI (1943-4):173.
33   I am indebted to Mr John Thompson, Director of Australian Collections, National Library of Australia, for these details.
34   ML, Brabourne, IX:79, Menzies to Banks, 5 May 1791.
35   Ibid., Menzies to Banks, 10 August 1791.
36   Willis Linn Jepson, 'The Botanical Explorers of California – VI. Archibald Menzies.' *Madrono*, I (1929):264.
37   Balfour, 'Archibald Menzies,' 179.
38   Dr Glyndwr Williams and Lt-Cdr Andrew David checked the watermarks on the British Library's manuscript, and Mr Graeme Powell, of the National Library of Australia, examined the Canberra manuscript on my behalf.

Chapter 12: Polynesia

1   I use the term *Polynesia* in its old-fashioned sense of delineating both a geographic region, roughly encompassed by the triangle formed by Hawai'i, New Zealand (Aotearoa), and Easter Island (Rapa Nui), and an assumed regional cultural identity. I do so because much of this chapter's scholarship is based on that assumption, although modern scholarship tends to reject the second aspect of this definition. While cultural affinities are certainly present within Polynesia, perhaps most notably in language and aspects of material culture, strictly speaking, no such 'Polynesian culture' exists because of the many variants and adaptations among the widely scattered 'Polynesian' communities. The term *Polynesia* in a modern context should delineate a particular geographic, but not a cultural, region of Oceania.
2   See, for example, Bernard Smith, *European Vision and the South Pacific*, 2nd ed. (Sydney: Harper & Row 1984); K.R. Howe, 'The Fate of the "Savage" in Pacific Historiography,' *New Zealand Journal of History*, IX (2) (1977):137-54.
3   See, for example, Alan Howard, 'Polynesian Origins and Migrations. A Review of Two Centuries of Speculation and Theory,' G. Highland et al. (eds.), *Polynesian Culture History. Essays in Honor of Kenneth P. Emory* (Honolulu: Bishop Museum Press 1967), 45-101; M.P.K. Sorrenson, *Maori Origins and Migrations. The Genesis of Some Pakeha Myths and Legends* (Auckland: Auckland University Press 1990).
4   Sorrenson, *Maori Origins*, 7.
5   For example, J.R. Forster (trans.), [Louis-Antoine de Bougainville] *A Voyage Round the World. Performed by Order of His Most Christian Majesty in the Years 1766, 1767, 1768, and 1769*

(London: J. Nourse & T. Davies 1772), 242-74; Beaglehole, *Banks Journal*, 1:258, 384-5.

6   Olive Wright (ed.), *New Zealand 1826-1827 from the French of Dumont D'Urville* (Wellington: O. Wright 1950), 126, 185.

7   Bernard Smith, *European Vision*, 43.

8   On Mai, see E.H. McCormick, *Omai. Pacific Envoy* (Auckland: Auckland University Press 1977).

9   For overviews of notions of the Pacific as paradise or otherwise, see Smith, *European Vision*; O.H.K. Spate, *Paradise Found and Lost: The Pacific Since Magellan*, III (Canberra: Australian National University Press 1988).

10   George Boas, *Essays on Primitivism and Related Ideas in the Middle Ages* (New York: Octagon Books 1978).

11   Ronald L. Meek, *Social Science and the Ignoble Savage* (Cambridge, England: Cambridge University Press 1976).

12   Lord Monboddo [James Burnett], *Of the Origin and Progress of Language*, 1:1773 (Menston: Scolar Press 1967), 234.

13   Ibid., 231.

14   J.R. Forster, *Observations Made During a Voyage Round the World, on Physical Geography, Natural History and Ethnic Philosophy* (London: G. Robinson 1778), 468, 471.

15   Ibid., 303-4.

16   Ibid., 538.

17   Michael E. Hoare, *The Tactless Philosopher: Johann Reinhold Forster 1729-1798* (Melbourne: Hawthorn Press 1976), 144, 311; Thomas Bendysche, *The Anthropological Treatises of Johann Friedrich Blumenbach* (Boston: Milford House 1973), 264-6.

18   J.J.H. de Labillardière, *Voyage in Search of La Pérouse, Performed by Order of the Constituent Assembly during the years 1791, 1792, 1793, and 1794*, translated from the French (London: Stockdale 1800), v.

19   Translator's preface to de Labillardière, vii.

20   Wright, *New Zealand*, 126-7.

21   Meek, *Social Science and the Ignoble Savage*.

22   Niel Gunson, *Messengers of Grace. Evangelical Missionaries in the South Seas 1797-1860* (Melbourne: Oxford University Press 1978), 206.

23   John Inglis, *In the New Hebrides. Reminiscences of Missionary Life and Work, Especially on the Island of Aneityum from 1850 till 1877* (London: T. Nelson & Sons 1887), 5.

24   John Rawson Elder (ed.), *The Letters and Journals of Samuel Marsden 1765-1838* (Dunedin, NZ: A.H. Reed 1932), 219-20.

25   Sorrenson, *Maori Origins*, passim.

26   William Ellis, *Polynesian Researches during a Residence of Nearly Six Years in the South Sea Islands* (London: Fisher & Jackson 1829), II:42.

27   George Turner, *Nineteen Years in Polynesia. Missionary Life, Travels, and Researches in the Islands of the Pacific* (London: John Snow 1861), 245-6, 249.

28   Thomas Williams and James Calvert, *Fiji and the Fijians* (New York: Appleton 1859), 196-9; Thomas West, *Ten Years in South-Central Polynesia. Being Reminiscences of a Personal Mission to the Friendly Islands and Their Dependencies* (London: J. Nisbet 1865), 253.

29   For an advocate of an entry into Polynesia via America see William Ellis, *Polynesian Researches*, II:47-52. A nice rebuttal is in John Williams, *A Narrative of Missionary Enterprises in the South Sea Islands* (London: John Snow 1839), 430-7. The case for a South American entry was aired periodically throughout the century. For example, see R.C. Barstow, 'Stray thoughts on Mahori or Maori Migrations,' *Transactions and Proceedings of the New Zealand Institute*, IX (1876):229-43. The other extreme was to argue that the Americas were settled from Polynesia, see John Dunmore Lang, *View of the Origin and Migrations of the Polynesian Nation:*

Demonstrating their Ancient Discovery and Progressive Settlement of the Continent of America (London: James Cochrane 1834), and Joshua Rutland, 'Traces of Civilization. An Inquiry into the History of the Pacific,' *Transactions and Proceedings of the New Zealand Institute*, xxix (1896):1-51.

30   By far the most perceptive study was by linguist Horatio Hale, *United States Exploring Expedition during the Years 1838, 1839, 1840, 1841, 1842. Ethnography and Philology* [first published 1846] (Ridgewood, NJ: Gregg Press 1968).

31   J.A. Moerenhout, *Voyages aux Îles du Grand Océan* (Paris: Bertrand 1837).

32   M. Russell, *Polynesia. A History of the South Sea Islands including New Zealand, with a Narrative of the Introduction of Christianity, etc.* (London: T. Nelson 1853), 63, 81.

33   For example, John Williams, *A Narrative*, 431; Ellis, *Polynesian Researches*, II:42-4; Russell, *Polynesia*, 63-4.

34   John Williams, *A Narrative*, 441.

35   Turner, *Nineteen Years in Polynesia*, 244, 249.

36   Ellis, *Polynesian Researches*, II:62.

37   Williams and Calvert, *Fiji*, 196.

38   Lang, *View of the Origin*, 231.

39   Judith Binney, *The Legacy of Guilt. A Life of Thomas Kendall* (Auckland: Oxford University Press 1968), Chapter 7.

40   Among the more useful surveys of these developments are Holger Pedersen, *The Discovery of Language. Linguistic Science in the Nineteenth Century* (Bloomington: Indiana University Press 1962); Leon Poliakov, *The Aryan Myth. A History of Racist and Nationalist Ideas in Europe* (London: Chatto & Windus 1974).

41   On Müller, see Nirad C. Chaudhuri, *Scholar Extraordinary. The Life of Professor the Rt. Hon. Friedrich Max Müller* (London: Chatto & Windus 1974). On Müller and comparative mythology generally, see Richard M. Dorson, *The British Folklorists. A History* (London: Routledge & K. Paul 1968).

42   The following material is discussed in more detail in K.R. Howe, 'Some Origins and Migrations of Ideas Leading to the Aryan Polynesian Theories of Abraham Fornander and Edward Tregear,' *Pacific Studies*, IX (2) (1988):67-81.

43   John Rae, 'Polynesian Languages,' *The Polynesian*, 27 September, 4, 11 October 1862.

44   Müller, *Lectures*, II:10-11.

45   Quoted in Müller, II:12.

46   Quoted in Coleman Phillips, 'Civilization of the Pacific,' *Transactions and Proceedings of the New Zealand Institute*, IX (1870):65.

47   W.W. Gill, *Myths and Songs from the South Pacific* (London: Henry S. King 1876), xiv-xv.

48   Adolf Bastian, *Die Heilige Sage de Polynesier. Kosmogonie und Theogonie* (Liepzig: Brockhaus 1881).

49   Edward Tylor, 'Notes on the Asiatic Relations of Polynesian Culture,' *Journal of the Anthropological Institute of Great Britain and Northern Ireland*, XI (1882):404.

50   Edward Shortland, *Maori Religion and Mythology* (London: Longmans, Green 1882), 3. Shortland had long argued the case for Polynesians' Aryan origins; see 'Sketch of the Maori Races,' *Transactions and Proceedings of the New Zealand Institute*, I (1868):337.

51   Abraham Fornander, *An Account of the Polynesian Race, its Origin and Migrations, and the Ancient History of the Hawai'ian People to the Times of Kamehameha I*, 3 vols. (London: Trubner 1878, 1880, 1885). Volume 3, subtitled 'Comparative Vocabulary of the Polynesian and Indo-European Languages,' contained the most substantive evidence for Aryan origins.

52   Edward Tregear, *The Aryan Maori* (Wellington: George Didsbury, Government Printer 1885).

53   Fornander's view was rather more complex than Tregear's. For Fornander, Polynesians descended from an Aryan people 'agnate to, but far older than ... Vedic Aryans.' They entered

India, 'mixed' with Dravidians, became 'moulded' to the Cushite-Arabian civilisation, and were eventually pushed out of India, *An Account*, 1:159.

54 Tregear, *The Aryan Maori*, 38.

55 K.R. Howe, *Singer in a Songless Land. A life of Edward Tregear 1846-1931* (Auckland: Auckland University Press 1991).

56 Tregear went on to become one of New Zealand's most active and internationally recognized scholars of Polynesia. He was author of the monumental *Maori-Polynesian Comparative Dictionary* (1891), a founding father of the Polynesian Society, and editor of its *Journal*. He was also a major public servant, as the controversial 'socialist' secretary for labour during the twenty years of Liberal rule.

57 Both Fornander (of Oland, Sweden) and Tregear grew up with an acute sense of their respective histories and folklores. Both were steeped in classical studies; lost their fathers in their mid-teens, leaving comfortable homes and studies for considerable physical hardship in remote parts of the world (Fornander went whaling before settling in Hawai'i); became influential government administrators; and were passionately interested in Polynesian studies, immersed in the comparative sciences, and particular devotees of Müller. See E.H. Davis, *Abraham Fornander. A Biography* (Honolulu: University of Hawaii Press 1979).

58 F.W. Christian, *Eastern Lands: Tahiti and the Marquesas Islands* (London: Robert Scott 1910), 16-17.

59 For the example of A.H. Keane, see Christian, 249; and for Arthur Vogan, see Vogan to Ngata, 24 Oct. 1947, in copy of Tregear, *The Maori-Polynesian Comparative Dictionary* (Wellington: Lyon and Blair 1891), ML, Sydney.

60 Basil Thomson, *The Fijians. A Study of the Decay of Custom* (London: Heinemann 1908), 12-20.

61 F.D. Fenton, *Suggestions for a History of the Origin and Migrations of the Maori People* (Auckland: H. Brett 1885).

62 Smith, 'Hawaiki. The Whence of the Maori Being an Introduction to Rarotonga History,' *Journal of the Polynesian Society*, VII (1898):137-77, 185-223; VIII (1899):1-48; revised and republished as *Hawaiki: The Original Home of the Maori; With a Sketch of Polynesian History* (Christchurch, NZ: Whitcombe & Tombs 1904); 'Aryan and Polynesian Points of Contact,' *Journal of the Polynesian Society*, XIX (1910):84-8; XX (1911):37-8, 170-2; XXVIII (1919):18-30. Smith is often regarded as one of the foremost advocates of Polynesians' Aryan ancestry, yet in fact he was not particularly supportive of this notion: 'If the Polynesians belong to the Aryan people, they must have separated off from them in very early times.' He preferred the term *proto-Aryan* if it was to be used at all. See 'Aryan and Polynesian Points of Contact,' XXVIII (919):21. Smith emphasized India as the formative homeland of the Polynesians though conceded that 'outward influences, beyond the limits of India, have greatly affected the race. There are traces of such influences to be found from East Africa, Egypt, and very strongly from some Semitic source, possibly Arabia. Dravidian and North Indian influences are to be observed in custom, physique and language. See 'On the Origin and Migrations of the Polynesians, Considered from the South Polynesian Point of View, delivered before the Hawai'ian Historical Society, December 14, 1897,' *Fifth Annual Report of the Hawaiian Historical Society 1897* (Honolulu: Hawaiian Historical Society 1897), 10.

63 John Macmillan Brown, *Peoples and Problems of the Pacific* (London: T.F. Unwin, 1927), II:152. On the extent and longevity of the tradition in New Zealand, see Sorrenson, *Maori Origins*.

64 E.S. Craighill Handy, Kenneth P. Emory, Edwin H. Bryan, Peter H. Buck, and John H. Wise, *Ancient Hawaiian Civilization. A Series of Lectures Delivered at the Kamehameha Schools*, rev. ed. (Rutland, VT: Tuttle 1965), 15.

65 Peter Buck (Te Rangi Hiroa), *Vikings of the Sunrise* (first ed. 1938, Christchurch: Whitcombe & Tombs 1954), 21, 26. Ironically, the race issue came to haunt Buck when the American government refused him U.S. citizenship on the grounds that naturalisation 'required proof of more

than fifty per cent Caucasian ancestry. Polynesians were classified as Asians.' However, Buck was offered a British knighthood and readily dropped efforts to become a U.S. citizen. See J.B. Condliffe, *Te Rangi Hiroa. The Life of Sir Peter Buck* (Christchurch, NZ: Whitcombe & Tombs 1971), 196-8n.

66 Félix Speiser, 'Les Polynésians sont-ils des Aryans?' *Archives Suisses d'Anthropologie Générale*, XII (1946), 68-91.

67 On the issues regarding the European impact on Polynesia see Howe, 'The Fate of the "Savage."'

68 Percy Smith, 'Hawaiki,' 138.

69 Russel Ward, *The Australian Legend* (Melbourne: Oxford University Press 1958).

70 See J.O.C. Phillips, 'Musings in Maoriland – or Was There a *Bulletin* School in New Zealand?' *Historical Studies*, XX (81) (1983):520-35.

71 D.R. Simmons, *The Great New Zealand Myth* (Wellington: A.H. & A.W. Reed 1976).

72 ATL, Tregear papers, MS 554, Tregear to his daughter, 30 June 1918.

73 J.O.C. Phillips, *A Man's Country? The Image of the Pakeha Male. A History* (Auckland: Penguin 1987); see also Keith Sinclair, *A Destiny Apart. New Zealand's Search for National Identity* (Wellington: Allen & Unwin 1986).

74 One further claimed use of Aryan Maori ideology in New Zealand social policy was as a 'model for social amalgamation' between Maori and *pakeha*. See Michael Belgrave [on Tregear's Aryan Maori], 'Archipelago of Exiles. A Study of the Imperialism of Ideas of Edward Tregear and John Macmillan Brown' (M.Phil. thesis, University of Auckland 1979), 54; see also 60, 62. Sorrenson makes similar claims for Aryan views on pp. 29-30. Although Aryan theory clearly supported those who viewed Maori with respect and favour, I find little evidence that it played any more direct role in supporting amalgamation policies. Such policies had been advocated/implemented in New Zealand since humanitarian times. And there is no evidence that Tregear, Percy Smith, and other such scholars took any active interest or part in legislative or other policies for Maori. Indeed their general assumption was that the Maori were on the verge of extinction. The scholars' concern was to salvage what they could of the Polynesian past before it was too late. It is also possible to argue that Aryan/Caucasian theory was, for some, a way to accept, rather than to prevent, the demise of the race. Fenton, summarizing his ancient history of the Polynesians, noted: 'We have been present at their cradle in the great Mesopotamian basin, before the races of men had dispersed themselves over the earth, and we or our children will, it can scarcely be doubted, stand over their grave ... Let, then, the great English nation treat the remnant of the race with gentleness, and learn from their varied career the transitory nature of all human greatness,' *Suggestions*, 122.

75 Peter France, 'The Kaunitoni Migration,' *Journal of Pacific History*, I (1966):107-13.

76 R.M. Daggett (ed.), [His Hawai'ian Majesty Kalakaua] *The Legends and Myths of Hawai'i. The Fables and Folklore of a Strange People*, with an introduction by the editor (New York: Charles L. Webster 1888), 65. Daggett seems to have had little real understanding of Fornander, erroneously claiming that Fornander gave Hawai'ians semitic origins. On Daggett see Davis, *Abraham Fornander*, 254-7.

77 George Grey, 'On New Zealand and Polynesian Mythology,' a paper delivered at the Museum of Practical Geology, London 1869, in *Polynesian Mythology and Ancient Traditional History* (2nd ed., Auckland: H. Brett 1885), Appendix II.

78 Edward Tylor, 'Phenomena of the Higher Civilisation Taceable to a Rudimental Origin among Savage Tribes,' *Anthropological Review*, V (1867):304-5.

79 Tregear, 'Old Stories of Polynesia,' *Report of the Australasian Association for the Advancement of Science for 1891*, III (1891):353.

80 Edward W. Said, *Orientalism* (London: Routledge 1978).

81 Tylor, 'Phenomena of the Higher Civilisation,' 303-4.

Chapter 13: The Burden of *Terra Australis*

1 Michael E. Hoare (ed.), *The Resolution Journal of Johann Reinhold Forster 1772-1775* (London: Hakluyt Society 1982), II:336.
2 W.P. Cumming, R.A.Skelton, and D.B.Quinn (eds.), *The Discovery of North America* (London: Elek 1971), 193, 200.
3 Phillip to Banks, 26 July 1790, in John Cobley, *Sydney Cove 1789-1790* (Sydney: Angus & Roberston 1963), 256.
4 Hoare, *The Resolution Journal*, 427.
5 E.H. McCormick, *Omai, Pacific Envoy* (Auckland: Oxford University Press 1977), 128.
6 Beaglehole, *Banks Journal*, I:341.
7 Spate, *Paradise Lost and Found*, 237.
8 J.G.A. Pocock, *The Machiavellian Moment* (Princeton: Princeton University Press 1975).
9 Beaglehole, *Banks Journal*, I:xliii.
10 A. Dalrymple, *A Collection of Voyages Chiefly in the Southern Atlantick Ocean* (London 1775), 6; G. Williams, *Search for the Northwest Passage*, 38.
11 Cumming, Skelton, and Quinn, *The Discovery of North America*, 73.
12 Cited in O.H.K. Spate, *The Spanish Lake* (Canberra: ANU Press 1979), 279.
13 Glyndwr Williams (ed.), *A Voyage Round the World by George Anson* (Oxford: Oxford University Press 1974), 115, xi.
14 Beaglehole, *Banks Journal*, I:472.
15 Sharp, *Journal of Jakob Roggeveen*, 103.
16 Ibid., 146.
17 Robert E. Gallagher (ed.), *Byron's Journal of His Circumnavigation 1764-1766* (London: Hakluyt Society 1962), lv-lviii.
18 Ibid., 109.
19 Cook, *Flood Tide of Empire*, 3, 461.
20 Williams, *Search for the Northwest Passage*, 6, 19.
21 Ibid., 37.
22 Cited in O.H.K. Spate, 'The Pacific. Home of Utopias,' in Eugene Kamenka (ed.), *Utopias* (Canberra: Oxford University Press 1987), 21.
23 Gallagher, *Byron's Journal*, xxxv.
24 HRNSW, I (2):1-2.
25 Ibid., 11-12.
26 PRO, Chatham, 30/8/361, fols. 34-7, Banks to R. Dundas, 15 June 1787.
27 For the breadfruit expedition, see Mackay, *In the Wake of Cook*, Chapter 5.
28 Spate, *Paradise Lost and Found*, 155.
29 Beaglehole, *Banks Journal*, I:lxxii.
30 Sharp, *Journal of Jakob Roggeveen*, 7-8.
31 Beaglehole, *Banks Journal*, I:lxxxii.
32 J.C. Beaglehole, *The Exploration of the Pacific* (London 1966), 181.
33 The story is recounted in Williams, *Search for the Northwest Passage*, 69-78.
34 Documented in Glyndwr Williams, 'Myth and Reality: James Cook and the Theoretical Geography of Northwest America,' in Robin Fisher and Hugh Johnston (eds.), *Captain James Cook and His Times* (Vancouver: Douglas & McIntyre 1979), 59-79.
35 Cited in Gallagher, *Byron's Journal*, xxxv.
36 Williams, *Anson's Voyage*, 96.
37 Ibid.
38 Cited in Gallagher, *Byron's Journal*, 161.
39 Some of these are discussed in Mackay, *Wake of Cook*, Chapter 2.
40 Ibid., 441.

41 Williams, *Anson's Voyage*, ix-x.

42 Spate, in Kamenka, *Utopias*, 29.

43 Leonie Kramer, 'Utopia as Metaphor,' in Kamenka, *Utopias*, 134.

44 Sharp, *Journal of Jakob Roggeveen*, 108.

45 Williams, 'James Cook and Theoretical Geography'; Beaglehole, *Banks Journal*, III:456.

46 Beverley Hooper (ed.), *With Captain James Cook in the Antarctic and Pacific. The Private Journal of James Burney* (Canberra: National Library of Australia 1975), 67.

47 P.J. Marshall & Glyndwr Williams, *The Great Map of Mankind* (London: Dent 1982), 285; Spate, *Paradise Lost and Found*, 263.

48 Cited in Spate, 268.

49 Beaglehole, *Banks Journal*, II:60.

50 Ibid., I:310.

51 Ibid., ccix.

52 *Gentleman's Magazine*, December 1786, cited in HRNSW, II:738.

53 The same problem beset Captain Stirling and the botanist Fraser in the Swan River almost sixty years later; see J.M.R. Cameron, *Ambition's Fire: The Agricultural Colonization of Pre-convict Western Australia* (Nedlands, Australia: University of Western Australia Press 1981).

54 Cited in G. Williams, 'New Holland: The English Approach,' in John Hardy and Alan Frost (eds.), *Studies from Terra Australis to Australia* (Canberra: Australian Academy of the Humanities 1989), 91.

55 HRNSW, I (2):1-2, Matra's Plan.

56 Ibid., 11-12.

57 Paul Fidlon and R.J. Ryan (eds.), *The Journal of Arthur Bowes Smyth* (Sydney: Angus & Robertson 1979), 57.

58 Rex Rienits (ed.), [John White] *Journal of A Voyage to New South Wales* (Sydney: Angus & Robertson 1962), 109-10.

59 Ibid., 112.

60 ML, Safe 1/121, 151, R. Johnson to Henry Fricker, 15 November 1788.

61 L.F. Fitzhardinge (ed.), [Watkin Tench] *Sydney's First Four Years: being a reprint of a Narrative of the Expedition to Botany Bay and a Complete Account of the Settlement at Port Jackson* (Sydney 1961), 155-6.

62 Cobley, *Sydney Cove*, I:248, Letter of female convict, 14 November 1788.

63 Fitzhardinge, *Tench Narrative*, 152.

64 PRO, CO 201/5, 15-23, Phillip to Sydney, 12 February 1790.

65 Michael Roe (ed.), *The Journal and Letters of Captain Charles Bishop* (Cambridge, England: Hakluyt Society 1967). Teast's instructions are on pp. 10-16.

66 Ibid., 37.

67 Helen Wallis (ed.), *Carteret's Voyage Round the World* (Cambridge, England: Hakluyt Society 1965), 136.

68 Roe, *Bishop Journal and Letters*, xxxiii, 237, 239, 285.

Appendix

1 NMM, Adm/A/2827.

2 CUL, RGO 14/9, fols. 64-4v.

3 The astronomical clock cost £89 5s, the journey-man clock £6 0s, and their common stand £21, CUL, RGO 14/17, fol. 231

4 Ibid., at a cost of £47 5s.

5 Amended to 'Two,' in the receipt signed by Gooch on 2 July 1791 in RGO 14/13, fols. 155-5v.

6 Ibid., amended to 'Three.'

7 Ibid., inserted in a later hand: 'called a station-pointer.'

8   Ibid., inserted in the same hand as above: 'A Hadley's quadrant, with two moveable clamps, for surveying in a boat or vessel in motion.'

9   Lamb, *Vancouver's Voyage* 1:287.

10 PRO, Adm 1/2629, letter dated 13 January 1793.

11 For another copy of these lists, see PRO, HO 28/11, fols. 212-21.

12 For a complete list of these charts, copied with minor errors from PRO, HO 28/11, see J. Holland Rose, 'Views and Charts of the Coasts of the "New Albion," etc.,' *The Mariner's Mirror*, x (1924):82-4.

Index

Margaret, ship, 108, 168
Marias Islands, 295
Marion du Fresne, Nicholas Thomas, captain, 30, 200, 279
Marquesas Islands, 25, 28-9, 196-8, 294
Marsden, Samuel, chaplain, 211, 250
Marshall, Yvonne, 16
Martínez, Esteban José, navigator: instigator of Nootka crisis, 44, 107-8, 117, 230; Native peoples' fear of, 146-8; plans for northwest, 138, 142, 154, 159; presence at Nootka Sound, 136-48; voyage in 1774, 110
Marvinas, 154
Más Afuera, 288
Maskelyne, Nevil, astronomer, 74, 77
Masson, Francis, collector, 228, 242
Mathews, Joseph, missionary, 225
Matilda, ship, 197-8
Matra, James Mario, former midshipman, 117-18, 264, 269, 272, 283
Matthews, general, 122
Maui, 210
Mawun, 165-6
Mayflower, ship, 259
Mazarredo, José de, admiral, 83
Meares, John, trader, 40-1, 44, 47, 106-8, 116, 152, 153, 161
Melanesia, 32
Mendaña, Alvavo de, captain, 29, 271
Menzies, Archibald, botanist: arrest and intended court martial, 235-7; and Banks, 116, 228-33, 235-41; comment on Russian voyages of exploration, 102; drawings, 297; journal, 17, 227, 234-44; and Vancouver, 9, 48, 232-9
Menzies Bay, 65
Mer de l'Ouest, 39. *See also* Juan de Fuca, Strait of
Merry, Anthony, diplomat, 108-10, 117
Mexicana, ship, 154, 161-2, 165-6
Mexico, 108, 120, 121, 131, 135-6, 153, 241, 273
Mexico City, 128, 159
Micronesia, 32
Middleton, Christopher, captain and explorer, 274
Middleton, Sir Charles, admiral (later Lord Barham), 117, 125
Milligan, R.R.D., 218
Miranda, Francisco de, soldier, 120, 122
Miranda, Louis, northwest coast Native historian, 3
Moerenhout, J.A., 250

Mohi Tawhai, Maori chief, 191
Moluccas, 283. *See also* Spice Islands
Monboddo, James Burnett, lord, jurist and anthropologist, 247
Montague Island, 136
Monterey, California, 8, 38, 79, 197-8, 241, 294-7
Moscow, 86, 91, 98
Moskvitin, Ivan, cossack leader, 87
Motukawanui, Cavalli Islands, 199-200
Mount George, Norfolk Island, 206
Mount Pitt, Norfolk Island, 206
Mount St Elias, 46
Mourelle, Francisco Antonio, first officer, 36, 46, 110, 130-5, 141
Mudge, Zacariah, lieut., 241, 296-7
Muka, 215. *See also* Flax
Mulgrave, Henry Phipps, earl, India Board member, 112-13, 120-1
Müller, Gerhard Friedrich, cartographer, 95, 274
Müller, Max, linguist, 253-5, 258, 260; *Lectures on the Science of Language*, 253; *Chips from a German Workshop*, 253
Mulovsky, Grigorii Ivanovich, captain, 96
Murimotu, 216, 219
Muriwai, Maori chief, 208, 217, 218
Muriwhenua, 216-17, 220-2, 225
Murmansk, 93
Mutiny: on *Bounty*, 114; at Norfolk Island, 224

Nadezhda, ship, 99
Nanaquius, northwest coast Native chief, 165-6, 173
Nanikius, northwest coast Native child, 152
Narborough, Sir John, buccaneer, 273
Narvaez, José, pilot, 44
National Library of Australia, Canberra, 241, 296
National Maritime Museum, Greenwich, 72
Native Land Claims Commission (Fiji), 25
Native people
– Alaska: Aleuts, 86, 102; Konyagas, 103
– Australia, 277
– Hawai'i: alleged Aryan origins, 255-7, 260; and Cook, 34; on *Daedalus*, 198, 201; language, 24; and Vancouver, 8, 10
– New Zealand: alleged Aryan origins, 255-7; cannibalism, 192, 207, 218, 265, 279; hierarchy and organization, 213-14, 216-18, 220; language, 23, 256; Maori and Europeans, 17, 21-2, 191-5, 200-1, 250, 259; Maori and King,

Valdés, Antonio, minister of navy (Spain), 45-6
Valdés, Don Cayetano, explorer, 44, 46, 154
Valparaiso, 79, 235, 240-1
Van Dieman's Land, 283
Vancouver (City), 7, 11, 75
Vancouver, George, captain: appointment to head expedition, 230-1; background, 8, 51-2, 79-80; chronometers, 15, 62, 64, 66-7, 70-2, 74, 77-8, 80, 82-4; death, 239; equipment, 291-2; exploration, 7-8, 37, 62, 69, 193, 197, 230-1; historical reputation, 6-7, 12-14, 18; instructions, 7, 14-15, 43-4, 54, 80, 194, 196, 197-8; involvement in Hawai'ian affairs, 10; kidnapping of Tuki and Huru, 17, 193, 196-8, 202; meeting with Gray, 47; and Menzies, 102, 232-9; and Native peoples, 3-6, 9-10, 167, 171, 173, 176, 193-4, 225-6; and northwest passage, 48-50, 123, 125; request for extra pay, 80; and Russians, 9, 85-6; and Spanish, 10-11, 16, 46-7, 197; survey methods and charts, 8-9, 51-4, 56-63, 65, 68, 294-7; A Voyage of Discovery to the North Pacific Ocean and Round the World, 7, 11, 18, 67, 158, 193, 196, 225, 239, 240-2, 296
Vancouver, John, 12, 82, 239-40
Vancouver Conference on Exploration and Discovery, 3, 6, 12
Vancouver Island, 9, 45, 131, 160, 295
Vancouver Maritime Museum, 75
Vanuatu, 33. See also New Hebrides
Varley, Samuel, scientist, 82
Vason, George, missionary
Venus: Cook's observation of, 19-20, 26
Venus, ship, 167
Vernacci, Juan, lieut., 63
Vestal, ship, 112
Virgil (Publius Vergilius Maro), poet, 263-4
Vladivostok, 93

Wafer, Lionel, surgeon and buccaneer, 278
Wager Bay, 274
Waitangi, Treaty of, 191, 225
Waitoa, Maori chief, 217-18
Wales, William, astronomer, 51, 53, 57, 80; Finding the longitude at sea, by Timekeepers, 79
Wallis, Samuel, captain, 26, 277, 293
Walpole, Robert, earl, prime minister of Great Britain, 266
War: Crimean, 103; likelihood between Great Britain and Spain, 10, 40, 43, 117-20, 138;

Russia with Turkey and Sweden, 96, 101
Warner, John, engraver, 67
Washington, ship, 39, 41, 43, 47, 139
Washington State Historical Society, 68
Webber, John, artist, 78, 188
Wentworth, D'Arcy, assistant surgeon, 211
West Indies, 121-122
Whaling, 105, 123, 125
Whangaroa, 217, 220
Whidbey, Joseph, shipmaster, 52, 64, 79-80, 241, 293-4
White, John, 201
White, John, surgeon, 284-5
White, Robert, 122
Whul-whul-LAY-ton, Squamish placename, 5
Wickaninish, northwest coast Native chief, 144, 145, 147-8, 158, 161-3, 167-74
William and Ann, ship, 204
Williams, Glyndwr, 14; Anson's Voyage, 274-6, 278
Williams, John, missionary, 251
Williams, Thomas, missionary, 251
Wilson, Samuel, missionary, 252
Woodoo, Maori native, 220
Wright, Ronald, Stolen Continents, 13
Wyatt, Victoria, 16
Wytete Bay, 295

Yakutat, 181
Yakutat Bay, 45. See also Port Mulgrave
Yakutia. See Siberia
Yakutsk, 92-3
Yakutsk-Okhotsk Track, 92
Yasak, 88. See also Fur trade, Russian
Yedso, 269, 271
Young, Sir George, captain (later admiral), 272, 283
Yuquot: 139-40, 143-4, 147-8, 151-4, 167, 173; Spanish garrison, 155-9. See also Friendly Cove

Contributors

CHRISTON I. ARCHER
Professor of History, University of Calgary, Calgary, Alberta

ANDREW DAVID
Retired Lieutenant Commander, Royal Navy, and Qualified Hydrographic Surveyor, Somerset, England

ALUN C. DAVIES
Professor of Economic and Social History, Queen's University of Belfast, Belfast, Northern Ireland

BEN FINNEY
Professor of Anthropology, University of Hawaii at Manoa, Honolulu, Hawaii

ROBIN FISHER
Professor of History, University of Northern British Columbia, Prince George, BC

ALAN FROST
Reader in History, LaTrobe University, Bundoora Victoria, Australia

JAMES R. GIBSON
Professor of Geography, York University, North York, Ontario

K.R. HOWE
Professor of History, Massey University, Palmerston North, New Zealand

CHIEF PHILIP JOE
Land Administrator for the Squamish Nation, North Vancouver, BC

HUGH JOHNSTON
Professor of History, Simon Fraser University, Burnaby, BC

W. KAYE LAMB
Former Dominion Archivist and National Librarian, Vancouver, BC

DAVID MACKAY
Professor of History, Victoria University of Wellington, Wellington, New Zealand

YVONNE MARSHALL
Anthropologist, University of Auckland, Auckland, New Zealand

CHIEF LOUIS MIRANDA (1892-1990)
Historian for the Squamish Nation, North Vancouver, BC

ANNE SALMOND
Professor of Maori Studies, University of Auckland, Auckland, New Zealand

GLYNDWR WILLIAMS
Professor of History, University of London, London, England

VICTORIA WYATT
Assistant Professor of History in Art, University of Victoria, Victoria, BC